SCHOOL LIBRARY MEDIA SERIES
Edited by Diane de Cordova Biesel

Taking Humor Seriously in Children's Literature

Literature-Based Mini-Units and Humorous Books for Children Ages 5–12

Patricia L. Roberts

School Library Media Series, No. 11

The Scarecrow Press, Inc.
Lanham, Md., & London
1997

SCARECROW PRESS, INC.

Published in the United States of America
by Scarecrow Press, Inc.
4720 Boston Way
Lanham, Maryland 20706

4 Pleydell Gardens, Folkestone
Kent CT20 2DN, England

British Library Cataloguing in Publication Information Available

Library of Congress Cataloging-in-Publication Data

Roberts, Patricia, 1936–
Taking humor seriously in children's literature : literature-based mini-
units and humorous books for children ages 5–2 / Patricia L. Roberts.
    p.   cm.—(School library media series ; no 11)
Includes index.
1. Children's literature—History and criticism. 2. Humor in literature.
I. Title. II. Series.
PN1009.A1R56   1997   809′.89282—DC21   97-15547 CIP

ISBN 0-8108-3209-7 (pbk. : alk. paper)

♾ ™ The paper used in this publication meets the minimum require-
ments of American National Standard for Information Sciences—Perma-
nence of Paper for Printed Library Materials, ANSI Z39.48–1984.
Manufactured in the United States of America.

To J. M., who has a fine sense of humor

Contents

Editor's Foreword

The School Library Media Series is directed to the school library media specialist, particularly the building-level librarian. The multifaceted role of the librarian as educator, collection developer, curriculum developer, and information specialist is examined. The series includes concise, practical books on topical and current subjects related to programs and services.

The benefits of humor are explored in *Taking Humor Seriously through Children's Literature: Literature-Based Mini-Units and Humorous Books for Children Ages 5–12*. Parts I and II include mini-units designed for children ages 5–12. The extensive bibliography of humorous literature comprises parts III and IV. Dr. Roberts has suggested activities that incorporate analyses of different types of humor.

Librarians, parents, and caregivers in many settings are certain to find this book a necessary addition to their collections.

Diane de Cordova Biesel
Series Editor

Introduction

A merry heart doeth good like a medicine.
—Proverbs 17:22

"What do they call it when you break out in tiny wrist watches?" " . . . Small clocks."

This is the kind of unexpected answer to joking riddles given by Joanne Bernstein and Paul Cohen in *Dizzy Doctor Riddles* (Whitman, 1989). Here are two more that may surprise children:

"Why are doctors often dizzy?"

" . . . From doing rounds and rounds."

"What's harder than making a child go to the hospital?"

" . . . Making the hospital go to the child."

Many children and adults, too, are charmed by surprise responses they haven't heard before such as those offered by Bernstein and Cohen—as well as anything else that's humorous and tickles their "funny bones." Related to the subject of jokes and other forms of humor for children, every conceivable area in which children and adults relate to humor has been explored through a collection of studies in the fields of education, medicine, and psychology (see bibliography). With this in mind, specialists in children's literature have urged us to take time to consider the humor in children's books more seriously and to foster humor awareness—and its benefits—for children ages 5 to 12. Thus, this book is in response to the clear pleas for the use of more humor in school curricula that have been made by many. As examples, Greenlaw (1983) has stated succinctly that more literary humor is needed in the curriculum and Monson (1983) has pointed out the value of humor—she said that laughter was a powerful response to literature. If children's literature that provokes laughter (and other benefits of humor) could be identified further in a resource such as this one, perhaps more literary humor would be seriously introduced in the school curriculum and children's books and the aspects of humor could be made more readily available to all children. This book is a step toward that end.

HUMOR AND ITS BENEFITS

Related to the positive aspects of humor, it seems that even in the most serious of situations, humor can be beneficial to adults and children alike. Inside or outside the classroom, many children and adults, faced with crucial health situations, work performances, academic situations, or being in conditions of great apprehension, confront their challenges staunchly and some cope best by using humor.

Work Performance

Related to work performance, humor and its accompanying laughter, appears to be good for children and adults—especially in the work place where some recent findings about humor have impressive implications:

- While once an employee might have been able to see no linkage between his or her performance at work and humor, the employee can now look forward to benefits from humor when the employee sees work as fun (Isen, 1987; Paterson, 1986; DeLuca and Natov, 1977; and Jurich, 1977).
- Additionally, humor appears to help a person think broadly and creatively. According to a thesis by D. Abramis at California State University, Long Beach, the employees who see their work as fun perform better and get along better with coworkers than the employees who do not see their jobs as fun.
- Further, humor helps a person gain a perspective in assessing one's self (Paterson, 1986); it can be a counterbalance for everyday life (DeLuca and Natov, 1977); and as an added bonus, has been found to help us learn about other cultures (Jurich, 1977).

Health Care

Related to health care, where once a child or adult might have been able to expect no connection between an illness and humor, he or she can now look forward to a medical interest in using humor in health care situations. Research findings (Nowell, 1989) are beginning to accumulate about this and suggest that laughter can be therapeutic when it is used to reduce certain disease symptoms. Humor seems to increase the quality of a patient's life; it relieves certain chronic symptoms such as painful muscle and bone disorders; humor in comic videos appears to relieve stress with accompanying drops in a patient's blood pressure, heart rate, and stress; and it also appears that humor and laughter can be a link between a patient's positive feelings and his or her physical body (Nowell, 1989).

Using humor as a pick-me-up in health care is not new. As a brief testimony to the early use of humor in health care in the 1800s, Edna B. Patterson in *Sagebrush Doctors* (Art City Publishing, 1972) recounts an anecdote about Joe Taber, male nurse and hunting companion of the skilled, straightforward Dr. Eby of Elko County, Nevada. An enthusiastic fun-loving man, Joe Taber, also a druggist, was a steward at Elko County Hospital. He entertained the townspeople as he drove around town in his open-top car with his favorite companion by his side—a skeleton mascot named Bones who wore a driving cap just like Joe's.

Using humor as a pick-me-up in health care continues today. To help a child or adult cope with illness, laughter is now being used as "good medicine" in several hospitals. As examples, ways to generate laughter are used in the University Hospital in Albuquerque, New Mexico, and in the Presbyterian Hospital in Charlotte, North Carolina (Esper, 1989). At Presbyterian Hospital, a 5-foot-tall yellow Laugh Mobile rolls to the cancer unit with videotapes, humorous books, audio tapes, games, and toys. Patients, young and old, report that the Laugh Mobile is a "real pick-me-up." In further support of the pick-me-up point of view for patients, Dr. Robert Karns, secretary of the Los Angeles County Medical Association, says, "laughter and happy feelings have been shown to be helpful to any situations, including terminal cancer." Karns emphasizes that he tells people to "be as up as you possibly can be." He goes on, "If you are more comfortable in your own mind, you're going to feel better."

As further testimony to the value and benefits of humor and laughter, Norman Cousins, in his book *Anatomy of An Illness,* tells us, "Even if we find that laughter produces no specific biochemi-

cal changes, it does accomplish one very essential purpose, it tends to help a person cope with apprehension and even panic that all too frequently accompany serious illness." For those who need to be as up as they can be, Jody Leader (1993), a practitioner of Norman Cousins's philosophy of laughter, sees laughter as the "best" medicine, and has become the editor and founder of the *Laughter Prescription Newsletter*. This is a letter filled with jokes and words of wisdom and articles from health and humor professionals. It is written in a folksy, informal way. Leader makes her newsletter available to adults and children interested in the topic of humor. They can write to the following address:

The HUMOR Project
  110 Spring St., Dept. BHG
  Saratoga Springs, NY 12866

Academic Situations

Related to the classroom, the author researched the responses of specialists to what benefits humor has for us that were discussed in the previous sections about work performance and health care. She also researched responses to the following question, "What are some of the studies that form the foundational underpinnings for the use of humor with children?"

Some specialists in literature for children have pointed out that appreciation for literature, including humor, seems to be developmental. Indeed, Huck, Hepler, and Hickman (1987) point out that if the children have not had the chance to laugh at the antics of humorous animal stories when they are 5 or 6, they need the experience at 7 or 8. If they have not met Mother Goose before they come to school, then early primary grades need to supply this "cornerstone" of literature. The authors go on to mention that educators need more research on the various phases of appreciating literature. And there is some evidence to show that children go through various stages of interest—including the nonsense verse stage.

Educators realize that if they are to improve children's awareness of humor and ways children select and interact with it in children's literature, they will want to know the following:

1. Humor helps form a literary side of knowledge for children and adults. The literary side of humor as a factor in children's literature written

since the mid-nineteenth century was investigated by Berding (1965) who concluded by identifying five criteria that were consistently found in quality humorous books. The criteria were as follows:

  a. A plot included related and dependent incidents.

  b. Some styles had repetition.

  c. Subtleties were evident.

  d. Originality was used.

  e. Graphic descriptions were humorous.

2. Humor also has been placed in categories related to what children find funny (Kappas, 1967). Here are the groups:

  a. Exaggeration

  b. Surprise, Incongruity

  c. Slapstick

  d. Absurdity

  e. Human predicaments

  f. Ridicule of adults

  g. Ridicule of society

  h. Human foibles or oneself (this becomes satire in its more sophisticated form)

  i. Defiance or rebellion against adult authority or expressing forbidden ideas

  j. Verbal humor

3. It appears that primary grade children chose "funny books" as their first choices when they are allowed to choose freely from the children's choices list of books that is prepared annually each October by teachers for *The Reading Teacher*. A yearly review of the entries indicates this interest.

4. It appears that middle school students select humor as a preference, too. Spiegel (1983) recorded the first-place preferences of reading interests of middle school students and found that humor was their preference. Students in higher elementary grades choose adventure books first—then jokes and humor books. Humor also had a strong attraction for seventh and eighth graders and widespread appeal for both females and males across all ability levels.

5. It appears that lists of humorous short stories and books suitable for middle school students are available (Cart, 1987). Many of the books appear to be beneficial for low-ability readers who show emotional disorders and levels of stress (Gentile and McMillan, 1987). Humorous books also appear to be suitable for gifted children who are looking for challenging material (Colwell, 1987).

6. In a related study, Landau (1955), who observed three social studies classes, completed a study of the ideas of humor expressed by sixth graders and the relationship to their social class status. Landau discovered that, in spite of their middle-class upbringing, children in the middle-class seemed more RETICENT in their reactions to humorous material than either lower- or upper-class children—thus seemingly supporting a need to introduce more humor awareness through children's literature. Some of the same points in Landau's study, however, were investigated again by Monson (1966) who found that there seemed to be few differences in the choices of categories of humor made by sex, intelligence, socioeconomic, and reading level groups.

FOR THE CLASSROOM

Humor, Laughter, and Delivery

In the classroom, humor and its accompanying laughter appear to be good for students as well as teachers. It seems that humorous words—jokes, for example, strengthen bonds between people. Teachers who weave humor about the topic into their material seem to be more effective in the classroom than those teachers who don't use humor. Humor that does not distort information generally enhances children's ability to master new material. This has been pointed out by Dolf Zillman (1973) of Indiana University in the *Handbook of Humor Research*. Additionally, humorous nonsense also appeals to the interests of children, is beneficial because of its bonding and attention-getting potential, and has various forms that can be used in the classroom. Interestingly, this type of humor relies on its *delivery* for part of its nonsense (Anderson and Apseloff, 1989), a skill many educators deliberately develop. It seems that deliberate delivery of humor has not only been accepted in the elementary and secondary schools, it also has been accepted in the university academic arena, as attested to by the recent publication of *The International Journal of Humor Research* by Lawrence E. Mintz, professor in the Department of American Studies at the University of Maryland.

Humor and Strong Teacher-Models

The positive benefits of humor can be actively used by developing children's awareness of the techniques of humor seriously considered by authors and artists in quality children's books. Such benefits need to be reinforced by a strong teacher-model who demonstrates his or her own conviction that humor is good, worthwhile, and beneficial.

In support of strong teacher-models, a professional group, the National Council of Teachers of English, indicated that humor was good, worthwhile, and beneficial. They selected "Humor and Laughter" as the theme of a recent conference. The council's literature stated that laughter was beneficial in school because it takes a teacher in the "direction of humanizing the learning atmosphere, makes it less threatening, and puts the learner in a receptive frame of mind." The theme that ran through the workshops and topics that were available was evident in one section called "Laughter: In and Out of the Classroom." This workshop was led by Jean Greenlaw who humorously promoted the use of laughter in school. Another session was "Language Arts: Using Great Happenings in Theater for English and Reading (LAUGHTER)," led by Adrian F. Klein, who presented ways to integrate fine arts with language arts. Several authors—Marc Brown, Patricia Reilly Giff, and Paula Danziger—writers who have used various techniques of humor in children's stories—also attended the conference and discussed their writing styles.

Through the professional development of such conferences as that sponsored by the National Council of Teachers of English, and others, benefits of humor can be reinforced by a strong teacher-model who demonstrates his or her own conviction that humor is beneficial. Such a model also can foster the use of humor in children's lives by introducing children to literature that has at its center main characters who are themselves using humor in a positive way. Discussions that follow readings of the literature can show children that there is value in using humor and its accompanying laughter as one of the ways to cope with problems. They, like literary characters, can become "humor specialists" and serious "comedians-in-residence" who know when, where, and how to use humor and how to gain in a positive way from its beneficial values.

Humor and Children's Books

With young children in the primary grades, an example of the techniques of an author-artist to create humor can be found in *Arthur's Family Vacation* (Joy St./Little,1993, ages 5–8) by Marc Brown, a story suitable for reading aloud. The story centers on Arthur who wants to go to camp with his best friend—but he has to go with his family, of course, when his parents schedule their vacation at the beach. For Arthur, the "vacation" has its disappointing moments—including spending an entire week with his sister. Disappointed, Arthur discovers that there is no view at the Ocean View Motel and he thinks the motel's swimming pool is smaller than the bathtub in their cinderblock cubicle the motel calls a room. When rain begins to fall nonstop for days, Arthur does his best to entertain himself. He recalls that at camp there was always something to do and he decides the family needs "something to do." To make the most of the situation, Arthur arranges family field trips to a Cow Festival, Flo's Fudge Factory, Gatorville, and Jimmy's Jungle Cruise. When the sun comes out on Friday, the vacation finally ends on an "upbeat" note when Arthur and his family enjoy a wonderful and perfect day on the beach.

For older children, comic ideas are found in *Kid Camping from Aaaaiii! to Zip* (Lothrop, Lee & Shepard, 1979, ages 10 and up), by Patrick McManus, former professor of English and journalism at Eastern Washington University. McManus's humor about kid camping are demonstrated by kids whose ideas about camping are quite different from those of grown-ups. The kid campers are the main characters who tell the entertaining anecdotes and give advice to adults on such things as how to keep your matches dry and what to do when encountering a cow or a bear. McManus gets a reader's attention right at the beginning of his book when he announces, "*Aaaaiii!* This is a sound often heard on kid camping trips. You won't have any trouble recognizing the *Aaaaiii!* sound because it will cause your hair to jump up and stand at attention." He tucks other bits of humor and jokes into his writing everywhere. For example, Oops! is what you should try not to say too often when it's your turn to cook.

Using children's literature such as *Arthur's Family Vacation* and *Kid Camping from Aaaaiii! to Zip* to present some of the features of humor can include the feature of contrast where Arthur's expectations are contrasted with the realities of the family's vacation. It can include the unexpected event when Arthur plans humorous field trips for the family or the contrastive ending that is "upbeat" after a dismal rainy day. Indeed, humor has been recognized and available in books

for children long before a formal type of biblio-
therapy came into use—this approach being the
use of books to help children understand and
cope with their problems and the problems of
others.

When children read about the humorous situations, such as the ones Brown and McManus
wrote, they can reach into themselves to recognize humor in their own personalities. Obvious
to many, the vicarious experiences of reading often can provide children with more humor than
the sober reality of everyday life. With humorous children's books there are additional values
too, for child-readers can reflect for days upon
the humorous words and actions of book characters and continue to come up with more humorous actions from slapstick, clever word play, idioms, and puns. Additionally, they can reflect on
the authors' humorous approaches and their use
of double meanings, switches, and exaggerations. They, too, can suggest humorous effects in
stories that could be added with sound effects
from records and tapes, with humorous words
they find in dictionaries and thesauri, or with
new words they create such as sniglets, buzz
words, slang, and jargon that would appear humorous to others.

HOW TO USE THIS BOOK

In the sections of the book, librarians, teachers,
parents, and others will find some helpful aids—
literature-based mini-units and an annotated bibliography of humorous books for children—that
will assist adults as they use children's literature as
a vehicle for presenting techniques of humor used
by authors and artists in quality books.

Literature-Based Mini-Units

Parts I and II cover "Mini-Units for Children Ages
5–8," and "Mini-Units for Children Ages 9–12."
These parts include literature-based mini-units for
various children's books accompanied by a variety
of ideas, activities, and discussion questions.
These are followed by additional humorous children's readings about the subject that reflect features of humor. Subjects for the mini-units in both
parts are as follows:

- Animals as Humans
- Family, School, and Community
- Humorous Humans
- Holidays
- Jokes, Riddles, Puns
- Nonsense
- Rhymes and Verses
- Unusual Characters and Creatures

Each mini-unit has the bibliographical information of a selected book, an annotation, some new
and unfamiliar words that could be introduced,
and specific features of humor in the book and
other books that can be discussed seriously with
children within a range of activities. With interested girls and boys, brief book talks can be given
about any of the books and their features of humor
to enable the children to become aware of the seri-
ousness that writers give to humor in their books.
Creative librarians and teachers may use the mini-
unit examples as models to adapt other books to
the children they work with daily.

Annotated Bibliography

Parts III and IV are annotated bibliographies on
"Humorous Literature for Children Ages 5–8,"
and "Humorous Literature for Children Ages 9–
12." In each subsection, brief numbered annota-
tions feature humorous characters from carefully
selected children's books and are entered by the
author's last name. The age levels for which the
book would be most suitable are indicated. In the
index, the entered numbers refer to the *entry* numbers in the bibliography, *not* the page numbers.
The annotated bibliographies are divided into the
same subjects reflected in the literature-based
mini-units sections.

SUMMARY

While even the most dedicated of librarians and
teachers cannot change a child's persona or
home or community environment, they can take
humor seriously in children's literature and can
provide positive models of humor for a child,
fully realizing that they need to avoid any mismatch between child humor and adult humor.
Further, they can enhance the reading and language arts curricula by selecting quality humorous children's literature for well-designed mini-
units and experiences that seriously guide all
children toward developing their sensitivity toward humor awareness.

Taking Humor Seriously in Children's Literature is intended to be a beginning place for librarians, teachers, parents, and others who find themselves interested in the benefits of teaching humor and are challenged by the increasing number of children who live day-by-day without recognizing its full value. With this guidance, children can be led toward recognizing the techniques of humor seriously used by authors and artists to be used as models and patterns as children themselves write and illustrate their own original books. Further, children can be encouraged to use humor as a way to respond to today's challenging social, economic, and political milieu. As mentioned earlier, this book is a resource dedicated to that goal.

Readings

Alfonso, Regina (1987). "Modules for Teaching about Young People's Literature—Module 4: Humor." *Journal of Reading* 30, 5 (February): 399–401. Describes a teaching unit that involves students in reading and analyzing elements of humor in young people's literature. Focuses on what makes quality humorous books funny as well as literary.

Anderson, Celia Catlett, and Marilyn Fain Apseloff (1989). *Nonsense Literature for Children*. Hamden, CT: Library Professional Publication. Discusses the idea that humorous nonsense appeals to the interests of children, is beneficial because of its bonding and attention-getting potential, and has various forms that can be used in the classroom.

Balzer, John A. (1978). *Fabulous Freaky Fun Fill-In for Fridays*. East Aurora, NY: DOK Publishers. A teacher shows ways to care about what students feel and what they have to say through a fun-filled activity for grades 4–9.

Baughman, M. Dale (1970). *Contemporary Education*. Terre Haute: Indiana State University. Editorial about the use of teacher humor.

Berding, Sister Mary Cordelia (1965). "Humor as a Factor in Children's Literature." University of Cincinnati. *Dissertation Abstracts* 26: 3691. Berding, after investigating humor as a factor in children's literature written since the mid-nineteenth century, concludes by listing five criteria for a good humorous book. Included are points of the plot of related and dependent incidents and the style involving repetition, subtleties, originality, and graphic descriptions.

Bennett, John E., and Priscilla Bennett (1982). "What's So Funny? Action Research and Bibliography of Humorous Children's Books—1975–80." *The Reading Teacher* 35, 8 (May): 924–27. This is a report on a research project in which students read books considered to be funny by media specialists and rated them for their humor. Presents a list of the books read and the ratings provided for each by the students.

Bleedom, Berenice, and Sara McKelvey (1984). *Humor: Lessons in Laughter for Learning and Living*. East Aurora, NY: DOK Publishers. Humor can be used to create a relaxed learning environment and to help the teacher detect the students' hidden creative talents.

Brumbaugh, F. (1940). "The Place of Humor in the Curriculum." *Journal of Experimental Education*. 8 (June): 403–9. Emphasizes that educators should avoid a mismatch between teacher humor and student humor.

Cart, Michael (1987). "A Light in the Darkness: Humor Returns to Children's Fantasy." *School Library Journal* 33, 7 (April): 48–51. Cart discusses the humor found in three fantasies: 1) *Up from Jericho Tell* (Atheneum, 1987) by E. L. Konisburg; *Howl's Moving Castle* (Greenwillow, 1987) by Diane Wynne Jones; and *The Hounds of the Morrigan* (Holiday, 1987) by Pat O'Shea.

Colwell, Clyde (1987). "Rationale for More Humor in Middle School Literature Programs." Greeley, CO: *SIGNAL:* Official Newsletter of IRA Special Interest Groups: A Network on Adolescent Literature. 11, 5 (May/June): 1–4. Emphasizes that gifted children look for challenging material.

DeLuca, Geraldine, and Roni Natov (1977). "Comedy in Children's Literature: An Overview." *The Lion and the Unicorn* 1, 1: 4. Emphasizes that humor can help children and adults learn another culture.

Esper, George (1989). "Humor: It's No Laughing Matter." *The Sacramento Union* (December 16): 35, 38. This is an article about Joel Goodman, head of the HUMOR project in Saratoga Springs, N.Y., and others who realize that humor has benefits for people—that is, "A sense of humor helps you take a step back from the problem that looks really terrible up close." Points out that research findings are beginning to accumulate that suggest laughter might be therapeutic and could be used to reduce disease symptoms.

Flinn, John (1989). "Cost of Comedy: the Joke's on Us." *San Francisco Examiner*. reprinted in the *The Sacramento Union* (March 27): 15. The 1989 Cost of laughing Index (a compilation of 18 leading humor indicators) is given by Malcolm Kushner, a humor consultant in Santa Cruz. The index reports on the use of humor in business. He teaches business leaders to break down the barriers between themselves and their audience by inserting some self-deprecating humor or personal anecdotes into their speeches. He has given seminars to IBM, Lockheed, Hewlett-Packard and ASK Computer Systems. He states that his biggest challenge was trying to teach humor to a group of Internal Revenue Service Managers. Kushner, a former lawyer, believes that telling a little story about how they botched up some project twenty years ago can help them connect.

Fry, William B. (1989). *A Study of Humor*. Palo Alto: Pacific Books. Emeritus associate professor of clinical psychiatry at Stanford, Fry supports the theory that laughter is good for you with research on respiratory activity maintaining that a hundred laughs are the cardiovascular equivalent of ten minutes of rowing.

Gallo, Donald R. (1978). *A Gaggle of Gimmicks*. National Council of Teachers of English. Interesting games and fun activities are contributed by twenty-eight college educators and teachers to enhance language skills in both elementary and secondary classes.

Gallo, Nick (1989). "Lighten Up: Laugh Your Way to Good Health." *Better Homes and Gardens* (August): 31–32. Research shows that humor is good for us. Humor increases some patients' tolerance for pain—it is like inner jogging and makes people happy. Laughter gets your facial, shoulder, and diaphragm muscles going and aspects of your heart, as well as your circulatory and respiratory systems. Hospitals are using laughmobiles, comedy workshops, and humor rooms for those who are ill. The author encourages readers to look for humor in situations, collect humor in cartoons, jokes, cards, tapes, and brighten up the surroundings with posters, bumper stickers, and signs. Suggests that people make time for a humor "break" daily, laugh when you are feeling low, encourage laughter in others, be playful, and avoid put-down humor. Points out that different items are humorous to different people—that is,

posters, clown noses, balloons, bubble soap, posters, comic tapes, funny books, games, and monologues by humorists.

Gentile, L. M., and M. M. McMillan (1987). *Stress and Reading Difficulties: Research, Assessment, Intervention*. Newark, DE: International Reading Association. Emphasizes that low-ability readers show emotional disorders and levels of stress.

Goleman, Daniel (1987). "You Can't Be Serious: A Little Laughter Goes a Long Way in Solving Problems." *The Sacramento Bee* (August 8): A16. This is a reprint from *New York Times* that discusses the use of humor in organizations.

Greaney, V., and J. Quinn (1978). "Factors Related to Amount and Type of Leisure Time Reading." Paper presented at the Seventh IRA World Congress on Reading, Hamburg, Germany.

Greenlaw, M. Jean (1983). "Reading Interest Research and Children's Choices." In Nancy Rosen and Margaret Frith, editors. *Children's Choices: Teaching with Books Children Like*. Newark, DE: International Reading Association. 90–92. Subjects were almost 10,000 students whose selections of 700 titles were ranked and categorized. Results indicated that books classified as funny were the first choice at the primary level. In second place were books designated as make-believe, those about people, and animal stories. The first levels of choice for grades 3–6 were books of adventure, jokes/humor, and information.

Heenan, Michael (1990). "Pelley: Laughter Can Make Work More Productive." *The Sacramento Union,* Monday, p. D2, August 13, 1990. This is an article about Jim Pelley, founder of Laughter Works, a company that instructs hard-edged business people on the art of being funny through such presentations as "Management by Horsing Around" and "Laughter: There's Nothing Funny about the Way It Sells." Pelley suggests the motto "laugh lines help the bottom line" and advocates putting humor into action with light heartedness in the office by having "play days."

Hitchens, Christopher (1988). "The Politician as a Wag: The Joke's on Him." *The Sacramento Bee* (January): 22. Hitchens, a *Newsday* reporter, reviews recent books by Morris Udall and Gerald Ford and says that the usual sign of the unfunny joke is when the teller prefaces the punch line by saying " A wag remarked . . . " or "One wit observed . . . ." This generally means that the story won't hold up on its own and needs padding and prompting. Both Ford and Udall resort to this all the time in their books. Hitchens writes that "few things are more gruesome than the politicians with a sense of humor."

Huck, Charlotte S., Susan Hepler, and Janet Hickman (1987). *Children's Literature in the Elementary School, Fourth Edition.* New York: Holt, Rinehart, and Winston. This is a source to share knowledge and enthusiasm for the literature of children with students, teachers, and librarians in the hope that they in turn will communicate their interest in books to the children they teach.

Jurich, Marilyn (1977). "Once Upon a . . ." *The Lion and the Unicorn.* 1, 1: 9. Discusses books.

Kappas, Katherine Hull (1967). "A Developmental Analysis of Children's Responses to Humor." *The Library Quarterly* 37, 1 (January): 67–77. Kappas has categorized what children find funny into ten types: exaggeration; surprise; slapstick; the absurd; human predicaments; ridicule of adults, society, human foibles or oneself (this becomes satire in its more sophisticated form); defiance or rebellion against adult authority or expressing forbidden ideas; violence; verbal humor; and incongruity.

Klause, Annette Curtis (1987). "So What's So Funny, Anyway?" *School Library Journal* 33, 6 (February): 34–35. Cites research of Katherine Hull Kappas and her developmental analysis of children's responses to humor as well as the classification of jokes for adults by Harvey Mindess, an instructor at Antioch West College in California. Mindess sees humor as freeing readers from controls and taboos imposed by society and classifies jokes for adults into ten categories: nonsense; philosophical; social satire; ethnic; sexual; scatological; hostile; degrading to women; degrading to men; and sick. Klause sees some parallels between the two lists and suggests that there is a seamier side of childhood humor that is not reflected in Hull's list. Suggests, for instance, that teens enjoy puns such as Piers Anthony's *Crewel Lye: A Caustic Yarn* (Ballantine, 1985) and the verbal humor in Douglas Adam's *The Hitchhiker's Guide to the Galaxy* (Crown, 1980); recommends Sue Townsend's *The Adrian Mole Diaries* (Grove Press, 1986).

Landau, Elliott D. (1955). "The Relationship Between Social Class Status and What Sixth Grade Children Say Is Funny in Selected Excerpts from Children's Literature." New York University. *Dissertation Abstracts* 16: 1401. This is the study of the relationship between social class status and ideas of humor expressed by sixth grade children after having read or heard selections. Three social studies classes were examined with the rather surprising finding that middle-class children seemed more reticent in their reactions to humorous materials than either lower- or upper-class children.

Leader, Jody (1993). "The Humor Project." 110 Spring St., Dept. BHG. Saratoga Springs, NY, 12866. Leader is the editor and founder of the *Laughter Prescription Newsletter,* an informal letter filled with jokes and articles from health and humor professionals. It is available to adults and children interested in the topic of humor and can be ordered from the humor project's address.

McGhee, Paul (1984). "What's the Sense of Humor?" *Science Digest* (February): 76. McGhee, the author of *Humor: Its Origins and Development* (Texas Tech University Press) says that in order for something to strike people as funny, it must be intellectually stimulating. "Kids love riddles," he says, "because they're just tackling the challenge of words with more than one meaning. Of course, for most adults, they are no longer funny. By the same token, most adults know that a pun isn't really very funny. But for the person who came up with the pun, who went through the cognitive process, it's much more humorous."

McNamara, Shelly Gail (1980). "Responses of Fourth and Seventh Grade Students to Satire as Reflected in Selected Contemporary Picture Books." Unpublished Ph. D. dissertation. Michigan State University. McNamara found that a majority of students responded to satire in a critical rather than literal manner. They expressed a positive response to it as humorous literature and recognized associational characteristics of stereotyping, superiority, moralizing, distortions, scorn, and exaggeration.

Monson, D. L. (1966). "Children's Responses to Humorous Situations in Literature." University of Minnesota. *Dissertation Abstracts* 27: 2448-A. There were few differences of humor by sex, intelligence, socioeconomic, and reading level groups among 635 fifth grade students in a strat-ified random sample.

———(1990). "Humorous Children's Books." *The Five Owls* (March/ April): 1–2. Discusses the many forms of humor in characters and a reader's reaction to the forms: 1) a discovery that the character is better or smarter than some-one else; 2) the stupid or absent-minded char-acter; 3) the technique of inversion where a character lays a trap and is caught in it; 4) dis-comfiture, horseplay, incongruity; and 5) con-fusion, surprise at the unexpected, and at any deviations from the ordinary.

Monson, D. (1983). "Literature in Programs for Gifted and Talented Children." In N. Rosen and Margaret Frith, editors, *Children's Choices: Teaching with Books Children Like.* Newark, DE: International Reading Association. 48–65. Discusses the view that laughter is a powerful response to literature.

Nowell, Paul (1989). "Laugh Mobile Brings Joy to Cancer Patients' Lives." *The Sacramento Union* (December 16): 35. Reviews the genesis of the Laugh Mobile at Duke University in 1986 by Ruth Hamilton, executive director of the Carolina Health and Humor Association. Med-ically, the mobile addresses the mind-body con-nection. It has also been introduced at Presby-terian Hospital in Charlotte, N.C.

O'Bryan-Garland, Sharon, and Stinson E. Worley (1986). "Reading Through Laughter and Tears: Developing Healthy Emotions in Preadoles-cents." *Childhood Education* 63, 1 (October): 16–23. Maintains that healthy emotional devel-opment in preadolescents can be enhanced when children vicariously experience laughter and tears (sadness) in their reading. A survey of 531 fifth graders indicated the favorite humor-ous and sad books for preadolescents.

Parker. *Wizard of Id.* Creators Syndicate, Inc., *The Sacramento Bee,* Thursday, August 4, 1994. F7. In answer to the king's question, "Okay . . .Why did you throw a tomato at me during my speech today?," the subject replies, " 'cause I couldn't reach you with the pumpkin."

Pasquet, Trinda (1989). "Self-Esteem Task Force Uses Humor, Hand Hugs to Get Message Across" in *The Sacramento Union* (August 26): 10. According to the California task force, which promotes self-esteem and personal and social responsibility, it seems that humor is an important part of increased self-esteem, which decreases problems of crime, drug and alcohol abuse, and school failure. Emphasizes that while laughter is instinctive, a sense of humor is an at-titude that is developmental and points out that self-esteem can be enhanced with humor. Em-phasizes that humor is a natural relaxant and healing facilitator. Medical research indicates that laughter releases endorphins—the body's natural pain killer—and oxygenates the blood.

Paterson, Katherine (1986). "Wednesday's Chil-dren." *The Horn Book Magazine* (May/June): 293. Makes the point that humor can be a coun-terbalance for everyday life.

Patterson, E. B. (1972). *Sagebrush Doctors.* Springville, Utah: Art City Publishing Co. This is an accounting of the early days of the west-ern health care professionals who served mainly in Nevada in the 1800s. Gives some in-formation about physicians who later practiced with the Elko Clinic—Drs. George Moore, James Monohan, Byron Benson, George Col-lett, and others.

Perlman, Lisa (1989). "What's So Funny?" In *Religion, The Sacramento Union* (March 25). Cal Samra's Fellowship of Merry Christians, a Kalamazoo-based (Michigan) ecumenical group, believes there is a serious lack of humor in faith. The group celebrates Easter Monday, the first day of what they call the Holy Humor Season, in different ways. There are festivities, sing-alongs, and joke telling. Samra, who says his 3-year-old group has 10,000 members, be-lieves humor and Christianity are thought often as mutually exclusive but emphasizes that peo-ple should focus on Christian humor, wit, and joy, and to this end, produces a bimonthly pub-lication, *Joyful Noiseletter.*

Perret, Gerie (1993). *Great One-Liners.* Illustrated by Myron Miller. New York: Sterling. Defines a one-liner as a humorous, creative, and clever response to a situation. There are thirteen chap-ters that begin with one-liners by famous peo-ple such as Woody Allen, Will Rogers, Mark Twain, *et al.* The chapters have titles that include "School Chums and Chumps" (about brains, dummies, and education); "The Sport-ing Life," (basketball, baseball, football, golf, hockey); "Boy Meets Girl and So On" (dating, bachelors, marriage); "King of the Road" (au-tomobiles, driving, traffic); and "Life and Its After Effects" (birth, old age, death, spiritual matters).

Rasgorshek, Beth (1990). "Laughing Is One Way to Learn." *Young American* 7, 2 (February): 1. Discusses the Kids Comedy Club where students, grades 1–6, in New York City in Public School 132 meet twice a week to laugh. They are divided into groups of comedians, artists, writers, designers, and critics. They tell jokes, draw funny pictures, and read funny books. They work on fun projects to improve their reading and writing skills, solve problems with the ideas that come from their heads, and use their imaginations to keep from getting grouchy. For projects, they read twenty joke books a year and make three joke books a year. Last year's favorite book was *Alf-A-Laugh-A-Bet Book* which was the result of collecting 5,000 of the funniest words in the English language and matching the words with drawings. They also made an antidrughead manual and did antidrug rap commercials based on real TV commercials.

The Sacramento Union (1990). "Practical Joking: Laughing All the Way to Good Health." *USA Weekend* (August 10–13): 7. Examples are given: 1) Dr. William Fry, emeritus associate professor of clinical psychiatry at Stanford, supports the theory that laughter is good for you. He reports research on respiratory activity maintaining that a hundred laughs are the cardiovascular equivalent of ten minutes of rowing; and 2) C. W. Metcalf, former health worker conducts business seminars on laughter for better productivity and cites a 25 percent decrease in employee downtime and 60 percent rise in job satisfaction.

Sadker, Myra Pollack, and David Miller Sadker (1977). *Now Upon a Time: A Contemporary View of Children's Literature.* New York: Harper. The authors link humor to general life experience and state: "Children laugh at characters, ideas, words, and events that do not fit, that are illogical and unnatural. But in order to appreciate the incongruity of a given situation, the child must understand the natural order, and therefore see the comedy in the grouping of incompatibles. Since children are generally much more limited in experience and background than adults, they are able to see few incongruities. Therefore, their sense of humor is somewhat different and more limited than adults" (p. 319).

Spiegel, D. L. (1984). "Preferences of Middle School Students in Humorous Literature." Unpublished masters thesis, Kansas State University. Discusses results of an interest inventory completed by middle school students that showed humor as a first-place preference in reading interests.

Spiegel, D. L. (1981). *Reading for Pleasure: Guidelines* (Reading Aids Series) Newark, DE: International Reading Association. Emphasizes that humor has an attraction for seventh and eighth graders and widespread appeal for both females and males across all ability levels.

Stanish, Bob (1983). *A Mouser's Shoe and the Cat Kangaroo.* East Aurora, NY: DOK Publishers. Discusses art, writing, and discussion activities as well as a "what happens next" form.

Sugarman, Joe (1994). "What's So Funny About Humor?" *College Park* Magazine (summer): 12–17. Gives examples and discusses the anatomy of a joke that includes the joke body, the punch line, and a cognitive map. The map diagrams how the joke body leads a listener to Concept A but the following punch line whips the mind over to Concept B—the idea that triggers the humor.

Udall, Morris K. (1987). *Too Funny to be President.* New York: Holt. As an example, one chapter is entitled "The Punch Line: Getting Laughs Almost Anywhere." Udall writes "this job has done wonders for my paranoia: now I have real enemies." He later refers to Erma Bombeck as the "first lady of humor" who has brought the "healing power of laughter to a whole country." In return, Bombeck says that Udall's humor is "drier than most humor. What did you expect from a state with less than ten inches of rainfall a year!"

Vance, Charles M. (1987). "A Comparative Study on the Use of Humor in the Design of Instruction." *Instructional Science* 16, 1 (September): 79–100. This study of fifty-eight first graders used audio cassette recordings of a familiar story to examine the effects of three integrated and contiguous instructional designs using incongruity humor on recognition and recall of information as measured by immediate learning and retention tests. Research methodology is discussed and sixty-eight references listed.

Weaver III, Richard L., and Howard W. Cotrell (1987). "Ten Specific Techniques for Developing Humor in the Classroom." *Education* 108, 2 (Winter): 167–179. Discusses techniques of humor—that is, smiling, being spontaneous, providing an informal climate, having a thought for the day, and using stories and experiences. Emphasizes that humor can also be developed by relating things to students, planning lectures with humor, having a give-and-take climate, and telling a joke or two.

Whitmer, Jean E. (1986). "Pickles Will Kill You: Use Humorous Literature to Teach Critical Reading." *The Reading Teacher* 39, 6 (February): 530–34. Argues that humorous books have the potential to brighten the classroom environment, motivate students, and develop reactive thinking readers in the classroom.

Yolen, Jane (1983). "To Make a Child Laugh." *The Writer* (August):15. Yolen believes that children have what a sophisticated humor palate would call "no taste" and says "Wit is the product of the cultivation of the funny bone." She warns "what may be hilarious to an adult writer may often go over a child's head" (p. 16).

Zillman, Doug (1973). *Handbook on Humor Research*. Indiana University. Educational Research Association Press. Humorous effects in stories also can be added with sound effects from records and tapes, with humorous words found in dictionaries and thesauri, and with new words such as sniglets, buzz words, slang, and jargon. Humorous actions can come from unintended slapstick, or from clever word play, the use of idioms, or puns. Additionally, humorous approaches can use double meanings, switches, exaggerations, and thinking of opposites to include in the writing. To engage in humorous writing, the girls and boys should have plenty of opportunities to associate words, exaggerate, make disparate words, and put unusual objects, services, and trends together in ways that will appear humorous to others.

I

Literature-Based Mini-Units
for Children Ages 5–8

Animals as Humans

Pigs Aplenty, Pigs Galore! (47)

WHAT'S THE BOOK?

Pigs Aplenty, Pigs Galore! Written and illustrated by David McPhail. New York: Dutton, 1993. Ages 5–6.

WHAT'S SO FUNNY?

It is the surprise behavior—the slurping, burping—and the clothing of the pigs. Piggy party-goers arrive in a wide variety of vehicles dressed in different costumes resembling kings, queens, members of a rock and roll band, and other eye-catching apparel.

WHAT'S IT ABOUT?

Happily for the young contemporary reader, *Pigs Aplenty, Pigs Galore!* is humorous and direct. As a man reads quietly, he hears noises—crunching, munching—that are preparatory signals for a pig invasion of party-hearty characters into his home. The pigs arrive by different means of transportation and have a good time all through the night. They are dressed in different outfits—ballplayers, bagpipe players, cowboys, and so on. Though initially patient, the man loses it, and commands the party pigs to clean up. After he feeds them pizza, all the chaos quiets down and the man falls asleep. As he sleeps, he dreams about counting pigs to fall asleep, an amusing ending.

WHAT'S THE MINI-UNIT PURPOSE?

Mention to children: "You are going to hear a story about a young man whose home is invaded by pigs dressed in different costumes—one is dressed as Elvis Presley—and who drive different vehicles to get to the party. Listen to find out how the pigs have a piggy celebration through the night and how their behavior surprises you. How does the young man finally get them to 'clean up'?"

WHAT NEW WORDS CAN BE EMPHASIZED?

Pigs, aplenty, galore, crunching, munching, slurping, burping.

WHAT'S THERE TO TALK ABOUT?

Before Reading Aloud

1. **Brainstorming about Pigs.** Different animals have been the subject of humor, and pigs are no exception. They seem to have comic characteristics that appeal to children as well as authors and illustrators of children's books. To emphasize this appeal, ask the children to seek out pig expressions from others at school during a recess or lunch hour. With the children back in the classroom, have them brainstorm any expressions they have heard about pigs—that is, "This little piggy stayed home; pigging out; this room looks like a pig pen," and so on. Write their expressions on the board. Have children get into groups and select one of the expressions to illustrate on art paper. Have children show their work to the whole group and display in the room.

2. **Piggy Predictions.** Have the children look at the illustrations as you show them and ask them to make predictions about the title and about the story based on the information they get from the pictures. Write the predictions on the board. Read the story and stop occasionally to check the predictions. Ask children to tell how the predictions on the board, especially the humorous ones, compare with what happened in the story.

3. Class Passes. Introduce the children to making their own "humorous class passes," a paper pass with space on it to write the classroom number and the teacher's name. Encourage the children to decorate the passes with sketches of pigs and their surprise behavior. The "Fall Fun" (Spring Fun, etc.) passes can be carried to enter the class each morning when humor is the topic of study; they can show permission to be in the bathroom, the hall, the library, the main office, and so on.

4. Humorous Illustrations from Newspapers and Magazines. Encourage children to cut out humorous pictures from discarded newspapers, flyers, brochures, and magazines. Have them dictate/write a sentence for each one—that is, I thought this was funny because . . . . Give the children time to read these aloud to the class. If desired, they can put the illustrations into groups or art collages, and create headings or categories for their collections. The collections can be mounted on chart paper for a class display. Have the contributors for each chart sign their names at the foot of the chart similar to the way cartoonists sign their names in the last frame of a cartoon strip.

For an optional activity, have children use the illustrations to decorate book marks, class passes, another class banner, booklets or pages in an individual humor scrapbook.

5. Humorous Bookmarks. Engage children in making their own humorous bookmarks (8 1/2″ × 2″) and a 6-foot classroom banner, "Welcome to Humor," from art paper or butcher paper. The banner and bookmarks can show humorous scenes and humorous books they have heard/read through the school year from September through June. Have children color both items with markers, crayons, colored pencils, or paints as a cooperative group project.

After Reading Aloud

1. Who Wanted What? With children, discuss the story, its elements, and the humorous surprise behavior:

Who:
Wanted What:
But what funny thing happened that surprised you?
And then what happened?

Have children dictate their ideas about these story elements. Write their responses on a chart or the board. Ask for volunteers to illustrate the children's ideas and make drawings for the chart or chalk sketches for the board.

2. One funny thing *Pigs Aplenty, Pigs Galore!* makes me think of is . . . Have each one turn to a child next to him or her and briefly discuss any or all of the following:

- "One surprise behavior that I saw in *Pigs Aplenty, Pigs Galore!* was . . . and it makes me think of. . . ." "This is what I would have said or done that would have been a funny surprise at the piggy party. . . ."
- How did the young man stop the party? What surprising behavior did he have?
- How is this piggy party different from your idea of what a party at your house should be?
- Describe how you think the pigs might have learned to dress in different costumes and drive different vehicles? What was it about the pigs' clothing that surprised you? About their transportation? How do you think the young man felt when the pigs arrived?

3. Reread a Funny Part. Reread a funny part of the story by dividing the selection into parts and having individuals or duets of students read the parts aloud in voices that are different from their own—that is, invite them to hold their nose while they talk in a character's voice. Have children identify things they think are funny by discussing them when they see them or hear them in the story.

If desired, take time to discuss the form of humor—that is, is humor in the paragraphs? What did you notice that was humorous to you? Have children give other examples of what they thought was funny to them.

4. Write a Class Pig Tale. Engage the children in writing a brief humorous pig tale and discuss the play on the words *tale* and *tail*. Have children suggest ideas for another adventure for the party-going pigs and suggest names for the characters, situation(s) in which the pigs would find themselves, and some surprise behavior. Write their ideas on chart paper or butcher paper. When the whole group has developed events for a story, ask partners to write one of the events in the plot. After each partnership has written their event, share them aloud with the group. Put the events together by pasting them on a long section of butcher paper—mural style. Ask the partnerships to illustrate their event and affix them to the mural. Fold up the butcher paper in accordion folds and unfold it to read it aloud to another class.

5. Independent Reading. Each week or two with a small group of children, choose several humorous books (among which is *Pigs Aplenty, Pigs Galore!*) from the school or public library for the independent reading shelf in the classroom. Skim through several of the books and place book marks in places where there is a humorous incident, a funny description, a cartoon-type illustration, scenes of zany characters, and so on. Point out and read from these selections each day to interest the children in independently reading the books.

6. Humorous New Words for a Familiar Tune. Refer to the title, *Pigs Aplenty, Pigs Galore!,* on the board. Have children suggest new words about the pigs to the tune of the chorus of "Skip to My Lou." For example, new words could include

Pigs Aplenty, one by one,
Pigs Aplenty, one by one,
Pigs Aplenty, one by one,
Pigs Galore . . . Pig fun.

7. A Book Banner: Going Hog Wild. With a book banner that says "Going Hog Wild," give brief book talks from a class display to interest children in other pig tales such as *Pigs Will Be Pigs* (1) by Amy Axelrod where pigs turn their house upside down looking for spare change so they can go out to dinner; *Oink, Oink* (22) by Arthur Geisert, which is the story of eight piglets who sneak away from a dozing mother to play in a cornfield; and *Pigs in Hiding* (19) by Arlene Dubanevich where a young child can look for hidden pigs on the pages.

Have children select a book of their choice from the display. Ask them to find something they think is humorous in one of the illustrations. Ask the children to tell why they selected the humorous illustration they did.

WHAT ACTIVITIES WILL EXTEND THE BOOK?

1. Piggy Pencil Mini-Posters

It is the behavior—slurping, burping—and clothing of the pigs that is surprising in the story and children can make colorful "Piggy Pencil Mini-Posters" to advertise the book. Have them sketch and color scenes of the pigs' surprising behavior on small squares of colored paper (5″ × 5″) and insert a pencil through the margins at the foot and the head of the sketch. This will make the scene look somewhat like a ship's sail with the pencil as the mast. Children can sketch some of the piggy party-goers, their transportation, and the different costumes. Have children use the mini-posters on the pencils for a fun experience while they write.

2. You Can't Be Serious: So What's So Funny to You Anyway?

Suggest that the children contribute humorous materials for the classroom. Elicit children in indicating what is funny to them and get an idea of their concepts of humor by distributing a half-sheet of paper to each child. Ask for something humorous to be sketched or written—a humorous response from each child. Read some of the responses throughout the week to begin the school day, to insert in lessons, to serve as humorous "commercial" breaks, and to close the end of the school day. The half-sheet could look like Figure 1.

It's Funny Funny Funny Funny Funny

To the Teacher:
The research of Katherine Hull (*Library Quarterly* 37 [January 1967]: 67–77) and her developmental analysis of children's responses to humor indicates what children find funny can be identified in ten categories: exaggeration, surprise, slapstick, the absurd, human predicaments, ridicule (of society, adults, human foibles, or oneself), defiance (against adult authority), and rebellion (or expressing forbidden ideas and violence), verbal humor, and incongruity. Group the children's responses into these categories as part of your classroom research. What results did you find?

Figure 1. Form for What's So Funny to You Anyway?

2. Hand Hugs in Class

With partners, invite the children to play the role of the young man who tells the pigs to clean up and then falls asleep to dream about pigs—ask the children to describe aloud a humorous scene where the young man shakes hands with the pigs as they arrive. Suggest that the children try creating some friendly and humorous hand hugs with their partners and others. For instance, while shaking the hand of another, they can use the other hand to cover, tickle, or hug the already clasped hands.

3. Tell Your Feelings about Humorous Actions

Taking the role of the young man, invite children to tell a friend how the young man might have felt about the humorous actions that happened at the party. Later, have each of the two children trade the roles with the friend taking the part of the young man.

4. Fortunately, I was there to help and I . . . .

Have the children retell their favorite humorous part of the story by taking turns in partnership discussions and putting themselves in the story somewhere by saying, "Fortunately, I was there to help and I . . . ." Ask them to make story changes as they say what they would do to help the young man during the piggy invasion.

5. A Chart Story and Pig Alphabet of Surprise Behavior

Invite children to dictate their interpretation of the story. Write their dictation on a chart and reread it as a group story. Engage the children in creating their own humorous art to make a "Pig Alphabet" to show surprise behavior as a border for the chart. The children can create a sketch of a pig with an object whose name begins with a letter of the alphabet. For example, a pig can polish an automobile for the letter A, another can blow shiny soap bubbles for B, and still another can frost a giant cupcake with chocolate icing for C.

6. A Party Pig Calendar

Introduce the monthly calendar and have the children imagine that the last day of the month is the day that the pigs plan to arrive at the man's house for their piggy party. They can brighten the calendar with humorous "Share-a-Smile" sketches that show their ideas of what surprise behavior the pigs were doing on the other days of the month to prepare for the party. Have the children paste the sketches on each of the boxes that represent the days of the month. There can be humorous weather seals to indicate days that are sunny, rainy, cloudy, partly cloudy, snowy, and windy.

Pigs at Christmas (19)

WHAT'S THE BOOK?

Pigs at Christmas. Written and illustrated by Arlene Dubanevich. New York: Bradbury, 1986. Ages 5–7.

WHAT'S SO FUNNY?

There are verbal and visual jokes. The drawings are cartoon panels filled with visual jokes and the word balloons have verbal humor.

WHAT'S IT ABOUT?

As six pigs prepare for Christmas, everything seems to go right for five pigs. For one pig, however, everything seems to go wrong. As an example, everyone else's cookies turn out fine, but his blueberry binkies burn. When he has other mishaps, he worries that Santa won't bring a present to him because he is not perfect. But, of course, Santa does bring a present and it is very special.

WHAT'S THE MINI-UNIT PURPOSE?

Mention to children: "You are going to hear a story about six pigs who are getting ready for Christmas. Listen to find out how everything goes right for five little pigs and everything goes *wrong* for one little pig. The little pig worries that Santa won't bring him a present because he is not perfect. Listen to hear how many verbal jokes you can hear and to find out what Santa does bring the little worried pig."

WHAT NEW WORDS CAN BE EMPHASIZED?

Pigs, Santa, Christmas, blueberry binkies.

WHAT'S THERE TO TALK ABOUT?

Before Reading Aloud

1. **What's Going on at Christmas?** Ask children to listen to an audiotape of some familiar holiday music. Have children close their eyes and listen. Ask them to think what time of year it might be and WHERE they might be while listening to the music. Ask them to tell any musical instruments they can identify. Replay the tape and ask the children to act out motions of things they would do at this time of year—that is, wrapping presents, baking holiday cookies and candies, etc. Have them suggest some musical sounds to add to the tape when it is replayed—perhaps sounds made by objects in the classroom that would sound humorous to them.

2. **Pigs Prepare for a Holiday.** Introduce the title of the book and write the words *Pigs at Christmas* on the board. Ask children to tell what the title might be saying to them. Have them divide into two groups and when a signal is given, have each group pantomime their interpretation of the title for the other group. Show several illustrations from the book that show humorous actions in the ways that the pigs prepared for the holiday. Have children identify the activities and relate them to their own experiences. Ask them to tell some kinds of things related to the holiday that they think will be mentioned in the book.

3. **Think of Amusing Holiday Ways.** Ask the children to think of some amusing ways that the pigs acting like humans could prepare for a winter holiday. Ask them to dramatize one or more of their suggestions. Invite the children to review their dramatization and tell more about what they did. If desired, introduce children to other fall and winter multicultural holidays—Chinese New Year, Hanukkah with candles, dreidels, gifts, and food representative of the holiday, and Kwanzaa

with candles, mats, gifts, food, and other significant symbols.

4. **Interpreting Humor in Your Own Way.** Ask children to think of ways to describe one or more of the pigs. Ask them to quickly make pencil sketches of their descriptions. As a contrast, show some of the humor in the illustrations. Ask the children to show them and turn to the child on their right (or left) and tell why they drew humor in their sketches the way they did. As a whole group, invite volunteers to show their descriptions and tell more about them to the entire group.

After Reading Aloud

1. **One Joke in *Pigs at Christmas* that I liked was . . . .** Return to the title on the board. Introduce children to the idea of a joke (a *brief* happening that is told, shown, or portrayed to make people laugh). Have each child turn to a child next to him or her and tell, "One joke in *Pigs at Christmas* that I liked was . . . ." Discuss:

- What might *you* have said or done to cheer the worried little pig?
- What did Santa bring as a gift for the little pig? If you had been a Santa's helper, what gift would you have selected for the little pig?
- What made Santa's gift for the little pig special? How do you think the little pig felt when Santa gave him a gift?

2. **More Verbal and Visual Jokes.** With *Pigs at Christmas,* point out that the drawings are cartoon panels filled with visual jokes and that the word balloons hold the verbal humor about the six pigs who prepare for Christmas. Much of the fun is in the idea that everything seems to go right for five pigs; but for one pig everything seems to go wrong. With an opaque projector, show some of the illustrations to the children and ask them to look for visual jokes—that is, the things that go wrong for the little pig or things that appear funny to the children.

3. **A Humorous Class Book Report.** Have children review the parts of the story that they thought were funny to them and list them. Discuss the examples of the humor. Choose one of the examples to describe aloud. Have children illustrate an example of their choice and write two phrases/sentences that describe the humor. Put the writing together as a humorous class book report.

4. Book Buttons to Wear. Introduce the title of the book again and ask children to tell what the words mean to them. Show several illustrations from the book that show the pigs doing holiday activities. Related to the books, engage children in creating humorous book awards they can wear—buttons that announce the title of the humorous book they are enjoying. Engage children in making their own buttons (about 2 1/2″ circle) cut from adhesive-backed shelf paper that can be worn on their clothing.

5. A Humorous Holiday: Torn-Paper Winter Pictures. Have the children describe how they *think* the pigs learned to prepare for the holiday. Engage them in brainstorming ideas for making torn-paper winter pictures of the pigs with a pig motif—that is, making snowpigs (instead of snowmen outside), gingerbread pigs, gingerbread barns, Santa Pig, pig elves, pigs to pull Santa's sleigh, etc. Write their ideas on the board as a reference list as they make their pictures. Encourage them to add any visual jokes they think should be in the pictures.

WHAT ACTIVITIES WILL EXTEND THE BOOK?

1. Gift Boxes with Humorous Drawings

With partners, invite the children to prepare gift boxes with humorous scenes of the pigs, or other animals, preparing for the holiday. Have children use discarded milk cartons and cover the outside with art paper. They can use markers, crayons, colored pencils or paint to make the scenes of pigs and humorous behavior. If desired, they can place an object for a gift inside—a favorite comic strip, a favorite pet rock, a length of ribbon, a special hand-written note, a slip of paper with a joke or riddle written on it, etc.

2. Something Funny Happened on a Holiday

Ask children to interview another classmate with, "Tell me about preparing for a holiday at your house where something funny happened."

3. Humorous Books of the Week

Ask children to tell about other stories they know where they saw animals as humans and where there were visual and verbal jokes that surprised them. Have them make a list of the stories and display the list in a reading area as "Humorous Books of the Week" so children can refer to it as needed and look for other books on the subject.

4. Humor-Go-Round Wheel(s)

Some children like to see what is going on and respond readily to a humor-go-round wheel (see figure 2) that lists different types of humor to read about. In some cases, children can limit their humor awareness to a single response—it's a joke. To encourage a more balanced awareness of humor, introduce a humor wheel (a circle with pie-shaped wedges). Encourage children to refer to the wheel—that is, to make decisions about different types of humor to read about and to talk about after their reading.

If desired, engage children in drawing their own individual wheels on a sheet of colored paper. With crayons, have children draw dark "spokes" for the wheel from paper to outline the pie-shaped wedges. In the wedges, have children label the space to represent various features of humor—cartoonlike illustrations, humorous details, exaggerations, misadventures, verbal and visual jokes, zaniness, etc. Additional wheels can be made when additional features of humor are identified. After a humorous book is read and a certain feature of humor is identified, a child can add an additional colorful spoke on the wheel in the appropriate space. Some wheels will have lots and lots of spokes.

5. Animals as Humans Who Acted in Surprising Ways

Ask the children to tell about other stories where they saw animals as humans who wore clothing that surprised them and acted in surprising ways. On a chart, list the titles of the stories along with the names of the children who made the suggestions:

- *When Bluebell Sang* (21) suggested by Vicki
- *Liverwurst Is Missing* (38) suggested by Margie

If desired, the chart can be used as a reading and browsing reference in the room's reading area. If an individual reading area is preferred, consider constructing a reading area from a large refrigerator box by cutting a door on one side, a large window on another, and a skylight on the top. Prepare a door latch so a child can close the door and have privacy while reading. For additional light, place an extension light cord through the skylight.

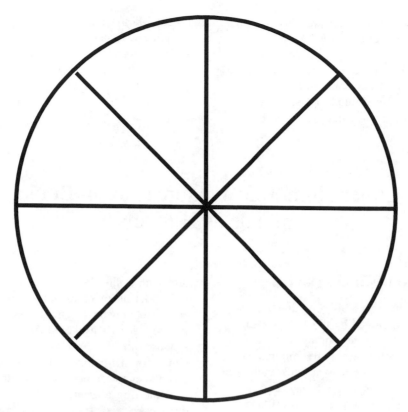

Figure 2. Form for Humor-Go-Round Wheel.

6. Recognizing Some Features of Humor

With third grade children (or older), reread parts of the story aloud to illustrate the idea that in the writing of humorous stories there are one or more of the following features incorporated in the writing. Discuss excerpts from Brown's story that are the author's examples of

- A funny opening
- A colorful narration
- Colorful character(s)
- A concise plot
- Putting in some surprises with things that don't "fit" together. One way to remember the value of "putting in some surprises" is to recall comedian Steven Wright's misfortune—"I'm not afraid of heights, I'm afraid of widths."

Further with third graders, discuss any or all of the four tips for writing short humor that have been offered by Patrick McManus (Finley, 1988). Write the tips on paper strips to display as headings on the board:

- Find a comic idea so your writing will have a single theme.

- Develop the characters who will tell the story.
- Make a list in a notebook of the bits of humor, the jokes, that you can fit into your writing.
- Begin writing and remember that the beginning is the hardest part.

Engage the children in offering suggestions of examples of the previously mentioned features to write under each of the headings. Encourage them to refer to comic strips or books that they have read or stories they have heard. Additionally, invite the children to work together with a writing partner in the class to do one or more of the following, and display their products under the appropriate sentence strip/tip:

- Write about or illustrate a comic idea that has made them laugh; for example, in the *Peanuts* (May 15, 1994, *The Sacramento Bee*) strip by Charles Schultz, Charlie Brown is yelling at Lucy because she missed a catch while they played ball. He tells her she is the "worst" player in the history of the game, that she is driving him crazy, and so on. Lucy responds with "Are you talking to me?"

- Write about or sketch a character who has made them laugh. In the *Marmaduke* (May 15, 1994, *The Sacramento Bee*) strip by Brad Anderson, the great dane digs a large hole to uncover a bone he had buried and a man yells "Hey!" The surprised dog turns around and sees the man holding a small green-leafed tree in a planting pot. Marmaduke hears him say, "That's a great hole . . . Thanks."
- Write about or make drawings of a humorous situation or a joke that made them laugh—perhaps they enjoy the escapades of *Calvin & Hobbes*. Take time to have the children show and discuss their work.

What Other Humorous Features Are in Books with Animals as Humans?

CARTOONLIKE ILLUSTRATIONS

Cartoonlike illustrations—often with exaggerations—are often employed by illustrators to draw or sketch to show something funny in children's books. Lisa Campbell Ernst shows children what cartoonlike illustrations add to a book in *When Bluebell Sang* (21). It is a very funny account of Farmer Swenson's attempt to showcase Bluebell, his singing cow. He takes her to town so all can hear her beautiful voice. With the help of her zealous talent agent, Big Eddie, Bluebell becomes a star overnight! When Bluebell becomes homesick, however, Swenson and his cow try to outsmart Big Eddie so they can return home.

HUMOROUS DETAILS AND EXAGGERATED EXPRESSIONS

The concept of exaggeration—the idea of making something seem more than it really is—is often used to create certain effects of humor. Steven Kellogg uses it as a technique in his book *Liverwurst Is Missing* (38). The funny details and exaggerated expressions help tell this humorous story of Farmer Appelard and his animal friends who pursue Liverwurst's kidnappers. The story, while wacky to some adults, could appear to some young children to be quite sensible in its ending. It is Liverwurst's gargantuan mother who rescues him just in the nick of time.

KNOWING THE JOKE OF THE PLOT

The idea of "being in on the joke" or knowing what can be done to be funny can be shown to children with Colin West's *"Pardon" said the Giraffe* (73). It lets a reader know the joke of the plot line early. Hopping on the ground, the frog asks the tall giraffe, "What's it like up there?" The giraffe responds with, "Pardon?" Time after time, the frog hops upon the animals—the lion, then the hippo, then the elephant, and finally on the giraffe. Each time the frog asks the same question, a question that can be predicted and repeated aloud. The surprise comes when the giraffe sneezes and makes the frog tumble to the ground. This time it is the giraffe who "turns the tables" and asks the question, "What's it like down there?"

UNUSUAL PREMISE: AN ANIMAL USES ITS UNIQUE CHARACTERISTICS

In Franz Brandenberg's *Otto Is Different* (8), Otto is different because he is an octopus. The idea of using eight arms all at once is what makes the story fun. Otto thinks he would rather be like his other animal friends and not have so many arms but his parents convince him that having eight arms can be a grand accomplishment. They point out he has more arms for hugging and he can play a game of hockey all by himself. The illustrations are done by James Stevenson with great comic action that show the various ways Otto uses all his arms as he does his homework, sweeps the floor, and practices the piano all at the same time. Children will be able to imagine many other possibilities for Otto's extra arms and they can consider what funny things might have happened if Otto had been another creature—a caterpillar, spider, giraffe, or anteater.

Leonard Kessler's *Old Turtle's Baseball Stories* (40) presents Old Turtle as a narrator who tells tall tales about baseball for his friends. His animal heroes, like Brandenberg's Otto in *Otto Is Different* (8), use their special characteristics and turn into unbelievably great achievers. There was

- Cleo Octopus, the greatest pitcher of all times
- Melvin Moose, the player who hit the ball with his antlers and invented Mooseball
- Carla Kangaroo, whose little baby, Joey, caught the fly ball when Carla tripped and fell
- Randy Squirrel, a good base stealer—literally

RIDICULOUS SITUATION

The idea of ridiculousness in everyday situations can be shown through some objects and actions that are *not* worthy of serious consideration. This technique is used in *The Wuggie Norple Story* (17) by Tomie de Paola. This is a picture book worth showing for its ridiculous situations about Lunchbox Louis. Louis is convinced that the kitten he brings home for his son, King Waffle, is rapidly growing bigger—bigger than a bulldog, a razorback hog, a horse, and—finally—an elephant. He brings home each of these animals to prove his point, until all finally agree that Wuggie Norple is, indeed, as big as the elephant. The whole satisfied crew troops off to picnic at Nosewort Pond.

TRICKY ENDINGS

The use of tricks that are humorous—acts that involve cleverness and skill—and intended to fool someone (or even to cheat a deserving villain) can be shown to children with Arnold Lobel's *Mouse Soup* (43). It is a narrative with a Scherazade-story twist and a tricky ending. It is about a captive mouse who tells four tales to keep himself out of the soup. Among the four tales, don't miss the mouse's story about the noisy cricket and the lady mouse who couldn't get to sleep.

The use of a clever, skilled trickster who fools someone is the main character found in *Tiger Soup* (69), a Jamaican tale. Tiger fixes a sweet soup for himself but Anansi distracts him from eating it, insisting that they go swimming together first. Tiger gets into the water, but Anansi sneaks off to eat the soup. Then, fearing the Tiger's revenge, he teaches some nearby monkeys a song about eating the soup. He disappears into the woods after encouraging the monkeys to sing the song loudly. Tiger wants revenge but the monkeys escape into the treetops.

ZANINESS

In keeping with the idea of zaniness, Fernando Krahn's *The Family Minus* (315) is a story that reflects some buffoonery, irrational words, and ludicrous behavior and antics to amuse readers. For one example, eight long-nosed odd-looking animal children and their inventive mother take part in several zany adventures—actions that will appear irrational, ludicrous, or even "mildly insane" to some viewers. For another, the children ride to school in their mother's latest invention, a caterpillarlike car with an open cab for each child. The caterpillar mobile becomes the family's novel transportation to school each day.

Family, School, and Community

I Don't Want to Go Back to School (122)

WHAT'S THE BOOK?

I Don't Want to Go Back to School. Written by Marisabina Russo and illustrated by the author. New York: Greenwillow, 1994. Ages 5–7.

WHAT'S SO FUNNY?

This is a story that combines humorous relationships in a family with kindness. The universal concern is a serious one about overcoming fears and going back to school and it is dealt with in a caring way. There is humor, however, in the contrast between the support of the boy's parents and the teasing taunts of his older sister.

WHAT'S IT ABOUT?

When summer is at an end, Ben does not want to go back to second grade. His parents offer him their assurances that everything will be fine, but this is contrasted with the dire predictions of Ben's big sister, Hannah. Hannah relies on her memories of second grade—all are apparently disastrous—and says that Ben will probably not know the answers to questions in class and he might fall asleep on the bus, missing his stop. This is a contrast to the support of his parents. The first day turns out fine, however, and it is Hannah who is the one who nearly sleeps through their bus stop—an unexpected ending that is humorous and pleasant.

WHAT'S THE MINI-UNIT PURPOSE?

Mention to children: "You are going to hear a story about a young boy, Ben, who doesn't want to go back to second grade. Listen to find out what his parents say to him in a positive way to tell him that everything will be OK at school and to find out what his big sister says about the negative side of second grade. Listen to find out how the first day of school *really* turned out for Ben."

WHAT NEW WORDS CAN BE EMPHASIZED?

Hannah, Ben, school.

WHAT'S THERE TO TALK ABOUT?

Before Reading Aloud

1. What the Title Means to Me. Introduce the title of the book and write the words, *I Don't Want to Go Back to School* on the board. With an opaque projector, show several illustrations from the book that reflect some of the conversations between Ben and his parents as they assure him things will be fine; and then show illustrations of Ben and his big sister as she recounts her own memories of disaster in second grade.

2. Schoolhouse Bulletin Board: Reasons for Not Going Back to School. Ask the children to think of reasons why someone would not want to go back to school. Ask them to tell what they could do to help the person who did not want to return to school. In what ways could they assure the person that things would turn out fine? After a discussion, have each child cut out and color schoolhouse shapes (about 2″) from art paper. Ask them to write a reason for going/not going back to school on the back of the shape. Display the shapes on a bulletin board beside a large schoolhouse (48 × 24″) cut from art paper. Have volunteers draw windows and doors on the large schoolhouse.

3. All about Me Mural: Fun Activities and Humorous Playmates. Ask children to think if they have looked forward to returning to school at the end of summer. Encourage them to share their feelings about any fun activities and humorous playmates that made them feel that way. Have them prepare a mural of sketches that show the activities and playmates. Use the mural to help children get to know one another as they introduce one another and some of the humorous events and friends they have encountered at school.

After Reading Aloud

1. Retelling the Story. Ask the children to help tell the story in sequence about the humorous family relationships, and emphasize the humorous ending. Discuss:

1. If you had been with Ben and Hannah, what might *you* have said or done that would have been funny?
2. How did the parents feel about Ben's feelings about *not* going back to school?
3. Is Hannah different from your idea of what a big sister should be? What ways? In what ways was Hannah funny/not funny?
4. Describe how you think Ben felt on the bus riding to school on the first day. How do you think Ben felt at the end of the school day and on the bus returning home?

2. Being Ben: Humorous Partnership Play. With partners, invite the children to get in pairs and play the roles of Ben who does *not* want to return to second grade and Hannah who makes her dire predictions of what could go wrong. Ask the children to take turns playing the roles of the two book characters and describe aloud anything humorous from their role-play to the whole group.

WHAT ACTIVITIES WILL EXTEND THE BOOK?

1. Put Your Own Personality into the Story

Have each child tell about their favorite part of the story, and somewhere insert their own personality into it by saying, "If I had been there as a friend of Ben's, I . . . . " Invite them to make story changes as they say what they would have done to bring humor into the situation to help Ben face his negative feelings about returning to school.

2. Classroom Door Decor: A Humorous Friend or Event at School

Ask the children to get into pairs and interview one another with "Tell me about a time you *wanted* to go back to school because of a humorous friend or event. What happened?" After the interviews, have children sketch their friends or the events. Cut out the sketches and mount them on a section of butcher paper about five feet tall to make a tall decoration for the classroom door.

3. A Going-Back-to-School Luncheon

Invite the children to a "Going-Back-to-School Luncheon." To prepare for the lunch, have each child bring his/her own lunch and provide the milk from the school cafeteria. Engage the children in listening to humorous books read aloud while they eat, in hearing one or two book talks about humorous books they can find in the school library or in the classroom reading area, and if desired, playing one or two humorous book games—acting out the titles in a charade-type game.

Not the Piano, Mrs. Medley (103)

WHAT'S THE BOOK?

Not the Piano, Mrs. Medley. Written by Evan Levine and illustrated by S. D. Schindler. New York: Richard Jackson/Orchard, 1991. Ages 5–7.

WHAT'S SO FUNNY?

The unexpected ending is a humorous one. Mrs. Medley, her grandson, Max, and her dog, Word, go to the beach for the day. Leaving home, she returns for other things she says are needed: first, an umbrella, a game of Monopoly, some folding chairs and table, drums, accordion, and more. Max begins to wonder if they will ever get to the beach.

WHAT'S IT ABOUT?

As Max wonders if he and his grandmother will ever get to the beach, he waits while she returns for various objects she says are needed for the day. He watches while she collects various objects that seem unrelated to the beach. Max wonders if the two of them will ever get to have fun under the sun, in the water, and on the sand. After they arrive, there is an unexpected ending that is humorous and pleasing.

WHAT'S THE MINI-UNIT PURPOSE?

Point out to children: "You are going to hear a story about a young boy, Max, and his grandmother who want to go to the beach. Listen to find out how his grandmother delays the outing as she returns to collect different items—an umbrella, a game, some musical instruments. When they get to the beach, listen for the unexpected humorous ending."

WHAT NEW WORDS CAN BE EMPHASIZED?

Piano, Mrs. Medley, umbrella, Monopoly, chairs, table, drums, accordion.

WHAT'S THERE TO TALK ABOUT?

Before Reading Aloud

1. What Humorous Connection Is There Between Mrs. Medley and the Word "Piano"? Introduce the title of the book and write the words *Piano* and *Mrs. Medley* on the board. Ask children to tell any connections they know of between the two words, *medley* and *piano*. Ask them to brainstorm other musical terms that would serve as a name for Max's grandmother—Mrs. Andante, Mrs. Ivory, Mrs. Whitekeys, Mrs. Baby Grand.
2. Colorful Classroom Border: Sketching Objects Taken to the Beach. Show several illustrations from the book that depict the various ob-

jects Mrs. Medley says she needs for the day. Ask children to think of ways to describe one or more of the objects and tell why taking these objects to the beach would be humorous. Ask them to sketch their descriptions on strips (12″ × 3″) for a classroom border. In partnerships, ask them to tell their partners why they drew their sketches the way they did. Back in the whole group, invite volunteers to show their artistic descriptions and tell more about them.

- Ask children to think if they have ever returned to their home to get something that had been forgotten and if anything funny happened.
- Encourage them to share their feelings about any humorous incidents that happened to them or that they know about.

After Reading Aloud

1. Mrs. Medley's Suitcase: A Pantomime. Have children imagine that you have carried Mrs. Medley's suitcase to the front of the classroom. In the suitcase are all the items she took to the beach. Have one child take an imaginary item from the suitcase and use in a pantomime. Ask the rest of the group to use three guesses to identify the object. The one who guesses it correctly first then gets to choose another imaginary object from the suitcase and describe with motions. If no one guesses the object correctly, then the child who is pantomiming can appoint the next child to continue the activity.

2. Add Sounds and Mime. Ask the children to help retell the story. Instead of telling the story with words, have children tell it with sounds, perhaps adding some pantomime. If desired, have the children in small groups work up the sounds and pantomime for each one of the following items: an umbrella, a game of Monopoly, some folding chairs and table, drums, accordion, etc. Back in the whole group, ask each small group to chime in with their sounds and pantomime actions when their object is mentioned in a rereading.

3. Joining Mrs. Medley. Ask children: Tell how you think Mrs. Medley and her grandson carried all of the objects to the beach? How do you think Max looked (and felt) when he helped carry all of the objects?

- What humorous thing might *you* have said or done if you had been with Mrs. Medley?

- How did the grandson, Max, feel about his grandmother's behavior?
- How was Mrs. Medley different from your idea of what a grandmother should be?

WHAT ACTIVITIES WILL EXTEND THE BOOK?

1. Humorous Role Play

With partners, invite the children to play the role of Max who helps his grandmother carry a multitude of objects to the beach—ask the children to describe anything humorous from their role-play aloud to the class. Taking the role of Max, invite children to tell a friend how they felt about Mrs. Medley's objects.

2. Humor Blocks: Something Funny Happened to Me

Ask children to interview another child in class with, "Tell me about a time you went to the beach with your family and something humorous happened to you or someone you saw." Ask children to tell about other stories where they saw humans acting in surprising ways that were comical to them. To make Humor Blocks to represent their stories, have children cover discarded milk cartons with art paper and sketch and color humorous scenes on each side. Display the blocks in the room.

3. Book Bingo

To establish student background for the theme of humor in the family, school, and the community, introduce Book Bingo. To prepare for the activity of Book Bingo:

1. Give several book talks over several weeks that introduce other books about humor in the family, school, or community.
2. Display the books for browsing and reading.
3. Ask the students to help you prepare a "bingo card" with 2″ squares on paper that is 10″ × 12″.
4. Make twenty-five squares. In the squares, have the children write in the titles of the books about humor related to the theme of the family, at school, and in the community, in a random fashion (this is to ensure that no two cards are alike).
5. Have the children measure and cut 2″ × 2″ colored paper squares so they can cover the squares. Have the children number the tokens in sequence so they have at least fifty or more. Keep the colored paper squares in a plastic baggie or an envelope.
6. To play Book Bingo: give a clue for the colored paper square #1. Ask the students who know the book to place the #1 colored square over the title on the bingo card. Have a student announce "Book Bingo" if he or she has covered five titles in a row. The direction can be either across or down.
7. Take time to match the numbers on the colored paper squares with the titles of the books represented by the clues. Let a Book Bingo winner be the one to choose a humorous book of his or her choice to take after school to share with an adult in the home.

4. What Are Some Other Surprise Endings?

Help the children become aware of an unexpected ending as a humorous technique used by authors and show examples of unexpected endings in other picture books. Point out the value of a surprise ending—one a reader was not expecting—to add humor to a story. Several humorous stories about the family and school distinguish themselves by having the characteristic of a surprise ending that can be shown in an illustration while the text is read aloud. For example:

- The surprise ending in *Good Night, Gorilla* (118) by Peggy Rathman is sure to be enjoyed by children. An added bonus of this zoo fancier's choice are the mischievous gorilla and other animals who parade behind a zookeeper too sleepy to notice they are out of their cages. In a final scene at the zookeeper's house, the animals are bedded down for the night in a silly finale.
- *The Day Jimmy's Boa Ate the Wash* (108) by Trinka Hakes Noble relates a series of nonsensical and zany happenings when Jimmy's pet boa constrictor escapes from the school bus on the class visit to the farm. The surprise ending is punctuated by a new pet pig and a new sweater for the boa.
- The title in *Night Noises* (95) by Mem Fox is a clue to the unexpected surprise in the ending. Grandmother discovers that the noises are caused by family members who are coming to give a surprise birthday party for her.

What Other Humorous Features Are in Books about the Family, School, and Community?

ANTICS AND PRANKS

Introduce children to the idea of "antics and pranks" as being synonymous with jokes and tricks with a book of your choice or with Eileen Christelow's *Jerome the Babysitter* (91) or *Old MacDonald Had a Farm* (84) by Holly Berry. Jokes and tricks are the basis of the pranks of Mrs. Gatorman's "little angels" in *Jerome the Babysitter*. During a babysitting job (which is the main source of the fun), Jerome has to come up with a creative solution to cope with the "angels." The fun is also in the antics of the animals during a jamboree in *Old MacDonald Had a Farm* that offers humor. Farmer MacDonald brings in the crops and calls the animals together for a harvest celebration. Each animal is named in turn in the verses of the song and MacDonald gives it a musical instrument to play at the hoedown in the barn—a jumping musical jamboree that shakes the rafters.

Another version of *Old MacDonald Had a Farm* (113) is by Tracey Campbell Pearson and it also shows the animals antics—the cat, dog, and rooster are in every illustration as they wake up Farmer MacDonald and his wife and follow them through the daily chores, hanging up clothes, feeding the pigs, and milking the cows. The cows have their names—Phyllis, Sue Anne, even Toby—at their places in the barn, and the mule is truly stubborn as it takes both the farmer and his wife to push-pull him from the barn. The stampeding mule frightens the other animals into a runaway and the farmer chases him with the tractor. When the mule is finally pulled back home behind the tractor, all settle down for a peaceful snooze.

EXAGGERATIONS

Exaggerations will entertain children as they listen to James Stevenson's *Worse Than Willy!* (130). This is grandpa's tall tale that explains to his grandson that there are things worse than Willy, the new baby. Grandpa tells his memories of all the things that happened to him including his version of what was once under his bed and his first day at school.

MISBEHAVIOR AT SCHOOL

The misbehavior of the worst kids in school in classroom 207 in Harry Allard's *Miss Nelson is Missing* (80) begins one day when sweet Miss Nelson does not come to school but is replaced by Miss Viola Swamp who means business. All this ensures great laughter. After the class is whipped into shape, Miss Nelson reappears and all that is left of Miss Viola Swamp is an ugly black dress and a wig in Miss Nelson's closet.

ONE-LINERS

You can introduce the concept of one-liners to children with Nancy Winslow Parker's story, *Poofy Loves Company* (112). Much of the fun is in the friendly actions of the big shaggy dog, Poofy, and the brief responses of Poofy's owner. The one-liners are the witty replies given when Sally and her mother visit Poofy's mistress. It seems that Sally doesn't mind the overfriendly dog but when her possessions begin to disappear during the visit, Sally's struggle is *on* with the huge canine.

SLAPSTICK

Show children what slapstick looks like with the illustrations in Jim Aylesworth's *Hush Up!* (82). A chain of unbelievable slapstick events begin on a hot lazy day after a huge horsefly bites the nose of a sleeping mule in Aylesworth's story. Jasper Walker, who has tilted his chair back, has propped up his feet and is snoozing. Rudely, he is awakened along with the barnyard animals who have also decided to nap.

Filmstrips of stories with slapstick elements can be shown so the children can see the illustrations. For example, close-ups of enlarged scenes of Paula Winter's two books *The Bear and the Fly* (134) and *Sir Andrew* (135) will assist the children in identifying the cause-and-effect situations. In *The Bear and the Fly,* a bear family's house is in turmoil by a buzzing fly that seems unaware of the commotion it creates. In *Sir Andrew,* an unusual and vain donkey dresses elegantly and takes an eventful stroll on a windy day. His self-admiration leads him to an accident which causes mishaps for others. The filmstrips of these books are available from Weston Woods, Westport, CT 06880.

SPOOFS

You can introduce children to a spoof with Harry Allard's *Miss Nelson Has a Field Day* (79). The fun is in the takeoff on school sports in the text by Harry Allard and in the humorous illustrations by James Marshall. For example, there is the full-length view of Coach Viola, the characterized football players, and the cafeteria ladies who have wide-line mouths. In the story, the students agree that they need Viola Swamp, the meanest substitute in the whole wide world, to whip the school's pathetic football team—the Smedley Tornadoes—into shape. When Viola does appear, she's in an ugly black sweat suit printed with the words "Coach and don't you forget it."

Humorous Humans

The Happy Hocky Family (195)

WHAT'S THE BOOK?

The Happy Hocky Family. Written and illustrated by Lane Smith. New York: Viking, 1993. Ages 5–6.

WHAT'S SO FUNNY?

There are parody and jokes in the illustrations with accompanying tongue-in-check humor in the text. The author parodies the "Dick and Jane" format of previous basal readers and uses a repetitive writing style to introduce the Hocky family and the family canine.

WHAT'S IT ABOUT?

There are eighteen brief stories that introduce humorous adventurous episodes of the Hocky family and their dog, Newton. In one episode on a family outing to visit the zoo, the family members visit the crocodiles in their habitat because Newton, the dog, likes them best. The subsequent illustration shows Newton's leash leading into the jaws of a crocodile—and Newton is nowhere to be seen—only the five Hockys are left.

WHAT'S THE MINI-UNIT PURPOSE?

Tell children: "You are going to hear some short stories about a family who has several humorous adventures. Listen to find out why the family seems so "happy" and why you think the book is called *The Happy Hocky Family*.

WHAT NEW WORDS CAN BE EMPHASIZED?

Balloon, string, happy, Hocky family, Newton.

WHAT'S THERE TO TALK ABOUT?

Before Reading Aloud

1. Pantomime Happy Actions. Introduce the title of the story and tell children you are going to entertain them with the Happy Hocky Family, or to say it another way, "I'm going to 'Happy Hocky' you for a little while." Show several illustrations from the book that portray the family where one can infer the family members are happy. Divide children into groups and have each group, in turn, pantomime some happy actions they predict might be related to the story.

2. Humor in Repetitive Words. Ask children to think if they have ever heard/read a story that also entertained them with the fun of hearing/reading repetitive words. Encourage them to tell the whole group about the stories that they know about.

After Reading Aloud

1. One Joke *The Happy Hocky Family* Makes Me Think of Is . . . . Write the title on the board. Have children turn to a a child next to them and briefly discuss, "One joke *The Happy Hocky Family* makes me think of is . . . . " For instance, discuss:

- What jokes might *you* have said or done that would have been funny at the zoo when Newton disappeared?
- In what ways would you say that the Hocky family was *happy?*
- How is this happy family different from your idea of what a happy family should be?
- Why do you think the author named the book *The Happy Hocky Family*?

2. Parody Is Imitating and Mimicking. With children, reread parts of the text where the writing style imitates or mimics a "Dick and Jane" story for a comic effect. Have the children suggest their favorite passages. If desired, read aloud some passages from a "Dick and Jane" story to help children see the connection with the writing in *The Happy Hocky Family*.

3. Jokes in the Illustrations. For one example of a joke in an illustration, cover up the illustration where the child's balloon bursts with a loud POP, and read the text, "I have a string. Do you have a string?" Ask if the words by themselves are funny to hear. Uncover the illustration to show the joke of the bursting balloon which shows a child with no balloon at all—just a string. Ask if the words become funny (a tongue-in-cheek joke) when the joke in the illustration is seen. Have the children select other examples of jokes they like in the illustrations.

WHAT ACTIVITIES WILL EXTEND THE BOOK?

1. Book-shapes for the Happy Hocky Family

Engage the children in cutting out book jacket shapes from art paper. Have them add the features of the members of the Happy Hocky Family (even Newton) that they want—faces, arms, legs—to the book jackets. Display the jackets on a bulletin board and let children add word-bubbles with dialogue to allow the family members to tell something humorous about the story.

2. A Bulletin Board Border: One of *Your* Trips to the Zoo

Ask the children to interview a classroom peer with, "Tell me about one of *your* trips to the zoo where something humorous happened." Have children write/dictate/sketch something from the interview on narrow strips of colored art paper for a border and place the borders on a class bulletin board.

3. First-Rate Humor Badges: Features of Humor in a Story

Ask children to tell about other places where they saw some of the features of humor found in this story. For example, the idea of a humorous human doing something to surprise a reader can be shown with a *Wizard of Id* comic (Parker, 1994). In the first frame, the king asks the subject, "Okay . . . Why did you throw a tomato at me during my speech today?" The subject replies, " 'cause I couldn't reach you with the pumpkin." After they share their examples, have children make award badges from colored paper (approximately 4″ × 2″) that say "First-Rate Humor Badges" and write on it the feature each child told about—that is,

- Humorous humans who did something that surprised them or acted in surprising ways
- Tongue-in-cheek humor
- Parody (writing style that imitates or mimics for comic effect)
- Jokes in the illustrations

Big Anthony and the Magic Ring (152)

WHAT'S THE BOOK?

Big Anthony and the Magic Ring. Written and illustrated by Tomie de Paola. New York: Harcourt, 1979. Ages 6–9.

WHAT'S SO FUNNY?

It is Big Anthony's protracted bumbling behavior and misadventures with a magic object that provide the humor in this one. In the story, Big Anthony, the misguided helper of *Strega Nona* (154) who fooled around with a magic pasta pot, is back.

It is springtime and he is restless, so Strega Nona diagnoses spring fever and recommends a little night life for her helper.

WHAT'S IT ABOUT?

Poor Anthony wonders who would dance with a dolt such as himself. Strega Nona assures him that Bambolona—the baker's rotund daughter—will. Feeling a bit restless herself, that night Strega Nona uses her magic ring, sings a magic chant, and poof—transforms herself into a beautiful young lady. Big Anthony observes all this, and follows her to the village square where the new Strega Nona dances until dawn. Big Anthony waits for his chance and when Strega Nona goes off to visit her godchildren, he finds the ring, places it on his finger, and sings the magic chant. A puff of smoke and poof—there stands handsome Big Anthony in elegant clothes. He goes to the village square where the ladies keep him dancing until he drops from exhaustion. He runs away, singing the chant to turn off the spell. But the ring is stuck fast to his finger. Anthony runs and the ladies chase him. Past the fountain, past the priest, past the sisters of the convent, out through the gate, past the goats and into the countryside. He escapes up a tree but the ladies shake and shake until Big Anthony flies off into the air and lands straight at Strega Nona's feet. A bit of olive oil removes the ring and he promises never to touch Strega Nona's magic again. "Never mind, Big Anthony," said Strega Nona with a smile. "There are other kinds of magic in the spring." And coming up the road is Bambolona.

WHAT'S THE MINI-UNIT PURPOSE?

State the purpose: "You are going to hear a story about Big Anthony, a bumbling assistant to Strega Nona, who fools around with a magic ring. As a result, the magic backfires on him. Listen to find out why Big Anthony has to escape from the ladies of the town."

WHAT NEW WORDS CAN BE EMPHASIZED?

Big Anthony, Strega Nona, magic ring, Bambolona, priest, convent.

WHAT'S THERE TO TALK ABOUT?

Before Reading Aloud

1. Title Tags to Laugh Over: Big Anthony and His Behavior. Introduce the title of the book and write the words, *Big Anthony and the Magic Ring,* on the board. Ask children to think of ways they would describe Big Anthony. Ask them to each make a book title tag (2″ × 3″) made from art paper with the name of the book on the front; on the back, have children sketch their humorous descriptions of Big Anthony. As a contrast to show

different ways people can illustrate the same story, show some of the illustrations by Tomie de Paola. In partnerships in class, ask children to tell their partners why they drew their sketches the way they did on their book title tags. Back in the whole group, invite volunteers to show their descriptions and tell more about them.

2. Look What Bumblers Can Do: A Basket of Bumbling Characters. Ask children to think if they have ever heard/read a story that had the humor of someone being a "bumbler" and doing something that backfired on the character. Encourage them to tell the whole group about any stories that they know about and write their suggestions on a chart labeled with the heading "Look What Bumblers Can Do." Beneath the chart, place a large basket to hold copies of the books.

After Reading Aloud

1. Sketch of the Week: One Bumbling Thing *Big Anthony and the Magic Ring* Makes Me Think of Is . . . . Have children reflect about the behavior of a bumbler and what makes it funny to them and tell, "One bumbling thing *Big Anthony and the Magic Ring* makes me think of is . . . ." Ask them to sketch their ideas and show the drawings to the whole group. Display the sketches under a heading, "Sketches of the Week." Discuss:

- In a humorous way, what might *you* have said or done at the town square when Big Anthony tried to run away?
- In what comical ways could you say that the ring was *magic?*
- How is Big Anthony and his humorous actions different from your idea of what an assistant/helper should be?

2. Another Amusing Adventure for Big Anthony and Bambolona. Ask children to tell in what ways they think that Big Anthony's promise *not* to touch magic again could be a hint of another adventure? Predict what could be a humorous happening:

- What humorous events could be predicted from the unbelieving look on Strega Nona's face?
- In what humorous ways could the children see Bambolona behaving in another story?
- What humorous words could be used to write a special chant for Big Anthony to say to escape from the magic of the ring?

WHAT ACTIVITIES WILL EXTEND THE BOOK?

1. Taking the Role of Humorous Big Anthony

Taking the role of Big Anthony, invite children to tell a friend in the class how the assistant felt when

- He goes to the village square where the ladies keep him dancing the tarantella until he drops from exhaustion
- He runs away and says the chant to turn off the spell
- The ladies chase him out into the countryside
- He climbs up a tree to escape but the ladies shake and shake the tree until he flies off into the air and lands right at Strega Nona's feet
- A bit of olive oil removes the ring from his finger and he promises never to touch Strega Nona's magic again

2. Replicating Big Anthony's Magic Ring

Engage children in groups in making their own replicas of Big Anthony's magic ring with a mixture of classroom dough made from 4 cups of flour, 1½ cup of water, and 1 cup of salt (add a little extra water if dough is too stiff). Have children mix and knead the ingredients to make the mixture. If the mixture is too stiff, add a small amount of water. Let them design their own interpretations of the magic object in de Paola's story. Have children think of a humorous happening where Big Anthony would wear the ring made by each child

and then sketch or write about the event on an index card. Display the rings and place each index card appropriately nearby.

3. Books to Laugh Over

Display a large replica of Big Anthony's face and have children look through magazines, newspapers, and brochures to find illustrations of people laughing to cut out and add to the display of Big Anthony. Place the cutout pictures around Big Anthony's face, and if desired, add some book jackets of humorous books about humorous humans and their bumbling behavior.

4. Humorous Book Week

Have children help plan a humorous book week and select a week for this from the calendar. This celebration will help interest and motivate the children in becoming more aware of the features of humor in children's literature. Engage the children in constructing announcement posters, window and door decorations, bulletin board displays, class mobiles, and other decorations to advertise features of humor and celebrate the week. Additionally, let children make decisions about other activities—having a humorous book parade and carrying book jackets of humorous books affixed to cardboard tubes (discarded from wax paper, etc.), decorating the school building with hall displays, showing large paintings of humorous scenes from favorite books, reciting humorous rhymes and poems, and exchanging humorous books to read.

What Other Humorous Features Are in Books With Humorous Humans?

CARTOONLIKE ILLUSTRATIONS

Jacquie Hann's *Up Day, Down Day* (165) is a humorous good luck-bad luck story with cartoon-style illustrations. When Jeremy and his friend go fishing, Jeremy catches three fish. His friend catches a shoe, a can, and a cold. On alternating pages, Jeremy's good luck is contrasted with his friend's bad luck. Monday when it is time to go to school, the cold has its advantages. There is a final twist as Jeremy

gives his friend a fish and his friend gives Jeremy his cold.

DISPROPORTIONATE OBJECTS

In *The King's Flower* (141) by Mitsumasa Anno, the king thinks that biggest is always best and wants objects that are disproportionate to human size. For example, his toothbrush is so big that it takes two men to carry it; there is a large pincer for pulling his royal tooth, and a fishhook large enough to catch a whale. The king changes his mind about size when he has a single tulip bulb planted in the world's biggest pot. Instead of one enormous bloom, the king finds the flower small and beautiful and realizes that not even a king can make the biggest flower in the world.

EXAGGERATIONS AND ANACHRONISMS

Help the children become aware of exaggerations—words or pictures that make something more that it really is—and anachronisms that are errors in chronology in which something, some event, or someone is misplaced, with Mitsumasa Anno's *The King's Flower* (141). In the story, the king surrounds himself with everyday objects that are disproportionate to human size. For example, his kitchen utensils have to be handled with ropes and pulleys. The king changes his mind about size, however, when he has a single tulip bulb planted in the world's biggest pot and the flower is small and beautiful. When the king realizes that he cannot make the biggest flower in all the world, he says, "perhaps that is just as well." There is also humor in the use of anachronism—there are objects that are misplaced out of their time period—the toothbrush and a chocolate bar.

HUMOROUS ACTIONS

In *Have You Seen Hyacinth Macaw?* (162), Abby Jones is trying very hard to be a detective. To practice, Abby fills a memo book with her notes about anything that seemed at all unusual. Because of her police friends and her observations, Abby finds herself involved in what seems to be four or more mysteries. Abby and her friend Potsie trail a suspect through the New York subway system, break into the apartment next door, capture an unusual bird, and realize that all the mysteries were linked together. After solving the mystery, Abby receives a reward for finding the bird, Hyacinth Macaw.

PARODY

Help the children become further aware of what a parody—writing in which the language and style of an author is imitated especially for comic effect or for ridicule—can be like with the words in Dale Fife's *Follow That Ghost!* (157). The story's language will remind some TV rerun viewers of the show *Dragnet*. In this parody, Chuck and Jason take on their first detective case and they follow people for practice when their next door neighbor, Glory, catches them following her home. Instead of being angry at the boys, Glory decides to hire them to find the ghost that she and her mother hear at 5 o'clock every morning. Despite their attempts to capture the ghost or to find a human reason for the ghostly sounds, the boys cannot rid the apartment of the ghost. The ghost turns out to be a displaced woodpecker looking for a new home.

PUNS

Develop the children's awareness of a pun—a joking way of saying something by using a word (or a saying) that has two different meanings—with the story of *Truman's Aunt Farm* (119) written by Jama Kim Rattigan. In the story, the pun is that the word *ant* is mistaken for *aunt*. Truman's Aunt Fran sends him a coupon for an ant farm for his birthday and he is sent—not "ants" but more than fifty aunts of all shapes and sizes. Truman has to decide what to feed them and to find the right nieces and nephews for them.

STRAIGHT-PERSON/FUNNY-PERSON TECHNIQUE

There is a straight-person/funny-person feature that builds the humor in *Perrywinkle and the Book of Magic Spells* (319) written by Ross Martin Madsen and illustrated by Dirk Zimmer. There are easy-to-read adventures about Perrywinkle, the son of a great wizard, who suffers from "overspelling." He tries the familiar rabbit trick and instead produces a thing that eats a table. Another example of Perrywinkle's overspelling happens when he spells the word *waterfall* for his teacher and a real waterfall tumbles out of the chalkboard and engulfs the class. The entertainment is increased by a crow named Nevermore, who is the straight-entity to Perrywinkle's funny-comic role.

VERBAL AND VISUAL JOKES

Help children become further aware of the use of verbal and visual jokes—something said or done to get a laugh—to create humor with *A Job for Wittilda* (306) by Carolyn and Mark Buehner. The delightful illustrations show Wittilda the witch when she applies for a job at the Dingaling Pizza. She needs the job because she has forty-seven cats and wants to buy food for them. When Wittilda and the other applicants are told, "the first one back gets the job," she balances five pizza boxes with one hand as she flies over the town on her broom. Of course, she delivers the pizzas in time to be the first one back and gets the job.

Holidays

The Witch Who Lived Down the Hall (201)

WHAT'S THE BOOK?

The Witch Who Lived Down the Hall. Written by Donna Guthrie and illustrated by Amy Schwartz. New York: Harcourt Brace Jovanovich, 1985. Ages 6–7.

WHAT'S SO FUNNY?

This is a tale with underlying humor—and a different twist—to read aloud for October reading. It is about Ms. McWee, a witch, who lives just down the hall from a young boy. As proof that his neighbor in the apartment house is indeed a witch, the boy describes her traits, one by one. He does so with the budding logic and earnest appeal of a young lawyer, but when his mother tries to dispel his suspicions, his reply, somewhat illogical, is "I'm not so sure." The illogical logic and subtle humor of this story make it a compelling tale to read.

WHAT'S IT ABOUT?

The boy knows that Ms. McWee down the hall makes click-clack noises at night. He knows that Ms. McWee just loves Halloween. He offers these traits as proof that the neighbor is a witch. The mother, however, refutes each bit of evidence, but this does little to dispel his suspicions.

WHAT'S THE MINI-UNIT PURPOSE?

Mention to children: "You are going to hear a story about a young boy who thinks that Ms. McWee, his neighbor down the hall in the apartment building, is a witch. It seems that Ms. McWee, the boy says, strangely seemed to know *all* about him before the two even met. Listen to find out what happens to help the boy overcome his suspicions."

WHAT NEW WORDS CAN BE EMPHASIZED?

Ms. McWee, witch, click-clack, neighbor, sure, Halloween.

WHAT'S THERE TO TALK ABOUT?

Before Reading Aloud

1. Imaginary Cauldron: *The Witch Who Lived Down the Hall.* Introduce the title of the book by writing it on the board. Ask children to tell what the title might be by suggesting it to them. Show several illustrations from the book that show the boy and Ms. McWee and have children mention the events in the scenes. Write their responses on the board. Have a volunteer pretend to carry a cauldron to the front of the room. From the cauldron, have volunteers pretend to select objects related to the character in the title or the responses on the board, and use the pretend object in a brief pantomime. If desired, introduce a rhyme for the whole group to say while a child reaches for the imaginary object—"Big pot, big pot, what do you hide? What will _____ (child's name) find inside?" Have the rest of the children use three guesses to name the object. The child who guesses the name of the object correctly becomes the next one to select an imaginary object and use it in actions. If no child names the object, have the pantomiming child select another to take part in the activity.

2. An Imagined Walk in an Imagined Apartment House. Ask the children to go on an imaginary walk in an imagined apartment house where they hear strange click-clack noises. Have some of the children line up at the writing board and others stay at their tables or desks to draw sketches of what they might see or like to do on a tour of the apartment house. Have them pretend that they leave the classroom and walk to an apartment house nearby. Have them identify what they would wear, what they might see, and what could happen to them.

After Reading Aloud

1. Share-a-String Story. Distribute lengths of different measurements of brightly colored ribbon, yarn, or nylon cord to each child. Have each one tie the length to the length held by the child sitting next to him or her. Roll the length into a ball and place inside an empty can that has a plastic lid. Make a small circular opening in the lid. Pull one end of the ribbon through the opening. Engage each child in turn in holding the Share-a-String Story Can while he or she retells the story. As the child is talking, have him or her pull the yarn out slowly from the lid's center. Have the child talk until he or she reaches a knot. When the child sees the knot, have the child turn the Story Can over to the next child who will continue the story.

2. I Was Walking Down the Hall: A Finger Snapping Rhyme. Have the children recall the events in the story and contribute words for a rhyme to which they can snap their fingers in rhythm:

I was walking down the hall the other day,
When I met Ms. McWee going my way.
I said, Ms. McWee, "Where have you BEEN?"
She said, "My dear boy, what do you mean?"

I was walking down the hall the other day,
When I met Ms. McWee going my way.
I said, Ms. McWee, "What have you SEEN?"
And this is what she said to me:

I've seen the ____ ____ ____ ____
and the ____ ____ ____ ____.
I've seen the ____ ____ ____ ____
and the ____ ____ ____ ____.

WHAT ACTIVITIES WILL EXTEND THE BOOK?

1. New Words for "Here We Go Round the Mulberry Bush"

Ask children to contribute new words about Ms. McWee and the boy to sing to the tune of "Here We Go Round the Mulberry Bush."

And here's Ms. McWee busy as a bee,
Busy as a bee,
Busy as a bee,
And here's Ms. McWee busy as a bee,
What did the little boy see?

2. Act It Out—Sound It Out

With partners, invite the children to play the role of the worried little boy who was suspicious of the neighbor down the hall. Ask one of the children to act out some of the boy's actions and the other child to contribute the sound effects— the creaking of a door, a suspicious clicking noise, etc. Have them trade roles and repeat the activity.

3. If I had been there, I would have . . . .

Have the children retell the funniest incident in the story, and somewhere say, "It was funny when . . . ." Add "If I had been there, I would have . . . ." Invite them to make story changes as they say what they would do to help the worried little boy in the story.

4. Jokes That Surprised Us

Ask children to tell about other stories that have holiday settings where they saw or read something humorous or where there were visual and verbal jokes that surprised them. Write their suggestions on a chart labeled "Jokes That Surprised Us." Discuss: How can these jokes help you enjoy your daily activities? How can these jokes help you learn to know other persons better?

Daniel O'Rourke: An Irish Tale (205)

WHAT'S THE BOOK?

Daniel O'Rourke: An Irish Tale. Written and illustrated by Gerald McDermott. New York: Viking Kestrel, 1986. Ages 6–8.

WHAT'S SO FUNNY?

This is a tale of lighthearted fun. It is about poor Daniel O'Rourke whose troubles start when he goes to a grand party at a great mansion on the hill. At the party, he stuffs himself with food—some green cheese and goose livers. He dances until he can dance no more and then starts off for his house early in the dark morning. Daniel stops to rest by a stone tower that is claimed by a pooka, a mischievous spirit creature that can change its shape.

WHAT'S IT ABOUT?

Daniel's lovely summer night turns into a nightmare as misadventures befall him. Just as he was about to cross a little brook near the tower, he missteps on a slippery stone and falls into the water that suddenly becomes a rushing river and sweeps him away out to sea. Other strange things happen to Dan. He's washed up on a strange island, given a ride, and left on the moon by a talking eagle. The man in the moon initiates Dan's freefall back to earth. Dan grabs hold of the leg of a flying gander who drops Dan into more water where a great whale bounces Dan up and down. When Dan hears the words "Get up" and opens his eyes, he finds his own mother throwing water in his face. She says, "Only a fool would fall asleep under the tower of the pooka. You've had no easy rest of it, I'm sure." And that was the last time Daniel slept under the pooka's tower and not in his very own bed.

WHAT'S THE MINI-UNIT PURPOSE?

Mention to children: "You are going to hear an Irish story about Daniel O'Rourke who falls asleep under the pooka's tower. It seems that the pooka is a spirit creature who is full of mischief and Daniel has some strange adventures. Listen to find out why this was the last time Daniel wanted to fall asleep somewhere that was *not* in his own bed."

WHAT NEW WORDS CAN BE EMPHASIZED?

Daniel O'Rourke, mansion, pooka spirit's tower, reaping hook.

WHAT'S THERE TO TALK ABOUT?

Before Reading Aloud

1. Daniel O'Rourke and the Pooka. Introduce the book by showing the book jacket or cover. Ask children to tell what the title and the cover illustration could be suggesting to them. Show the initial illustrations in the book that shows Daniel waving good-by to his mother as he leaves for the grand party at the mansion, the grand mansion on the hill, and the dancing that Daniel did, and the pooka spirit's tower by which Daniel paused to rest after the party. Mention that the pooka is one of the many Irish creatures believed to inhabit the land and have children imagine what they think one would look like. The pooka is supposed to be responsible for some of the mischief and bizarre things that happen to "ordinary" people.

After Reading Aloud

1. Daniel's Lighthearted Story. Ask some of the children to take the role of Daniel and pantomime some of Daniel's actions. If desired, have other children add sound effects for any or all of the following actions:

- Dan danced and danced until he could dance no more.
- Then he dined on green cheese and goose livers until he thought he would burst.
- He missed his footing on a slippery stone and fell headlong into the water; he was swept away on a wild ride that carried him far out to sea.
- Dan found himself being carried high up into the sky on the back of the eagle until they reached the moon; there was a reaping hook sticking out of the moon and the eagle dropped Dan on the end of the handle; there Dan stayed, hanging from a hook on the moon.
- Whap! The man in the moon chopped the handle of the reaping hook in half with his kitchen cleaver and Daniel O'Rourke went falling and tumbling through the clouds.
- Whoosh! A wild goose let Dan grab hold of its leg and then let Dan tumble down into the bottom of the sea.
- Whish! Dan shot up into the air from the bottom of the sea because a whale was bouncing him up and down so that Dan got thoroughly soaked.
- Dan heard the words "Get up," and when he opened his eyes, he saw his mother throwing a

bucket of water in his face. Dan had been sleeping under the tower of the pooka.

2. Because of a Mischievous Pooka . . . . Because of a pooka spirit, Daniel went on a fanciful journey but both Daniel and the creatures he met talked with realistic words. Have children explore some of the language in the book by repeating the phrases aloud. If desired, have them experiment with an Irish accent while repeating the words on an audiotape recorder:

- "Death Alive! I'll be drowned now!" cried Daniel.
- "Dan," said the eagle. "Hold on tight to the reaping hook, for I'll be saying goodnight to you now."
- "'Tis a lovely tale, Dan," said the man in the moon. "But here you must not stay. So be off in less than no time."
- "This is a pretty pickle for a decent man to be in," said Dan as he fell.
- "I think 'tis falling you are, Dan," said the gander.
- "Get up, Daniel!" she said. "Only a fool would fall asleep under the tower of the pooka. You've had no easy rest of it, I'm sure."

WHAT ACTIVITIES WILL EXTEND THE BOOK?

1. On Daniel O'Rourke's Path

Ask children to trace a path on a butcher paper mural to help Daniel O'Rourke get from the great party at the mansion on the hill back to his house. Have each child draw and color the character of Daniel. Ask children to cut out their characters to paste on the mural to highlight different actions in the story. Along the path, have children volunteer to use crayons or markers and embellish the scenes of what happened to Dan on his fanciful adventure before his mother found him sleeping near the pooka's tower.

2. Stage a Class Production

Show children that a tale from Ireland can be exciting and invite the children to take part in a group production of the story of Daniel O'Rourke. Ask the children to make finger puppets of characters they choose from the story and have them cut and color the puppets themselves. Decide on which children will

- Lead the whole group in an Irish song to open and close the puppet production
- Develop different "voices" for the characters
- Put the characters' words into their own words to give brief "speeches" for the characters
- Insert lively Irish dialogue
- Try to involve the whole group by asking for a dialogue exchange with a character
- Be the narrator and describe the actions

3. A Pop-up Shamrock Card as a Book Report

Help children recognize celebrations that Irish people acknowledge and engage them in constructing a pop-up shamrock card (see figure 3). Show the shamrocks in the illustrations in *Daniel O'Rourke*. For those who need a pattern for a pop-up card, the following one is included. Have children cut out a card and fold along the dotted lines. They can color or paint the shamrock green. Have children dictate/write a simple message about the story to someone inside the card. Encourage children to decorate the card in a humorous way with cut-out paper shapes, crayons, or markers.

What Other Humorous Features Are in Books about Holidays?

BLENDING OF HUMOR AND MYSTERY

Help increase the children's awareness of the mingling of humor with nonhumor in a story—in this case with *Something Queer at the Haunted School: A Mystery* (204) written by Elizabeth Levy and illustrated by Mordecai Gerstein. The story is quite suitable for October reading. In this

Pop-up Shamrock Card

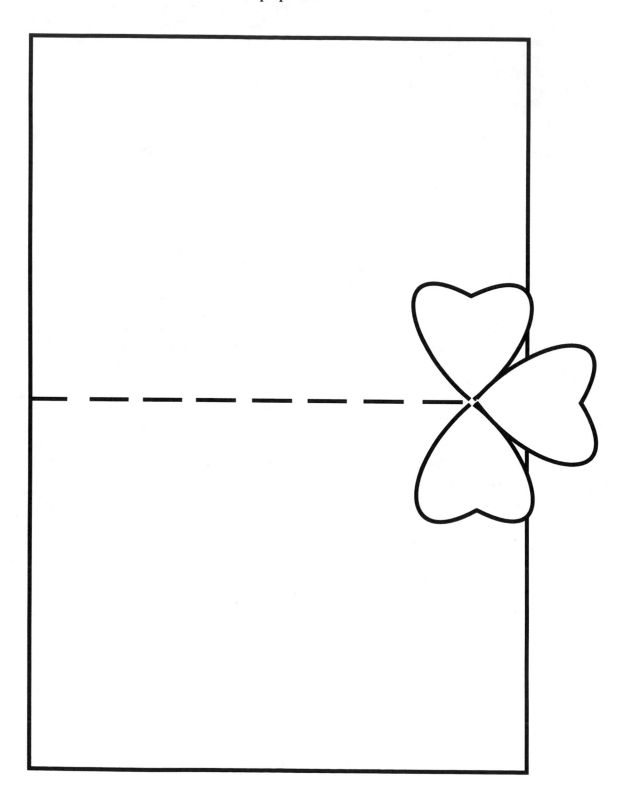

Figure 3. Form for Pop-up Shamrock Card.

story, Gwen and Jill are trying to discover the identity of the werewolf haunting their school before Halloween. Young readers particularly like Fletcher, the dog, dressed as a vampire, in this spooky but humorous mystery.

CARTOONLIKE ILLUSTRATIONS

With children, begin reading aloud *Funnybones* (197) by Allan Ahlberg by showing the frolicking skeletons on the title page and the end pages. Emphasize the clever comic strip format that helps tell what happened when three skeletons decide to go out and scare someone. This is a great read-aloud story with lines for children to chime in on such as "In the dark, dark street, there was a dark, dark house."

EXAGGERATIONS

In *The Witch Baby* (325) by Wendy Smith, Wanda is the baby who has a broom that won't fly. She has her troubles with spells too, and her attempt to turn a wicked witch into a worm results in an exaggeration—a spotted unicorn.

HUMOROUS PERSPECTIVE

Present children with a humorous perspective of what Washington did by reading aloud Edward Bangs's *Yankee Doodle* (198), illustrated by Steven Kellogg. This is about the day Washington took command of the American army and the story is illustrated with humorous details. Both the text and the illustrations let a child in on some of the excitement, patriotism, and spirit of the event. This is a book suitable for celebrating the 4th of July or any of America's patriotic holidays related to history. The rhythmic text of the story may remind a listener of the upbeat familiar melody of the song.

MISDEEDS

A giggling ghost is the unusual creature in Steven Kroll's *Amanda and the Giggling Ghost* (316). Amanda's encounter with the ghost leads to a chase through town as she attempts to retrieve her possessions. Amanda has a hard time convincing the townsfolk that it is a ghost, not she, who is responsible for all the humorous misdeeds. An "I told you so" ending makes the book especially satisfying to children.

PARODY

Prairie Night Before Christmas (282) by James Rice is a parody spiced with the local dialect from a prairie setting. This is an account of what happens when Santa becomes stranded in the southern panhandle country. With the help of two cowhands, he hitches up eight longhorn cattle and is able to deliver his holiday gifts and surprises.

PUNS

Examples of entertaining puns are found in *Wags to Witches: More Jokes, Riddles, and Puns* (212) by Victoria Gomez. This is a collection of jokes and riddles that are suitable for both attracting reluctant readers and challenging gifted ones.

SURPRISE ENDINGS

Show children the value of a surprise ending to create humor by reading aloud Marc Brown's *Arthur's April Fool* (199). This story contributes unexpected humor and includes one of the best April fool jokes written for young readers as Arthur performs his best magic trick to prove he is a hero. He concludes the story in a satisfying manner.

Jokes, Riddles, and Puns

Wags to Witches: More Jokes, Riddles, and Puns (212)

WHAT'S THE BOOK?

Wags to Witches: More Jokes, Riddles, and Puns. Written by Victoria Gomez and illustrated by Joel Schick. New York: Lothrop, Lee and Shepard, 1981. Ages 7–8.

WHAT'S SO FUNNY?

This book is a collection of riddles, jokes, and puns that have answers with plays on words— What kind of dog has the most germs (*a bac-ter-rier*). The answers rely on plays on words that have the same sound but different meanings as well as plays on words that have the same sound but are used differently for a humorous effect in the joke.

WHAT'S IT ABOUT?

The riddles are placed in sections entitled "Beasts, Bugs, and Birds," "Musicale," "On the Waterfront," "By Hook or by Crook," "Munchtime," "Here and There," and "Witches and Company."

WHAT'S THE MINI-UNIT PURPOSE?

Mention to children: "You are going to hear several riddles with answers that play on words. Listen for the humorous words and decide which ones you think are the funniest to you."

WHAT NEW WORDS CAN BE EMPHASIZED?

Wags, puns.

WHAT'S THERE TO TALK ABOUT?

Before Reading Aloud

1. **What's a Pun?** Invite the children who are interested in being stand-up comics to tell their favorite joke or one-liner and introduce the *pun* and its comic use.

Ask children to tell what, if anything, the word means to them. Point out that some words that sound alike (hare-hair) are played with to make a joke called a pun. As an example, read aloud a riddle from the book and then the answer—What does a mother rabbit read? (*Hare-raising stories*). Have children talk about how the words are used together—played upon—to make the joke. Ask them to tell why the pun is/is not funny to them.

After Reading Aloud

1. **This Pun Is Funny/Not Funny Because . . . .** With the permission of the book's publisher, photocopy some puns from one or more of the cartoon-style illustrations to make an overhead transparency of the jokes in *Wags to Witches* and discuss them with children. For example, show the cartoon where a snake is calling on a friend and is told by another snake at the door, "I'm sorry—Alfie isn't home." Unmask the last cartoon frame and read the visiting snake's response, "That's okay—I'll just leave my crawling card." Have children talk about why the pun is funny/not funny to them. Continue to show other cartoons and keep the mask on the final frame of each one until the children have had a chance to predict several ways to complete the joke. Remove the mask and discuss the pun in each joke.

2. **Completing a Pun.** Puns to amuse and challenge children can be made from copies of the first

frame of an illustrated pun from the book. Have children sketch and color a scene for the ending frame with humorous words of their choice. For example, give them a copy of the illustration of Santa Claus who says, "Sorry I sounded grouchy—I've been cooped up making toys all day!" With partners, have them think of some humorous words that make a play on Santa's name, his traits, or activities (*Oh— you must have claustrophobia!*).

WHAT ACTIVITIES WILL EXTEND THE BOOK?

1. If You're a Pun Lover

Invite the children who want to hear more jokes, riddles, and puns to make an audiotape of some of their favorites from the book. Have them leave the tape at the reading area for others to hear and enjoy.

2. More Puns

Another riddle book that is worth showing for its outlandish jokes and puns is *Grime Doesn't Pay: Law and Order Jokes* (218) compiled by Charles Keller and illustrated by Jack Kent. The humor focuses on the theme that, indeed, "grime doesn't pay" and provides more material over which children can chuckle—or groan.

Bennett Cerf's Book of Animal Riddles (209)

WHAT'S THE BOOK?

Bennett Cerf's Book of Animal Riddles. Written by Bennett Cerf and illustrated by Roy McKie. New York: Random House, 1964. Ages 6–7.

WHAT'S SO FUNNY?

This book provides unexpected bursts of humor about domestic and wild animals and their traits— "How do you stop a dog from barking in the back seat of a car?" (*Have him sit in front with you.*)

WHAT'S IT ABOUT?

This is a collection of riddles about animals—specific ones such as jokes about dogs, geese, and fish, and general ones—"Which animals need to be oiled?" (*Mice do. They squeak.*)

WHAT'S THE MINI-UNIT PURPOSE?

Mention to children: "You are going to hear several riddles about animals. Listen for the humorous words and try to figure out the answer before I turn the page and read the answer aloud."

WHAT NEW WORDS CAN BE EMPHASIZED?

N/A.

WHAT'S THERE TO TALK ABOUT?

Before Reading Aloud

1. What's a Riddle? Let children explore the ways in which riddles make them smile and have them entertain one another with a riddle and joke time. Introduce the word *riddle* to the whole group and ask children to tell what the word means to them. Show the first illustration from the book and read aloud the accompanying riddle about a barking dog and others. Have children guess what the answer might be. Ask them to tell why the riddle is/is not funny to them.

2. What Makes You Laugh? Invite volunteers to read (or tell) some favorite jokes, puns, poems, or anecdotes after which the members of the classroom audience indicate their rating of how much they enjoyed it—laughed out loud or were tickled. Invite the children to assign a "10" to the joke they enjoyed most, a "9" to the next joke they liked, and so on. If desired, have the children design index cards for laughter ratings based on the titles of humorous books they have read or heard and assign phrases from the titles to the ratings. After a joke, pun, poem, anecdote is told, children can hold up their index cards and show the ratings of how much they enjoyed the joke. Examples of ratings are

- **10** best joke (this is a Count Draculations joke; the phrase is taken from Keller's *Count Draculations*)
- **9** next best joke (this is a howl; taken from Maestro's *Halloween Howls*)
- **8** etc. (this is batty; taken from *Batty Riddles*)

After Reading Aloud

1. 3-D Animal Riddles: One riddle that *Bennett Cerf's Book of Animal Riddles* Makes Me Think of Is . . . . Invite each child to turn to a child next to them and tell a favorite riddle about a four-legged animal that *Bennett Cerf's Book of Animal Riddles* makes them think of. Engage children in folding a sheet of paper in half to make a "tent" and then drawing a four-legged animal on the side that is related to their animal joke. Have them cut out the head (and tail) and then add details with crayons. They can trim around the legs so the animal will stand up when the legs are spread apart. Have them write their animal riddle inside the 3-D animal, sign their work, and display the animals at the reading area for others to read.

2. Super Humorous Joke Award: What Should Humorous Riddles about Animals Be Like? *Discuss* how *you* think the author developed his or her humorous riddles about animals? How did this book of riddles seem different from your idea of what riddles about animals should be? Have the children tell some of their favorite animal riddles and then make funny Super Humorous Joke Awards (see figure 4) to give to their classmates to recognize them for the extra special accomplishment of a riddle well told.

WHAT ACTIVITIES WILL EXTEND THE BOOK?

1. Laughs on a Mural of Riddles

With partners, invite the children to select three favorite riddles and have them talk about what makes each riddle funny to them. Write their ideas on a list headed "The Riddle Is About" and then have them describe the riddle. Write their ideas

about this in a second list headed "What Makes It Funny to Me." Have children use their ideas in the second list to make groups with headings for a large mural of butcher paper. Write children's ideas on the mural and put their ideas in groups with headings such as "Using an Animal Trait," "A Natural Enemy Situation," "Using a Common Trait of Two Animals or Objects," and so on. This is a sample list:

The Riddle Is About	What Makes It Funny
A dog barking in back seat	Changing the location to front seat
Oiling animals	Using an animal trait—mice squeak
Making a comparison between a bird and a car	Using a common trait of the two
It's bad luck for a cat to follow you when . . .	. . . you're a mouse; this is using a "natural enemy" situation for the joke.

Here is a sample mural of riddles:

Using an animal trait	A natural enemy situation
Why is it hard to talk with a goat around? (*Because it always butts in.*)	_____

Invite children to select their favorite riddles, write each riddle and the answer on adhesive-backed notepaper, sign the riddle with their name, and affix the riddles in the appropriate categories on the mural. Encourage the children to read and browse by walking along the mural to read the riddles.

2. Oral Interpretation of a Riddle: Choral Reading

Invite children to suggest an oral interpretation for a selected riddle to make the riddle more humorous to them. Use their suggestions (holding their noses to make their voices sound funny) and reread the riddles together as a choral reading as the group members suggested.

3. Giant Humorous Puzzles

Invite children to turn to a puzzle as an entertaining way to add to their enjoyment of humor. Distribute large sheets of art paper (12″ × 18″) and have chil-

Super Humorous Joke Award

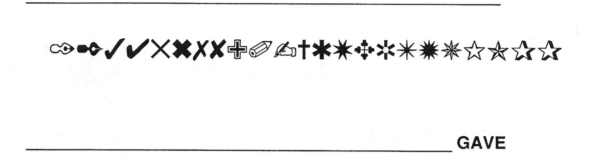

_____ **GAVE**

100%

IN HUMOR TODAY

Figure 4. Form for Super Humorous Joke Award.

dren work with partners to illustrate brightly colored jokes or riddles. Let the children draw the puzzle lines and cut the illustration apart. Place the puzzle pieces in a large manila envelope with the humorous subject written on the outside. Place the puzzle in the reading area for others to put together. This is a craft time activity that can feature a variety of humorous subjects and develop humor awareness.

4. Classroom Hall of Humorous Jokes and Riddles: Share a Laugh with Someone

Introduce children to collections emphasizing jokes with books by Charles Keller, Sam Schultz, Joanne Oppenheimer, and Paul Cohen, four popu-lar authors. All of their books are entertaining pre-sentations that many children will pick up over and over. Ask the children to tell jokes to one another and have them find the answers to some joke-ques-tions you have printed on slips of paper—"Do you know what to do with a green monster?" and "Do you know why vampires are like stars?" Introduce them to the source of the answers—one hundred riddles in Sam Schultz's book, _701 Monster Jokes_ (226). After children have gotten involved with joke and riddle books, initiate a classroom hall of humorous jokes and riddles. Have children nomi-nate their favorite author (collector, compiler) of humorous jokes and riddles, and prepare nominating speeches to suggest their favorite to the whole group. If desired, stage an election to determine the favorite and display the name of the winner(s) on a bulletin board in the room.

What Other Humorous Features Are in Books with Riddles, Jokes, and Puns?

CARTOONLIKE ILLUSTRATIONS

In *Batty Riddles* (210) written by Lisa Eisenberg and Katy Hall and illustrated by Nicole Rubel, the humorous comic illustrations are paired with the silly riddles of word play related to the topic of bats. Young readers can find at least one or two riddles that will be fun to ask others—"Why did the little bat walk around in his pajamas?" (*He didn't have a bat-robe.*)

PERSONIFICATION

Personification—giving an inanimate object some human attributes for a comic effect—is the joke in Dee Lillegard's *Do Not Feed the Table* (219). The illustrations feature a young boy, his dog, and quite often his father. Both appliances and foods have human characteristics. For examples, the appliances grin and the potatoes each have two eyes and peer over the edge of a bowl, warily eyeing the potato peeler.

QUIRKINESS

Introduce children to the idea of quirkiness—a sudden humorous turn or twist in language or behavior, with some selected riddles from Sam Schultz's *701 Monster Jokes* (226). The riddles can help introduce children to quirkiness as a technique used by writers to achieve humor for readers. In the book, the children will find many riddles that are suitable for October reading—they are about such things as monsters and other creatures. Some children will be entertained by reading the questions and answers to friends, browsing and selecting riddles to tell, and asking riddles to others in the classroom. This book

of riddles would also support a unit on humor in holidays and celebrations.

SILLINESS

The concept of silliness is shown in the answers to the jokes in Victoria Hartman's *The Silliest Joke Book Ever* (215). A child can choose jokes from such categories as "food funnies," "gruesome giggles," and "techie ticklers." There are over eighty jokes in a question-and-answer format. The answers lack sense as we know it and include some absurdities in the words and deeds—"How did the dragon devour the computer?" (*in one byte*).

WORD PLAY

Soon to be a favorite of some children, *A Very Mice Joke Book* (213) by Karen Jo Gounaud and illustrated by Lynn Munsinger, is a collection of riddles that play on the word *mice*. The mice names and related jokes are humorous to read and the illustrations are in keeping with the title.

ZANINESS

Zaniness is a good aspect of humor to discuss because it lends itself so well to buffoonery and ludicrous behavior. The idea of zaniness is shown in Charles Keller's *Norma Lee I Don't Knock on Doors: Knock Knock Jokes* (218). In keeping with the idea, the jokes reflect irrational words and behaviors that amuse young readers. The wild jokes will have special appeal for those children who have developed a fine sense of humor as well as a sophisticated vocabulary.

Nonsense

Wacky Wednesday (172)

WHAT'S THE BOOK?

Wacky Wednesday. Written by Theo LeSieg and illustrated by George Booth. New York: Random House, 1974. Ages 6–8.

WHAT'S SO FUNNY?

There are humorous mistakes in the illustrations. A child wakes up and discovers that everything is really wacky.

WHAT'S IT ABOUT?

When a boy wakes up, he discovers that everywhere he turns, he finds a shoe on the wall that shouldn't be there, and more and more things are wacky—he seems to be the only one who notices.

WHAT'S THE MINI-UNIT PURPOSE?

Mention to children: "You are going to hear a story about a young boy who wakes up and discovers that everything is really wacky. First, he sees a shoe on the wall, then a shoe on the ceiling, and bananas in the apple tree. As I show the pictures on the overhead, hunt for all the wonderfully silly things that are wrong on each page."

WHAT NEW WORDS CAN BE EMPHASIZED?

Wacky, Wednesday, window, bathroom, dress, things.

WHAT'S THERE TO TALK ABOUT?

Before Reading Aloud

1. **Wacky Weekly Calendar.** Introduce the title of the book and write the words *Wacky Wednesday* on the board. Ask children to tell what the words mean to them. Have them imagine what might happen to make a day become "wacky" to them and write their suggestions on a chart labeled "Wednesday and Other Days: A Wacky Weekly Calendar."

2. **Classroom Border: A Wacky Time.** Ask children to think if they have ever felt that a day was "wacky" and things were not as they should be. Encourage them to share their feelings about the wacky time. Engage them in drawing and coloring scenes of the wacky times they mentioned. Have them cut out the scenes and paste an "L" shaped piece of art paper to the scenes to make the scenes stand out similar to "pop-out" illustrations. Have children adhere the scenes to art paper strips for a classroom border.

After Reading Aloud

1. **Title Fun.** Review the title *Wacky Wednesday*. Have children use the title as the focus of a writing/dictation activity and suggest a seven-day week of book titles. If the children have difficulty in finding books with names of weekdays in the titles, have them suggest titles that reflect activities for the day. Examples:

- Sunday: *Alexander Who Used to Be Rich Last Sunday*
- Monday: *One Monday Morning*
- Tuesday: *Horton Hatches the egg*
- Wednesday: *Wacky Wednesday*
- Thursday: *It Could Always Be Worse*
- Friday: *Freaky Friday*

2. A Shoe on the Wall? Ask children: "What might *you* have said or done if you had been with the boy and seen a shoe on the wall?" "What are some of the wacky things the boy saw in the bedroom, yard, kitchen?" "How is this wacky day different from your idea of what a wacky day might be?" "What wacky thing (mistakes) might happen if you had a wacky day?"

WHAT ACTIVITIES WILL EXTEND THE BOOK?

1. Role-Play Ways That Things Are Wacky

With partners, invite the children to play the role of the young boy who woke up to discover that things were wacky and ask the children to describe something wacky—humorous mistakes—aloud to the audience.

- Taking the role of the young boy, invite children to tell a friend how they felt about seeing the wacky things in his bedroom.
- Have the children tell about their favorite illustration of the story, and somewhere, say, "If I had been there, I would have . . . "
- Ask children to interview a neighbor in the class with, "Tell me about something wacky you would like to discover at your house."
- Ask children to tell about other stories where they saw something wacky in the illustrations that surprised them.

2. Exhibits of Characters in Other Wacky Stories

Have children use clay to make likenesses of characters from other wacky stories they have read. Invite them to display the models along with copies of the books in the reading area.

Bartholomew and the Oobleck (245)

WHAT'S THE BOOK?

Bartholomew and the Oobleck. Written and illustrated by Dr. Seuss. New York: Random House, 1949. Ages 6–8.

WHAT'S SO FUNNY?

There are humorous exaggerations in the illustrations. A child discovers that everything is covered with oobleck.

WHAT'S IT ABOUT?

A page boy named Bartholomew Cubbins saves the kingdom of Didd when the king gets angry with the sky and wishes for something to fall from the sky that no other kingdom had ever had before.

WHAT'S THE MINI-UNIT PURPOSE?

Mention to children: "You are going to hear a story about Bartholomew Cubbins, a young page boy who keeps the king from wrecking his kingdom when he growls at the things that come down from the sky and asks for something different to fall from above. The magicians promise to make oobleck—a greenish cloud like green molasses. Listen to find out how Bartholomew helped solve the king's problem when the oobleck covered everything in the kingdom.

WHAT NEW WORDS CAN BE EMPHASIZED?

Bartholomew Cubbins, oobleck, kingdom of Didd, King Derwin, his majesty, sputtering, growled, magicians.

WHAT'S THERE TO TALK ABOUT?

Before Reading Aloud

1. What Will Oobleck Look Like? Introduce the title of the book and write the words *Bartholomew and the Oobleck* on the board. Ask children to tell what the words mean to them. Have them imagine what oobleck might look like after you read aloud the magicians' description of the greenish goop—"Won't look like rain. Won't look like snow./ Won't look like fog./ That's all we know./ We just can't tell you any more./ We've never made oobleck before." Write the children's predictions on a chart labeled "What will oobleck look like?" Have children sketch and color their own original illustrations of oobleck (as they think it might be) to affix as a border to the chart.

2. The Oobleck Is Falling. Ask children to think if they have ever imagined what it would be like if oobleck fell in their yard and things were not as they should be. Encourage them to talk about what they would think and what might happen.

After Reading Aloud

1. One Funny Thing Oobleck Made Me Think of Was . . . Have children turn to a child next to them and briefly discuss, "One funny thing oobleck made me think of was . . ."

2. I Think Oobleck Was Like . . . Ask children: "What might *you* have said or done if you had been with Bartholomew the page boy and seen the first little greenish cloud?" Reread some of the descriptions of the oobleck that follow and have children sketch their own interpretations to cut out and mount on hanging oobleck mobiles in the classroom:

- A little greenish cloud
- A wisp of greenish steam
- Tiny little greenish specks that shimmered
- Queer little greenish blobs, just about the size of grape seeds
- Blobs as big as greenish peanuts
- Blobs like greenish molasses
- As gummy as glue
- As big as greenish cupcakes
- As squiggly as a slippery potato dumpling made of rubber
- As big as greenish baseballs
- As plump and big as greenish footballs
- As big as greenish buckets full of gooey asparagus soup

WHAT ACTIVITIES WILL EXTEND THE BOOK?

1. Some Oobleck Is Falling

With partners in the classroom, invite the children to play the role of the young page boy in the kingdom of Didd who first saw the oobleck falling from the sky. Ask the children to describe to one another how the oobleck affected something in the kingdom. As Bartholomew, have children tell a friend what they saw and how they felt when

- Bartholomew held out his hand to catch one of the oobleck blobs that first fell from the sky.
- Bartholomew, at King Derwin's command, asked the royal bell ringer to ring the bell and proclaim a holiday, and nothing happened.
- Bartholomew asked the royal trumpeter to blow the alarm about the "green things," and one of the green things flew inside the trumpet.
- Bartholomew asked the captain of the guards to do something and the captain *ate* some of the green stuff.
- Bartholomew ran for the king's horse so he could ride through the kingdom and warn the people. He found that outside the royal stables there were great greenish tons of oobleck, deeper and deeper, and farmers in the fields were stuck to hoes and plows, and goats were stuck to ducks, and geese were stuck to cows.
- Bartholomew ran through the palace and warned the lords and ladies to get to their beds and get under the blankets for the oobleck was springing leaks in the palace. He saw the royal cook stuck to stew pots, a tea cup, and a cat; he saw the royal laundress stuck to the clothesline; and he saw the royal fiddlers stuck to their royal fiddles.
- Bartholomew ran and found the king with his royal crown stuck to his head and the seat of his royal pants stuck to his throne; he helped the king think of some special words to make the oobleck stop falling.

2. Make Your Own Version of Oobleck

Set up an activity center with materials (mixing bowl, water, cornstarch, and green food coloring) so children can make their own version of oobleck (see figure 5). Have children experiment to see what versions of oobleck they can create. If desired, copy the directions that follow for making oobleck on a large chart or the board so children can read and follow them. For those who want to use an overhead projector, use the subsequent form to make an overhead transparency at the activity center.

OOBLECK OOBLECK OOBLECK

OOBLECK POURS LIKE A LIQUID BUT IT FEELS LIKE A SOLID. HERE IS THE RECIPE:

- POUR ONE CUP OF WATER INTO A MIXING BOWL.
- PUT IN FOUR DROPS OF GREEN FOOD COLORING.
- ADD ONE BOX OF CORNSTARCH (16 0Z).
- ADD 3/4 CUP MORE WATER AND MIX BY HAND.
- MIX TO CREATE AN EVEN TEXTURE.

OOBLECK WAS THE SUBSTANCE FROM THE STORY, *BARTHOLOMEW AND THE OOBLECK* (RANDOM HOUSE,1949) BY DR. SEUSS. DEFINE ITS PROPERTIES:

1.

2.

3.

Figure 5. Form for Directions For Mixing Oobleck.

What Other Humorous Features Are in Books with Nonsense?

ABSURDITIES

Introduce children to the concept of absurdity and the idea of being foolish, silly, and preposterous, with John Caldwell's *Excuses, Excuses: How to Get Out of Practically Anything* (229). This is a collection of witty excuses and strategies that are offered for getting out of things like how to get out of walking the dog or doing homework. There are also black-and-white sketches that emphasize the absurdity of the excuses.

CARTOONLIKE ILLUSTRATIONS

Show children the cartoonlike illustrations In *The Stupids Die* (228) written by Harry Allard and illustrated by James Marshall. In the story, the power fails and the lights go out. When all becomes dark, the stupids are sure they have died. When the lights come on again, they are convinced they are in heaven. The humor is found in several features—the colorful cartoonlike illustrations, the funny things that happen, and the humorous names for the characters.

HUMOROUS FANTASY

William Joyce's *Santa Calls* (235) lets a child in on a humorous fantasy set at the North Pole. Santa Claus invites Art Atchinson Aimesworth, his little sister Esther, and his friend Spaulding, to visit him. The reason for the invitation is not revealed until the last pages. On the way, the three children are confronted by Ali Aku, captain of the santarian guard, along with the dark elves and their evil queen in scenes that will remind some children of *The Wizard of Oz*. At long last, they enter Santa's toyland until they are magically returned to their beds. Two letters that are attached to the last pages reveal the reason the children received Santa's invitation.

RIDICULOUS SITUATIONS

Help a child recognize some of the ridiculous situations—such as ridiculousness in everyday situations that can be shown through objects and actions that are not worthy of serious consideration—in *Hugo and the Spacedog* (238) by Lee Lorenz. The story is about Hugo, a wandering canine, who decides to settle down on a farm as a watchdog. In his encounter with a space dog, he proves to be quick-witted and comes up with some unique approaches to the situations he faces. Through all this, Hugo emerges as a brave and endearing hero and is shown in bold cartoon-style drawings.

SILLINESS

Introduce children to silly humor with *As: A Surfeit of Similes* (236) written by Norman Juster and illustrated by David Small. The book shows the use of a simile as a figure of speech where one object, action, behavior, or relationship is compared to something of a different kind of quality. It also shows some of the powers of similes to help children learn about what something *isn't* to also learn about what something *is* (children may not know what nonsense is unless they can recognize sense). An example of a simile from the text is: "as exciting as a plateful of cabbage." If desired, pair this book with one of Marvin Terban's humorous books that focuses on humorous word use: *Guppies in Tuxedos: Funny Eponyms* and *The Dove Dove: Funny Homograph Riddles* (both 236).

SPOOF

Sometimes a person writes something humorous that is similar to another writing or portrays something humorous in a semiserious manner—it's a spoof. With children, discuss some of the examples of the humor of a spoof in Hudson Talbott's *Your Pet Dinosaur: An Owner's Manual* (248). This is a chaptered book that is a spoof on raising dinosaurs written by an unknown Dr. Rex who gives readers tips on the choosing and home care, feeding, training, discipline and exercise of the dinosaurs—the intellectual giants of their time. Dr. Rex answers questions in the "Dear Dr. Rex" column where the owners mail in their letters of concern about their dinosaur's behavior. For example, one owner is concerned about his dino-pet who keeps jumping on the mail carrier.

UNEXPECTED SIGHTS

Unusual sights are found in Bernard Most's *Whatever Happened to the Dinosaurs?* (241). This is a humorous collection of some fanciful explanations of where the dinosaurs went. The illustrations are simple watercolor illustrations that depict the author's conjectures.

UNUSUAL PREMISES

Several authors use imagination and humorous details to illustrate their unusual premises. You can introduce children to this approach with *If the Dinosaurs Came Back* (240) by Bernard Most. In the book, the author's imagination and humorous details help illustrate the premise about what would happen if the intellectual giants of prehistorical times returned to today's society. For example, the dinosaurs could scare away robbers, give dentists plenty of teeth to work on, provide transportation, and so on. Many young readers will want to offer their own predictions (guesses, hunches) about what would happen if the creatures returned.

Another book that has imaginative ideas is Judi Barrett's *Cloudy with a Chance of Meatballs* (143) illustrated by Ron Barrett. In Chewandswallow people didn't have to buy or grow food because their meals always rained down from the sky. One day, things turned sour. That day there was only broccoli, all overcooked, and eventually huge foodstorms forced an evacuation on oversized peanut butter and jelly sandwich rafts. For more imaginative ideas, select Barrett's *Animals Should Definitely Not Wear Clothing* (5) and *Animals Should Definitely Not Act Like People* (5).

WEIRD AND WACKY

The concepts of "weird and wacky" are shown through very unusual, uncanny, somewhat crazy, and definitely mixed-up inventions in *Weird and Wacky Inventions* written and illustrated by Jim Murphy. The detailed drawings present ingenious inventions, many of them humorous. Most children will smile when they see an eye protector for a chicken, a diaper for a bird, a mouthpiece to prevent snoring, and a hunting decoy shaped like a cow. Additionally, there are some thoughtful items too, such as a parachute for escaping from the top of a burning building. This book can motivate some of the readers to draw sketches for humorous inventions of their own.

Rhymes and Verses

Edward Lear's ABC: Alphabet Rhymes for Children (263)

WHAT'S THE BOOK?

Edward Lear's ABC: Alphabet Rhymes for Children. Written by Edward Lear and illustrated by Carol Pike. Topsfield, Maine: Salem House, 1986. Ages 5 and up.

WHAT'S SO FUNNY?

There are nonsense combinations of words and ideas.

WHAT'S IT ABOUT?

This rhyming alphabet of Lear's first appeared in *Nonsense Songs, Stories, Botany and Alphabets,* 1871. With sound associations, the rhymes introduce the letters. For example, sound associations for A, apple pie, include pidy, widy, tidy, widy. Both upper- and lower-case letters are in bordered inserts in full-color illustrations beginning with apple pie, little bear, little cake, and ending with Xerxes, yew, and zinc. All ages.

WHAT'S THE MINI-UNIT PURPOSE?

Mention to children: "You are going to hear some verses about a rhyming alphabet. The poems have some silly combinations of words and ideas. Listen to find out which nonsense combination of words and ideas gives you the most pleasure when you hear it."

WHAT NEW WORDS CAN BE EMPHASIZED?

Words that rhyme with the key words in the verses—for example, pidy.

WHAT'S THERE TO TALK ABOUT?

Before Reading Aloud

1. What's Your Pseudonym? Lear used the pseudonym of Derry Down Derry to write his first *Book of Nonsense* that included made-up words, funny rhymes, and punch lines for his limericks. Invite children to select their own pseudonyms and use them later when they dictate/write their own original nonsense verses for a class *Book of Nonsense*. For a final page, they may list their pseudonyms and give written clues to their real identities for others to guess.

2. Where Would You Travel? Because of poor health, Lear spent most of his time traveling to the warm countries of Egypt, Greece, Italy, and the Middle East. Invite children to look at travel brochures for one or more of these countries. Ask them to tell what they would have seen had they been with Lear when he traveled.

Ask them to *retell* what they would have seen with *humorous* words or actions.

3. Get Ready for Lear's Animals. At one time, Lear was employed by the Zoological Society of London to do animal drawings. With the children, plan a bulletin board that will display the children's versions of some of Lear's animals from alphabet verses: busy old ants, crafty old cat, dear little duck, stately and wise elephant, lively old fish, good little goat, quaint little quail, and so on.

4. Blue Paper-Blue Markers. Lear promised an alphabet to a child and drew it in deep blue ink on pale blue linen. Show it to the children in *Edward Lear: A New Nonsense Alphabet* (499) by Hyman. Point out the photograph of Lear on the title page, a sample of Lear's letter that accompanies the alphabet, the reproductions of the original alphabet pages, and his original sketches.

As mentioned Lear wrote a nonsense alphabet on light blue linen in dark blue ink. Invite children to choose a favorite verse and write it on blue paper with blue markers or crayons.

After Reading Aloud

1. Mouse Mask—Mouse Actions. Reread the book and show illustrations. Discuss with children how they might show Newsom's mouse in the illustrations. Invite some to mime poses of the mouse. Engage children in creating mouse masks from art paper or brown paper bags. Depict mouse actions by wearing the masks and holding a brief mouse production.

2. Oral Interpretation of a Poem. Invite children to dictate their interpretation of one of the poems (loud voices, soft voices, one-child-a-line, unison, and so on). Write their suggestions on the board. Repeat the poem using their suggestions.

3. Entice Others to Read Lear's Verses. Show *An Edward Lear Alphabet* (262) illustrated by Newsom and *Edward Lear's ABC* (263) illustrated by Pike. Ask children to discuss/write reasons why they prefer one over the other. Discuss features of preference—"It reminds me of a personal experience; tells me something I did not know; it brings senses from real life (hear, see, smell, taste, touch); it has creative use of words, attractive illustrations, and shows what the author looked like." Engage children in designing a poster to entice others to read Lear's verses from one of the versions.

4. Lear's Inventive Words. Lear delighted in using made-up words. Invite children to dictate/write words for categories in a word map for any or all of the following groups. Write the children's suggestions on the map on the board. Keep the map on display and have children make up their own words to place in the different categories and use in their writings. Here are some possible categories.

- **Hidden Meanings:** The ending "able" was added to words ending in *t:* for example, carrot became carrotable. Have the children suggest words that end in t and write them on a list on the board. Ask the children to work together and create a definition for the words and then illustrate them for a Lear's glossary.
- **Onomatopoetic Sounds:** Examples are bosh-blobberbosh; meloobious, and growlygrumble.
- **Transposed Letters:** Rejoice becomes erjoice; publisher becomes buplisher; bedtime becomes

ted bime. Mixed-up letters resulted in the following: dragon becomes dragging; officers becomes ossifers.

- **Unusual Spellings:** *A* was added to looking, going, etc., and made alooking, agoing. *F* words began with ph—thus, fog becomes phogg and fortunate becomes phortschnit. Silent g as in gnat was added to other *n* words: gnatural. *H* words began without *h:* happy becomes appy; words beginning with vowels had an *h* beginning: opposite becomes hopposite; enemies becomes henemies. *Ph* words began with *f:* physical becomes fizzicle.

WHAT ACTIVITIES WILL EXTEND THE BOOK?

1. Illustrate a Phrase

Introduce other verses by Lear and invite the children to illustrate one of the phrases—"On the top of the Crumpetty Tree, the Quangle Wangle sat . . . ," and then compare the interpretation with a published artist's rendition of the character in the poem.

2. Original Endings

Invite the girls and boys to finish one of Lear's phrases with original endings. Possibilities include the following:

- Now, this letter will be neither a nice one nor a long one, but just the *hopposit* for it is to say that I am . . .
- The knock-shock-sprain which I got in that South Hampton train bothered me a good deal and . . .
- You see therefore in how noxious a state of knownothingatallabout whatimgoingtodo-ness I am in.

3. Cheerful Rhymes for a Flannel Board

Lear used cheerful rhymes and sound associations. To promote this use, engage children in making flannel board figures for retelling the verses or for acting out individual rhymes with movements or movements and words.

4. Limerick Models

Read aloud some of Lear's limericks from *There Was an Old Man . . . A Gallery of Nonsense Rhymes* (500) illustrated by Michelle Lemieux.

Some were written for the grandchildren of Lear's financial patron, the Earl of Derby. One limerick begins with "There was an old man of the west/ who never could get any rest. . . . " This limerick can be a pattern for children interested in writing original ones, and they can insert their own names or the names of their peers in the limerick.

5. Move to the Words

As Lear's rhymes are read, invite students to move to the words, to dramatize the actions silently, to say the verses in refrains, to think of ways to sing the words, and to write Lear-type alphabet rhymes of their own. They can create different shapes of poetry books, make word webs of narrative poems, and sing songs that were popular during Lear's time—*The Battle Hymn of the Republic* (1861), *John Henry* (1872), and *Sixteen Tons* (1900s).

6. An Edward Lear Center

Create a Lear center in the room and have children place books written by Lear there. They can visit a nearby library to find versions they want to check out for the center. Decorate the center with children's work about Lear—their posters, puppets, verses, and art compositions.

Further, with the help of the school librarian, engage the students in locating different works by Lear—limericks, narrative poems, tongue twisters, and alphabet rhymes—and discuss the language usage. For example, there is *A Learical Lexicon: A Magnificent Feest of Boshlobberbosh and Phun from the Vorx of Edward Lear* (502) with "vords" selected by Myra Cohn Livingston and "piggchurs" by Joseph Low. The selections focus on Lear's rhymes and letter substitutions in words.

The Dragons Are Singing Tonight (277)

WHAT'S THE BOOK?

The Dragons Are Singing Tonight. Written by Jack Prelutsky and illustrated by David Sis. New York: Greenwillow, 1993. Ages 6–8.

WHAT'S SO FUNNY?

Playful imagination and unexpected bursts of humor. This is a collection of verses that show ways the author plays with his thoughts and ways he surprises readers with something comical.

WHAT'S IT ABOUT?

This is a collection of seventeen verses about dragons—ancient, contemporary, real, and fanciful.

WHAT'S THE MINI-UNIT PURPOSE?

Mention to children: "You are going to hear several verses about dragons—some ancient, some modern, some real, and some imaginary. Listen for the unexpected words of humor."

WHAT NEW WORDS CAN BE EMPHASIZED?

Dragons, singing, tonight, and words from selected verses.

WHAT'S THERE TO TALK ABOUT?

Before Reading Aloud

1. The Dragons Are Singing Tonight. Introduce the title of the book and write the words *The Dragons Are Singing Tonight* on the board. Ask children to tell what the words mean to them. Have them imagine what sounds dragons make when they sing and perform their sounds for the whole group. Display several illustrations from the book that show various dragons and discuss what meaning the word *singing* might have for the children after they see the illustrations.

2. Dragon Chart Look-Over Shapes. Ask children to think of ways to describe one or more of the dragons. Ask them to sketch their descriptions as extra-large dragon shapes that can be displayed partially behind a chart and placed to look as if each dragon is looking over the edge of the chart. In partnerships, ask the children to tell their partners why they drew their sketches of dragons the way they did. Back in the whole group, invite volunteers to show their sketches and tell more about the dragons they drew. As a contrast to show ways people artistically describe dragons, show the illustrations by David Sis.

After Reading Aloud

1. **"One Imaginative Thing (Unexpected Humor) that *The Dragons Are Singing Tonight* Makes Me Think of Is. . . . "** Return to the title written on the board. Have each child turn to a child next to them and briefly discuss "One imaginative thing (unexpected humor) that *The Dragons Are Singing Tonight* makes me think of is. . . ."

2. **Describing Dragons in Humorous Ways.** Discuss: How might *you* have humorously described a real dragon? An imaginary dragon? An ancient dragon? A modern dragon? How might you include other funny things to say?

3. **What Should Humorous Poems about Dragons be Like?** With children, ask them the following:

- How do *you* think the author/poet developed his humorous ideas about dragons?
- How did this book of poems seem different from your idea of what poems about dragons should be?

WHAT ACTIVITIES WILL EXTEND THE BOOK?

1. Singing Dragon Week: Laugh Lines in Poems

With partners, invite the children to select a favorite humorous poem by Prelutsky and identify their favorite words from Prelutsky's rich language. Have the children write their favorite words in a visual graphic and place the words in groups with headings. Also, invite children to tell a friend how they felt about their favorite poem.

2. A Jack Prelutsky Title Invitation

Have children use the title of Prelutsky's books to be the center of a writing/dictating activity. For example, the children can suggest guests they want to visit the classroom. For the first guest, they may want to pretend to invite A.

Nonny Mouse from *Poems of A. Nonny Mouse* (278) and prepare their handwritten invitations. A second guest might be Baby Uggs from *The Baby Uggs Are Hatching* (278) and a third, the sheriff from *The Sheriff of Rottenshot* (278). Since the guests are different personalities, ask children what ways they should decorate the room and prepare humorous questions for the "guests." If desired, ask one or two students in the upper grades to role play one of the guests and visit the classroom.

3. Find the Humor in Other Rhymes: Start with Mother Goose

Read aloud humorous Mother Goose rhymes from a version of your choice to enrich children's awareness of humor around them. They can listen to the verses in Walter Crane's *An Alphabet of Old Friends and the Absurd ABC* (259). Show a copy of one of the verses on the overhead or on the board, and ask children to say the verse together. Reread it and ask children to tap their fingers to the rhythm of the words. Ask children in what ways they would draw and color a picture to illustrate the verse in a humorous way? What colors would they select to help the drawing stand out and show the humor? Have the children draw their pictures and then display them on a bulletin board with a caption, "Mother Goose on the Loose."

4. Funny Rhymes and Verses Create Humorous Mental Pictures

With children point out that humorous rhymes and verses help them see funny pictures and hear the accompanying sounds. Some humorous words can make them laugh and keep them in a happy mood. Have children close their eyes and listen to a selected rhyme or poem. Ask them to feel the fun, laughter, and happiness as they listen. After the poem, ask children to share their reactions and then reread the rhyme or verse again so that children can listen for one or more of the following:

- Some words that are the most interesting to them
- Some pictures that come to their minds
- Some words that relate to sounds that could accompany the rhyme or verse, when the rhymes are reread aloud

What Other Humorous Features Are in Books With Rhymes and Verses?

NONSENSE

The idea of nonsense—words, language, or actions that have no sensible meaning—can be introduced with *Ride a Purple Pelican* (280) written by Jack Prelutsky and illustrated by Garth Williams. In the collection, there is an ear-catching group of new verses with plenty of alliteration, interior rhyme, and bouncing rhythms of Mother Goose. The humor is mainly in the happy, nonsensical verses with prominent names of places such as "Justin Austin/ skipped to Boston"; "A white cloud floated like a swan/high above Saskatchewan"; "Grandma Bear from Delaware/ rocked in a rockety rocking chair," and so on.

PERSONIFICATION

A Frog Inside My Hat: A First Book of Poems (285), edited by Fay Robinson and illustrated by Cyd Moore, has over thirty lighthearted poems. It includes selections such as "The Purple Cow" by Gelett Burgess, "The Furry Bear" by A. A. Milne, and others in categories labeled animals, food, nonsense, weather, and the seasons.

RIDICULOUS SITUATION

A simple yet ridiculous presentation based on animals in unusual situations is the premise in Fritz Eichenberg's *Ape in a Cape: An Alphabet of Odd Animals* (260). This book can generate many additional situations on paper by amused children.

SURPRISES

A House Is a House for Me (216) by Mary Ann Hoberman is a collection of colorful illustrations, filled with lots of detail and many surprises in the text that add fun and interest to the rhymes about houses. Some of the houses will be familiar ones to children while others are quite unique. For example, roses are houses for smells, pods are houses for peas, and pockets are houses for pennies.

TONGUE TWISTING WORDS

Fun in hearing and saying alliterative tongue twisters can be provided with *Peter Piper's Principles of Plain and Perfect Pronunciation with Manifold Manifestations* (256) retold by Marcia Brown. In the rhyming text, there is lilting nonsense rhyme with tongue twisting lyrics.

WITTINESS

Wittiness—saying amusing congruities (harmonious things, things in agreement) and incongruities about things—can be found in the fifty-plus clever poems in *Oh, Such Foolishness* (258) by William Cole. There are amusing things said in agreement as well as those *not* in agreement, which makes this a good introduction to wittiness for children learning to appreciate the amusing words of others.

Unusual Characters and Creatures

The Cow Who Wouldn't Come Down (313)

WHAT'S THE BOOK?

The Cow Who Wouldn't Come Down. Written and illustrated by Paul Brett Johnson. New York: Orchard, 1993. Ages 6–8.

WHAT'S SO FUNNY?

There is a unique situation, surprise expressions, and surprise behavior. Gertrude, the contented cow, doesn't know that cows don't fly and she glides over the farmland showing off her figure eights.

WHAT'S IT ABOUT?

Miss Rosemary, an elderly woman, is determined to bring Gertrude down from her flights and uses several ways to resolve her problem—but all end in near disaster. When Miss Rosemary tries a more subtle approach, it works.

WHAT'S THE MINI-UNIT PURPOSE?

Mention to children: "You are going to hear a story about Gertrude, a cow that doesn't realize she can't fly and so she glides over the countryside. Miss Rosemary, an elderly lady, wonders how she will milk the flying cow. Listen to find out the ways Miss Rosemary tries to get Gertrude to come down."

WHAT NEW WORDS CAN BE EMPHASIZED?

Gertrude, wouldn't, Miss Rosemary.

WHAT'S THERE TO TALK ABOUT?

Before Reading Aloud

1. Flying Cows. Have children think of a time when a flying cow might be something humorous—yet valuable to have around. Ask for volunteers to share their ideas. Show several illustrations from the book that show Gertrude, the cow, in flight. Have children turn to a child next to them and briefly discuss, "One surprise behavior about cows that I think might be funny is. . . . "

2. Artists Show Humor in Various Ways. Ask children to think of ways to describe Gertrude or Miss Rosemary from the cover of the book. Ask them to sketch the descriptions they talked about in the discussion. In partnerships, ask the children to tell their partners why they drew their sketches the way they did. Back in the whole group, invite the children to display their descriptions and tell more about what they drew. Elicit suggestions as to ways they could make their descriptions more humorous. As a contrast to show ways artists interpret characters differently, show more illustrations by Johnson.

3. Flying Excitement. Ask children to think if they have ever wanted to experience the excitement of flying. Encourage them to share their feelings about flying or about any flying incidents—in a plane, a hot air balloon, a glider—that happened to them or that they know about.

After Reading Aloud

1. Humor Graph: Favorite Animals for Flying. Ask children to describe how they think Gertrude learned to fly and do figure eights. Have them reflect about how Miss Rosemary felt when she discovered Gertrude could fly. Ask children to identify her or his favorite nonflying animal that should learn to fly and why. Record the information on a humor graph:

1. Make a bar graph to record the information.
2. List each animal's name. Have each child vote for a favorite animal.
3. Draw a humorous cow face as a tally beside each child's choice of animal.
4. Vote on the favorite animal from the top three and list on the board all the reasons why that animal was the favorite.
5. Have children brainstorm ways they could help teach the nonflying animal to fly and some humorous things that might happen.

2. The Feel of Flying. Have children think of ideas about how flying feels and write the ideas in a column on the board. In another column, think of *humorous* words that describe how flying feels.

WHAT ACTIVITIES WILL EXTEND THE BOOK?

1. Gertrude the Cow: A Milk Carton Alert

To make a milk carton alert for Gertrude the cow, a discarded milk carton can be used. Have children make *wanted* posters for Gertrude and paste them to the four sides of the carton. Display the cartons along with a copy of the book in a reading area.

2. Gertrude's Flying Mobile

With partners, invite the children to take turns and describe their favorite illustrations of Miss Rosemary who wants Gertrude to stop flying and come down so she can milk the cow. Encourage the children to use words to tell about a unique situation they liked, some of the surprise expressions, and any behavior that surprised them. Ask the children to sketch and color a scene from the story to make a hanging mobile about Gertrude the cow.

Three-Star Billy (312)

WHAT'S THE BOOK?

Three-Star Billy. Written and illustrated by Pat Hutchins. New York: Greenwillow, 1994. K–1.

WHAT'S SO FUNNY?

The chaos that occurs because of a young monster's behavior at nursery school when he throws things and scares others.

WHAT'S IT ABOUT?

At first Billy, a young green monster, does *not* want to go to nursery school. Once there, however, he throws the paint, hollers instead of singing, and scares the others in the class. The teacher, however, is not upset because it seems that this is a nursery school for monsters and she gives Billy gold stars for his "monstrous" behavior. By the end of the day, Billy does *not* want to go home.

WHAT'S THE MINI-UNIT PURPOSE?

Mention to children: "You are going to hear a story about Billy, a young monster, who does *not* want to go to nursery school. Consequently, he throws the paint and hollers out loud during group singing. This does not cause chaos in the class because all the children are young monsters. Listen to find out why the teacher *rewards* Billy with gold stars."

WHAT NEW WORDS CAN BE EMPHASIZED?

Billy, stars, three-star.

WHAT'S THERE TO TALK ABOUT?

Before Reading Aloud

1. Before-the-Story Interest Builders. Engage children in one or more of the following activities to help build interest:

- Tell information or related experiences they know about related to unusual characters and creatures.
- Discuss a previous read or heard story about unusual characters or creatures.
- Look at illustrations related to unusual creatures and characters.
- Cut out illustrations from magazines and newspapers that depict unusual creatures or characters.

2. A Vest of Stars. Introduce the title of the book *Three-Star Billy,* and ask the children to tell what the title means to them. Discuss what stars are given for at school. What are some things for which stars are awarded or given? Make a list of the responses the children give. Show several illustrations from the book that show the children in the nursery school with their round faces, sharp teeth, and long fingernails, to see if any of the children's responses about actions are shown in the illustrations. Have children cut out large stars from art paper and draw and color actions for which stars are awarded or given. Affix the stars to the vests made from brown paper grocery bags and display them in the room.

3. A Monster Description. Ask children to think of ways to describe Billy, the young monster, and his behavior. Ask them to sketch the descriptions they talked about in the discussion. As a contrast, show the illustrations by Pat Hutchins. In partnerships, ask the children to tell their partners why they drew their sketches of Billy the way they did. Back in the whole group, invite the children to display their descriptions and tell more about what they drew.

4. Humorous Going-to-School Stories. Ask children to think if they have ever read other books about going to school, and list their suggestions on a chart. Encourage them to share their thoughts about the stories and place the chart of titles near a reading area for future reference.

After Reading Aloud

1. Off to Nursery School. Describe how you think Billy felt when he did not want to go to nursery school? How do you think Ma, Pa, and sister Hazel felt when they had to pry his little green fingers off the garden gate and drag him to nursery school?

2. If You're Good, You Might Get a Star. If someone said to you, "If you're good, you might

get a star," what do you think you would have to do to get one? What might *you* have said or done to help Billy feel good about going to nursery school when his sister Hazel said, "If you're good, you might get a star?"

3. A Different Type of Nursery School. What might *you* expect Billy to do at nursery school that was good enough to get a star? What did the nursery school teacher think was "good" behavior? How is this nursery school for young monsters different from your idea of what a nursery school should be?

WHAT ACTIVITIES WILL EXTEND THE BOOK?

1. Monster Masks

With partners, invite the children to illustrate Billy's classmates creatively with "Monster Masks." The masks can be made from brown paper bags and painted. If desired, fill the inside of the masks with crumpled newspaper to make the masks full and plump before displaying them in the room.

2. Make Lift-Up Paper Doors for Mural Scenes

With butcher paper and painting materials, have the children engage in making a mural of Billy and his behavior through the day. Invite children to interpret and fingerpaint different scenes from the story. Ask the children to identify the most exciting part of each scene and mask it with a sheet of art paper hinged with tape similar to a door. Let children lift the paper doors to review the "surprise" drawings that they drew to tell about Billy's behavior.

3. Humorous Preferences

With children, ask them to divide into groups related to their interest for a particular humorous story related to unusual creatures or characters. Engage them in selecting ways to extend the book. For example, one group might decide to read aloud sections from the story and another group might recite a related poem about another unusual creature or character. Another group might prepare a chart of humorous events, while still another group might design and construct items for a bulletin board based upon the unusual character or creature in the humorous story they read.

4. A Monster Puppet

Introduce the title of the book with a monster puppet. Have the puppet announce the title and ask the students to tell the puppet what the words mean to them. Show several pictures from the book to illustrate the words *monster, star,* etc. Invite the students to tell the puppet what they could do to be good listeners during the reading of the story. List their suggestions on the board. At the end of the story, use the puppet to summarize the important events in the story. Engage the students in making their own finger-ring monster puppets from art paper and talking to a friend in the classroom about their favorite humorous part in the story.

What Other Humorous Features Are in Books with Unusual Characters and Creatures?

ABSURD SITUATIONS

Absurdity and silliness is shown through the character of Imogene, a young girl, who realizes that there is nothing wrong with being different and that there may even be some advantages—when she awakens one morning wearing full-size antlers in the story *Imogene's Antlers* (324) by David Small. And what a fine set of antlers they were! Undaunted after coping with the problems of dressing and getting downstairs, Imogene and the cook and the kitchen maid realize that there are pluses in having antlers—they can be used as a drying rack, a bird feeder, and a candelabra. Her hefty mother, not quite so attuned to this new situation, reacts to her daughter's predicament by fainting over and over. The matter appears to resolve itself the next morning, when an antlerless Imogene appears at breakfast, proudly displaying something else—a new peacock tail.

ANTICS

Laurent de Brunhoff's *Babar and the Ghost* (307) lets a reader in on the encounter with a friendly ghost that happens when Babar and his children are on a picnic to the black castle. It seems that only the children can see the nice ghost and many humorous antics occur before Babar has had enough of the tricks and catches on.

BIZARRE BEHAVIORS

A humorous, imaginative approach is seen when Russell Baker, the author, makes fun of Dr. Frankenstein, the mad scientist and his creations in *The Up-side-Down Man* (297). In the kingdom of delirium, Dr. Frankenstein, with the help of his bungling assistant Lazlo, attempts to create a man and his results turn into an upside-down man as well as a girl with cow's ears.

COLLOQUIAL DIALOGUE

In *Leprechauns Never Lie* (298) by Lorna Balian, there is a refrain of "Leprechauns never lie" for the children to chant to help tell the story when the rhythmic, catchy text is read aloud. With bits of humor in the text, Lazy Ninny Nanny tries to find a captured leprechaun's gold. Highlighted in green, the leprechaun is easy to find on the pages.

DETAILS

In *The Dwarks at the Mall* (299) by Michael Berenstain, action and fun help tell the story of the Dwarks, a small, furry, fun-loving family. During the day, they live in a cozy old car in a junkyard. Every night, however, they disguise themselves as possums and raid the houses of humans for their favorite food—garbage. One day, Mamma Dwark wants a different adventure and they visit a gigantic new mall.

EXAGGERATIONS

The humor of exaggeration is shown through overspelling in *Perrywinkle and the Book of Magic Spells* (319) by Ross Martin Madsen. This story is an easy-to-read adventure. In it, Perrywinkle is the son of the great wizard who tries the old rabbit trick, and instead produces a thing that eats a table. The humor is increased by a crow named Nevermore, who serves as the straight man for Perrywinkle's comic adventures with overspelling. The worst example of overspelling occurs when he spells the word *waterfall* for his teacher—a *real* splashing waterfall tumbles out of the chalkboard and engulfs the class.

NONSENSICAL CREATURES

There is an outlandish array of rare and ridiculous birds to be found in another nonsensical book—*The Ice-Cream Cone Coot and Other Rare Birds* (317) by Arnold Lobel. Using objects like ice-cream cones and electric plugs, the author-artist has created such unusual fowls as the garbage canary who lives in conditions quite unsanitary and the key crane looking for doors that might need unlocking. Another collection of nonsensical creatures is found in Bill Peet's *No Such Things* (481). These creatures—the Snoof, a Fandango, a Mopwaggin, and others—are accompanied by explanations for their existence. There are simple rhymes and humorous illustrations.

UNEXPECTED SIGHTS

Robert Bright's *Georgie's Christmas Carol* (305) presents an unusual character—Georgie, the friendly ghost. Georgie organizes an unusual Christmas surprise for two children and their gloomy uncle, Mr. Gloams. Readers will enjoy the unexpected sight of a cow with evergreen antlers pulling a sleigh and the sight of Georgie coming down the chimney.

UNUSUAL SIZES

In Patricia Brennan's *Hitchety, Hatchety, Up I Go!* (303), Hitchety, Hatchety is smaller than an elf—a tiny sprite who says a refrain, "Hitchety, Hatchety, Up I Go! Up I Go! Up I Go! and down I go, down I go, down I go," whenever he leaves his teacup home by climbing up his ladder. He plans to take some ingredients for a pancake feast from a cranky old woman down the lane, but his craving for olives does him in.

II

Literature-Based Mini-Units
for Children Ages 9–12

Animals as Humans

The Champions of Appledore (328)

WHAT'S THE BOOK?

The Champions of Appledore. Written and illustrated by Romayne Dawnay. New York: Four Winds, 1994. Ages 9–10.

WHAT'S SO FUNNY?

There is slapstick humor as Grunwinkle, a worn-out dragon, and a Scottish mouse named Iona, help rid the town of pests. The residents of Appledore Manor are being invaded by smelly polecats and hungry wolves. The silly schemes of some of the townspeople and the Lord of the manor, Sir Pomfrey de Pomme, to get rid of the pests go awry until Grunwinkle and Iona get involved.

WHAT'S IT ABOUT?

This is a lighthearted fantasy about Sir Pomfrey de Pomme, the lord of the manor of Appledore, and the residents who faced a terrible situation. It seems that the manor's village is being invaded by smelly polecats and hungry wolves. With the declaration that "something must be done," Sir Pomfrey initiates his first silly scheme and builds a trap. He baits it with Stilton cheese. He discovers that he has captured a Scottish mouse named Iona. In another scheme, Sir Pomfrey decided to hire the dragon Grunwinkle, to get rid of the pests. Grunwinkle is in a worn-out state with broken wings and needs to be touched up with colorful paint and have his wings mended. Grunwinkle has back-up reinforcements against the pests with Sir Pomfrey, his cook, Iona, and a boy named Tom.

WHAT'S THE MINI-UNIT PURPOSE?

Mention to older students that "You are going to hear a story about Sir Pomfrey de Pomme and his friends who have some silly schemes to get rid of the smelly polecats and hungry wolves that are invading their village. Listen to find out how they did this with the help of a Scottish mouse named Iona and a worn-out dragon named Grunwinkle."

WHAT NEW WORDS CAN BE EMPHASIZED?

Champions, Appledore, Sir Pomfrey de Pomme, Iona, Grunwinkle.

WHAT'S THERE TO TALK ABOUT?

Before the Reading

1. What Are Champions to You? Ask students to think of ways they would define the word *champions.* Ask them to offer their descriptions. Write the word *Champions,* on the board. Have students turn to a partner and discuss, "One thing the word *champions* makes me think of is. . . . " As a contrast, ask them to think of ways they would define *nonchampions.* Have them brainstorm ways to describe the two words. Show the illustrations of Iona, the Scottish mouse, and Grunwinkle, the worn-out dragon, and ask in what ways the two look like/do not look like champions to them.

2. Who Was a Champion You Knew? Ask students to think if they have ever known a person who was a champion to them. Encourage them to share incidents about knowing a person who was a champion in their eyes.

3. Slapstick Makes Me Think of. . . . Ask students to think if they have ever seen a slapstick situation that was entertaining to them. Encourage them to share their experiences about seeing a situation from a book, a movie, or television that had slapstick comedy from their points of view. Discuss some of the features of slapstick:

- the rapid, physical activity that is used for comic effect;
- rough-and-tumble actions;
- striking quickly or sharply in a humorous way;
- and some cause-and-effect situations.

After the Reading

1. Humor Search. Engage students in a fifteen-minute humor search. Each student must find one other student who can tell him or her something humorous in the story and then write it down (sketch it) for the searching student. At the end of the fifteen minutes, ask for the names of the students who have given written information or sketched drawings, and have those students tell about the humor they found in the story.

2. Put Yourself in the Story. How do you think Iona felt when the mouse became trapped by the Stilton cheese in the wolf trap? What might *you* have said or done to Sir Pomfrey de Pomme when Iona was discovered in the trap?

3. Design Your Own Fanciful "Wolf Trap" to Catch a Mouse. Invite students to create their own version of a fanciful wolf trap that was needed to rid the town of Appledore of the pests. Ask them to work with partners to sketch their designs and make decisions about what bait would be used. Ask them to explain their designs to the whole group and discuss, "How did Sir Pomfrey's 'Wolf Trap' eventually help the townspeople?"

4. A Double Collage: What Should a Humorous Dragon Look Like? Have students in small groups discuss, how was Grunwinkle different from your idea of what a dragon should be? Ask the students to fold a sheet of art paper in half. On the leftside of the paper, engage the students in sketching and coloring their version of Grunwinkle (and characteristics that are humorous to them) and on the righthand side, sketch and color their *own* version of what they think a humorous-looking dragon should be like.

5. Dramatize Dragon Grunwinkle's Touch-Ups. Invite students to imitate the work that was needed to touch-up the sorry-looking dragon, Grunwinkle. Ask them to take turns and pantomime some of the actions that were needed to get Grunwinkle ready to confront the town pests.

WHAT ACTIVITIES WILL EXTEND THE BOOK?

1. Mimicking the Smelly Polecats

With partners, ask students to role play events in the story and take turns mimicking the accents of the smelly and smart-mouthed polecats as they slink into houses to take food and get warm by the fires.

2. How Do You Hire a Dragon?

Taking the roles of Sir Pomfrey and Grunwinkle, invite students to act out the discussion that Sir Pomfrey had with Grunwinkle to "hire" him to rid the town of pests and the possible arguments/reasons that the worn-out Grunwinkle could have given to turn the offer down.

3. Create a Time Line of Appledore and the Slapstick Encounters

Have girls and boys track the events from the story on butcher paper by sketching them from left to right, and at appropriate places, color the first event, the second, and so on. Encourage them to insert humorous details. The students can map the events of the story from the point of view of Sir Pomfrey; or Iona; or the biggest character of all, Grunwinkle. If desired, the events also can be sketched from the point of view of an inanimate object—the fanciful wolf trap or the Stilton cheese.

4. Write Your Own Slapstick Event to Add to the Story

With students, reread excerpts from the story aloud and discuss the idea that slapstick humor is the hit-them-on-the-head and the fall-down kind. Suggest that they reread a favorite part of the story and then write drafts of their own slapstick event that could be included in the story.

5. What's So Funny about Slapstick?

With the students, write the word *slapstick* on the board or chart, and ask them what meanings the word has for them now that they have heard/read the story. Write their interpretations of the word on the board before reading the meaning from a dictionary. Review other slapstick situations from the wordless books *The Bear and the Fly* (134) and *Sir Andrew* (135) by Paula Winters. Elicit examples from the students about ways the author used slapstick in the stories.

Willy the Champ (10)

WHAT'S THE BOOK?

Willy the Champ. Written by Anthony Browne and illustrated by the author. New York: Knopf, 1985. Ages 9–11.

WHAT'S SO FUNNY?

Surprise behavior. Willy, the scrawny little chimpanzee goes through life apologizing—even when it is not his fault.

WHAT'S IT ABOUT?

Scrawny Willy says "I'm sorry" when the big gorillas knock him down and is a whiner through most of the story. He sends for a "Don't Be a Wimp" kit. Feeling better about himself after dieting and exercising, he rescues his friend Millie from the Gorilla gang and takes on the biggest bully of all, Buster Nose. Buster punches at him. Willy ducks—and Buster smashes his fist into a brick wall. Wally stands back up and crashes into Buster's chin. The children carry Willy on their shoulders as their thanks to him for saving them from Buster.

WHAT'S THE MINI-UNIT PURPOSE?

Mention to older students that "You are going to hear a story about a Willy, a small chimpanzee who seems to be a wimp and goes through life apologizing—even when it is not his fault. Listen to find out what happens when he sends for a 'Don't Be a Wimp' kit."

WHAT NEW WORDS CAN BE EMPHASIZED?

Wimp, kit, diet, exercise, Millie, Gorilla, Lassie movies, Buster Nose, chin.

WHAT'S THERE TO TALK ABOUT?

Before the Reading

1. Surprise Behavior: Describe and Draw Willy the Champ. Ask students to think of humorous ways they would describe Willy, the apologetic chimp, from the cover of the book. Have them identify a behavior that Willy could do that would surprise them. Ask them to draw their descriptions. As a contrast, show the illustrations where Browne depicts Willy and the rest of the characters. In small groups, ask students to tell their classmates why they drew their drawings the way they did. Display the drawings in the room.

2. Accordion Book: Five Faces of Willy. Have students work together as partners and make an accordion book about Willy that shows their original illustrations of Willy and five scenes of some surprise behavior. For example, the students can use strips of art paper (12″ × 18″) and fold them concertina-style to make the "pages" for the book. Have students finish their illustrations about Willy and then write about the chimp in their own words beneath the drawings.

After the Reading

1. Dramatize Willy's Apologies. Invite students to imitate Willy's apologetic "I'm sorry" in different tones of voice. Ask them to take turns and say something in a "whiney" voice—in a voice that is different from their own.

2. Design Your Own "Don't Be a Wimp" Kit. Taking the role of Willy, invite students to tell a friend how they felt about the "Don't Be a Wimp" kit. Invite students to design and draw their own ideas of what should be in an antiwimp kit. Ask them to tell *why* they selected the ideas they did for the kit. Have them advertise their ideas of the kit on posters to display in the room.

WHAT ACTIVITIES WILL EXTEND THE BOOK?

1. Humorous Diorama

After reading several humorous books and discussing the features of humor they noticed, older students can seek out other features of humor in supplementary books. Invite the students to further extend the features of humor in the books they have read. Construct a shoe box diorama to show a humorous scene from the story that students liked best. If desired, have the students label the scene with its main feature of humor—slapstick, surprise behavior, and so on.

2. Humor Glossary

Have students begin their own glossaries of humorous words, words they think are funny, and unusual character's names or story titles that strike their funny bones. Invite them to illustrate the words with humorous sketches, if desired.

3. Invite Someone to a Humorous Book Party

Engage students in writing and addressing invitations to a humorous book party for parents or guardians at which time a humorous book program will be presented. The invitations can be the person's ticket for admission to the presentation and written on ticket-shaped paper. If desired, encourage students to use titles of humorous books in the text

---

It's *Paddy's Evening Out!* There will be a Humorous Book Party and book program with *Castaways on Chimp Island* (really the fourth grade students in the fourth grade classroom, room ____) at 2:30 P.M. on the last day of school, June 6. There will be *Willy the Champ, Catastrophe Cat,* and *Jolly Roger: A Dog of Hoboken* for all to meet.
R. S. V. P.

Signed
*The Frog Band and the
Onion Seller*
_____ student name

---

of their invitations. For example, an invitation/ticket might include titles from humorous books where animals act like humans and look like this:

4. Create a Game Board of Willy and His Encounters

Have girls and boys retell an event from the story on a game board, and somewhere, insert their name and personality with the words "Suddenly, there I was with Willy and I . . . . " Encourage them to see how the story changes as their personality helps Willy or makes choices different from Willy's. The students can map the events of the story from the point of view of Millie, or a member of the Gorilla gang, or the biggest bully of all, Buster Nose. If desired, an event also can be written on the board from the point of view of an inanimate object—the event where Buster Nose throws a punch at Willy and smashes his fist into a brick wall can be told by one of the bricks.

5. Dear Author: The Surprise Behavior That I Liked Best Was . . . .

Invite students to write a humorous letter to the author and tell him the funny parts—especially the surprise behavior—they liked about the story.

What Other Humorous Features Are in Books with Animals as Humans?

PARODY

Several stories where the animals act like humans are humorous mystery stories that are parodies. Write the word *parody* on the board and ask students what meaning the word has for them. Write their ideas on the board, or a chart, or an overhead transparency. Turn to the dictionary and read the word's meaning and then return to the children's

ideas on the board and identify the ideas that are closest to the definition in the dictionary. Discuss with students what they have learned about a parody after reading aloud a humorous mystery story—either *Bunnicula: A Rabbit Tale of Mystery* (333) written by Deborah and James Howe, or *Piggins* (341) by Jane Yolen. Brainstorm with students some ideas about how more humor could be put into the story and write the ideas on the board. Ask students to choose one of these ideas and draw or write about it to show what the mystery would be like if this bit of humor was included.

Parody of Dracula Mystery

Bunnicula: A Rabbit Tale of Mystery (333) written by Deborah and James Howe and illustrated by Alan Daniel is a parody of the Dracula story. Harold, the family dog, narrates this humorous tale of a bunny who was found by the Monroe family in a Dracula movie. Chester and Harold attempt to "save" the family from the suspected bunny vampire. Chester tries to rid the house of the long-eared beast with help of garlic and other information he finds in *The Mark of the Vampire*.

Parody of an English Mystery

Piggins (341) by Jane Yolen and illustrated by Jane Dyer is a parody to show students. It is based on the typical English mystery. It has a great deal of fun and begins when the Reynards throw a dinner party to show off Mrs. Reynard's new diamond lavaliere and to explain why they must sell

it. As Mr. Reynard tells the story of the necklace's curse, the lights go off. When the lights go back on, the necklace is gone. All the dinner guests are stumped, but Piggins, the very proper butler, explains to Professor T. Ortoise, an elderly turtle, and the other guests how it was done and who did the evil deed (the thieves are the rats, you know).

SATIRE

Piggybook by Anthony Browne (327) is a picture book suitable for older students that reflects satire. In the book, Browne uses satire as a way to ridicule and humorously discredit male chauvinism. Mr. Piggott, who has a *very* important job, lives with his two sons, Simon and Patrick, who attend a *very* important school, in a nice house with a nice garden, and a nice car in the nice garage. Inside the house also lives Mrs. Piggott who finally reacts to the chauvinism in this pig family! Mr. Piggott and the boys shout commands at Mom who cleans, cooks, and washes before she has to go off to work. One day, however, she is not there when the males return. They find a note from her stating, "You are pigs."

Family, School, and Community

The Magic School Bus at the Waterworks (357)

WHAT'S THE BOOK?

The Magic School Bus at the Waterworks. Written by Joanna Cole and illustrated by Bruce Degen. New York: Scholastic, 1987. Ages 9–12.

WHAT'S SO FUNNY?

Surprise behavior. Wearing scuba suits and snorkels, the students in Ms. Frizzle's class have a fanciful journey on the magical school bus and visit the waterworks. The students follow Ms. Frizzle and experience what it is like to be raindrops and go through the water cycle.

WHAT'S IT ABOUT?

Cole and Degen have an exciting, attractive, and informative science book. The students in Ms. Frizzle's class have an adventure from school to the waterworks and back again that is a fanciful journey. Wearing scuba suits and snorkels, the students follow Ms. Frizzle along the water cycle. The students find surprises as they begin as raindrops from clouds. They follow the water's course through the purifying process at the waterworks before they are expelled from water pipes and they arrive back at school. The illustrations are in watercolor in a cartoon-style format, and word balloons contain pertinent information as well as the students' asides. There is a tongue-in-cheek section at the end of the story that discusses the real and fanciful aspects of the book.

WHAT'S THE MINI-UNIT PURPOSE?

Mention to children: "You are going to hear a story about a teacher, Ms. Frizzle, who takes her class to the waterworks in a humorous way. Listen to find out what the children learned about the way water is treated after they got into their scuba suits."

WHAT NEW WORDS CAN BE EMPHASIZED?

Waterworks, Ms. Frizzle, scuba suits, snorkels, sedimentation pond.

WHAT'S THERE TO TALK ABOUT?

Before the Reading

1. The Bus. Tell the title of the book to students and ask, what surprising things do you think a magic school bus could do? What makes you think so? What do you think will be seen when the students get to the waterworks?

2. Ms. Frizzle. From looking at the cover of the book, ask students to think of ways to describe Ms. Frizzle, the teacher. Ask them to quickly sketch their descriptions. In groups of two, ask them to tell their partners why they drew their sketches the way they did. Back in the whole group, invite volunteers to show their descriptions and tell more about them. As a contrast to show ways artists interpret humorous characters differently, show the illustrations by Bruce Degen.

3. The Magic School Bus. Have students turn to someone in class next to them and briefly discuss, "One surprise behavior that *The Magic School Bus* made me think of was . . . . "

4. What I Know about the Waterworks. Have students brainstorm what they know about a waterworks plant and write their thoughts in a list on the board. Once the list is made, have the students review the list and group similar thoughts together in clumps on a diagram on the board. Once several thoughts are written in a group, ask students to think of a label for the group of thoughts.

After the Reading

1. **Discussion.** Discuss *surprise behavior* with students:

- *Now* that you know the story, what surprise behavior do you think a magic school bus can have? Were your ideas about the bus right? What does the school bus have to do with the story?
- Which behavior in this story could have *really* happened? Which parts were surprise parts? Which parts were the most humorous to you? Why do you think so?

2. **A Humorous Everyday Act.** Suggest that students create another tale of the magic school bus that begins with an everyday occurrence. For example, a tale might begin with, "I was waiting for the school bus. I reached up to grab the door handle to get aboard the bus. Suddenly, a hand inside the bus reached out and grabbed me and . . ." Have students work with partners to write the story, act it out to one another if desired, and then sketch the pictures that tell the story. In the whole group, ask students to reflect upon which idea came first when they thought about their stories. Ask students to meet again with new partners and tell one another the way in which the events in the story were written and illustrated. Have them tell which came first—the illustrations or the words. Ask the new partners to create another humorous tale in the reverse way—either words first or pictures first. Back in the whole group, have partners report on ways the second tale differed from the first tale.

3. **Hard Hats and a Humorous Book Corner.** In an area designated "Humorous Book Corner," display another adventure about Ms. Frizzle and the students with *The Magic School Bus: Inside the Earth* (359), an adventure from school to a volcano and back again, a fanciful journey to the center of the earth. Have interested students read the book and put on hard hats as they take turns and tell others what they learned about the inside of the earth. Carrying picks and wearing hard hats, the students in the story follow Ms. Frizzle among the stalactites and stalagmites inside the earth to begin their journey. The students find surprises in

each strata down to the very inner core where it is hot, hot, hot. They collect rock samples before the bus is expelled from the core in a volcanic eruption and they arrive back at school.

WHAT ACTIVITIES WILL EXTEND THE BOOK?

1. A Humorous Field Trip

With partners, invite the children to play the role of one of the students who goes on the field trip to the waterworks or to the center of the earth. What will the student say, tell, and do that could be humorous? What does it feel like to wear a scuba suit and a snorkel? (carry a pick and wear a hard hat?) What is it like to see what happens at the waterworks? (to see the surprises in each strata?) What is it like to be in the school bus when it flies up into the sky? (is blown from the core of the volcano in the eruption?)

2. If I had been there, I would have. . . .

Have the students tell their favorite part of the fanciful field trip in the story, and somewhere, say, "If I had been there, I would have. . . . " Invite them to make humorous story changes as they say what they would have done on the field trip.

3. Humorous Thought of the Week Posters

Have students collect humorous sayings to use as a springboard for group discussions about humor. Encourage awareness of humor by having students copy the humorous sayings they find on posters to display in the room.

4. Humorous Cards

Have students think of occasions where they can create humorous cards to send to others in the classroom. There can be postcards, fold-over cards, mini-messages, cards that are "tented" (folded in half to stand up), thank-you cards, and award cards.

5. Humor Check List

In the list that follows are examples of features of humor listed on the left-hand side. Have the students identify features of humor that they enjoy the most (e.g., comic asides, word balloons) and write the features in a list. Ask the students to select a different colored crayon for the two books (such as green for *The Magic School Bus* and brown for one of the books that the students select). With a green crayon, read down the list, and put a check on the line where they believe *The Magic School Bus* has that humorous feature. After the students have rated *The Magic School Bus* on the features, then ask them to check the same features for the other book. Engage students in showing others in the school how to "read" the check list and how to get information from it.

Bel-Air Bambi and the Mall Rats (378)

WHAT'S THE BOOK?

Bel-Air Bambi and the Mall Rats. Written by Richard Peck. New York: Delacorte, 1993. Ages 10–12.

WHAT'S SO FUNNY?

This is a spoof narrated by Buffie, a sixth grader new from Los Angeles, about Hickory Fork, a small town and its high school cheerleaders and football team members who call themselves the "Mall Rats." They dress in leather and "take over" the local mall. However, the Babcock family use their show business talents (and hence Bel-Air Bambi) and do what they can to save the mall and the town whose people have almost given up all control to the kids.

WHAT'S IT ABOUT?

Television producer Bill Babcock is in debt in Los Angeles and takes his family back to his hometown, Hickory Fork. Once there, the Babcock family, which includes Buffie, a sixth grader, and Bambi and Brick, discover that the high school kids are "into" tearing up the local mall and use it as a meeting place. They decide to do something about the leather-wearing kids who call themselves the "Mall Rats."

WHAT'S THE MINI-UNIT PURPOSE?

Mention to students: "You are going to hear a story about a sixth grader, Buffie, whose family moves to a small town, Hickory Fork, and tries to fight back against a gang called the "Mall Rats" who are trying to destroy the local mall. Listen to find out how the Babcock kids get together to save the mall and the town.

WHAT NEW WORDS CAN BE EMPHASIZED?

Bel-Air Bambi, Mall Rats, Hickory Fork, Buffie, Brick, spoof.

WHAT'S THERE TO TALK ABOUT?

Before the Reading

1. Bel-Air Bambi. Introduce the title of the book and write the words *Bel-Air Bambi* and *Mall Rats* on the board. Have them think of ways to describe their idea of a "mall rat." As a contrast, read a description by Peck. Have them predict what the humorous story might be about. Write their predictions on the board and after the story is read, return to the list of predictions to determine how many were accurate.

2. Humorous Incidents at a Mall. Ask the students to share any feelings about humorous incidents that have happened to them in a mall or that they know about.

After the Reading

1. Humorous Events in the Story. Ask students to describe how the Babcock kids get together to save the mall and the town. What humorous things happened in the story? How do you think the Babcocks felt when they first found out about the Mall Rats? Here are some other questions:

- What might *you* have said or done in a humorous way to add to the story of the Babcock kids?
- How did the Babcock kids save the mall?
- How is the humor in the story about the Babcock kids different from/or the same as your idea of humor?

2. What's a Spoof? Discuss the idea of a spoof as a takeoff on a subject. Have the students turn to a student next to them and briefly discuss the spoof connection between the story and Hollywood. Have them say, "One thing from the story of *Bel-Air Bambi* that made me think of Hollywood was. . . . ."

WHAT ACTIVITIES WILL EXTEND THE BOOK?

1. If I had been there to add humor to the story. . . .

Have the students retell their favorite part of the story, and somewhere, say, "If I had been

there to add humor to the story of the Babcock kids, I would have. . . . " Invite them to make funny story changes as they say what they would do.

2. Tell Me Something Humorous. . . .

Ask each student to interview another with, "Tell me something humorous you have done in your neighborhood or community."

What Other Humorous Features Are in Books about Family, School, and Community?

CARTOONLIKE ILLUSTRATIONS

Only a few writer-illustrator teams, such as Cole and Degen, combine fanciful fiction with realism and humor in cartoonlike illustrations. In *The Magic School Bus: Inside the Earth* (359) by Joanna Cole, the humorous cartoonlike illustrations by Bruce Degen show a one-of-a-kind field trip with Ms. Frizzle and her students. When the class begins a study of earth science, the old school bus of *The Magic School Bus at the Waterworks* is brought out to take them on a rock-collecting trip. When the bus spins around, the students find themselves magically equipped for exploration with jump suits and jackhammers, and are off for a wild ride through the earth's crust and into the core, up through a volcano, down a lava flow into the sea, and up in a cloud of steam where the bus sprouts a parachute and lands them safely back in the school parking lot. Through it all the cool Ms. Frizzle calmly explains vocabulary, rock formation, and the inner dynamics of earth. Illustrations claim every page; the text is printed within. Cartoon balloons from Ms. Frizzle and the children carry part of the information as well as comic asides. Other facts are represented in hand-lettered student reports, charts, or displays. This is one of a growing number of books to offer information to children through a combination of narrative and explanations. The characterization of the teacher and the energetic humor in the illustrations makes it a great deal of fun.

COMIC ASIDES, DETAILS, AND WORD BALLOONS

Word balloons from Ms. Frizzle and her students carry part of the information as well as comic asides in Joanna Cole's *The Magic School Bus in the Time of the Dinosaurs* (358). Like *The Magic School Bus at the Waterworks,* this is the story of a one-of-a-kind field trip with the teacher, Ms. Frizzle. She begins a study of prehistory, and the old school bus is brought out to take them all back in time. When the dial on the windshield of the bus spins around, they find themselves magically equipped for exploration with safari suits, hard hats, and magnifying glasses, and are off for a wild journey back into the time of the dinosaurs. Through it all the cool Ms. Frizzle calmly explains vocabulary, flora and fauna, and facts about dinosaurs. Illustrations are on every page and the text is printed within. Other facts are represented in hand-lettered student reports, charts, or displays—all part of the fun.

HILARIOUS ENDEAVORS

In Sue Townsend's *The Adrian Mole Diaries* (383), nothing goes right for Adrian as his diary writing attests. He is worried about the lack of morals in society, and is afraid of turning into an intellectual so he thinks he will "join the library and see what happens." One time, when he is tempted to sniff glue while making a model airplane he writes: "nothing happened, but my nose stuck to the plane!"

Another boy, Andy, has his own hilarious endeavors in Phyllis Reynolds Naylor's *Beetles, Lightly Toasted* (376). In his fifth grade essay contest, Andy doesn't think the topic, conservation, will be a fun thing to write about. So he decides to write about "How Beetles, Bugs, and Worms Can Save Money and the Food Supply . . . . " and does enough research to discover three topics: toasted beetles in brownies; breaded earthworms to deep fry; and boiled mealworm larvae to add to egg salad. Andy, a picky eater, humorously tests his products on his unsuspecting family members and his classmates. Winning the contest "hoists him on his own petard," for in order to get his picture in the paper, Andy has to be photographed eating the food—beetle brownies, deep-fried worms, and boiled mealworm larvae in egg salad.

Humorous Humans

A Small Tall Tale from the Far Far North (439)

WHAT'S THE BOOK?

A Small Tall Tale from the Far Far North. Written and illustrated by Peter Sis. New York: Knopf, 1993. Ages 9–12.

WHAT'S SO FUNNY?

It's irony. Both the text and pictures can show older students some examples of irony—situations of light ridicule or light sarcasm where the intended implication is the opposite of the literal sense of the words.

WHAT'S IT ABOUT?

This is the story of Jan Welzl, a Czech folk hero, who journeyed to the cold Arctic regions in the late 1800s. Close to freezing to death in the harsh environment, Welzl is rescued by native people. He lives with them and develops a great deal of respect for their survival ways as they cope with the weather and icy surroundings. They learn that gold hunters are traveling into their environment, and Welzl predicts that the newcomers will bring troubles along with their greed for gold, guns, and thirst for whiskey. He devises an ironic solution for his prediction.

WHAT'S THE MINI-UNIT PURPOSE?

Mention to students: "You are going to hear a story about a folk hero who explored the harsh, cold regions of the Arctic in the late 1800s. Listen to find out how he was rescued from freezing to death in the ice and snow, and how he repaid his rescuers."

WHAT NEW WORDS CAN BE EMPHASIZED?

Jan Welzl, Arctic, Eskimos.

WHAT'S THERE TO TALK ABOUT?

Before the Reading

1. What Humorous Action Does the Title Suggest? Introduce the title of the book and ask students to identify where they think the "far far north" might be on a map and globe. Ask them to tell what climate they imagine for the "far far north." Show several illustrations from the book that show the environment so the students can see a visual presentation of what the surroundings are like.

2. An Explorer of the Artic. Ask students to think of humorous ways to describe the way they think an explorer of the Arctic might look. Ask them to sketch their descriptions. In partnerships, ask them to tell their partners why they drew their sketches the way they did. Back in the whole group, invite volunteers to show their descriptions and tell more about them. In contrast, show one or two illustrations of Jan Welzl by Sis to show his interpretation of the northern explorer.

3. Features of Humor You Like/Dislike. Ask students to think if they have ever been around someone who was lightly sarcastic—making a cutting remark or rebuke or a taunt that stings—or who used ridicule—they were eliciting laughter at a person or thing with jesting and joking words, caricature (ludicrous exaggeration), and mockery—to make sport of, or to imitate or mimic. Also encourage them to see that irony can be any situation of light ridicule or light sarcasm where the intended implication of someone's words is the exact *opposite* of the literal sense of the words. Elicit the children's experiences with ridicule, sarcasm, and irony. Have them locate some humorous words, phrases, and illustrations. What do they mean to the students?

4. A Humorous Action. Write the complete title, *A Small Tall Tale from the Far Far North,* on the board. Have students turn to someone next to them and briefly discuss, "An ironic action this title makes me think of is. . . ." and "Something that could happen next might be. . . ." and "The reasons *why* this could happen is. . . ."

After the Reading

1. What's Irony? Use both the text and pictures to show older students some examples of irony—situations of light ridicule or light sarcasm. For one example, show the students the illustration of Jan Welzl, the Czech folk hero who explored the Arctic in 1893, where he is looking out into the vast emptiness of a snowstorm and says, "I am very much alone." Let the students discover the irony of his words when you project the illustration on an opaque projector for their careful observation. Have them look at the blowing puffs of snow to discern the carefully crafted cats' faces and eyes—enough to show that Welzl is not "alone."

2. "Question Slips." With students review the meaning of *irony*—any situations of light ridicule or light sarcasm where the intended implication of someone's words is the exact *opposite* of the literal sense of the words. Type the following questions on slips of paper and distribute them to the students. Have them join in partnerships and discuss their questions about *irony* together:

* What was the situation that appeared most ironic to you?
* Describe how you think Welzl might have thought of his ironic solution to the arrival of the gold hunters.
* How do you think the native people felt when they saw Welzl's solution?
* How do you think Welzl was feeling?
* What might *you* have said or done to add more irony (light ridicule or light sarcasm where your meaning is intended to be the *opposite* of your literal words) to the situation?

3. Author's Sense of Humor. With the whole group, ask the students, "What does the use of irony tell you about the author's sense of humor?" and "How is Jan Welzl's solution different from your idea of what the solution could be?"

WHAT ACTIVITIES WILL EXTEND THE BOOK?

1. Ironic Feature

Have the students discuss an ironic part in the story, and encourage them to suggest the story changes they would make if they were writing or illustrating a second version of the story.

2. Irony in My Own Experience

Ask students to interview a student-neighbor in class with, "Tell me something ironic that has happened to you or that you know about."

3. An Original Humorous Tall Tale

Introduce the idea of writing original tall tales by reading aloud *The Morning the Sun Refused to Rise* (435). This is an original Paul Bunyan tale by Glen Rounds who tells of the time when the sun refused to rise one morning. It seems that the bitter cold of a blizzard had frozen the axle of the Earth to its bearings and brought the world to a total stop. Paul Bunyan and his Blue Ox, Babe, were called in to help repair the damage and get the globe spinning again. Reread some selected lines to emphasize the humor in the author's words:

* When the sun didn't shine, "the desks of Kings, Presidents, Prime Ministers, and even Senators were piled high with telegrams asking what had happened to sunrise."
* When the specialists in the government looked in their books "they found instructions for dealing with such things as revolutions, typhoons, hurricanes, forest fires, and hundreds of other kinds of disasters—but not a word about what to do when the sun refused to rise."
* When lumberjacks tried to measure how big Babe really was, they found that the distance between the Blue Ox's eyes was "seven-hundred-and-fifty-four ax handles, two-hundred-and-four cans of tomatoes (no. 10s) and a plug of Star chewing tobacco laid edgewise."

Attack of the Killer Fishsticks (445)

WHAT'S THE BOOK?

Attack of the Killer Fishsticks. Written by Paul Zindel and illustrated by Jeff Mangiat. New York: Bantam, 1993. Ages 9–11.

WHAT'S SO FUNNY?

Jokes and trivia. Five friends call themselves the Wacky Facts Lunch Bunch because they always eat lunch together and entertain one another with jokes and trivia.

WHAT'S IT ABOUT?

The Lunch Bunch—Dave, Liz, Johnny and Jennifer nominate Max to be the student council representative and support him as he runs against Nat, a Nasty Blob bully. Max, who is suffering from the recent death of his mother, receives needed understanding and support of the bunch.

WHAT'S THE MINI-UNIT PURPOSE?

Mention to older students: "You are going to hear a story about five friends who always ate lunch together at school. They told jokes and trivia facts and called themselves the Wacky Facts Lunch Bunch. Listen to find out what wacky facts they told and how they supported their friend Max when he ran for student council representative."

WHAT NEW WORDS CAN BE EMPHASIZED?

Wacky, bunch, Nasty Blob, council, representative.

WHAT'S THERE TO TALK ABOUT?

Before the Reading

1. Humorous Image of Killer Fishsticks. Introduce the title of the book and write the words *Killer Fishsticks* on the board. Ask students to tell what different meanings that the words could have for them and what the story might be about.

2. Jokes Related to Killer Fishsticks. Have students relate jokes about food that they have heard or read. Have students turn to a student next to them in class and briefly discuss, "One joke this title makes me think of is. . . . "

3. Humor among Friends. Ask students to think if they have ever been a member of a group of friends such as the *lunch bunch*. Encourage them to share their feelings about the humorous incidents that happened to them in the group of friends. What jokes about food did they tell one another?

After the Reading

1. The Fishstick Chain Story. Divide the students into groups of three and have them create their own version of the story in a chain story format. To begin, one student writes the title on an index card that is meant to resemble a fishstick. The next student dictates/writes the first event on an index card and so on. Each event is written and illustrated on a different fishstick (index cards). When completed, have the students punch holes on opposite ends of the cards and string them together with cord or yarn and hang them to display them in the room. Encourage the students to discuss the story as they write the events:

1. Describe how you think that Dave, Liz, Johnny, Jennifer, and Max became friends. How do you think Max felt when his friends nominated him to run for student council representative?
2. What might *you* have said or done at lunch with the lunch bunch?
3. How did Nate, the Nasty Blob bully, show he *was* a bully?
4. How is this group of friends different from your idea of what a group of friends should be? the same?

2. Lunch Bunch. Ask students to think of ways to describe one or more of the friends in the lunch bunch. Ask them to transform their words into sketches of their descriptions. In partnerships, ask students to tell their partners why they drew their sketches the way they did. Back in the whole group, invite volunteers to show their sketches and describe one of the friends.

WHAT ACTIVITIES WILL EXTEND THE BOOK?

1. Student Council Election

With partners, invite the students to briefly play the role of Max who is running for student council representative and give a humorous "Elect Me" speech. Ask the students to describe a humorous scene, conversation, or action related to the election that they liked.

2. Lunch Bunch Roles

Taking the role of one of the friends, invite students to tell a classmate how they felt about the humor among the friends in the lunch bunch.

3. Humorously, there I was to help lighten things up. . . .

Have the students retell their favorite humorous action in the story, and somewhere, respond to, "Humorously, there I was to help lighten things up. . . . Invite them to make humorous story changes as they say what they would do to help the lunch bunch during the election process.

4. Humorous Revenge on a Bully

Ask students to interview a neighbor with, "Tell me about a bully you know," and about anything humorous that happened to the bully—tricks that others played on him or her.

What Other Humorous Features Are in Books with Humorous Humans?

DAFFY, ECCENTRIC, AND QUIRKY CHARACTERS

In *Bagthorpes Unlimited* (394) by Helen Cresswell, a slightly off-balance family is led by Grandma—the quirky head of the clan who discovers the theft of several prized but absolutely worthless family possessions. It seems that, fearing such a break-in, Grandma left on her dresser a note to any would-be burglar listing each of the family's most treasured possessions and the locations. Her note instructed the burglar to leave these untouched—definitely quirky behavior.

In Daniel Pinkwater's *Alan Mendelsoh, the Boy from Mars* (427), there are more quirky characters. This is a story narrated by short and portly Leonard Neeble, the first quirky character who considers himself a slow fatso and a misfit at Bat Masterson Junior High School. Leonard's grandmother, the second quirky character, wants to be called "The Old One." The third quirky character is Leonard's friend, Alan, who announces he is from Mars. They meet a fourth quirky character, Mr. Klugarsh, head of Klugarsh Mind Control Associates, who sells Omega Meters for locating omega thought waves that have the added feature of playing jingle bells when the waves are produced.

EXAGGERATION

Judy Blume's *Tales of a Fourth Grade Nothing* (349) provides the humor that goes along with the exaggeration of a common idea—an older child thinks his life is in constant chaos because of a somewhat younger sibling. Peter's problems with his three-year-old brother Fudge become worse with each chapter of the story until the final disaster when Fudge swallows Peter's pet turtle.

EXAGGERATIONS IN A TALL TALE

The Morning the Sun Refused to Rise (435) by Glen Rounds is a tall tale full of exaggerations. It begins the day the sun didn't shine and the Earth froze on its axel and stopped turning. Paul Bunyan and Babe, the Blue Ox, are asked to remedy the situation.

HILARIOUS ENDEAVORS

Helen Cresswell's *Absolute Zero* (392) is about what happens when the world of advertising arrives at the home of the funny Bagthorpe family. The resulting competition among family members to win as many contests as they can leads to an all-out furor—and hilarious endeavors. And the winner is Zero, the family's mongrel dog.

HILARIOUS PEER CHARACTERIZATION

There is humorous peer rivalry in Stephen Roos's *Twelve-Year-Old Vows Revenge!* (434). When twelve-year-old Shirley Garfield escalates her rivalry with Claire Von Kemp, Claire tries to get Shirley's job and fails. Shirley retaliates by writing a humiliating article about Claire. Claire gets back by starting her own newspaper and running a lead story about Shirley and her date with a Martian. Shirley sues and the girls go before the judge where the verdict is that both the girls are guilty and the judge orders them to apologize and lay off one another.

HUMOROUS ANTICS

In Judy Blume's *Tales of a Fourth Grade Nothing* (350), one of the humorous antics takes place when Peter Hatcher's pet turtle, Dribble, is missing and Fudge, Peter's two-year-old brother, known as Farley, is questioned. He insists he did not chew the turtle and says, "No chew, no chew, gulp . . . gulp . . . all gone turtle. Down Fudge's tummy" (p. 111). It takes a trip to the hospital, castor oil and and prune juice before the turtle is out. In Blume's sequel, *Superfudge* (349) Peter tells more about his life when his family moves to New Jersey. The antics continue revolving around his new baby sister, Tootsie, his new friends, and his new school. His encounters with his brother go "public" when Fudge begins kindergarten.

HUMOROUS DIALOGUE

Humorous dialogue goes along with a sensitive look at Toby, a sixth grade bully who has a behavior problem in David Gifaldi's *Toby Scudder, Ultimate Warrior* (399). Best suited for individual reading because of the included profanity, the story portrays Toby as a charmer who pulls pranks, acts out, and gets into fistfights. Toby has his best relationships with his pet goldfish, and with Megan, his first grade partner in the school's mentoring program. At the end of the story, Toby

comes to terms with his life, his distracted mother, the memory of his father who deserted the family, his uncaring teenage half-brother, and his twenty-year-old sister.

IRONY AS HUMOR

There is some irony in Greenwald's book, *Give Us a Great Big Smile, Rosy Cole* (402). It seems it was Rosy's turn to be the subject of her Uncle Ralph's book. He needed to earn money again and Rosy had just turned ten—the same age each of her sisters had been when her uncle wrote *Anitra Dances* and *Pippa Prances* about them. However, Rosy could not dance like her sister Anitra or ride horses like Pippa. In fact, Rosy had no talent that was appropriate for a book and what she did to discredit the whole idea lends itself to irony.

ONE-LINERS AND WACKY COMIC SITUATIONS

One-liners and comic situations are found in Gordon Korman's *The Toilet Paper Tigers* (415). Cory Johnson finds himself on a little league team of misfits, led by a nuclear physicist coach who is more than a little distracted all the time. The toilet paper tigers seem destined to get clobbered at every game. However, when Professor Pendergast's granddaughter Kristy, an aggressive, tough-talking know-it-all from New York City, becomes the assistant coach, things change dramatically. She blackmails them with an embarrassing photograph of the players standing around in their jockstraps and "motivates" them to improve their performance on the field.

SLAPSTICK AND PRANKS

There is a laughing, joking "Mary Poppins" type character in Robert Burch's *Ida Early Comes Over the Mountain* (388). It is humorous Ida who takes charge of the four motherless Sutton children. Ida, who talks about taming lions and the other outrageous things she has done, is over six feet tall, wears overalls, and has unruly red hair. She reads the funnies aloud and does many other things that entertain the children.

Holidays

The Best Christmas Pageant Ever (448)

WHAT'S THE BOOK?

The Best Christmas Pageant Ever. Written by Barbara Robinson. New York: Harper & Row, 1972. Ages 9–12.

WHAT'S SO FUNNY?

The humor is mainly in the outrageous behavior of the worst kids in the history of the world, the Herdmans—Ralph, Imogene, Leroy, Claude, Ollie, and Gladys. They are six skinny stringy-haired kids all alike except for being different sizes and having different black-and-blue places where they had choked each other. Their idea of a game was banging a garage door up and down just as fast as they could and trying to squash one another. They had a sign in their yard that said "Beware of the Cat." The mailman wouldn't deliver anything to the Herdmans because of it.

WHAT'S IT ABOUT?

It was a surprise to everyone in town when the Herdmans wanted to participate in the town's Christmas program. The Herdmans had never heard of the Christmas story and their interpretation was humorous—they called the wise men a bunch of dirty spies.

WHAT'S THE MINI-UNIT PURPOSE?

Mention to students: "You are going to hear about the worst kids in the history of the world—the Herdman kids. Listen to find out what happened when the Herdmans wanted to take part in the town's Christmas program. Some people in town thought it would be the first Christmas pageant in

history where Joseph (Ralph Herdman) and the Wise man would get in a fight and Mary (Imogene Herdman) would run away with the baby."

WHAT NEW WORDS CAN BE EMPHASIZED?

Ralph, Imogene, Leroy, Claude, Ollie, Gladys.

WHAT'S THERE TO TALK ABOUT?

Before the Reading

1. The Best Christmas Pageant. Write the title of the book on the board. Ask students to tell what the words mean to them. Have them imagine how a pageant might be "the best" from their point of view. To develop further interest in the story and to contrast with the students' ideas of a "best" program, read a brief excerpt from the book about what was going on backstage on the night of the pageant. For example, page 71 could be read since it describes the mess behind the stage and the way that the baby angels were getting poked in the eye by the wings of other angels. Other things happened, too:

- Some of the shepherds were grumpy and stumbled over their bathrobes.
- The swooping spotlight made some of the children sick at their stomachs to look at it.
- As usual each year, the person who was playing the piano played "Away in a Manger" so high the children could hardly hear it, let alone sing it, and the children sounded like a closetful of mice.

After the Reading

1. Outrageous Behavior at the Pageant. If desired, have students re-create part of the pageant with their own ideas of outrageous behavior. To do this, the students may, as the angel choir did, begin and sing "Away in a Manger." Then, they can add their quiet pranks:

- Sing two verses of "O Little Town of Bethlehem" while Mary and Joseph come in from a side door. When the two fail to appear, have students hum and hum and hum.
- When Mary appears, she is not carrying the baby doll the way she is supposed to, cradled in her arms. Mary carries the doll slung up over her shoulder and before she puts it in the manger, she thumps it twice on its back.
- Sing "While Shepherds Watched Their Flocks by Night" and have shepherds bang their crooks around like a lot of hockey sticks.
- Have an angel from the angel choir announce as Gladys Herdman did, "Hey! Unto you a child is born," and have the angel choir sing three carols of their choice about angels.
- Have the boys sing "We Three Kings of Orient Are" while the wise men march into the room—not carrying gold, frankincense, and myrrh—but a large ham with a ribbon wrapped around it reading, "Merry Christmas."
- Have the angel choir sing "What Child Is This?" and "Silent Night" with candy canes for all, for a finale.

2. Making Humorous Pictures in the Mind's Eye. Have students listen to a description of the day Claude Herdman emptied the whole class in three minutes flat when he took his mean old cat to show-and-tell. It seems that Claude didn't feed it for two days so it was already mad, and then he carried it to school in a box. Ask students to sketch their ideas of the funny scene while some descriptive words about the event are read aloud (see p.5):

- Claude opens the box and the cat shoots out—right straight up in the air.
- The cat comes down on the top blackboard ledge and claws four big long scratches all the way down the blackboard.
- The cat tears around all over the place. It sheds its fur and scatters books and papers everywhere.
- The teacher yells for everybody to run out in the hall. She pulls a coat over her head and grabs a broom, and tries to corner the cat.
- The teacher can't see with the coat over her head, so she just runs up and down the aisles hollering, "Here, Kitty!" and she smacks the broom down whenever the cat hisses back at her voice.
- The teacher knocks over the happy family dollhouse and a globe of the world and breaks the aquarium filled with twenty gallons of water and about sixty-five goldfish.

Have students trade sketches and look at the sketches they received while the descriptive words and sentences are read aloud again. Have them look for things in the sketches that were mentioned in the descriptive words.

WHAT ACTIVITIES WILL EXTEND THE BOOK?

1. Other Humorous One-liners of Description

Type up lines of description on slips of paper and distribute them to the students. Have students work in pairs and put the descriptions into their own humorous words. Ask them to turn the slips over and write their own sense of comedy on the back. Examples:

- The Herdmans moved from grade to grade through the Woodrow Wilson School like those South American fish that strip your bones clean in three minutes flat . . . which was just about what they did to one teacher after another.
- Fat camp is a place where they feed you lettuce and grapefruit and cottage cheese and eggs for a month, and you either give up and cheat or give up and get skinny.
- My friend Alice was so nasty clean that she had detergent hands by the time she was four years old.
- The first pageant rehearsal was usually about as much fun as a three-hour ride on the school bus and just as noisy and crowded.
- Imogene pulled on her earrings, which made you shudder—it was like looking at the pictures in *National Geographic* of natives with their ears stretched all the way to their shoulders.

Bunnicula: A Rabbit Tale of Mystery (333)

WHAT'S THE BOOK?

Bunnicula: A Rabbit Tale of Mystery. Written by Deborah and James Howe and illustrated by Alan Daniel. New York: Atheneum, 1979. Ages 9–12.

WHAT'S SO FUNNY?

The humor is mainly in the technique of parody related to the Dracula story. In this hilarious tale, suitable for reading anytime but especially in the month of October, Harold, the family dog, narrates the story of a bunny who was found by the Monroe family in a movie theater while watching *Dracula*.

WHAT'S IT ABOUT?

The well-read pet cat, Chester, observes strange nighttime behavior by the bunny and Chester uses some clues—the rabbit's nocturnal behavior and his long fangs instead of buckteeth—to conclude that the rabbit is a vampire. Chester and Harold attempt to "save" the family from the suspected bunny vampire. Chester tries to tell the human owners of the danger, but fails, and then tries to rid the house of the beast with help of the information he finds in his book, *The Mark of the Vampire*.

WHAT'S THE MINI-UNIT PURPOSE?

Mention to students: "You are going to hear about Chester the cat and Harold the dog who are concerned about a bunny who was found by the Monroe family while watching the movie *Dracula* in a theater. Chester and Harold think the bunny is a vampire and call him Bunnicula. Harold tells the story. Listen to find out how the two try to rid the house of Bunnicula with help of the information Chester finds in a book entitled *The Mark of the Vampire*."

WHAT NEW WORDS CAN BE EMPHASIZED?

Bunnicula, vampire, Chester, Harold.

WHAT'S THERE TO TALK ABOUT?

Before the Reading

1. What Does the Title Mean to You? Introduce the title of the book and write the words *Bunnicula: A Rabbit Tale of Mystery* on the board. Ask students to tell what the words mean to them. Have them imagine how the characters might look—especially Bunnicula—and then show several illustrations from the book that show Chester and Harold and the bunny.

2. Describe and Draw Your Idea of Bunnicula. Ask students to think of ways to describe Bunnicula further. Ask them to sketch their descriptions. As a contrast, review the illustrations by Alan Daniel to see his interpretation. In partnerships, ask them to tell their partners *why* they drew their sketches the way they did. Back in the whole group, invite volunteers to show their drawings and tell about them.

After the Reading

1. A Parody: This Makes Me Think of. . . . Write the title *Bunnicula: A Rabbit Tale of Mystery* on the board. Have students turn to someone next to them and briefly discuss the parody connection, "One thing from the story of *Dracula* that *Bunnicula: A Rabbit Tale of Mystery* makes me think of is. . . . " Discuss:

- If you had been in this story, what might *you* have said or done related to the story of *Dracula?*
- In what ways did this story remind you of the story of *Dracula?*

2. Humor Couplers. With students in groups of three, invite them to play "humor couplers" and take the roles of Chester and Harold who try to get rid of Bunnicula. Have the third student add sound effects for the actions of the other two students while they are role-playing. Have students trade roles so all have a turn providing the sound effects.

WHAT ACTIVITIES WILL EXTEND THE BOOK?

1. Bulletin Board Border of Clichés and Puns

With the book, have students locate some humorous puns and clichés related to vampire movies and write them on adding machine tape to make a border for the bulletin board. For more about these humorous characters, suggest that the students read *Nighty Nightmare* (334), where Harold and Chester go on a camping trip with the Monroes and pitch camp near an unusual trio.

2. Being Bunnicula

Taking the role of the bunny as a vampire, invite students to tell a friend in class how the bunny felt about what Chester and Harold were doing. Taking the reversed role of the bunny as a nonvampire, ask students to tell a friend how the bunny felt about what Chester and Harold were doing.

3. Bunny Control: Helping Chester and Harold

Have the students retell their favorite part of the story, and somewhere say, "Fortunately, there I was to help and I. . . . " Invite them to make story changes as they say what they would have done to help Chester and Harold during their efforts at bunny control.

What Other Humorous Features Are in Books about Holidays?

HUMOROUS DETAILS

There are humorous details in the funny account of *The Witches of Hopper Street* (447) by Linda Gondosch. In the story, three not-so-popular girls try to use witchcraft to ruin a Halloween party because they were not invited to attend. Have students identify the humorous details they notice— especially those in the final confrontation scene at the end.

PRANKS

There is humor in the pranks of Ida, the Mary Poppins-type character, in *Christmas with Ida Early* (446) by Robert Burch. Ida has a love for life—she likes to read the comics instead of washing dishes—and tries to do anything and everything. The children are impressed by her—they discover that Ida can toss hats and coats perfectly onto the rack and rope cattle.

The Best Christmas Pageant Ever (448) by Barbara Robinson is a fine read-aloud about the pranks of the meanest kids in town who take over the leads in the Christmas pageant. The six Herdman children are the terror of the school, so it is not surprising that they extend their reign of terror into Sunday school and take over the Christmas Pageant. The substitute teacher cannot understand why only the Herdmans volunteer for the parts, unaware that they have threatened to stuff pussy willows down the ears of any children who raise their hands. Since the Herdmans have never heard of the story before, their interpretation is contemporary and humorous.

Jokes, Riddles, and Puns

Home on the Range: Ranch-Style Riddles (460)

WHAT'S THE BOOK?

Home on the Range: Ranch-Style Riddles. Written by Diane and Andy Burns and illustrated by Susan Slattery Burke. New York: Lerner, 1994. Ages 9–10.

WHAT'S SO FUNNY?

Surprise words and subtle humor that answer riddles in a joking manner. Additionally, there are zany riddles that relate to a regional theme accompanied by cartoon-type illustrations.

WHAT'S IT ABOUT?

This is a collection of riddles involving the wide open spaces and ranch living.

WHAT'S THE MINI-UNIT PURPOSE?

Mention to students: "You are going to hear some jokes and riddles about ranchers and their life on the wide open range. Listen to find out if you can answer some of the questions in the riddles before they are read aloud."

WHAT NEW WORDS CAN BE EMPHASIZED?

N/A.

WHAT'S THERE TO TALK ABOUT?

Before the Reading

1. Dreaming Up a Humorous Home on the Range. Ask students to imagine they are planners of new humorous homes and can start all over with some range land that will be given to them. What kind of "Home on the Range" would they like? Distribute paper so the students can sketch their ideas. They will want to plan the following:

- What size will their home on the range be?
- Who will be the people living there?
- What will the home look like?
- What work will need to be done?
- What recreation will be available?

2. Adding to the Humor. Invite students to "Choose some event in your life and make it more humorous." Have students relate the humorous event(s) to a theme—life in the city, country, at sea, in the air, etc. For an option, have students imagine that they could rename the days of the week according to something humorous—Wacky Wednesday. Ask them to give each day a new name that reflects something humorous related to where they live. If desired, repeat the activity with the months of the year and the seasons.

After the Reading

1. Surprise Words: Putting Funny Things First. Invite the students to consider, "If you could select some surprise words from this book of riddles, what would they be?

Have students write down their suggestions and then discuss them with the whole group and determine from their points of view why the surprise words were really surprises to them.

2. Finding Humor Where I Live. Sometimes people don't appreciate the humor around them but pay attention to other things. At other times, people do see the humor in situations that are nearby. As an example, Diane and Andy Burns wrote about the humor they saw in a regional area in *Home on the Range: Ranch-Style Riddles*. Mention to students that now it's their turn to write about humor they see in their area. Have students make a list of the humorous things in their community, city, region, or state. Remember, everyone will have a different idea of what is funny. The students might want to turn the list into a verse for a free verse poem or a song—Humor about San Francisco, What's Funny about My Town, etc.

WHAT ACTIVITIES WILL EXTEND THE BOOK?

1. You Must Be Joking

Have the students listen to several of the regional jokes from the book or from another in the *You Must Be Joking series* (Lerner)—*Out to Dry: Riddles about Deserts* (460) by June Swanson and illustrated by Susan Slattery Burke. Invite the students to try to answer the jokes on their own before reading the answers at the bottom of the page, and then select one or more to tell a friend.

2. Humor Then and Now

Sometimes it is hard for students to imagine what was humorous in times "before," and one way for the students to explore this is to find old cartoons found in libraries, history museums, and newspapers. If students can find an old cartoon, have them paste a photocopy of it on a poster and ask them to figure out what was humorous then and in what way they think humor has changed. Do they like humor better the way it was before or the way it is now?

3. "Ye Old Humor Faire"

Once the students have become familiar with examples of cartoons that were humorous in days "before," invite them to display their knowledge at a humor faire. The students can wear humorous costumes. Have them use an old cartoon to make a slide show. A tape cassette or record player can play humorous "Spike Jones" type music. There can be "side shows" that feature humorous acts and there is always room for homemade humor—Rube Goldberg-type inven-

tions and student-created cartoon strips, comic books, etc.

4. Jokes in Every Language

Display a map of the world on the bulletin board and have students search for jokes from other countries. Invite students who speak a second language to contribute some they know. Ask students to interview people they know who speak a second language at home and in the neighborhood to contribute jokes. As the students collect the jokes, they can write them and attach them to the border of the map. A length of colorful yarn can lead from the joke to the related country.

5. Joke Festival

Using student suggestions, organize a joke festival as a forum for a discussion of humor and its meaning for the students. Engage students in preparing a program based on the favorite jokes they select. For instance, part of the preparation can include using a tape recorder to record the jokes that would be told and then selecting the ones that would be finally used; on deciding on ways to present the jokes—by categories; and collecting props for jokes if needed. To decorate the room, have the students illustrate riddles (conundrums) where the question is answered by a pun—a play on words that is part of the joke. Posters can show the answers to such questions as "What does an insect wear to bed?" (*a gnat-gown*) and "What kind of cars do owls drive?" (*Owls-mobiles*). Have students talk about the ways they would illustrate a gnat-gown and an owls-mobile. Additionally, musical selections can be played to determine which ones, if any, would be suitable for background music. Encourage the students to include a discussion at the end of the program where they can talk about what was funny to them and why.

6. Joke Panel Discussion

With students, plan a panel discussion related to jokes that the students have heard or read about in class. Ask them to reflect on their thoughts about ways the jokes might have been created; reasons why they think the jokes are used; reasons why they think people tell the jokes; and reasons why the jokes are popular with some people. Do the jokes serve any purposes?

Hello, Mr. Chips! (459)

WHAT'S THE BOOK?

Hello, Mr. Chips! Computer Jokes and Riddles. Written and illustrated by Ann Bishop and Jerry Warshaw. New York: Dutton, 1993. Ages 9–12.

WHAT'S SO FUNNY?

Surprise words that answer riddles in a joking manner with innuendoes, anecdotes, and satire. Readers may laugh or groan of course. The book opens with a flow chart on how to use the book beginning with turning to any page of riddles, trying to answer it, finding the answer at the bottom of the page, and then laughing or groaning.

WHAT'S IT ABOUT?

This is a collection of riddles involving computers. For example, What's a computer's favorite song? (*Thanks for the memory*). Why was the computer cranky? (*It was out of sorts*). Which way did the programmer go? (*He went data way*).

WHAT'S THE MINI-UNIT PURPOSE?

Mention to students: "You are going to hear some jokes and riddles about computers. Listen to find out if you can answer some of the riddles before the answers are read aloud."

WHAT NEW WORDS CAN BE EMPHASIZED?

Chips, programmer, systems engineer; there is a list of computer terms on the last two pages of the book.

WHAT'S THERE TO TALK ABOUT?

Before the Reading

1. Hello, Mr. Chips. Introduce the book *Hello, Mr. Chips!* If the students had been the author(s), would they have selected the name, Mr. Chips, for a joke and riddle book about computers? What other names could be selected?

2. Daffy Computer Definitions. Introduce definitions about the subject of computers prepared in a joking manner as one approach to humor. Ask students to think of ways to describe a scene that includes one or more of the following daffy computer definitions:

Word	Meaning
Algorithm	Why Al is such a good drummer
Bugs in the system	Terminalities
Data	Something that brings two computers together on Saturday night
Keypunch	What keys drink at a party.
Microcomputer	Not your cro-computer, or hiscro-computer, or hercro-computer either

Ask students to draw and color their descriptions. In partnerships, ask them to tell their partners why they drew their sketches the way they did. Back in the whole group, invite volunteers to show their descriptions and tell more about them.

After the Reading

1. What's Your Favorite? Ask students, "What one joke or riddle in the book would you select to tell a computer enthusiast to pick up his or her spirits?" Have students in groups write their favorite jokes and riddles on a slip of paper and tie it with string to a coat hanger over their desks. Have the groups take turns and, in turn, each read aloud one riddle or joke to the whole group. Have each explain *why* they selected the one that they did.

2. In the Shoes of the Author. Invite students to tell how they think the author learned to think of all the questions and answers to make this riddle and joke book. How do they think the author felt when she started the book?

WHAT ACTIVITIES WILL EXTEND THE BOOK?

1. Cross-Hatching Jokes

Have students meet with partners and distribute a list of cross-hatching statements to them from the book to make their own jokes, for example, What do you get when you cross a computer with a (1) refrigerator; (2) blender; and (3) onion? Ask them to try to answer the jokes in the riddles with their own words. Examples: (1) very cool answers; (2) a mixed solution; and (3) answers that bring tears to your eyes.

2. Knock-Knock Jokes

Have the students listen to several of the knock-knock jokes from the book—for example, Who's there: Hardware. Hardware Who? (*Hard where you run up a hill, easy where you run down*). Invite them to try to answer the jokes on their own before reading the answers at the bottom of the page, and then select one or more to tell a friend.

3. What Joke and Riddle Books Do You Recommend?

Ask students to tell about other joke and riddle books where they saw and read questions and answers that surprised them. Write their suggestions on a chart and place it near the reading area. Have the students refer to it for further reading recommended by their peers.

4. Tips on Writing Riddles

In *Funny Side Up!* (227) by Mike Thaler, the riddle writer shares his process of creating riddles. Read aloud excerpts from Thaler's helpful tips on writing, illustrating, and publishing riddles.

5. Humor in the Year 2000

Have students take a look at a daily newspaper to identify two or three major news items and have them identify which events are humorous items. Have them predict which current events might interest people in the year 2000 and become humorous items. Have students select several news stories that they think might trigger some humorous comments in the year 2000.

6. Jokes-to-Know Flash Cards

Have students work with partners to make colorful flash cards with the questions of their favorite jokes and riddles on one side and the answers on the other side. They can write the author and title of the source along with the answer. If the jokes and riddles are arranged by subject headings in a shoe-box file, appropriate cards can be used daily for five-minute humorous warm-ups before lessons. Make the cards available in the reading area near the humorous books.

What Other Humorous Features Are in Books with Jokes and Riddles?

CARTOON-STYLE ILLUSTRATIONS

Simple cartoons enhance the play on words and knock-knock jokes in *Monster Knock Knocks* (227) by William Cole and Mike Thaler. Invite the students to read the jokes in this book aloud to others in a joke-a-thon or joke olympics setting in the classroom.

PARODY

The title of *How Do You Get a Horse Out of the Bathtub? Profound Answers to Preposterous Questions* (472), compiled by Louis Phillips, is a parody of a newspaper advice column. The "profound answers" of the faux-advice columnist are arranged in eight categories and the "advice" stretches from "Questions Concerning Matters Strictly Personal" to "A Little Bit of History Goes a Long Way."

SURPRISE ENDINGS

Jon Agee's *Flapstick: 10 Ridiculous Rhymes with Flaps* (451) is a group of short, silly rhymes featuring surprise endings under the flaps. The last line of each joking rhyme is not complete until the flap is lifted so a reader can see the exaggerations in the illustrations. Agee also uses words imaginatively, grabs at nonsense, and adds comical cartoon drawings.

SATIRE

There are joking anecdotes about the injustices of life in *Life Is No Fair!* (470) by Stephen Manes and it is satirically packed. For example, there is an anecdote about a boy's fears coming true: on one page, Bronislow Babuska's parents told him he'd never grow up big and strong. A reader turns the next page and reads, "They were half right." (The illustrations show Bronislow strong enough to lift weights but still *very* short.) Another anecdote is about Professor Chuzzlewit who says "There is no such thing as a flying saucer" and the next page reads, "He wasn't wrong." The illustration shows two blue-bodied aliens with green eyes taking him away—not in a saucer but in a flying coffee cup.

VERBAL AND VISUAL JOKES

In *Never Tickle a Turtle!* (227) written and illustrated by Mike Thaler, there are black-and-white illustrations that show pictorial jokes. He has written delightful new verbal jokes too—puns and riddles—about familiar subjects such as ants, mice, and pigs.

Nonsense

Weird and Wacky Inventions

WHAT'S THE BOOK?

Weird and Wacky Inventions. Written and illustrated by Jim Murphy. New York: Crown, 1978. Ages 8 and up.

WHAT'S SO FUNNY?

It is ingenuity that surprises the reader in this book. Here are descriptions and detailed drawings of more than fifty inventions based on the files of the U. S. Patent Office.

WHAT'S IT ABOUT?

Some of the inventions in this informational book include an eye-protector for chickens, a bird diaper, a mouthpiece to prevent snoring, and a hunting decoy shaped like a cow.

WHAT'S THE MINI-UNIT PURPOSE?

Mention to students: "You are going to read about some inventions that may surprise you. For instance, would you be surprised to learn that someone has invented an eye-protector for chickens? Why do you think an inventor would want to do this? Read this book to find out more about unusual inventions. Find out which ones you like the most."

WHAT NEW WORDS CAN BE EMPHASIZED?

Weird, wacky, inventions, patent.

WHAT'S THERE TO TALK ABOUT?

Before the Reading

1. Weird and Wacky Drawings. To begin, ask students, "What are the weirdest and wackiest drawings you have ever seen in a book?" Have them discuss what they have found and ask for their opinions on what is weird and wacky to them and why it is that some people do *not* laugh at things that other people find funny. Introduce the book *Weird and Wacky Inventions*. Show several pictures from the book that illustrate the concept of a "weird" invention.

2. What's Your Personal Definition? Ask students to think of ways to describe something that is weird *and* something that is wacky, and suggest different ways of describing something to others in the class—using words, showing a picture or drawings, demonstrating before the group, and referring to a dictionary. Have the students suggest their own definitions of the words *weird* and *wacky* as a way to recap the discussion. Ask them to compare their definitions with those in a classroom dictionary and read the definitions aloud. Emphasize that a sense of what is weird and wacky is an individual decision.

After the Reading

1. Something Weird and Wacky. Have students turn to a student next to them in class and briefly discuss, "How is this collection of weird and wacky inventions different from your idea of what something weird and wacky should be?"

2. What's Weird and Wacky to You? Ask students to think if they have ever seen something that they thought was weird and wacky. Encourage them to share their experiences. Have the students look over the inventions in the book as the pages are shown on an opaque projector and laugh at the ones they like. Ask each student to choose a funny invention as a favorite and tell others why it was selected.

WHAT ACTIVITIES WILL EXTEND THE BOOK?

1. If I had been there to help invent this, I. . . .

Have the students tell about their favorite humorous invention in the book, and somewhere in the telling, say, "If I had been there to help invent this, I would have added (subtracted). . . . " Invite them to make changes in the invention as they say what they would have done to help the inventor.

Have them consider changes related to some of the following:

- Substituting something on the invention
- Changing something
- Adding something
- Magnifying or minifying a feature
- Extending something
- Rotating something

2. What Humorous Invention Is Needed?

Ask students to interview a neighbor in the class with, "Tell me about a humorous invention that is needed at your house." Invite them to discuss ways to make the needed invention. To summarize their thoughts, have them draw a sketch of their ideas to show others in the whole group.

The Best of Rube Goldberg (478)

WHAT'S THE BOOK?

The Best of Rube Goldberg. Compiled by Charles Keller. Illustrated by Rube Goldberg. Englewood Cliffs N. J.: Prentice-Hall, 1979. Ages 9 and up.

WHAT'S SO FUNNY?

It is tongue-in-cheek humor about the wonderfully complicated mechanical solutions in Goldberg's cartoons.

WHAT'S IT ABOUT?

Some of the inventions in this collection include a pencil sharpener, a self-watering palm tree, and a solution related to how to scrub your back when you take a bath.

WHAT'S THE MINI-UNIT PURPOSE?

Mention to students: "You are going to read about some inventions that may surprise you. For instance, would you be surprised to learn that Rube Goldberg, a cartoonist, has invented a way to scrub your own back when you take a bath that begins

with rain running through a hose? Why do you think someone would think of this? Listen to the information in this book to find out more about this unusual solution to the problem of scrubbing your own back. Find out which solutions you like in the cartoons."

WHAT NEW WORDS CAN BE EMPHASIZED?

Acrobatic, manikin.

WHAT'S THERE TO TALK ABOUT?

Before the Reading

1. Goldberg's Cartoons. Introduce the name of Rube Goldberg and ask students to tell what the name means to them. Show several cartoons from the book that illustrate the concept of the "best" of Rube Goldberg.

2. What's Your Solution? Ask students to think of ways to solve the problem of scrubbing your own back in a humorous way before showing them Goldberg's cartoon (p. 15). Have them compare their ideas with those in Goldberg's cartoon.

After the Reading

1. Goldberg Humor. With partners, have students engage in the discussion of one or more of the following:

- Select one of Goldberg's mechanical solutions and describe *why* you think he thought of the idea.
- With partners, describe your favorite mechanical solution from the book.
- Taking the role of Rube Goldberg, tell a friend how you thought up the need for a mechanical solution in the book.

2. What's a Solution You Need? Ask students to think if they have ever needed a solution to a problem they faced in their daily lives. Encourage them to share their experiences and any solutions they have.

WHAT ACTIVITIES WILL EXTEND THE BOOK?

1. What Humorous Solution Is Needed?

In pairs, ask students to interview a neighbor in the class with "Tell me about a humorous mechanical solution that is needed at your house." Invite them to discuss ways to assemble the mechanical solution. To visualize their thoughts, have them draw a sketch of their ideas (as Goldberg did) to show others in the whole group. With the whole group, have students show and discuss their sketches and ask for additional humorous improvements from the group. Ask students to return to their pairs and label their sketches with the letters A, B, C, etc., to indicate the order in which the mechanics would operate. Have them write the A, B, C, etc., steps (as Goldberg did) to describe how the mechanical solution would work.

What Other Humorous Features Are in Books With Nonsense?

CHARACTERS

Nonsense is seen not only in the ingenuity of inventions and mechanical solutions but also in characters such as those found in *Nonstop Nonsense* (479) by Margaret Mahy, a collection of short stories and poems. For example, in the narrative entitled "The Cat Who Became a Poet," Mahy lets the cat, who thinks that poetry is "very tricky stuff," talk about his genesis as a poet—"I became a poet through eating the mouse. Perhaps the mouse became a poet through eating the seeds." When the cat reflects further he muses that "poetry stuff is just the world's way of talking about itself."

UNUSUAL SIGHTS

There are nonsense rhymes in *No Such Things* (481) by Bill Peet. The book has unusual sights in nonsensical illustrations of such imagined things as the "blue-snouted twumps." For instance, it seems that when the twumps eat weeds and seeds, the seeds sprout into weeds on the twumps' backs.

This causes the twumps to look like walking "haystacks" to those that see them.

WORD PLAY

In *If I Ran the Zoo* (483) by Dr. Seuss, there are different words and names to describe the animals in a nonsensical rhyming text. Gerald McGrew imagines a fanciful zoological habitat that has an elephant-cat, a bird called a bustard, a beast called flustard, and bugs with names of thwerils and chugs. He searches for the imaginary animals in their imaginary habitats—called Motta-fa-Potta-pa-Pell and the Wilds of Nantasket, and the Desert of Zind.

ZANINESS

There are zany pictures (more nonsense) in Marvin Terban's *Guppies in Tuxedos: Funny Eponyms* (236) and *The Dove Dove: Funny Homograph Riddles* (236). In the books, words are used in humorous ways. They are shown in the illustrations and described to show students a comical way to learn how words are used in speech.

Rhymes and Verses

Roomrimes: Poems about Rooms (494)

WHAT'S THE BOOK?

Roomrimes: Poems about Rooms. Written by Sylvia Cassedy. New York: HarperCollins, 1993. Ages 9–12.

WHAT'S SO FUNNY?

Creative word play and humorous twists in poems.

WHAT'S IT ABOUT?

This is an ABC collection of twenty-six poems about places from an attic to a zoo. The poems—some metered rhymes and others free verse—are fun to read aloud and introduce children to ways to see ordinary spaces in extraordinary ways.

WHAT'S THE MINI-UNIT PURPOSE?

Mention to students: "You are going to hear some rhymes about rooms and places. Listen to find out how the writer makes some humorous twists in the words and plays with words in a creative way."

WHAT NEW WORDS CAN BE EMPHASIZED?

Roomrimes, vestibule, widow's walk, free verse.

WHAT'S THERE TO TALK ABOUT?

Before the Reading

1. An Imaginary Room of Your Own. With students, discuss "How many of you have ever wanted an imaginary room of your own?" Have stu-

dents tell what they *imagine* it would be like. Introduce the title of the book *Roomrimes,* and write it on the overhead or on the board. Ask students to tell what the book might be about. Write their predictions about the book's title on the board and then show several of the black-and-white illustrations from the book that accompany the poems.

2. A Special Place You Know About. Ask students to think if they have ever felt like writing—perhaps humorously—about rooms and places. Encourage them to share their feelings about special places from their experience or that they know about.

After the Reading

1. Group Reading. Distribute a copy of one of the poems where you have added numbers beside certain lines in the margin. Assign the numbers to groups of students and have the groups sit together. Ask the students to read the poem as groups for their parts.

- Discuss the humor in the poem with the whole group.
- Ask the students to give examples of something funny from the poem.
- Have the students circle the humorous words on their copies.
- Discuss the special parts the students circled on their copies.

2. Group Writing. Have students name some special rooms or places that have not been mentioned in the book. Record the ideas on the board. Have students select one thing and ask what words would rhyme with that word if they were to write their own verse about a special room or place. Write the verse the students develop on the board or chart paper.

Have students return to the original group they were in when they read the poem as groups for the parts and write a cooperative verse of their own using one of the things that go from the list on the board.

3. Presenting Humor Your Own Way. Ask students to think of ways to describe one or more of the poems after hearing the title(s) and listening to/reading the poem. Ask them to sketch their descriptions. In partnerships, ask them to tell their partners why they drew their sketches the way they did. Back in the whole group, invite volunteers to show their descriptions and tell more about them. As a contrast to show ways artists present humor differently, show the illustrations by Michele Chessare in the book.

WHAT ACTIVITIES WILL EXTEND THE BOOK?

1. Laughable and Singable Limericks

With interested students, engage them in singing some of the limericks they find and then in writing their own original ones. In the final section of *Laughable Limericks* (491) compiled by Sara Brewton and John E. Brewton, called "Try Singing These," the Brewtons suggest that readers try singing some of the limericks. They include the words and music for "There Was a Young Girl, A Sweet Lamb" and "There Was an Old Lady of Steen."

2. Laughable and Writable Limericks

Some instructions on how to write your own limericks—humorous five-line verses—are provided in "Writing Limericks" in *Laughable Limericks* (491) compiled by Sara Brewton and John E. Brewton. For example, they pass along David McCord's directions that include taking "an old man" of wherever and then telling what he does or doesn't do. He reminds writers about putting in five lines—two long ones, two little short ones, and then one quick last one.

Dr. Knickerbocker and Other Rhymes (490)

WHAT'S THE BOOK?

Dr. Knickerbocker and Other Rhymes. Written by David Booth. New York: Ticknor & Fields, 1993. Ages 9–12.

WHAT'S SO FUNNY?

Parodies of traditional rhymes and nonsense along with taunts and jump rope songs.

WHAT'S IT ABOUT?

This is a collection of playground rhymes collected from school yards and written sources. The text is written not only on white space but on word bubbles, on banners, on the bases of statues, on signs, and on postcards.

WHAT'S THE MINI-UNIT PURPOSE?

Mention to students: "You are going to hear some jump rope rhymes 1) your mother said that are still heard today; 2) today; and 3) from long ago. Listen to find out rhymes you have said or heard and which ones you like best."

WHAT NEW WORDS CAN BE EMPHASIZED?

Knickerbocker, parody, taunt, nonsense.

WHAT'S THERE TO TALK ABOUT?

Before the Reading

1. Tell a Jump Rope Rhyme. Ask three volunteers to jump rope at the front of the classroom and to chant a jump rope rhyme they know. Introduce the book and show the cover and read aloud one jump rope rhyme. Ask the volunteers to jump rope and chant the new rhyme. Show several of the black-and-white illustrations from the book that accompany the rhymes.

2. What's Funny from Your Point of View? Ask students to think when they have repeated jump rope rhymes that are humorous to them. What made the rhyme funny from their point of view? Encourage them to talk about their experience with different jump rope rhymes.

3. Nonsense. Have students turn to a student next to them and briefly discuss, "One nonsense thing (or parody) that the rhymes in *Dr. Knickerbocker and Other Rhymes* makes me think of is. . . . ."

After the Reading

1. Humor in Rhymes. With students, show a copy of a jump rope rhyme on an overhead transparency, chart paper, or on the board, so all can see the words. Read the words aloud and invite students to chime in as they feel they know the words. Reread the words again. Divide the class into two groups and ask each group to read a line aloud. Identify the humor. Have the students point out the humorous parts in the words. Have volunteers underline or circle the funniest part with a brightly colored crayon or chalk. Ask, what could *you* have added to the words of one of the jump rope rhymes to make it more humorous?

2. Write a Group Rhyme. *Discuss:* How is the writer's humorous ideas about jump rope rhymes different from your ideas about the rhymes? With the students' ideas, write a group jump rope rhyme and read the rhyme aloud as a choral reading. Invite students to write and illustrate the rhyme if desired.

3. Make Your Own Word Changes. Have the students chant their favorite humorous jump rope rhyme in the book, and ask them to make word changes to make another humorous remark about jumping rope.

WHAT ACTIVITIES WILL EXTEND THE BOOK?

1. How Does Nonsense Make You Feel?

Have students tell a friend in class how they felt about hearing the nonsense in one of the jump rope rhymes. Invite them to contribute additional nonsense rhymes they know.

2. Verse Slam: Rhymes and Verses in Your Own Way

Invite students to wipe the dust off any dry poetry and turn their attention to rhymes and verses for a "Verse Slam." Ask them to recite a favorite verse or rhyme and take part in a "Verse Slam," where they perform and ask the other students to respond to words, to phrases, etc. Other students can clap along, stomp their feet, cheer at words they like, or give out loud "Whoops."

3. What Made You Laugh?

Ask the students to interview a classroom student with "Tell me what made you laugh when you heard the nonsense rhymes (or parodies of rhymes) about jumping rope."

What Other Humorous Features Are in Books with Rhymes and Verses?

ACTIONS

In Jack Prelutsky's *Something Big Has Been Here* (506), humorous actions occur in several poems. Read some aloud and have the students identify some of their favorites and write the titles on the board in a list. Add a second list entitled "Funny Behavior" and have the students put themselves into the verses and suggest additional humorous actions for the poem. (See figure 6).

ANECDOTES

In Ernest Lawrence Thayer's *Casey at the Bat* (509), the classic Casey first appeared in *The San Francisco Examiner* in June 1888. Tripp illustrated the original version with his fresh whimsical drawings. His line drawings alternate with colorful two-page spreads and add humor to this funny poem of mighty Casey and his loyal fans.

Poems	Funny Behavior
1. "I Am Growing a Glorious Garden"	How I could get attention in a humorous way.
2. "I Am Wunk"	How I could show I had a hobby or talent.
3. "I Want a Pet Porcupine, Mother"	How I could convince someone I needed an unusual pet.
4. "Kevin the King of the Jungle"	How I could show I was king or queen of something.
5. "My Brother Is as Generous as Anyone Could Be"	How I act with my brothers and sisters.
6. "My Family's Sleeping Late Today"	How I act with my parents.
7. "My Uncle Looked Me in the Eye"	How I act with my aunts, uncles, and cousins.
8. "A Remarkable Adventure"	How I would describe a funny adventure.

Figure 6. Form for Poem Titles and Funny Behavior.

PLAYS ON WORDS

In *Hurry, Hurry, Mary Dear! and Other Nonsense Poems* (488) written and illustrated by Neils Mogens Bodecker, there are appealing words and humorous line-drawn illustrations. Bodecker's delightful play on words is seen in his series of "if" verses—consider "If I were an Elephant" as a way to introduce students to making their own rhymes.

RIDICULOUS SITUATIONS

The idea of ridiculousness in everyday situations can be shown through objects and actions that are not worthy of serious consideration in *The New Kid on the Block* (506) written by Jack Prelutsky and illustrated by James Stevenson. This is a book of nonsense worth showing to children for its ridiculousness in daily happenings. The verses "shout out" that nonsense can be taken from what goes on around children and adults every day.

TONGUE TWISTERS

In *Let's Marry said the Cherry and Other Nonsense Poems* (489), also written and illustrated by Neils Mogens Bodecker, there are tongue twisters along with other words of happy nonsense and examples of irony to find in the rhyming verses. The poems are humorously illustrated with line drawings.

WITTY SUBTLETIES

Doodle Soup (496) written by John Ciardi and illustrated with pen-and-ink sketches by Merle Nacht features witty words that are entertaining when read aloud. Perhaps introduce the book by asking children to take parts and read aloud "All I Did Was Ask My Sister." In addition to several anecdotes about children's misbehavior, this collection includes "A Lesson in Manners" ("*You should never be bad until you've been fed*"); and some advice on trapping moose ("*leave them alone/unless you are braver than you are bright*").

Unusual Characters and Creatures

The Devil and Mother Crump (511)

WHAT'S THE BOOK?

The Devil and Mother Crump. Written by Valerie Scho Carey and illustrated by Arnold Lobel. New York: Harper & Row, 1987. Ages 9–10.

WHAT'S SO FUNNY?

Colloquial dialogue and read-aloud cadence. A stingy, mean old woman is unwelcome in heaven but she tricks her way in.

WHAT'S IT ABOUT?

This is an original folktale about a stingy baker woman, Mother Crump, who gets three wishes from the Devil and uses them as tricks to escape him. When she dies she finds that her mean reputation has preceded her. So, she has to trick her way into Heaven and once there, builds a bake oven among the clouds. Some say it still glows in the form of heat lightning on warm summer nights.

WHAT'S THE MINI-UNIT PURPOSE?

Mention to students: "You are going to hear a humorous story about a woman who gets three wishes and uses them to trick herself out of the devil's clutches. Listen to find out how she tricks her way into heaven."

WHAT NEW WORDS CAN BE EMPHASIZED?

Mother Crump, bake oven, Lucifer, heat lightning, "get shut of her."

WHAT'S THERE TO TALK ABOUT?

Before the Reading

1. What Might the Humor Be About? Introduce the title of the book and write the words *Mother Crump* and *Lucifer* on the board. Ask students to tell what the words mean to them and what the humor in the story might be about.

2. Sketch Humorous Descriptions. Ask students to think of humorous ways they would describe Mother Crump if they had been asked to be the illustrators of the story. Ask them to sketch their descriptions. In partnerships in class, ask them to tell their partners why they drew their sketches the way they did. Back in the whole group, invite volunteers to show their humorous descriptions and tell more about them.

After the Reading

1. The Colloquial Dialogue That I Liked in *The Devil and Mother Crump* Was.... Write the title *The Devil and Mother Crump* on the board. Have students turn to someone next to them and briefly discuss, "The dialogue that I liked in *The Devil and Mother Crump* was...." In the whole group, have them retell the humorous dialogue they liked and write excerpts on the board. Reread the list and have students suggest humorous actions to go with the dialogue. Write notes about the actions on the board.

2. Talking about Humor in the Story. Have students discuss any or all of the following:

- What might *you* have said in a humorous way to Mother Crump?
- How did Mother Crump trick her way into heaven? What did you think was humorous in the story?

- Did you think that the explanation of heat lightning was humorous? Why or why not?

WHAT ACTIVITIES WILL EXTEND THE BOOK?

1. Be a Humorous Chronicler

In groups of three, invite the students to take turns and play the role of a chronicler who tells about one of the three wishes that Mother Crump gets from the Devil. Have them tell how she uses each wish to trick herself out of his cluthches.

2. Playing Tricks

Ask students to tell about other stories where they read/heard about humorous tricksters or someone who plays a trick on someone else.

3. One-a-Day: Humorous Books about Unusual Characters and Creatures

With students, read aloud from a humorous book/chapter once a day. Invite other school personnel in to the class to read aloud. If desired, provide time for the students to reread their favorite books. Keep and display a list of each student's favorite read-alouds. For an option, ask students to select a book to read aloud at home to a younger family member.

4. A Laugh-in Afternoon

With students in on the planning, establish a laugh-in afternoon and ask the older students to read humorous stories to the younger children at school. Invite students to set the stage for the afternoon and use art work to develop a mural of humorous characters, plan informal drama to act out parts of selected stories, and create and design a humorous announcement flyer about the afternoon. If desired, the students can write and bind their own humorous books for the class and be the authors for an autograph party. The authors can interview one another and write up an interview feature article for the school or class newspaper.

During the laugh-in afternoon, have the older student discuss the younger child's favorite humorous books and record some information about the visiting younger child on index cards for future reference. Have each pair discuss the humorous books they like.

5. A Funny Committee: More Humorous Books about Unusual Creatures

With a committee of four or five students, select several humorous books about unusual characters and creatures from the school library and make them available for browsing and reading in the room. Have the committee make humorous bookmarks and put them in the books at the page where something humorous happens. Read from one of these selections every day to interest the students in the stories.

6. Draw a Picture from Information

Select an illustration and describe the scene to the students. Ask them to draw a picture from the information you give them. Have the students exchange their drawings with a classroom neighbor and restate your description. Ask them to look for the objects that you described.

Helga's Dowry: A Troll Love Story (309)

WHAT'S THE BOOK?

Helga's Dowry: A Troll Love Story. Written and illustrated by Tomie de Paola. New York: Harcourt, Brace, Jovanovich, 1977. Ages 8–9.

WHAT'S SO FUNNY?

Humorous writing and illustrating. Helga, a lovely but penniless troll, discovers that her husband-to-be is very fickle.

WHAT'S IT ABOUT?

Penniless, Helga, the troll, works like a tornado to earn a dowry of cows, gold, and land to seal her marriage contract with Lars, a handsome troll. When she discovers the gold digging Lars is quite fickle, she wisely considers a bigger and better life.

WHAT'S THE MINI-UNIT PURPOSE?

Mention to students: "You are going to hear a story about a beautiful young troll, Helga, who wants to marry the handsome troll, Lars. She needs a dowry, however, to seal the marriage contract and works very, very hard to earn gold, land, and some cows. Listen to find out what Helga does when Lars changes his mind about the marriage.

WHAT NEW WORDS CAN BE EMPHASIZED?

Helga, troll, Lars, fickle, dowry.

WHAT'S THERE TO TALK ABOUT?

Before the Reading

1. *Troll* **Can Be a Special Word.** Choose the word *troll* as the special word of the day and ask students to listen for the word and, as soon as anyone hears it, to say aloud "special word." If desired, the child who hears it first can receive the privilege of choosing another word from Helga's story that will be the second special word of the day.

2. Pictures about Troll Actions in Your Mind. Ask students to brainstorm action words about trolls by imagining a troll and his or her daily troll activities. For example, what actions come to mind when they think of a troll getting up out of a troll bed in a troll house and getting dressed in troll clothes, brushing the teeth and combing the hair. On a winter holiday, trolls might make troll cookies, trollmen in the troll snow, and look forward to a visit from Santa Troll. Write the students' thoughts in a list on an overhead transparency, a chart, or on the board. Reread the list and ask the students to describe pictures about the actions in their minds and tell their descriptions aloud.

After the Reading

1. What Would You Ask Helga and Lars? Begin a discussion about the story by asking the students to think of questions they would ask Helga and Lars. Write their responses on chart paper or on the board. Ask students to think of something friendly they could do for Helga or Lars when they meet them. Ask students to sketch their ideas on paper and place the sketches on a bulletin board.

2. A Time Line about Helga and Her Dowry. Invite the students to review the ways that Helga earned something for her dowry. Write their ideas in a list on the board and then turn the list into a time line of her actions. Ask students to select the actions they want to illustrate with drawings.

3. What Humorous Things Might Happen if You Lived as a Troll? After the story is heard, ask students to discuss with others reasons why they would or would not enjoy living as a troll with Helga and Lars.

4. If I Had a Dowry, I Would Want . . . . After reading the story to the whole group, ask students to recall the three things that Helga wanted in her dowry. Ask the students to discuss with partners, "If I had a dowry, I would want . . . ."

WHAT ACTIVITIES WILL EXTEND THE BOOK?

1. What *Could* **Come Next?**

Read a brief page and stop in the middle of a sentence or at a critical part in the story and have students determine something humorous that *could* come next.

2. A Troll's Clap

Reread the story and ask the students to give a "troll's finger-snap" when they hear Helga's name. Repeat the activity with variations—snap fingers when they hear Lars' name, when they hear an action word, and when they hear the name of something special—dowry.

3. Make a Map of the Setting

After reading the story, tape a sheet of colored paper to the board and ask students to suggest features for a map of the setting in Helga's story. Using the students' comments, draw features on the map.

4. Suggest Sounds for a Story Rereading

Invite students to suggest sounds that could accompany the story and reread it. Have the students insert the sounds as the text is read aloud.

5. Troll Music

Play two or three selections of mood music and ask the students to paint or fingerpaint pictures that the music brings to their thoughts. Ask them to tell which selection impressed them the most as "troll music."

6. Attitude Survey about Humor

Engage students in responding to an attitude survey about humor. The items can be read aloud if desired. The survey, given as a prestudy activity as well as a poststudy data collection technique, might look something like the one pictured in figure 7.

What Do You Think about Humor?

Name _____

Date _____

Place a √ to show how you feel:

	It's Great!	Yes!	O. K.	Well, . . .	No Way

1. When someone reads something funny to you.
2. When reading humorous poems.
3. When listening to funny poems from books.
4. When reading humorous stories.
5. When listening to humorous stories.
6. When reading humor in your free time.
7. When reading humor and writing humor.
8. When reading humorous alliteration.
9. When reading exaggerations.
10. When humorous characters are animals.
11. When humorous characters are humans.
12. When humorous characters are imaginary or unusual.
13. When there are ridiculous situations.
14. When there are tricksters.
15. When there are tongue twisters.
16. When there are plays on words.
17. When there are caricatures of situations and people.
18. When there is zaniness.
19. When there are unusual sights.
20. When reading something humorous you wrote.
21. When writing humor with a partner.
22. When writing humor by yourself.

Figure 7. Form for Humor Attitude Survey.

7. Humorous Sayings Mural

Have students listen to some humorous sayings to use as a springboard for group discussions about humor. The sayings can be from *A Monster is Bigger Than 9* (512) edited by Claire Ericksen and illustrated by Mary Ericksen, or another favorite source. *A Monster* is a faithful recollection of the humor of preschoolers as recorded by their teachers. There are several related to unusual creatures and characters: Want to know where dwarfs live? (*The dwarfs live in a little cottage-cheese*). Or what polka dots on the arm mean? (*The polka dots on my arm mean they are shivering*). Or what is bigger than nine? (*A monster. A monster is bigger than nine*). Have students write and illustrate the humorous sayings they find on a mural to display in the room.

What Other Humorous Features Are in Books with Unusual Characters and Creatures?

HUMOROUS ALLITERATION

Rootabaga Stories (518) by Carl Sandburg is a collection of brief stories in a setting called Rootabaga Country where the train tracks zig and zag. The largest village is called Liver and Onions; the countryside is called Over and Under and some animals wear clothing; the residents have names that are tongue twisters such as Ax Me No Questions, Henry Hagglyhoagly, and Miney Mo; and they all talk in alliterative words.

EXAGGERATIONS

Humorous exaggerations are found in *Pippi Long-stocking* (515) by Astrid Lindgren. Pigtailed Pippi, a nine-year-old parentless child of "supergirl" fame, is the strongest girl in the world—she can lift her horse up onto the porch of her house or throw a man into the air. She scrubs the floor with brushes tied on her feet and wears stockings of different colors. She also sleeps on a bed with her feet where her head should be and decides to go to school so she won't "miss" having a Christmas and Easter vacation when school is "out."

HUMOROUS CHARACTERS

Natalie Babbit's *The Devil's Other Storybook* (510) presents the devil as a sly and vain character. The black-and-white drawings show him in a humorous way—slightly paunchy with a very long pointed tail. When not inviting the world's inhabitants to be uncomforatble in hell, he likes to jour-ney through the world causing trouble and misfortune wherever he goes. Sometimes the tables are turned on him, however, and the devil gets a surprise. A surprise is just what he gets in most of these humorous stories. For those students interested further in this vain character, suggest *The Devil's Storybook* (510).

IMAGINARY CREATURES

All of the fearsome critters in *Kickle Snifters and Other Fearsome Critters Collected from American Folklore* (519) compiled by Alvin Schwartz are imaginary beasts of the tall tale variety. Wisely included, there is a list of illustrated definitions with notes on sources included at the back of the book.

RIDICULOUS SITUATIONS

There is a humorous warning against dependence on gadgetry in *Lazy Tommy Pumpkinhead* (517) by William Pene du Bois. Tommy—who does nothing for himself—lives in an all-electric house. In a Rube Goldberg mechanical solution arrangement, an electric bed wakes him up and slides him into a tub of warm water. The tub tips him out and into a harness that holds him up while other machines dry him. Still other gadgets comb his hair, brush his teeth, dress him, and feed him. One day, his life changes because the gadgets are affected by a storm—his clothes are put on upside down and the machines feed his feet instead of his mouth.

Extensions for Mini-Units

If teachers or librarians are interested in considering what the children's previous experiences with humor has been, they may want to take an informal survey or inventory of the children's backgrounds in humor in children's literature. Additionally, they may be interested in keeping individual portfolios for the children, in providing opportunities for children to write in journals about the humorous material they enjoy, in participating in ways to extend humorous literature through the expressive arts and other means, in scheduling individual interviews, and in keeping anecdotal notes related to guidelines for evaluating children's understanding of humor in children's literature.

INFORMAL SURVEY

To take an informal survey, they can construct an inventory just to see what kind of exposure children have had to humor in their literature. If desired, the survey can be read aloud to young children and middle grade children. The survey will help teachers/librarians identify the features in children's exposure to humor and would, in turn, help them plan ways to include humor in a literature program for the children. For example, a survey would determine the extent to which the children showed their knowledge of some of the features of humor you wanted to emphasize. Perhaps the features would be similar to the following:

- A funny opening
- A colorful narration
- Colorful character(s)
- A concise plot
- Putting in some surprises with things that don't "fit" together

If the children demonstrated a lack of knowledge of some of the features of humor, you could plan a brief study of a feature/features through a mini-unit and several examples that are provided in this book. If a survey indicated that some students did not know about humorous personification or another humorous technique or had never heard of the writing of Dr. Seuss, teachers and librarians would have gained information on what to read aloud or what books to introduce to the children.

INDIVIDUAL PORTFOLIO

If desired, after information has been gathered from a survey, teachers and librarians can provide children with experiences of humor in children's literature and gather information that shows growth and progress in humor awareness of the children by keeping individual portfolios for the children, by providing opportunities for children to write in journals about the humorous material they enjoy, by participating in ways to extend humorous literature through the expressive arts and other means, by scheduling individual interviews, and by keeping anecdotal notes related to guidelines for evaluating children's understanding of humor in children's literature.

A manila folder can become a portfolio for each child. It can be designated for saving dated copies or originals of the child's work related to humor to begin a record-keeping system to keep information through the year. Such a folder will provide a child access to his or her work and be a record to take home at the end of a study on humor or at the end of the school year. In the folder, you can place notes about what the child was reading or put index cards on which the child has written the title and author of each humorous book he or she has read during the unit of study.

JOURNALS

Teachers and librarians can ask children to respond to their reading in writing and "just talk" on the page with the words they write. If desired, they can ask some guiding questions—"Tell what your humorous reading was this week," or "Tell about a funny part in the book you have read," or "Write about a book character who showed a fine sense of humor."

EXPRESSIVE ARTS

There is a variety of projects in which children can participate to extend their interaction with humorous literature. Here are some examples related to the expressive arts and crafts:

- Advertisements
- Art gallery
- Artifacts and realia
- Awards
- Board games
- Bulletin boards
- Card games
- Charts
- Clock decorations
- Collages
- Collections of objects
- Comic strips
- Cooking
- Costumes
- Dances
- Decor around the classroom door
- Detailed illustrations
- Diaries
- Dioramas
- Displays
- Dramas
- Essays
- Experiments
- Exploring media used by illustrators
- Exploring writing of authors' language patterns
- Fables
- Fairy tales
- Family trees
- Felt or flannel board (story retelling prop)
- Filmstrips
- Flat pictures
- Games
- Graphs
- Greeting cards
- Illustrated stories
- Journals
- Labeled diagrams
- Letters
- Making books
- Making objects
- Maps

- Mobiles
- Models of diaries, letters, and journals
- Movies and videos
- Murals
- Pencil decorations
- Pamphlets
- Pantomimes
- Poems
- Posters
- Puppets and shows
- Reports
- School subject signs for bulletin boards
- Scrapbooks
- Sculptures
- Sewing objects
- Short stories
- Slides and tape presentations
- Songs
- Stencils
- Story maps
- Surveys
- Taped recordings
- Time lines
- Transparencies

INTERVIEWS

If desired, a personal interview can give teachers and librarians time to reflect in what ways a child is aware of humor. Most suitable, the interview can include a book—such as a humorous book by Dr. Seuss that the child has read and around which questions can be asked:

- "What humor in the book do you want to talk about?"
- "Is there any other humor in the book other than the humor we have talked about?"
- "Now that you have read this nonsense story by Dr. Seuss, could you recognize one he wrote even if you didn't see his name as the author?"
- Show the child another nonsense story by Dr. Seuss and see if the child recognizes it as a story by Dr. Seuss. "In what ways can you tell this humorous story is by Dr. Seuss?"

EVALUATING CHILDREN'S UNDERSTANDINGS OF HUMOR

Guidelines. A librarian, teacher, or parent, may want to keep anecdotal notes on a child related to the following questions. Does the child demonstrate that he or she

- Reads humor voluntarily?
- Becomes involved in reading a humorous book independently?
- Likes one humorous book specifically?
- Likes many humorous books in general?
- Has certain understandings and awarenesses from reading humorous material?
- Can make predictions and ask related questions while reading a humorous book?
- Can recognize some of the characteristics of humor in reading material?

- Can visualize settings? Can visualize characters?
- Notices certain features of humor that are used in humorous writing?
- Uses certain features of humor verbally and in writing that are found in humorous material?
- Can make connections between humorous literature and his/her life?
- Makes humorous statements voluntarily?
- Is responding to a wider range and complexity of humor as the academic year progresses?
- Is changing positively in his/her appreciation of humor as the academic year progresses?

III

Humorous Books
for Children Ages 5–8

Animals as Humans

1. Allard, Harry (1981). *There's a Party at Mona's Tonight*. Illustrated by James Marshall. New York: Doubleday. Ages 5–8.

   There's a Party . . . is a slapstick story about Potter Pig. He tries to crash Mona's lovely party with her animal guests and learns that insults can *hurt*. When read aloud to a young child, an adult should discuss the extent to which Potter's costume changes confuse (or do not confuse) any of the young listeners.

2. Allen, Jeffrey (1975). *Mary Alice Operator Number 9*. Illustrated by James Marshall. New York: Little, Brown. Ages 5–6.

   Allen offers a humorously written story about Mary Alice, the duck, who is sick and can no longer "quack" the correct time for callers. The other animals try to substitute for her but fail to bark or oink the time correctly or pleasantly. At last, Mary Alice gets well and the callers are happy to hear her familiar quack again since the service of Operator Number 9 is the service they like. In *Mary Alice Returns* (Little, Brown, 1986), Mary Alice gets a mysterious call for help and she does her best to meet the emergency.

3. Asch, Frank, and Vladimir Vaglin (1989). *Here Comes the Cat!* New York: Scholastic. Ages 6–7.

   Asch and Vaglin have developed irony as an unexpected conclusion in this bilingual story. The words in Russian and English and pictures lead the readers to believe that the cat will harm the mice as in "The Belling of the Cat." The surprise ending happens when the cat brings cheese as a gesture of friendship and the mice repay him by offering milk and combing his fur.

4. Axlerod, Amy (1994). *Pigs Will Be Pigs*. Illustrated by Sharon McGinley-Nally. New York: Four Winds. Ages 6–8.

   The humor in *Pigs Will Be Pigs* is in the actions of the gaily dressed pigs who turn everything upside down in their house as they look for extra change so they can go out to dinner at the Enchanted Enchilada. Students can figure out what the pigs can afford to eat when they see the prices on the reproduced menu. The multiplication and addition necessary to find the answers about how much money the pigs will have left over are found on a final page.

5. Barrett, Judi (1970). *Animals Should Definitely Not Wear Clothing*. Illustrated by Ron Barrett. New York: Atheneum. Ages 6–7.

   In Barrett's book, the illustrations show most of the obvious fun that answers the question "what *might* happen if animals dressed in clothes? The pictures make it humorously clear. With broad humor, a moose would get tangled up in his trousers. A chicken would get an egg caught in her stretch pants. The oposums would wear their clothes upside down. A snake would wiggle out of his trousers. As an example of subtle humor, a large lady and a larger elephant might wear identical dresses made from the same material. For some children, it's possible that some of the humor in this book may need to be discussed with the question "why might this be funny?" The Barretts have a humorous sequel, *Animals Should Definitely Not Act Like People* (Atheneum, 1980), another picture book with unexpected illustrations of animals that make it entertainingly clear what *might* happen if animals acted like humans.

6. Berenstain, Stanley, and Janice Berenstain (1983). *The Berenstain Bears and the Messy Room*. Illustrated by the authors. New York: Random House. Ages 5–6.

   Humor is shown through the cooperation of comic characters of the Berenstain Bears. The story shows the problems that Papa Bear has when he sees the bear cubs' room. Brother Bear and Sister Bear have "messy buildup" among their belongings and they find out that cleaning up can be a satisfying thing to do. Young readers interested further in this family can turn to:

   • *The Berenstain Bears Get in a Fight* (Random House, 1982) where the usually compatible

Brother Bear and Sister Bear are fighting—all day long! Mama Bear helps them realize that everyone argues once in a while, even with loved ones.

- *The Berenstain Bears Go to Camp* (Random House, 1982) where the story shows the fun that brother and sister discover at Grizzly Bob's Day Camp. They overcome their apprehension and find out that camp is an exciting place with interesting things to do and enjoy the big sleep-out on Skull Rock.
- *The Berenstain Bears in the Dark* (Random House, 1982), where Brother Bear enjoys scaring Sister Bear with spooky stories and frightful sounds in the dark. But Brother Bear finds out that he, too, can be frightened.

7. Blundell, Tony (1992). *Beware of Boys.* New York: Greenwillow. Ages 5–8.

Blundell's story is slapstick comedy with the wolf as a naive chef-in-the-wild. When a boy finds himself taken off by wolf to his cave, the boy convinces him that it would be a *cooked* boy (not a raw one) that would be the tastiest for dinner. With wolf convinced, the boy sends him on a shopping trip for the ingredients for Boy Soup. There are quite a few items to shop for that include one *cartload* of carrots, one *oodle* of onions, one *ton* of potatoes, one *wellfull* of water, one *barrel* of bricks, and one trowel. Additionally, the boy reviews the method for preparing Boy Soup that includes catching the boy, washing him thoroughly (especially behind the ears), and sitting on the barrel of bricks and stirring with a trowel until Thursday.

Of course, wolf thinks this sounds *delicious* and hurries around to get the heavy items. Later, wolf is sent out to find a different list of ingredients to make a new dish—Boy Pie. The items for the pie are silly, too, and include a *cowboy* hat, three *foothills* of flour, and six *sacks* of cement. A third time, wolf is sent out again to find still more ingredients to make yet another dish—Boy Cake. The ingredients include a bathtub, a blob of butter, and a couple of barn doors. Wolf is now staggering from carrying the weight of the ingredients and looks worn out, pretty woeful, and pathetic. At the end, it is some of the main ingredients that enable the boy to trick wolf and make his escape back to his home.

8. Brandenberg, Franz (1975). *Otto Is Different.* Illustrated by James Stevenson. New York: Greenwillow. Ages 5–8.

If a child likes exaggerated animal characteristics, then this story will be enjoyed. Otto is different because he is an octopus. He thinks he would rather be like his other animal friends, but his parents convince him that having eight arms can be a fine characteristic. Even though he has more arms for getting tired he also has more arms for hugging. The illustrations are done with great comic actions. Otto uses all his arms as he does his homework, sweeps the floor, and practices the piano at the same time or plays a game of hockey all by himself. The idea of using eight arms at once is what makes it fun. Children will be able to imagine many other possibilities for extra arms. They might also consider how the story would have turned out if Otto had been a giraffe with an extralong neck or an anteater with an extralong nose.

9. Brown, Marc (1982). *Arthur Goes to Camp.* Illustrated by the author. New York: Atlantic/Little, Brown. Ages 5–7.

Brown's amusing illustrations help tell the story of Arthur and his adventures at Camp Meadowbrook. In one adventure, there is a competitive activity between the boys and the girls. When Arthur stumbles around, he saves the day at the scavenger hunt. Young readers interested further in Arthur and his adventures can turn to one of the following:

- *Arthur's Family Vacation* (Little, Brown, 1993), where Arthur makes the best of a boring rainy vacation without his friend Buster who is away at camp. Arthur organizes field trips for his family and they visit Jimmy's Jungle Cruise, Flo's Fudge Factory, and Gatorville.
- *Arthur Babysits* (Little, Brown, 1992) where Arthur takes care of the terrible Tibble twins. As soon as their mother leaves, the twins, dressed as cowboys, lasso the plants, shoot off their toy guns, and tie Arthur up. He finds he can control them with a spooky story about the green swamp thing, always hungry, who likes to eat only twin boys.
- *Arthur's Nose* (Little, Brown, 1976) and *Arthur's Glasses* (Little, Brown, 1979) where Arthur is the subject of a good deal of teasing by others in both stories.

- *Arthur's Baby* (Little, Brown, 1987) where Arthur is unhappy about the new baby but helps out when his sister asks him to help with the holding. When the baby cries, Arthur interprets and says she is trying to tell them something— a burp.
- *Arthur's Teacher Trouble* (Atlantic, 1986) where Arthur is chosen by Mr. Ratburn, the third grade teacher, to be in the school spellathon where Arthur is challenged with the word *preparation*.

10. Browne, Anthony (1985). *Willy the Champ*. Illustrated by the author. New York: Knopf. Ages 5–8.

What is scrawny and little? Why, it's Willy, a little chimpanzee, who goes through life apologizing—even when it is not his fault. Though Willy is not too good at sports, he *tries,* but his gorilla pals laugh at him every time. He sends for a "Don't Be a Wimp" kit. After diet and exercise, Willy feels better about himself and rescues his friend Millie from the gorilla gang. He inadvertently becomes a hero, too, when the biggest bully of all, Buster Nose, starts to hit him and Willy ducks at just the right time. Buster Nose's fist hits a brick wall—not Willy—and Willy is the champ. More humorous episodes of Willy are in *Willy the Chimp* (Knopf, 1984) and they tell how Willy's self-esteem becomes vastly improved when he takes a body-building course.

11. Calhoun, Mary (1991). *High-Wire Henry*. Illustrated by Erick Ingraham. New York: Morrow. Ages 6–8.

Henry, a Siamese cat, feels threatened by a new cute puppy, so he is anxious to prove himself more clever than the dog in the eyes of those around him. Henry does so in a humorous way, but then he decides to become a high-wire walker. During his act, he has a fall, which embarrasses him and almost makes him totally give up his idea of trying to be clever. When the exploring puppy climbs out on a window ledge, however, Henry, with his high-wire abilities, is the one to rescue him by walking the telephone line and is highly praised—a response that gives Henry a feeling of total satisfaction.

12. Carlstrom, Nancy White (1986). *Jesse Bear, What Will You Wear?* Illustrated by Bruce Degen. New York: Macmillan. Ages 5–6.

Jesse Bear, a cub (dressed in his underpants) puts on his clothes in unusual ways before his day's activities. His day begins when he answers the title question and says, "My shirt of red/ Pulled over my head/ Over my head in the morning." The story follows Jesse through a sunny day with Mom at home as he sees a butterfly and plays in the sandbox and the verses always ask the question, "Jesse Bear, what will you wear?" At noon, Jesse answers that he'll wear pear juice and rice in his hair and in the evening, Jesse says that he will wear "dreams" in his head. Young children will enjoy seeing how he dresses creatively and will laugh along with the rhymes in this story and other stories about the cub:

- *Better Not Get Wet, Jesse Bear* (Macmillan, 1988) has rhythmic words about Jesse's cheery attitude as he plays in the water and puddles.
- *It's about Time, Jesse Bear and Other Rhymes* (Macmillan, 1990) is a series of vignettes that follow the cub through the day. He gets up laughing and feeling fine. He builds with blocks, makes mudpies, and takes his medicine that really makes him sick but he says, "I mean I'm getting better./This medicine is quick." At bedtime, he wants a story before he goes to sleep and says, "One more kiss/And now it's time! Good-night."

13. Cazet, Denys (1994). *Nothing at All*. Illustrated by the author. New York: Orchard Books. Ages 5–6.

In Cazet's story, the barnyard animals react in humorous ways when they are awakened by the rooster who crows through his megaphone. For instance, the cow puts on a flowered shower cap and, still sleepy, turns on the shower to wake up. Seeing all of the animals' reactions, the scarecrow in the meadow wants to know what is going on and repeatedly asks about the animals' confusion. The repetitive response is one for a child to chime in on during a read-aloud time— "Nothing at all!"

14. Christelow, Eileen (1989). *Five Little Monkeys Jumping on the Bed*. New York: Clarion. Ages 5–6.

Humorous drawings show the silly little monkeys best as they get ready for bed and say goodnight to their mother. They jump on the bed and ignore her warning, "No more monkeys jumping on the bed," a repeated refrain. When the predicted accident happens, mother consults the doctor who bandages the wounds. Finally, all five fall asleep and mother can go to bed.

15. Christian, Mary Blount (1986). *Penrod's Pants*. Illustrated by Jane Dyer. New York: Macmillan. Ages 6–8.

Some low-key humor is shown in selected everyday situations with the idea that a reader has more logic than the characters, Penrod Porcupine and his friend, Griswold. For example, Penrod tries to trick Griswold out of the very last cookie at the tea party.

16. de Paola, Tomie (1978). *Bill and Pete*. Illustrated by the author. New York: Putnam. Ages 6–7.

The best of de Paola's humor is found in the surprise ending in this story. In Egypt with pyramids and lotus flowers in the setting, William Evert, a crocodile, meets a bird he nicknames Pete and they become fast friends. Pete enters school with William Evert where together they learn crocodile history, reading, and writing. Life is just fine for the two until a villain captures Bill and decides to turn him into a suitcase. It is Pete's beak, however, that saves the day.

17. de Paola, Tomie (1980). *The Wuggie Norple Story*. Illustrated by the author. New York: Four Winds. Ages 5–8.

De Paola's full-color illustrations add a great deal of punch to the humor in this story about Lunchbox Louis. Louis is convinced that the kitten he brings home for his son, King Waffle, is rapidly growing bigger—bigger than a bulldog, a razorback hog, a horse, and—finally—an elephant. He brings home each of these animals to prove his point, until all finally agree that Wuggie Norple is, indeed, as big as the elephant, and the entire satisfied group troops off to picnic at Nosewort Pond.

18. de Regniers, Beatrice Schenk (1964). *May I Bring a Friend?* Illustrated by Beni Montresor. New York: Atheneum. Ages 5–6.

Several humorous details are found in Montresor's illustrations of a small boy who goes to tea with the king and queen and each time he takes an animal friend. The friends—a giraffe, monkeys, lions, and, hippo—are not very po-lite. For example, the monkey swings on the chandeliers, the hippo puts his foot in the cake, the lions roar, and the seal plays "Long Live Apple Pie" on his bugle. All through the passing guest list of animal activities, the royal rulers keep their calm and patient manner.

19. Dubanevich, Arlene (1986). *Pigs at Christmas*. Illustrated by the author. New York: Bradbury. Ages 5–7.

Much of the humor is shown in the bright color cartoon panels and word balloons about six pigs who are busy with their Christmas preparations. For five of the pigs, everything seems to go right, but for one pig, everything seems to go wrong. He worries that Santa won't bring him a present because he is not "perfect." But, of course, Santa does bring him a special present.

20. Eastman, Philip D. (1958). *Sam and the Firefly*. New York: Random House. Ages 6–7.

Sam, the owl, goes looking for a playmate one night but finds everyone is asleep except a mischievous firefly named Gus. The amusement is in Gus's silliness and the catastrophes he causes. When Sam shows Gus how to write words with his light in the dark sky, Gus goes wild. First, he tries to direct auto traffic and then airplane traffic. Finally, the Hot Dog Man, a victim of one of Gus's tricks, captures him. When the man tries to take Gus out of town, however, his truck becomes stuck on the railroad tracks in front of an oncoming train. Gus, now free, quickly writes the word "stop" in the sky and saves everyone.

21. Ernst, Lisa Campbell (1989). *When Bluebell Sang*. Illustrated by the author. New York: Bradbury. Ages 6–8.

Farmer Swenson finds out that Bluebell, his cow, can sing and he takes her to town so the people can hear her beautiful voice. With a talent agent, Big Eddie, Bluebell becomes a star overnight! Bluebell and Swenson get homesick on the tour and have to outsmart Big Eddie when he wants to extend Bluebell's contract past the last date of the month's concert tour.

22. Geisert, Arthur (1983). *Oink, Oink*. Illustrated by the author. Boston: Houghton Mifflin. Ages 6–7.

Instead of napping, eight piglets sneak away from their dozing mother to play in a cornfield. Finally, they hear the "oink" of their mother's call but they want to play further and retreat to an island. Mother is alert and soon they see their mother swimming down the river toward them. Eventually, she gets the piglets back home for a much needed rest.

23. Goodall, John S. (1975). *Naughty Nancy*. Illustrated by the author. New York: Atheneum. Ages 5–6.

   Nancy, a small mouse, causes a lot of trouble in this book without words. She is in the house, then out the door, and into an automobile and headed for an elegant mouse wedding. She is the flower girl at her sister's wedding with disastrous, although humorous, results. Once there, she goes down the aisle of the church on the bride's train and then up the side of a reception tent. She even becomes an uninvited guest on the honeymoon.

24. Goodall, John S. (1985). *Naughty Nancy Goes to School*. Illustrated by the author. New York: Atheneum. Ages 5–6.

   Mother has to drag Nancy, the mouse, to school. During a day at school, Nancy continues to be naughty—in fact, a terror. Nancy has quick wits and a class visit to the seashore becomes a chance for her to rescue a stranded swimmer and become the heroine of the day. Nancy imitates the teacher behind the teacher's back, and later falls off the roof. During a field trip, Nancy buries the sleeping teacher in the sand. Nancy disrupts a puppet show. Closing her trip with a good deed, Nancy rescues some classmates from an attack by sharks.

25. Goodall, John S. (1983). *Paddy Pork: Odd Jobs*. Illustrated by the author. New York: Atheneum. Ages 5–7.

   Paddy, the very active Edwardian pig, does odd jobs in this book without words. Paddy works a water pump, washes a window, fixes a chimney, and wallpapers a room. Humorously, of course, he makes a mess of each job and runs away and leaves the owner with a mess. To redeem himself, Paddy finds a lost baby. Paddy will appear to have redeemed himself to the young child looking at the book.

26. Goodall, John S. (1984). *Paddy Underwater*. Illustrated by the author. New York: Atheneum. Ages 5–7.

   In Goodall's wordless book, half-pages artfully alternate with full-page watercolors to add to the sense of drama. Paddy Pork's adventure places him in perilous positions. He decides to go skin diving. Captured by an octopus, Paddy frees himself, and is befriended by sea serpents and mermaids who lead him to a sunken ship where he finds a treasure chest. Helped by friendly porpoises, he brings the chest to the surface to the happy amazement of his family. If a child is interested in another wordless adventure of Paddy's, suggest *Paddy to the Rescue* (Atheneum/ McElderry, 1986). In an English seaside setting, Paddy chases a robber rat who has stolen jewels from around the neck of a mistress pig. He chases him over the rooftops and down to the docks where Paddy at last gets the rat. He traps him under an empty barrel and turns him in to Constable Hound.

27. Goodall, John S. (1980). *Paddy's New Hat*. Illustrated by the author. New York: Atheneum. Ages 5–8.

   Paddy Pork, accident-prone, has quite a long adventure in this wordless picture book. Paddy buys a new straw hat and when a sudden wind blows his hat into the police recruiting station, he is signed up. Joining the force, Paddy is given a handsome uniform and tall bobby's helmet. He botches his new duties, however, in a series of misadventures. He makes such a tangle of directing traffic during a royal visit that he has to flee in disgrace. Handcuffed to a burglar twice his size, he ends up face down in a rain barrel. In a last encounter, he becomes a hero when he discovers a theft of royal jewels, foils the robbery in the royal apartment, and is awarded a royally bestowed medal.

28. Gray, Libba Moore (1994). *Small Green Snake*. Illustrated by Holly Meade. New York: Orchard. Ages 5–7.

   Gray's story is told in a rhyming text with lots of alliterative s's and ear-catching phrases that is illustrated with Meade's torn-paper collages. Disobeying his mother, a small green snake wiggles off to explore. He faces several dangers and is finally caught (true to his mother's warning) and put in a glass jar. A curious cat, interested in the small snake in the jar, pokes with its paws and accidentally releases the small snake. When the snake returns home, he interests the members of his family with his enticing tales of adventure and convinces his entire family to join him on his next wiggling outing.

29. Gretz, Susanna (1982). *Teddy Bears Go Shopping*. Illustrated by the author. New York: Four Winds. Ages 5–6.

Gretz's humor is shown in a trip to the grocery store as four bears shop for a homecoming party. When their list is lost, all of them remember the last item and end up with three kinds of ice cream, because "that's what they like best." Young readers who want to see more of the teddy bears can turn to Gretz's *Teddy Bears ABC* (Follett, 1974) where the bears and their dalmatian, Fred, meet some animal passengers traveling to the zoo. They invite the animals home with them for some fun—the giraffe with a sore throat has to gargle, the yak takes a shower, and the kangaroo helps paint a mural.

30. Hartelius, Margaret A. (1977). *The Birthday Trombone*. Illustrated by the author. New York: Doubleday. Ages 6–7.

The fun is shown in the illustrations in this wordless book about a small monkey who plays her birthday trombone and causes mishaps with her terrible tunes: the hippos capsize, an elephant's umbrella breaks down, the zebra falls into her washing, the rhino, giraffe, and lion all collapse. All are relieved when the snake comes to the rescue. The problem of another animal character is shown in another book by Hartelius, *The Chicken's Child* (Doubleday, 1975), as a hen faces danger until she relies on the rapid growth of her child to rescue her.

31. Hass, E. A. (1986). *Incognito Mosquito Takes to the Air*. Illustrated by Don Madden. New York: Random House. Ages 6–8.

Hass's tongue twisters and word play add to the humor in this spoof of the David Letterman show. In the story, Incognito Mosquito, a famous crime stopper, tells about his sleuthing fun and his successes as a private insective.

32. Hayward, Linda (1988). *Hello House!* Illustrated by Lynn Munsinger. New York: Random House. Ages 6–7.

The humor is found both in the illustrations and the text about ways Brer Rabbit plays tricks and fools Brer Wolf. As an example of the lighthearted approach, the small rabbits are called "Little Rabs."

33. Heide, Florence Parry (1994). *The Bigness Contest*. Illustrated by Victoria Chess. Boston: Little, Brown. Ages 5–7.

With a large sense of determination, Beasley is a hippopotamus whose goal is to grow as large as possible. His Aunt Emerald holds a "bigness contest" which he enters. To Beasley's surprise, the contest is won by his huge cousin Borofil. Naturally, Beasley is disappointed until he wins a second contest—for being the laziest of all.

34. Hendrick, Mary Jean (1992). *If Anything Ever Goes Wrong at the Zoo*. Illustrated by Jane Dyer. New York: Harcourt Brace Jovanovich. Ages 5–7.

Hendrick's understated humor is found in the illustrations by Dyer that accompany this story about Leslie who visits the zoo every Saturday. Unknown to her mother, Leslie tells the animal keepers that "if anything goes wrong at the zoo," she will take in the animals. When heavy rains cause flooding at the zoo, the animal keepers surprise Leslie and her mother when they arrive at her house with the animals. Mother agrees to let the animals stay but wants Leslie to ask permission first before inviting friends over "next time."

35. Hoban, Lillian (1981). *Arthur's Funny Money*. Illustrated by the author. New York: Harper and Row. Ages 6–7.

Hoban's humor is focused on the outcome of this story about Arthur, the chimp, and his little sister, Violet. Violet suggests a way for Arthur to earn the money he needs. When Arthur buys five licorice sticks to help Violet with her math, it turns out that he gets one stick and Violet gets four. More comedy about Arthur unfolds through the idea of sibling rivalry in another story, *Arthur's Prize Reader* (Harper and Row, 1978). It seems that Arthur's little sister is the best reader in the first grade—but to hear his side of it, he taught her everything she knows, even the hard words. A child finds out differently as the story is read to its end.

36. Johnson, Angela (1993). *Julius*. Illustrated by Dave Pilkey. New York: Orchard. Ages 5–7.

When Maya's granddaddy brings home a big crate from Alaska, she hopes for a horse (or an older brother), but is happy to welcome a huge, pink Alaskan pig named Julius. Maya's parents are *not* thrilled by the pig's behavior: he makes a mess of the newspapers, leaves crumbs on the sheets, doesn't like to take a bath, and plays records too loudly while he swings Maya around to a jazz tune. However, she knows another side of Julius who sneaks into stores and tries on clothes (he likes white underwear with hearts), spends hours playing at the playground, and protects her from scary "night" things.

37. Kellogg, Steven, reteller (1985). *Chicken Little*. Illustrated by reteller. New York: Morrow. Ages 5–6.

Kellogg's fun is introduced in this contemporary version of the familiar story of "Chicken Little" through Hippo Hefty, a sky-patrol officer. The humorous details in the illustrations add to the comedic version of the-sky-is-falling theme and include some animal characters wearing jogging shorts and running shoes, and others riding in a police car and helicopter.

38. Kellogg, Steven (1981). *Liverwurst Is Missing*. Illustrated by the author. New York: Four Winds. Ages 5–7.

Kellogg's animal romp has a wackiness that includes funny details, exaggerated expressions, and bold colors. When Liverwurst is kidnapped, Farmer Appelard and his animal friends take off in fast pursuit. Liverwurst's gargantuan mother rescues him just in the nick of time and everyone gathers to celebrate.

39. Kent, Jack (1984). *Joey*. Illustrated by the author. New York: Prentice-Hall. Ages 5–7.

Kent's absurdity begins when Joey, a young kangaroo, invites his friends into his mother's pouch to play. As more and more toys are brought into the pouch, the pouch expands and expands until. . . well, what can a reader predict? In the sequel, *Joey Runs Away* (Prentice-Hall, 1985), the amusement is found in Joey's setbacks as he hunts for a house after the young kangaroo runs away from his home in his mother's pouch. Finally, he decides to return home and clean his room.

40. Kessler, Leonard (1982). *Old Turtle's Baseball Stories*. Illustrated by the author. New York: Greenwillow. Ages 6–7.

Kessler's entertainment is in the exaggerations in the tall tales told by Old Turtle. Old Turtle is a narrator who tells tales about baseball for his friends. His tall tale animal heroes turn into baseball greats to the amusement of all who listen to him. His exaggerated animal heroes—Cleo Octopus, Melvin Moose, Carla Kangaroo, Randy Squirrel—use their special characteristics and become the greatest pitcher of all times, the inventor of Mooseball, catcher of fly balls, and a good base stealer.

41. Kraus, Robert (1987). *Come Out and Play, Little Mouse*. Illustrated by Jose Aruego and Ariane Dewey. New York: Greenwillow. Ages 5–6.

Kraus's humor is found in a surprising rescue after a determined cat invites a little mouse to play each day. But on Monday, the little mouse says he must go shopping with his mother; on Tuesday, he helps his father paint the kitchen, and so on through the week. But on Saturday, his little brother agrees to play with the cat. As expected, the cat chases little brother mouse, and just when it seems the mouse is caught, the surprising rescue takes place.

42. Krensky, Stephen (1983). *Perfect Pigs: An Introduction to Manners*. Illustrated by Marc Brown. New York: Joy Street. Ages 5–7.

Krensky's humor is supported by Brown's cartoon-style drawings. The drawings of pigs doing do's and don'ts are related to everything a child needs to know to have good manners. The messages about manners are delivered through the humorous actions of the pigs that help develop an awareness that older people will enjoy being with children more if they have good manners. The messages are divided into subjects in chapters that are focused on the family, the home, school, and other public places. Related to the family and home are "Around the House," "With Your Family," "On the Telephone," "During Meals," "With Pets," and "Giving a Party." Focusing on school and other public places are "At All Times," "With Friends," "At School," "During Games," and "In Public Places."

43. Lobel, Arnold (1971). *Mouse Soup*. Illustrated by the author. New York: Harper and Row. Ages 8–9.

Lobel's humor prevails in this narrative with a Scheherazade twist and a tricky ending. It is a frame tale—stories within a story—about a captive mouse who tells four stories in the main tale to keep himself out of the soup—from being dinner's main course.

44. London, Jonathan (1993). *Hip Cat*. Illustrated by Woodleigh Hubbard. San Francisco: Chronicle Books. Ages 5–8.

In London's story, the amusement of the story is strengthened by the upbeat style in Hubbard's illustrations. Oobie-do John, a feline musician from the country goes to the city to find his fame and fortune by playing the saxophone. To earn a living, he is a short-order cook at the Doggie Diner and plays his sax for pennies at the town's tourist places. Eventually, his music becomes known along with other jazz musicians and he finally becomes the "coolest cat" of all.

45. Lorenz, Lee (1985). *A Weekend in the Country*. Illustrated by the author. New York: Prentice-Hall. Ages 5–7.

   In Lorenz's story, there is a theme of the "grass-is-always-greener-on-the-other-side." Pig and Duck imagine that they can escape the heat of the city by visiting their friend the moose in the country. The two, however, begin speculating about the possible difficulties of the trip. Young readers should enjoy the entertaining dialogue and accompanying humorous cartoon-type illustrations.

46. McLeod, Emilie Warren (1975). *The Bear's Bicycle*. Illustrated by David McPhail. New York: Atlantic/Little, Brown. Ages 5–6.

   Much of the amusement in McLeod's story is in McPhail's colorful pictures of a small boy's teddy bear who becomes real—a huge brown bear—and takes on the hazardous consequences of ignoring bicycle safety rules. The small boy obeys the rules when he rides his bike, but the bear does not. The contrast in bike safety is shown in side-by-side illustrations. For example, the boy says "When I go down a hill, I don't go too fast" and the next illustration shows the bear with a silly expression, not only going down a hill fast, but getting additional momentum by using his bike as a scooter and pushing with one foot to get more speed. A double-page spread shows the changes in the bear's expression over the consequences—the bear can't stop and goes through a stop sign, lands on his backside, and finally is on his back with only the handlebars in his paws. A final scene shows the boy having milk and cookies with his bear—now shown as a teddy with a band-aid on his head.

47. McPhail, David (1993). *Pigs Aplenty, Pigs Galore!* Illustrated by the author. New York: Dutton. Ages 5–6.

   As a man reads quietly in his home, portly pigs arrive for a party in a wide variety of vehicles. They are dressed as cowboys, kings, queens, a rock and roll band, and other personalities. They slurp, burp, and crunch and eventually the man commands the party pigs to clean up. When the noise quiets down, the man falls asleep and dreams about counting pigs.

48. Marshall, Edward (1982). *Fox in Love*. Illustrated by James Marshall. New York: Dial. Ages 6–7.

Marshall's humor is shown in three stories where the characters share the ups-and-downs of friendship. Fox reluctantly takes his sister Louise to the park but perks up when he meets a pretty white fox, Raisin. Complications arise, however, when Fox has a photo session and tries to enter the big dance contest.

49. Marshall, James (1980). *George and Martha Tons of Fun*. Illustrated by the author. Boston: Houghton Mifflin. Ages 5–6.

   Created by Marshall, the funniest hippos ever are George and Martha, true friends. They star in five brief stories about the ways their friendship persists in spite of gluttony, conceit, and carelessness. The titles offer clues to what happens—"Misunderstanding," "The Sweet Tooth," "The Photograph," "The Hypnotist," and "The Special Gift." Young readers interested in following the adventures of the two hippos further can turn to *George and Martha One Fine Day* (Houghton Mifflin, 1978) for more jokes about the hippos and their days that are filled with tightrope walking, stamp collecting, playing practical jokes, and visiting amusement parks.

50. Marshall, James, reteller (1987). *Red Riding Hood*. Illustrated by the reteller. New York: Dial. Ages 5–8.

   Marshall's deadpan humor and vernacular language are included in this familiar tale. Mother tells Red: "Granny isn't feeling up to snuff today so I baked her her favorite custard." Warned not to talk to strangers, Red starts out on her short trip and *does not* wander off to pick flowers by herself but instead flings herself on a tall sunflower plant in order to pick the largest bouquet for Granny. She eventually meets the wolf who is a charmer. He offers to escort her to Granny's house and she accepts. At the house, Granny is a reader and is angry with the wolf for interrupting her reading—and the wolf still eats her up. After his meal and dessert, the wolf (Red) sits in a large comfortable chair, pats his stomach and says: "I'm so wicked . . . so wicked." It seems that Red has learned a lesson since the text reads: "Red Riding Hood promised never ever to speak to another stranger, charming manners or not." However, there is a double ending when the page is turned to see Red rejecting the advances of a charming looking crocodile.

51. Marshall, James (1986). *Wings: A Tale of Two Chickens*. Illustrated by the author. New York: Viking Kestrel. Ages 5–7.

Harriet loves to read but Winnie would rather swat flies. So Winnie is the foolish chicken who gets taken for a balloon ride by a hungry fox. In the end, it is Winnie who is put to bed with a good book about foxes in order to develop her survival skills.

52. Mayer, Mercer (1977). *Oops*. Illustrated by the author. New York: Dial. Ages 5–8.

Mayer's humor is in anticipating the impending catastrophe that makes the fun about Mrs. Hippo on a trip to the city. In this wordless book, the large hippo ends up causing disaster for everyone she meets. As she innocently makes her way from a china shop to a museum, she leaves a trail of destruction behind her.

53. Miles, Miska (1978). *Mouse Six and the Happy Birthday*. Illustrated by Leslie Morrill. New York: Unicorn/Dutton. Ages 6–7.

Miles's humor in the story, backed up by Morrill's illustrations, evolves as Mouse Six goes off to find a birthday present for his mother. He tells no one what he is up to do and the rumor spreads that he has run away from home. When his animal friends visit his parents to cheer them up, they provide an unexpected birthday party for Mother Mouse.

54. Muntean, Michaela (1983). *Bicycle Bear*. Illustrated by Doug Cushman. New York: Parents' Magazine Press. Ages 7–8.

Most of Muntean's humor is in the accumulation of the objects in this tale as they become larger and larger each time Bicycle Bear delivers something. This makes the story become more outrageous with each delivery in each of Cushman's illustrations. First, the bear delivers something small—green pickles; then something larger—a suitcase filled with shoes; and eventually—a moose. It ends with Bicycle Bear trying to figure out how to deliver a whale.

55. Newman, Nanette (1994). *There's a Bear in the Bath!* Illustrated by Michael Foreman. New York: Harcourt Brace Jovanovich. Ages 5–8.

Newman's tale, illustrated by Foreman, has lots of silliness that begins when Jam, a roly-poly brown bear, arrives in the garden to visit Lisa, a small girl. Lisa invites Jam inside the house where Jam drinks coffee (and shampoo), dances the tango, solves a crossword puzzle, and takes a bath. Later in her real world, Lisa turns to her homework—the task of writing about her day—and realizes that if she writes about Jam's visit no one will believe the silliness.

56. Numeroff, Laura Joffe (1991). *If You Give a Moose a Muffin*. Illustrated by Felicia Bond. New York: HarperCollins. Ages 5–6.

This is Numeroff's circular story about a child who makes the mistake of giving a moose a muffin. Now, since the moose has a muffin, he is going to want something else, and makes numerous requests. (The child always gives the moose what he wants.) As the chain of events continue, the moose eventually makes puppets for a puppet show. The story circle is completed in a style similar to *If You Give a Mouse a Cookie*.

57. Numeroff, Laura Joffe (1988). *If You Give a Mouse a Cookie*. Illustrated by Felicia Bond. New York: HarperCollins. Ages 5–6.

This is another circular story of what happens when a boy makes the mistake of giving an energetic mouse a cookie. The humor is in the antics—since the mouse has a cookie, he is going to want some milk. (The boy gives him a glass of milk.) When the mouse is finished, he'll ask for a napkin to wipe his mouth and he'll want to look in the mirror to see that he does not have a milk moustache. (The boy gets a napkin and holds the mouse up to the bathroom mirror so the mouse can see himself.) As the chain of events keep going, the house is a mess—the mouse trims his hair, washes the floors, draws pictures and puts them on the refrigerator. Eventually, the story circle is almost complete when the mouse, now near the refrigerator and thirsty, asks for a glass of milk. And of course, since the mouse has a glass of milk, he is going to want a cookie to go with it.

58. Oppenheimer, Joanne (1986). *You Can't Catch Me!* Illustrated by Andrew Schachat. Boston: Houghton Mifflin. Ages 5–7.

Oppenheimer's fun is in the lively verses that are similar to the rhythm of "The Gingerbread Boy," "The Three Little Pigs," and "This is the House That Jack Built." Schachat's illustrations help tell the story of an arrogant fly who uses a small boy's refrain as he teases first a cow, then a goat who lowers his head and says: "I swear by the hair of my chinny chin chin, I'll catch you, fly, and do you in!" and a horse all dappled and gray. After annoying a fox, a bear, a pig, it is the turtle, finally, who gives the fly a come-uppance as a final surprise.

59. Pomerantz, Charlotte (1989). *The Piggy in the Puddle*. Illustrated by James Marshall. New York: Aladdin. Ages 5–6.

Pomerantz's humor is in the silliness of a little pig's situation. Holding a balloon, a young pig is dressed in clothes and bonnet, and is sitting happily in the middle of a mud puddle. The words announce, "See the piggy. See the puddle. See the muddy little puddle. See her dawdle, see her diddle, in the muddy, muddy middle. See her waddle, plump and little, in the very merry middle." In turn, her father, mother, and brother come along and urge her to use soap and wash up. In the end, the whole family plays merrily in the mud.

60. Preston, Edna Mitchell (1978). *Where Did My Mother Go?* Illustrated by Chris Conover. New York: Four Winds. Ages 5–6.

There are humorous details in Conover's illustrations—especially the details on the map that shows Gojumpina Lake and Bow-Wow Boulevard—the site of Little Cat's adventure. Little Cat tricycles off to town to look for his mother. He somehow always fails to see her tail as she leaves the shops or see her back as she browses in the library, but a young child will enjoy being in on the joke of it all.

61. Rayner, Mary (1987). *Mrs. Pig Gets Cross: And Other Stories*. Illustrated by the author. New York: Dutton. Ages 7–8.

A great deal of Rayner's fun is found in the adventures of the ten childlike siblings in this pig family. Most children enjoy the story where the pigs use reverse psychology on a contrary Benjamin Pig. In another story, Mr. and Mrs. Pig try to sleep after all ten piglets squeeze into their bed. In still other adventures, the boys play against the girls in different events on sports day, Garth Pig's siblings save him from Mrs. wolf (who has crashed their parents' party) and Benjamin (the contrary one) and Alan try to help with the gardening.

62. Remkiewicz, Frank (1994). *The Bone Stranger*. Illustrated by the author. New York: Lothrop, Lee & Shepard. Ages 7–8.

Remkiewicz's story is a parody of *The Lone Ranger* that includes jump ropes for lassos and salamis for weapons. Shown in cartoon-style illustrations of the old Wild West, Boney, a canine business owner, runs a delicatessen where he serves salamis and bagels, and his faithful companion is not Tonto but a wolf named Wolfgang. After two thieving raccoons steal a strongbox full of doggie bones intended for the orphans of the town, Boney and Wolfgang set out to get it back.

63. Sadler, Marilyn (1986). *P.J. the Spoiled Bunny*. Illustrated by Roger Bollen. New York: Random House. Ages 5–7.

Most of the enjoyment is in Bollen's cartoon-style illustrations about P. J., a spoiled little rabbit. For instance, P. J. has always insisted on blowing out the birthday candles at others' birthday parties, insisted on having his favorite pieces—the red ones—in checkers, and insisted on playing the game *he* chooses. By the end of Sadler's story, the child sees the reform of this self-centered rabbit through several humorous events.

64. Schindel, John (1994). *What's for Lunch?* Illustrated by Kevin O'Malley. New York: Lothrop, Lee & Shepard. Ages 5–7.

This is Schindel's humorous accumulating tale of Sidney, a cocky little mouse, shown in O'Malley's colorful double-page illustrations. Sidney is threatened by a cat who says he will eat him, but Sidney, cool-headed and knowing he has a lunch date with a friend, replies, "I don't think so." The cat is surprised when a dog rushes in to give chase; the dog is surprised when a goose comes in to bite him; and so on. The animals vary in size until finally, Sidney's lunch-date, Shirley, arrives just in time to scare away the last animal—a very large elephant.

65. Sharmat, Majorie Weinman (1994). *Genghis Khan: A Dog Star Is Born*. Illustrated by Mitchell Regie. New York: Random House. Ages 5–8.

Sharmat's humor is supported by Regie's black-and-white drawings that center on the canine Duz Shedd, the look-alike replacement for a retiring dog star, Genghis Khan. Arriving in Hollywood, Duz and his human family are housed in an elegant mansion suitable for a star and all seems fine when Duz is scheduled to begin his part in the next movie, *Genghis Khan: The Challenge*. An unsettling note arrives, however, and Duz reads that his contract will soon be invalid when his real owner arrives to claim him. All are shocked when soon after, Duz disappears. The culprit is finally caught—it's a cat owner who wants to replace Duz in the movie with her feline.

66. Shaw, Nancy (1994). *Sheep Take a Hike*. Illustrated by Margot Apple. Boston: Houghton Mifflin. Ages 5–7.

The humor is in both Shaw's rolling rhythmic narrative and in seeing the silly sheep in Apple's illustrations. The sheep go exploring and lose their way. Confused, they wander (sheepishly) around in various settings—the dense fog, a wet swamp, and some brambly undergrowth. By the end of the story, they get serious and decide to find the trail again by following the "wooly fuzz they left behind."

67. Stadler, John (1979). *Cat at Bat*. Illustrated by the author. New York: Dutton. Ages 6–8.

Much of the delight is in the actions of the animals—such as a cat playing baseball—in Stadler's humorous assortment. There is a short, easy text that tells the improbable adventures of several unlikely animals engaged in humanlike behavior—a feline playing ball, mice on ice, a crocodile who runs a mile, and a sheep deep in sleep.

68. Stevens, Janet, reteller, (1984). *The Tortoise and the Hare*. Illustrated by the author. New York: Holiday. Ages 6–7.

The giggles will probably start with Stevens's illustrations when young children see the tortoise in a turtleneck sweater and sneakers. This is a contemporary version of the familiar fable, "The Tortoise and the Hare," where the tortoise's enduring effort still wins the race. For a child interested in this race, pair this one with another enjoyable version, *Harry and Shelburt* (Macmillan, 1977) by Dorothy O. Van Woerkom. Shelburt, the tortoise, shares his dinner with his good friend, Harry, the hare. Harry tells him that once, because of a certain race, hares didn't like tortoises at all. An ensuing challenge is given and ends in a different new twist for this old fable.

69. Temple, Frances, reteller (1994). *Tiger Soup*. Illustrated by the reteller. New York: Orchard Books/Richard Jackson. Ages 5–7.

This is Temple's telling of Anansi, a clever, skilled trickster who fools Tiger. In this Jamaican tale, Tiger fixes a sweet soup for himself, but Anansi distracts him from eating it, insisting that they go swimming together first. Tiger gets into the water, but Anansi sneaks off to eat the soup. Then, fearing the Tiger's revenge, he teaches some nearby monkeys a song about eating the soup. He disappears into the woods after encouraging the monkeys to sing the song loudly. Tiger wants revenge but the monkeys escape into the treetops and Anansi escapes, too.

70. Tompert, Ann (1979). *Three Foolish Tales*. Illustrated by Diane Dawson. New York: Crown. Ages 5–7.

Tompert's humor in the stories is also shown in Dawson's illustrations of actions of the clever and crafty fox who uses his wily ways to get the best of the situation. Raccoon and Skunk want Fox's lovely purple umbrella, and when they fail to steal the umbrella, they devise a contest telling tales and ask Fox to be the judge. Here's their idea: *whoever tells the finest tale about someone foolish will be the winner and Fox's umbrella will be the prize.* The fox agrees. First, Raccoon's tale is about a beaver who tries to make his dark and dreary new home bright by catching sunlight and moonlight, and finally by building so many windows that the house collapses. Next, Skunk's tale is about a fat and foolish rabbit who gets into trouble when his overstuffed body won't fit through the hole in the garden wall. When Fox declares that both stories are fine tales and both deserve a prize, he sets off for the fair to get another umbrella. Only after a very long wait do Raccoon and Skunk realize that they have been tricked and are the biggest fools of all.

71. Waber, Bernard (1994). *Lyle at the Office*. Illustrated by the author. Boston: Houghton Mifflin. Ages 5–7.

Lyle, the crocodile (and Lyle's mother), enter the world of work and Lyle reports to Mr. Primm's office in an advertising agency. Lyle makes new friends as he delivers memos, sharpens pencils on his rounds, notices the company's children's care center, and even catches the attention of the boss, Mr. Bigg, when Lyle enjoys some cereal—Krispie Krunchie Krackles. Mr. Bigg wants Lyle to pose in an ad for the Krackles and be the cereal's croc-rep. Mr. Primm steps in, refuses to let Lyle pose, and is fired. It is only after Lyle responds to a cry for help from a seemingly empty house and rescues Mr. Bigg from a light fixture in the ceiling that there is a happy ending—Mr. Primm is asked to come back to the office.

72. West, Colin (1986). *Have You Seen the Crocodile?* Illustrated by the author. New York: Harper and Row. Ages 5–7.

Most of West's humor is seen in the illustrations that show a unique set of green bumps on the right edge of each page in a setting of cattails, lily pads, and other vegetation in and around a pond. In this tale, bumble bee, butterfly, dragonfly, frog, hummingbird, and parrot in turn ask the question,"Have you seen the crocodile?" As each one asks the question, a few more green bumps emerge on successive illustrations, until all the creatures blissfully are sitting unaware upon or hovering above the crocodile innocently saying, "No one's seen the crocodile!" But on the next page, the crocodile snaps, "I've seen the crocodile!" and the animals quickly scatter. The last page shows a grinning crocodile alone in the pond. There is a similarity between the grinning crocodile in this story and the sly-looking crocodile in *The Elephant's Child* by Kipling.

73. West, Colin (1986). *"Pardon" said the Giraffe*. Illustrated by the author. New York: Harper and Row. Ages 5–7.

    West's story brings the young reader into the joke of the plot and offers bright colors, a patterned text, and a predictable story line. Hopping on the ground, the curious frog asks the proud lion, "What's it like up there?" The lion responds with, "Pardon?" Time after time, the frog hops upon other animals—the hippo, then the elephant, and finally the giraffe. Each time the frog asks the same question, a question that the child can predict and repeat in the reading. The surprise for the child comes when the giraffe sneezes. The frog tumbles to the ground. This time it is the giraffe who asks the question and it becomes "What's it like down there?"

74. Williams, Jay (1977). *Pettifur*. Illustrated by Hilary Knight. New York: Four Winds. Ages 6–7.

    Here is some fun from Williams and Knight for young children in a story about Pettifur, an excellent mouse catcher. He is so good, in fact, that there are no more mice in his house to catch. Subsequently, he spends his time indulging in a favorite pastime, eating, until he gets so fat that he cannot chase mice when they reappear. Pettifur decides to go on a diet and he leaves all his food for the mice. In turn, the mice get so fat that they decide to leave and move someplace else.

75. Wiseman, Bernard (1978). *Morris Has a Cold*. Illustrated by the author. New York: Dodd. Ages 6–8.

    Wiseman has included both verbal and visual jokes in this story. For example, Morris the moose has a cold but says that he has a walking (*not running*) nose. He refuses to have his fore-

head felt because he insists that he has just *one* head not *four*. He is fortunate to have Boris the bear for a friend, for Boris forgives Morris's *faux pas* (*to say nothing of four hoofs*). If desired, suggest some companion reading with Wiseman's *Morris and Boris* (Dodd, 1974), three silly stories with more slapstick humor about Morris the moose and Boris the bear. In one story, Boris tries to interest Morris in telling riddles but Morris frustrates Boris and Boris goes off angrily. In another, Boris tries to teach Morris a tongue twister and ends up in total confusion. In the third, Boris tries to teach Morris to play hide-and-seek, which turns out to be a disaster, too.

76. Wood, Audrey, and Don Wood (1990). *The Little Mouse, the Red Ripe Strawberry, and the Big Hungry Bear*. Illustrated by Don Wood. New York: Childs Play. Ages 5–6.

    After a mouse harvests a strawberry as big as he is, he discovers that there is a big hungry bear who will do anything to get it. The mouse has a problem—it is going to be difficult to hide the big strawberry in a good place in his small world. The humor is in the antics the mouse goes through to keep the bear from getting the berry.

77. Yolen, Jane (1980). *Mice on Ice*. Illustrated by Laurence DiFiori. New York: E. P. Dutton. Ages 7–8.

    The "Mice on Ice" show has a star who is kidnapped and the formula for making ice is demanded as a ransom. Using mouse energy and ingenuity, Horace and Little Ruby find the kidnappers, rescue the star of the ice show, and toss the crooks in jail. Yolen's story has eye-catching illustrations by DiFiori that emphasize the fun in the easy-to-read text.

78. Yolen, Jane (1987). *The Three Bears Rhyme Book*. Illustrated by Jane Dyer. New York: Harcourt Brace Jovanovich. Ages 6–7.

    Yolen has written poetic rhymes about the Three Bears and Goldilocks. The words, along with Dyer's illustrations, bring the characters to life to highlight "Poppa Bear's Hum," "Bears Chairs," "Three Bears Walking," and other aspects of the bears and their visitor. There is gentle humor and satisfaction in the repetition of the words.

Family, School, and Community

79. Allard, Harry, and James Marshall (1985). *Miss Nelson Has a Field Day.* Illustrated by James Marshall. Boston: Houghton Mifflin. Ages 7–8.

The main amusement by Allard and Marshall is in the spoof on school sports and on school in general—the caricatured mouths of the cafeteria ladies show they have lost their get-up-and-go, the illustrations of the football players are a definite spoof, and the full-length view of Coach Viola Swamp shows her appropriately in charge. In this story, Miss Nelson, one of the most popular teachers in school (who was introduced in *Miss Nelson Is Missing* [Houghton Mifflin, 1977]), tackles the genesis of the school's unhappiness—the Smedley Tornadoes, the school's pitiful, pathetic football team. When the coach has to go home for a nice long rest, the students agree they need Viola Swamp, the meanest substitute in the whole wide world, to come back and whip the team into shape. The principal tries to pass himself off as Miss Swamp but that doesn't work. When Miss Swamp finally appears, she's in an ugly black sweat suit printed with the words "Coach and don't you forget it." Some children will recall Miss Nelson was replaced by Miss Viola Swamp, a substitute teacher dressed in a dark black dress, who announced lots of rules and homework in *Miss Nelson Is Missing.*

80. Allard, Harry, and James Marshall (1977). *Miss Nelson Is Missing.* Illustrated by James Marshall. Boston: Houghton Mifflin. Ages 7–8.

Miss Nelson, a sweet young teacher, cannot make the students in her class behave. One day, she is replaced by a substitute teacher, Miss Viola Swamp, who wears an ugly black dress and the children think she is a witch. Miss Swamp has rules, gives homework, and after five days the children are glad to see Miss Nelson return. A final scene shows Miss Nelson at home and she takes off her coat and hangs it next to a dark black dress.

81. Arnold, Tedd (1987). *No Jumping on the Bed!* Illustrated by the author. New York: Dial. Ages 5–8.

Walter, a small boy, lives near the top floor in a tall apartment house in the inner city. He has a nightly habit of jumping on his bed even when his father tells him he'll be in trouble. One night, when he comes down with a mighty jump, the bed crashes through the floor to start an exciting nighttime free fall as he falls past some of the other people in the apartment building. In his descent, Walter lands directly in Miss Hattie's dining room, then falls into Mr. Matty's TV room, sends Aunt Batty's stamp collection in all directions, and then bumps into Patty and Natty's house of blocks. When Walter reaches the basement, it is dark and quiet. After opening his eyes, he finds himself back in his own bed with the lights out and promises to do "no more jumping on the bed."

82. Aylesworth, Jim (1980). *Hush Up!* Illustrated by Glen Rounds. New York: Holt, Rinehart and Winston. Ages 7–8.

Aylesworth's comical tale is embellished by Rounds's pen-and-ink sketches. One hot, lazy day, Jasper Walker tilted his chair back, propped up his feet, and snoozed. The barnyard animals decide to nap too. However, there is a chain reaction of incredible slapstick events that begin when a huge horsefly bites the nose of a sleeping mule who reacts in a hurry.

83. Aylesworth, Jim (1985). *Shenandoah Noah.* Illustrated by Glen Rounds. New York: Holt, Rinehart and Winston. Ages 5–8.

Aylesworth has subtle humor in this tall tale. Rounds's line drawings are in rustic brown and emphasize many of the subtleties in this exaggerated story—there is the sad-faced house, Noah's long johns drying on the bush, and the scene of Noah peeking out from under the bearskin rug. Work was something Shenandoah Noah didn't care for—his kin knew that—and when they saw smoke from Noah's place, his nephew Johnny went to check on what was going on at Noah's. And that started a chain of events that led to the humorous finale which put a hole in Noah's roof. To this day, Noah still hasn't fixed the hole in his roof because fixing the roof means work and his kin know that work is something that Noah just doesn't care for.

84. Berry, Holly, reteller (1994). *Old MacDonald Had a Farm*. Illustrated by the reteller. New York: North-South Books. Ages 6–8.

In Berry's version, Farmer MacDonald brings in the crops and calls the animals together for a harvest celebration. Each animal is named in turn in the verses of the song and MacDonald gives it a musical instrument to play at the hoedown in the barn—a jumping musical jamboree that shakes the rafters. Other humorous versions of this familiar song are found in the interpretations by Tracey Campbell Pearson (Dial, 1984) and Glen Rounds (Holiday House, 1989). Both include the familiar verses about Mr. and Mrs. MacDonald and their large group of farm animals. Most of the amusement is in the comical exploits seen in the illustrations of the two books.

85. Berson, Harold (1982). *Barrels to the Moon*. Illustrated by the author. New York: Coward. Ages 6–7.

Berson offers a humorous idea to capture the moon that turns into fun reading for a young child. Because the townspeople enjoy looking at the moon, they decide to hook it to their local church steeple, a decision that turns into a hilarious situation. Comparing what is happening in the story to what can really happen makes this a favorite for a know-it-all young reader.

86. Bird, Malcom (1981). *The Sticky Child*. Illustrated by author. San Diego: Harcourt Brace Jovanovich. Ages 6–7.

Bird has created a wordless book that shows some "sticky" child situations. The antics begin between a child and the babysitter when the sitter comes to "live-in" while the parents are on vacation. The babysitter tries to figure out a sticky solution of her own to bring order into the household.

87. Bonsall, Crosby (1974). *And I Mean It, Stanley*. New York: Harper & Row. Ages 6–7.

A little girl builds the very best thing "I ever made," but all the while tells Stanley not to look and to stay on the other side of the fence. Stanley pays attention only long enough for the thing to be completed and then crashes through the fence and bounds to the thing. The little girl is not angry because Stanley is an enormous, loveable mutt. Told through both the pictures and print, Bonsall's story will bring smiles to

young children, especially dog lovers. Bonsall's *The Amazing Incredible Super Dog* (Harper & Row, 1986) is another "little girl and her dog" story where the girl gets excited about the tricks her super dog can do.

88. Bunting, Eve (1980). *The Skate Patrol*. Illustrated by Don Madden. Chicago: Albert Whitman. Ages 7 and up.

The amusement is in the clever entertainment that is woven into Bunting's mystery. In the hopes that Mrs. Crump and their other neighbors would be grateful and allow the boys to roller skate in the neighborhood again, two friends decide to capture a local thief. James and Milton even know who the thief is and think they only have to capture the mysterious man (who sits daily in the park) in the act of stealing to prove that they are correct. They watch him continuously. Then the day comes when they hear Mrs. Crump scream that her purse has been snatched. The boys go after the mysterious man on their skates who declares that he is an undercover policeman. Off they skate again and this time they catch the right person and are rewarded just the way they had hoped. Mrs. Crump promises that the boys will be allowed to roller skate any time they wished.

89. Carlstrom, Nancy White (1994). *What Would You Do If You Lived at the Zoo?* Illustrated by Lizi Boyd. New York: Little, Brown. Ages 6–7.

Carlstrom includes silly animal sounds from the zoo in this one—"I would romp with the tiger/ Toogooliwa Toogooliwa/ And chomp with the ape/ Smack Smack!" The response is an answer to the title question about animals that continues with, "Would you romp with the tiger?/ And chomp with the ape?" There are also peek-holes in the pages to enable young readers to anticipate "which animal is next?" in Boyd's bright illustrations.

90. Chapman, Carol (1977). *Barney Bupple's Magic Dandelions*. Illustrated by Steven Kellogg. New York: E. P. Dutton. Ages 7–8.

When this story is read, most of the smiles will come from Kellogg's humorous illustrations. Six-year-old Barney Bupple is full of ideas about things he would like to change. His neighbor, Miss Minerva Merkle, has a lawn covered with magic dandelions that grant wishes to those who know their secret. Barney's adventures, courtesy of the magic flowers, provide some surprises for the young boy.

91. Christelow, Eileen (1985). *Jerome the Babysitter*. Illustrated by the author. New York: Clarion. Ages 6–7.

Christelow includes colorful, cartoonlike illustrations that provide most of the entertainment. When Jerome needs money, his sister gives him a babysitting job that nobody else wants—babysitting Mrs. Gatorman's "Little Angels." Many young readers will laugh out loud when they see the little pranks of the angels and they will enjoy Jerome's creative solution.

92. Cleary, Beverly (1981). *Ramona Quimby, Age 8*. Illustrated by Alan Tiegreen. New York: Morrow. Ages 7–8.

Ramona begins third grade in a new school and becomes famous for her statement "I can't believe I read the whole thing," a word play on a line in a TV commercial in real life in the 1980s. She adds the line after she gives her book report in the format of a television commercial. She is determined to help her family, which is struggling on one and a half paychecks. In humorous ways, the everyday occurrences are never so bad that they can't be made right by a Sunday dinner at the Whopperburger. A young child who wants more episodes about Ramona can select Cleary's *Ramona the Pest* (Morrow, 1968), a story where Ramona waits for kindergarten to begin so she can show others "Chevrolet," her doll with green hair. It seems the doll's hair turned green when it was washed with soap and Dutch Cleanser.

93. Dahl, Roald (1961). *James and the Giant Peach*. New York: Knopf. Ages 8 and up.

The amusement offered by Dahl is mainly in a "What if?" situation, a few absurdities, and some exaggerations—such as giant insects. James, an unhappy child, changes his attitude when a peach grows large enough for him to enter. With the peach as transportation, James makes his getaway by floating through the air over the countryside. He rides inside the giant fruit and is propelled by hundreds of seagulls.

94. Dobrin, Arnold (1973). *Jillions of Gerbils*. New York: Lothrop, Lee and Shepard. Ages 9–10.

Right after his family moved into a big and very old house, David (a somewhat old-fashioned character from the 1970s) realizes that his gerbil has disappeared. Before long, the replacement gerbil disappears too. The house was very old and did have strange creakings. Could there also have been secret hiding places for ghosts? Determined to find out, Davis searched the entire house until he found a secret room. In that room, he found his two gerbils with their new family—the beginnings of David's millions and billions and jillions of gerbils.

95. Fox, Mem (1989). *Night Noises*. Illustrated by Terry Denton. New York: Harcourt Brace Jovanovich. Ages 6–7.

The humor from Fox and Denton comes from the unexpected surprise in the ending. Grandmother hears some frightening night noises that turn out to be pleasant ones instead of scary ones. She discovers that the noises are caused by family members who are coming to give a surprise birthday party for her.

96. Hague, Kathleen, and Michael Hague (1981). *The Man Who Kept House*. Illustrated by Michael Hague. New York: Harcourt Brace Jovanovich. Ages 6–7.

Absurd situations provide the humor in this version of the familiar folk tale, *The Man Who Kept House*. One comical event after another happens when a husband tries to prove that his wife's housework is easier than his own farm chores. After they exchange jobs, the baby tosses oatmeal on the ceiling, the clean laundry is soiled, the goat gets into the house and creates chaos, and the husband almost inadvertently hangs himself and the cow.

97. Johnston, Tony (1986). *Farmer Mack Measures His Pig*. Illustrated by Megan Lloyd. New York: Harper & Row. Ages 6–8.

Johnston's humor is in a crazy contest over the fattest pig. Farmer Mack and Farmer Tubb argue over who has the fattest pig. Goldie, Farmer Mack's Pig, won't cooperate with being measured. Running away, the pig leads the farmer on a hilarious, wild chase. Lloyd's illustrations are quite expressive and play up the fun of the whole idea.

98. Jukes, Mavis (1984). *Like Jake and Me*. Illustrated by Lloyd Bloom. New York: Knopf. Ages 6–8.

Most of the amusement in Jukes's book lies in the hilarity of the antics even though the story deals with a problem common to some children—a strained relationship with a stepparent. Alex's new red-headed stepfather and former rodeo cowboy, Jake, seems to shun Alex (even though his small stepson likes wearing his small-size cowboy boots) and refuses to let Alex help with some of the household chores. A large hairy spider, however, helps turn things around when he crawls into Jake's clothes. It leads Alex and Jake on a humorous frantic search for the critter right down to Jake's underwear. The two become closer together in this "story within a story" about bonding as Jake finds out that though his stepson is small, Alex can be a great help, and Alex discovers that a big strong bearded man like his stepfather can be afraid too.

99. Kline, Suzy (1985). *Herbie Jones*. Illustrated by Richard Williams. New York: Putnam. Ages 7–8.

This is a funny and exciting mainly-at-school adventure. It is about the school experiences of Herbie Jones, a third grader who is anything but a star student. He goes through third grade with his best friend, Raymond. His experiences continue in Kline's *Herbie Jones and the Monster Ball* (Putnam, 1988) where Herbie and Raymond plan to spend the summer fishing after finishing third grade. Herbie dislikes baseball until his Uncle Dwight comes to town and coaches the team for eight- and nine-year-old boys *and* girls. Herbie and Raymond learn to like baseball—Herbie even has lessons from his older sister. They also reach the conclusion that Uncle Dwight is marrying their teacher, Miss Pinkham—an idea that becomes horrifying to the boys.

100. Kuskin, Karla (1986). *The Dallas Titans Get Ready for Bed*. Illustrated by Marc Simont. New York: Harper and Row. Ages 5–8.

In this humorous presentation, the author-artist team that portrayed the musicians preparing for a concert in *The Philharmonic Gets Dressed* (Harper, 1982) have turned to a far different setting. Simont's illustrations exaggerate the huge athletes just enough to be humorous. Kuskin's text tells about the rough actions of a profootball locker room after a game. The language—especially when the players step out of their jockstraps and into the showers—has a rolling rhythm: "They look like small wet whales." For a child who is interested in joining a pro's football team one day, there are facts about the equipment—face masks, hip pads, and shoes whose "soles are studded with mud between the studs."

101. Lancome, Julie (1994). *I'm a Jolly Farmer*. Illustrated by the author. New York: Candlewick. Ages 5–6.

Lancome's story is an "it's fun to imagine" story. A little girl pretends to be many different personas and enlists the help of her favorite playmate, her dog Fred. She harnesses Fred to a chair with a blanket and becomes a jolly farmer guiding the reins of the "horse." She places a doll on Fred's back and the dog is transformed into an elephant with a princess on his back. She becomes a wildlife ranger and keeps an eye on the dog when Fred decides to lay down and sleep. Fred becomes a resting lion. She becomes Little Red Riding Hood and Fred becomes the wolf disguised as Granny. Appropriately, Fred shows his teeth and the little girl decides she'll return "home" and play with something less scary—Fred, the dog, as himself.

102. Lawler, Ann (1977). *The Substitute*. Illustrated by Nancy Winslow Parker. New York: Parents. Ages 6–7.

Lawler's humor is in the fantasy in a school setting. An eccentric substitute teacher urges the class to dance like a series of animals while she plays the piano. A young child will enjoy Parker's pictures of student-animals as they dance around their classroom.

103. Levine, Evan (1991). *Not the Piano, Mrs. Medley*. Illustrated by S. D. Schindler. New York: Richard Jackson/Orchard. Ages 5–7.

Mrs. Medley, her grandson, Max, and her dog, Word, go to the beach for the day. Leaving home, she returns for other things she says are needed: first, an umbrella, a game of Monopoly, some folding chairs and table, drums, accordion, and more. Max begins to wonder if they will ever get to the beach. When they arrive, the unexpected ending is humorous and pleasing.

104. Levine, Evan (1994). *What's Black and White and Come to Visit?* Illustrated by Betsy Lewin. New York: Orchard. Ages 7–8.

Levine's story's fun is mainly in Lewin's cartoonlike pen-and-ink drawings. Lily's family is surprised when a skunk hides in the rain gutter and no one knows how to get the skunk to leave (without leaving its fragrance behind). Discussions about what to do increase and soon the family's front lawn is crowded with people—the mayor, representatives of the fire and police departments, and for no known reason, Miss Duffin, the town's yodeling expert. It seems that the problem of the skunk has generated a town picnic. Lily's mother, in the spirit of it all, makes lemonade and sandwiches. Opinions about the family's dilemma are continually offered but no one has a solution. When Miss Duffin entertains the crowd with her high-pitched yodeling, however, the skunk (seemingly with a "I vant to be alone" attitude) decides to leave on its own, and with no hesitation, quickly scampers from the gutter and heads for some nearby trees.

105. Lindbergh, Reeve (1994). *If I'd Known Then What I Know Now*. Illustrated by Kimberly Bulcken Root. New York: Viking. Ages 5–8.

In Lindbergh's tall-tale type story full of absurdities, an inexperienced man tries to build, furnish, and then manage his farm. His ineptitude results in a variety of things; first, his roof is finished—but it is full of holes; the baby's cradle is finished—but it will only rock one way. The plumbing in the house won't work properly and his wiring nearly electrocutes the family cat. At the end of the tale, the man's family, neighbors, and farm animals join in to show the man that he is "appreciated" by them despite his bumbling attempts on the farm.

106. Lobel, Arnold (1979). *A Treeful of Pigs*. Illustrated by Anita Lobel. New York: Greenwillow. Ages 7–8.

This is a story by Arnold Lobel that asks, What happens when there is a treeful of pigs on the farm? That question reflects just one of the pranks the farmer's wife must resort to in her attempts to get her lazy husband to help with the chores around the place. There is a good deal of fun in this folktale and Anita Lobel's colorful illustrations help add to the humor.

107. Lorimer, Janet (1982). *The Biggest Bubble in the World*. Illustrated by Diane Patterson. New York: Watts. Ages 5–6.

Lorimer has developed a funny adventure for a child beginning to read. It is based on the premise of chewing lots of gum—can a child imagine what would happen after chewing hundreds of pieces of gum? Can a child predict what would happen if two young boys chewed four hundred pieces of bubble gum? In the story, Harvey and Jeremy start chewing gum because they want to try and win a bubble-blowing contest. Their efforts as they collect the gum, take the time to chew all the pieces, practice blowing bubbles—and then what happens when some bubbles burst and others don't—cause an uproar throughout the town.

108. Noble, Trinka Hakes (1989). *Jimmy's Boa and the Big Splash Birthday Bash*. Illustrated by Steven Kellogg. New York: Dial. Ages 5–7.

This is Noble's modern tall tale that is a good read-aloud about Maggie who returns home from Jimmy's birthday party at the seaside. She tells a wild tale to her mother about why she is wet and smelly. It seems that when Jimmy's mother gives him a goldfish, it sets off a chain of events that incudes being in a whale's mouth to escape from sharks and playing a game of "keep-away" with penguins. The humor is mainly in the rapid-fire conversations between Maggie and Mother. It is backed up by the actions in the illustrations that show not only Jimmy's boa but the children playing with seals, sharks, and whales. For additional contemporary tall tales about Jimmy's boa, consider:

- *The Day Jimmy's Boa Ate the Wash* (Dial, 1980). There are nonsensical and zany happenings when Jimmy realizes that his pet boa constrictor has escaped from the school bus. Of course, the boa causes havoc in the henhouse during the class' visit to the farm. But in a surprise ending, Jimmy goes home carrying a new pet pig under his arm and the farmer's wife is seen happily knitting a sweater for the boa.
- *Jimmy's Boa Bounces Back* (Dial, 1984). More amusement is in the slapstick actions of the boa at a sedate garden party. Jimmy's pet boa constrictor causes chaos at the gathering and panics the guests, which results in flying wigs and poodles landing in the punch.

109. Oppenheimer, Joanne (1980). *Mrs. Peloki's Snake*. Illustrated by Joyce Audy dos Santos. New York: Dodd. Ages 7–8.

The amusement is mainly in the illustrations by dos Santos that show the humorous classroom and the related comic captions. In Oppenheimer's story, Mrs. Peloki's classroom erupts when the students hear one of their own say that a snake was in the boys' bathroom. Mrs. Peloki musters up her courage and takes her yardstick to fight the out-of-place reptile. It is fearless Stephie, however, who discovers that a gray string mop was masquerading as the snake.

110. Ormerod, Jan (1986). *The Story of Chicken Licken*. New York: Lothrop, Lee and Shepard. Ages 5–7.

Ormerod's story is a modern school play with the parents as the audience members who watch *Chicken Licken*. While the production goes on, however, the audience plays a humorous story of its own. For example, a bearded father falls asleep and gets a nudge from his wife. A curious toddler quietly goes through the contents of the purse of an unknowing neighbor—and cleans it out.

111. Parish, Peggy (1982). *Mr. Adam's Mistake.* Illustrated by Gail Owens. New York: Macmillan. Ages 6–7.

Parish's story is a read-aloud and laugh-out-loud school story. Mr. Adams has a special job—to see that all children go to school. Since he is nearsighted, he often takes strange things to school by mistake. One day, he takes a chimpanzee back to school which is a *big* mistake—for the chimp starts some humorous misadventures.

112. Parker, Nancy Winslow (1980). *Poofy Loves Company.* Illustrated by the author. New York: Dodd. Ages 5–6.

Much of the amusement is in the humorous one-liners of the owner of Poofy, the shaggy dog, in Parker's story. When Sally and her mother visit Poofy's mistress, Sally doesn't mind the overfriendly maneuvers of the big dog. Sally's possessions, however, begin to disappear, and her battles begin with Poofy.

113. Pearson, Tracey Campbell (1984). *Old MacDonald Had a Farm.* Illustrated by the author. New York: Dial. Ages 6–8.

This is a picture book of the familiar American folk song but Pearson has added some of her own verses about the animals on Old MacDonald's farm that are described in the verses. The cat, dog, and rooster can be found in every scene. When a mule runs away, the farmer follows in his tractor with the words, "With a putt-putt here, and a putt-putt there." The cat and dog hitch a ride on top of the tractor and the mule is guided back home behind the tractor. In closing, there is a finale to MacDonald, "He worked all day, then said goodnight, e—i—e—i—o! With a snooze, snooze here, and a snooze, snooze there. . . ."

114. Peters, Lisa Westberg (1994). *When the Fly Flew In . . .* Illustrated by Brad Sneed. New York: Dial. Ages 5–7.

In Peters' story, a young boy does *not* want to disturb his four sleeping pets—the cat, dog, hamster, and parakeet—and so he decides not to clean up his room, a tedious chore. A pesky buzzing fly invades the room and in turn irritates each pet during its nap. In their ambitious attempts to catch the noisy winged invader, the four pets all unknowingly manage to clean up the boy's entire room. Humorously, they rearrange the clutter into a semblance of tidiness and get everything back in its proper place. How the pets do this can be seen over and over as the pages are turned back and forth to look again at the cluttered bedroom scenes and are compared to the tidy ones.

115. Polacco, Patricia (1987). *Meteor!* New York: Dodd, Mead. Ages 5–7.

Polacco uses exaggeration to create the humor in this story. After a meteor lands on a farm, the townspeople in the nearby town react and each one exaggerates the power of the meteor. For example, some individuals claim that it gives one the ability to play the trumpet, others say it can help one create a marvelous recipe, and still others claim it helps one see extraordinary distances.

116. Polushkin, Maria (1987). *Baby Brother Blues.* Illustrated by Ellen Weiss. New York: Bradbury. Ages 5–7.

There is amusement in Polushkin's subtle humor that contrasts between the fussing of the adults and the big sister's casual words—"Hiya kiddo, what's the matter?" In this story, the big-sister narrator does the describing *and* the complaining. She tells about her contemporary family with the visiting grandparents and another couple who might be a visiting aunt and uncle. After such comments as "This is baby brother? What a mess!/ Everybody thinks he's so cute," the big sister's text is a description of the baby's shortcomings (Sometimes he smells/ Sometimes he squirts") rather than a list of complaints and jealous feelings. The ending could be a familiar one to some children—the big sister is able to quiet the crying infant when no one else can.

117. Pulver, Robin (1991). *Mrs. Toggle and the Dinosaur.* Illustrated by R. W. Alley. New York: Four Winds. Ages 5–7.

Pulver's story is tongue-in-cheek humor. Mrs. Toggle (the teacher), Mr. Abel (the custodian), and Mr. Paige (the librarian), and Mrs. Roggle's ethnically diverse students, all prepare for a new student—a dinosaur. They diligently research dinosaur habits and the custodian builds a special desk. Further, the school cook plans to make the right lunch as soon as she finds out if it is a plant-eater or a meat-eater. Finally, the principal explains the misunderstanding—the new student is a small girl named Dina Sawyer.

118. Rathman, Peggy (1994). *Good Night, Gorilla*. Illustrated by the author. New York: Putnam. Ages 5–7.

In Rathman's story, a mischievous gorilla at the zoo picks the pocket of the zookeeper to get his keys. That evening, as the zookeeper bids each animal good night, the quiet gorilla on tiptoes opens each animal's cage. Quietly, they all follow along behind the zookeeper as he walks home—he's too sleepy to notice he has a long parade of animals behind him. In a final scene at the zookeeper's house, the animals are bedded down for the night in an ending of silliness.

119. Rattigan, Jama Kim (1994). *Truman's Aunt Farm*. Illustrated by G. Brian Karas. Boston: Houghton Mifflin. Ages 5–7.

In Rattigan's story, the humorous pun is that the word *ant* is mistaken for aunt. Truman's Aunt Fran sends him a coupon for an ant farm for his birthday and he is sent—not "ants" but more than fifty aunts of all shapes and sizes. Truman has to decide what to feed them and to find the right nieces and nephews for them.

120. Roberts, Sarah (1983). *Bert and the Missing Mop Mix-Up*. Illustrated by Joe Mathieu. New York: Random House. Ages 7–8.

Roberts relates a fun story about a chain of antics that begins when Bert, a familiar Sesame Street character, spills the milk. When Bert spills the milk, he needs a mop and the fun starts. Everyone, including Ernie, misinterprets what Bert needs as they all try to help clean up the spill.

121. Rogers, Mary (1973). *Freaky Friday*. New York: Harper & Row. Ages 7–8.

Rogers' humor in this story takes a "what if" situation, exaggerates it, and makes events turn absurd as the story considers the idea "what if a mother and daughter exchanged their minds?" The conversations are believable as Annabel wakes up and finds she has changed into her mother. She looks like her mother and must meet her mother's obligations and appointments. However, she still thinks and acts like Annabel.

122. Russo, Marisabina (1994). *I Don't Want To Go Back to School*. Illustrated by the author. New York: Greenwillow. Ages 5–7.

Russo offers a story that combines funny relationships in a family with kindness. The universal concern is about overcoming fears about going back to school and it is dealt with in a caring way. There is humor in the contrast between the support of the boy's parents and the teasing taunts of his older sister. When summer is at an end, Ben does not want to go back to second grade. His parents offer him their assurances but this is contrasted with the dire predictions of Ben's big sister, Hannah. Hannah relies on her memories of second grade—all are apparently disastrous—and says that Ben will probably not know the answers to questions in class and he might fall asleep on the bus, missing his stop. When the first day finally arrives—it turns out fine for Ben but it is Hannah who is the one who nearly sleeps through their bus stop—an unexpected ending that is humorous and pleasant.

123. Samuels, Barbara (1985). *Faye and Dolores*. Illustrated by the author. New York: Bradbury. Ages 5–7.

Samuels's story portrays the humorous activities of two sisters, Faye and Dolores, as they engage in playtime, snacktime, and bedtime. For example, at snacktime, Dolores puts an elephant cookie on her sandwich. Through it all, the sisters fuss, have fun, and share—activities with which many children can identify. If young readers are interested in a sister's humorous activities further, suggest Samuels's book *Duncan and Dolores* (Bradbury, 1986) where Dolores is unsuccessful in her efforts to win over her new cat, Duncan. There is humor in the illustrations that show Dolores, dressed in ribboned hat, polka dot dress, tennis sneakers, and her purse over her arm, pushing a baby carriage with Duncan inside. The spotted Duncan, with his one black eyepatch, holds his paws tightly to the side of the carriage, hind feet up in the air, with tail dropping outside the carriage, with a look of dislike about the entire affair. Then, after a final feline rebuffing, Dolores has to change her strategies.

124. Schwartz, Amy (1994). *A Teeny Tiny Baby*. Illustrated by the author. New York: Orchard. Ages 5–6.

Set in an apartment in Brooklyn, a baby comically tells about the things he wants and needs and about his family, always doting, who give him what he wants—jiggling, patting, and tickling. He remarks, "I'm a teeny tiny baby and I know how to get anything I want." Sometimes he wants to be burped and sometimes he wants to see his family's apartment (especially in the early morning hours), and other times he wants to go outdoors and see what's happening in the parks and children's playgrounds. Still other times, he wants to be with his mother, father, or grandmother, and go where they go around the city. When out, he says he likes the praise and compliments different people offer him—however, he's not happy when an older child refers to his bald head—his hair is still missing. In a final sequence of events, the gentle humor continues as "Teeny Tiny" screams (for something) and his sleepy mother shows him his reflection in the mirror in the bathroom for a diversion. His own image eventually intrigues him and he smiles and is content at what he sees.

125. Sharmat, Marjorie, and Mitchell Sharmat (1980). *The Day I Was Born*. Illustrated by Diane Dawson. New York: E. P. Dutton. Ages 7–8.

The main amusement is in the humorous dialogue by Sharmat and Sharmat. At Alexander's sixth birthday party, his three guests look bored as they listen to Alex talk about all the important events that happened the day he was born. On each facing page, his older brother provides the humorous contrast—he has another version of what really happened. The story ends with the older brother saying, "In the past six years, I got to like my turtle a lot, but I like Alexander even better."

126. Spier, Peter (1978). *Oh, Were They Ever Happy!* Illustrated by the author. New York: Doubleday. Ages 6–8.

In a quiet suburban home, the sitter doesn't show up—so the Noonan children help out by painting the outside of their house. The contrast of a pastoral suburban street with the splashy mess they make is uproarious to see in the illustrations. While giving nearly every indication of what's happening, the author-illustrator keeps young readers waiting until the last page for a good look at the entire house. Spier's bright colors—blue, orange, red—certainly surprise their parents!

127. Stevenson, James (1985). *Are We Almost There?* Illustrated by the author. New York: Greenwillow. Ages 5–8.

This is a Stevenson's story of a family going to the beach and listening to the children's familiar question, "Are we there yet?" The dad in this book yells and struggles like anyone's dad. The seemingly endless trip to the beach is interrupted by an accumulation of obstacles—there are requests for drinks of water, stops at the bathroom, and food to eat, accompanied by pushing, spilling, and arguing by the family—all obstacles that humorously mar the trip.

128. Stevenson, James (1977). *Could Be Worse*. Illustrated by the author. New York: Greenwillow. Ages 6–8.

The amusement is mainly in Stevenson's exaggerations in Grandpa's humorous story. Grandpa does the same things and says the same things day after day. When someone complains, he says, "Could be Worse." Naturally, when he overhears his grandchildren talking about his dull existence, he tells them a whopper of an adventure. He tells exactly what happened to him the previous evening: it seems that he was captured by a huge bird and dropped into the mountains where he encountered an abominable snowman. Then he crossed a burning desert, escaped from a giant animal, landed in the ocean, and finally returned home on a paper airplane. After the children hear this tale, they respond with the expression, "Could be worse!"

129. Stevenson, James (1987). *Will You Please Feed the Cat?* Illustrated by the author. New York: Greenwillow. Ages 6–8.

The fun is mainly in Stevenson's comic strip format and the "What Now?—Oh, No!" theme. Once again, Grandpa entertains Mary Ann, Louie, and readers with a tale from childhood. Agreeing to take care of the neighbors' pets and plants for two weeks puts him and his little brother Wainey in the path of one disaster after another; the gerbils escape, and then the rabbit; dozens of cats wander in through an open door. Wainey falls into both aquaria and is just a bit too small to control the hose in the greenhouse. Naturally, Grandpa rises to the occasion and works out a device for the feeding of all the animals at once, and when they all make a bid for freedom, he corrals them and gets them back into their cages just as the neighbors return.

130. Stevenson, James (1984). *Worse Than Willy!* Illustrated by the author. New York: Greenwillow. Ages 6–8.

The fun is mainly in Stevenson's exaggerations. Grandpa's tall tale humorously explains that there are things worse than Willy, the new baby. Wainey, Grandpa's baby brother, is one of those things—but baby brothers can surprise you. Read the tall tale of *Could Be Worse!* or read *That Terrible Halloween* both about Grandpa's memories of all the things that happened to him; or *What's Under the Bed* for Grandpa's version of things that might frighten a child or read *That Dreadful Day*, Grandpa's first day of school.

131. Viorst, Judith (1978). *Alexander Who Used to Be Rich Last Sunday*. Illustrated by Ray Cruz. New York: Atheneum. Ages 6–7.

Viorst's understated humor provides the focus of the text. Alexander receives a dollar from his grandparents and intends to save it for a walkie-talkie. His intentions go astray in the drugstore, in foolish bets. Whenever he loses his money, Cruz's illustration features his coins flying away and forlorn Alexander sighing "Bye, bye, eight (or twenty) cents." For those children interested further in what happens to Alexander, there is *Alexander and the Terrible, Horrible, No Good, Very Bad Day* (Atheneum, 1972) where the boy experiences a series of "bad" incidents during a particular day—he gets gum in his hair, has to go to the dentist, and gets lima beans for dinner.

132. Weinthrop, Elizabeth (1986). *Shoes*. Illustrated by William Joyce. New York: Harper & Row. Ages 5–6.

There is humor in Joyce's illustrations of the adults who are seen as pictures of midsections and torsos, and a funny ending by Weinthrop that announces itself on two pages of this brochure about the kinds of footwear that a young child might have. Uses for shoes are proclaimed, too, as there are "shoes to skate in, shoes to skip in, shoes to turn a double-flip in" plus bunny slippers, ballet shoes, and even stilts. All are worn by four determined, active children who declare that the very best "shoes" are those from nature that will not pinch or get handed down, or be too hot—your very own "skinny-boned, wiggly-toes feet."

133. William, Joyce (1985). *George Shrinks*. New York: Harcourt Brace Jovanovich. Ages 5–8.

The laughter is mainly in William's comic actions after George dreams he is small and wakes to find it true. He discovers a note from his parents listing chores he must do while they are out. The words of the note become the text and the illustrations show how miniature George deals with the chores. He washes the dishes by surfing across them on a sponge. He takes out the garbage in a little red wagon hitched to his crawling baby brother.

134. Winters, Paula (1976). *The Bear and the Fly*. New York: Crown. Ages 5–8.

In this wordless book, Winters offers slapstick humor that will help children in identifying some cause-and-effect situations. The bear family's house is in turmoil from the fly who seems unaware of the commotion it creates. The fly intrudes on the family as they eat breakfast and Father Bear chases the noisy buzzing insect with a swatter. The swatting chase causes chaos—food and dishes fly everywhere—and Mother Bear, in her chair at the table, seems stunned by it all.

135. Winters, Paula (1980). *Sir Andrew*. New York: Crown. Ages 5–8.

There aren't any words at all in this story but Winters has packed it with slapstick humor. Sir Andrew is an unusual and vain donkey. He preens in the mirror and dresses elegantly in his shirt, vest, suit, and top hat. He takes an eventful stroll on a windy day. His self-admiration is noted when he admires himself by looking at his image in the store windows. Not watching where he is walking, he slips on a banana peel and this leads him to an accident, which causes mishaps for others.

136. Wood, Audrey (1985). *King Bidgood's in the Bathtub*. Illustrated by Don Wood. New York: Harcourt Brace Jovanovich. Ages 6–8.

In this original tale by Wood and Wood, various members of the king's court are clothed in elaborate Elizabethan dress, and they all try to get the king out of his bubbly tub. Instead, they are drawn into the tub with the king to "do battle" with toy ships and warriors, to eat a lavish feast, to fish, and to dance. Finally, it is the young page who finds a solution by pulling the plug. The amusement is mainly in the illustrations, which contrast the overdressed court members and their shocked expressions with the King's twinkling, playful manner. For example, the red-haired naked king frolics while the fully-clothed courtiers emerge dripping from the bath water with literally all their starch taken out.

137. Wood, Audrey (1984). *The Napping House*. Illustrated by Don Wood. New York: Harcourt Brace Jovanovich. Ages 5–7.

On a rainy afternoon, the amusement is in the cumulative rhyme by Wood and Wood that is full of fun about the napping inhabitants of Granny's house: "There is a house/ a napping house,/ where everyone is sleeping." Everyone is napping, including Granny, on a cozy (yet increasingly bending) bed. Granny, a child, and the others—the dog, cat, mouse, and the flea—all sleep while it quietly rains until the wakeful flea starts a chain reaction—it bites the mouse, who scares the cat, who claws the dog, who thumps the child, who bumps Granny, who breaks the bed and wakes them all up. Amid the activity of the flea and the others leaping into the air with surprise, the bed's inhabitants tumble out "in the napping house, where no one now is sleeping" as the sun comes out.

138. Wright, Freure, and Michael Foreman, retellers (1981). *Seven in One Blow*. Illustrated by the authors. New York: Random House. Ages 8 and up.

Much of the amusement is found in the cartoon-style illustrations by Wright and Foreman that convey the fun in the actions. This is the retelling of the story of the little tailor who kills seven flies in one blow. The tailor then has the confidence and wit to capture seven giants and win the hand of the lovely princess.

Humorous Humans

139. Ahlberg, Allan, and Andre Amstutz (1989). *Ten in a Bed*. New York: Viking. Ages 5–8.

Most of the humor is mainly in the double entendres and the parodies of fairy tales that Ahlberg and Amstutz have included. Every night, Dinah Price goes to bed and finds one of the fairy tale characters (such as a sarcastic old wolf) in her bed. They do *not* want to leave until Dinah promises to tell them a story. So on eight different nights, Dinah tells each fairy tale visitor an original story (actually Dinah's version of a fairy tale), and eventually, the character does leave. For example, one night the three bears are in her bed and they refuse to leave until Dinah tells them a humorous version of Goldilocks that includes a new character—a hunter. There is more humor in Dinah's telling as Baby Bear hears the tune of a nearby ice-cream truck and says he would leave the story for a cone. During the story, Baby Bear doesn't know exactly what a hunter is and asks Dinah to explain. Additionally, all three bears constantly interrupt Dinah to give her their suggestions about the story and make it their own. Each night, the same scenario is repeated with a new fairy tale character.

140. Allan, Ted (1991). *Willie the Squowse*. Illustrated by Quentin Blake. New York: Hastings. Ages 5–8.

There is understated humor in Allan's story and Blake's illustrations. Willie, a mouse-squirrel combination (squowse), is bright, talented, and sensitive. In addition, he is a great acrobat and his human trainer tries to get Willie's act accepted by an agent. The act is rejected on the grounds, however, that it is too weird and Willie finds himself all alone living in the wall between two families in a duplex. The Smith family, somewhat slovenly, lives on one side and the newly wealthy Pickerings live on the other. Mrs. Pickering uses the wall as a private bank and stuffs new hundred dollar bills into a hole each week and with Willie's help, the Smith family benefits.

141. Anno, Mitsumasa (1979). *The King's Flower*. Illustrated by the author. New York: Collins. Ages 7–8.

This is Anno's comical story that addresses the question "Is biggest always best?" The king thinks so and surrounds himself with everyday objects that are disproportionate to human size. His toothbrush is so big that it takes two men to carry it. The king changes his mind about size when he has a single tulip bulb planted in the world's biggest pot. Instead of one enormous bloom, the king finds one that is small and beautiful. The king realizes that he cannot make the biggest flower in all the world and says,"perhaps that is just as well." Though the illustrations suggest a European setting from the Middle Ages, there are some contrasts—some anachronisms—seen in the toothbrush and chocolate bar. The concept of relative size is comically introduced—there are large pincers for pulling the royal tooth, a fishhook large enough to catch a whale, and huge kitchen utensils that have to be handled with ropes and pulleys.

142. Bang, Betsy (1975). *The Old Woman and the Red Pumpkin*. Illustrated by Molly Garrett Bang. New York: Macmillan. Ages 7–8.

Betsy Bang's folktale is a good read-aloud about cleverness and has some comical Indian folk art in the illustrations by Molly Garrett Bang. It has a rhythmic text about a skinny old woman who meets several hungry animals—a bear, a jackal, and a tiger—on the way to her granddaughter's house. She gets fat at her granddaughter's and then, with the help of her granddaughter, outwits the animals on the way home by rolling inside a pumpkin. There are Bengali inscriptions for animal names in a glossary.

143. Barrett, Judi (1978). *Cloudy with a Chance of Meatballs*. Illustrated by Ron Barrett. New York: Atheneum. Ages 6–8.

In the small town of Chewandswallow, the weather came three times a day—at breakfast, lunch, and dinner. The weather rained things like soup and juice, and when it snowed, it dropped potatoes. The clouds were fried eggs and the wind blew in storms of hamburgers. One day, the weather took a turn for the worse—there was even a tomato tornado and a giant meatball storm—and the people decided to leave town to escape a flood. They glued bread slices together and made rafts to sail away to a new coastal town which welcomed them. There they realized that there *can* be too much of a good thing—and learned to buy food at a supermarket. For children interested further in Barrett's sense of humor, locate *Animals Should Definitely Not Wear Clothes* (Atheneum, 1970) and *Benjamin's 365 Birthdays* (Atheneum, 1974). The first is about what happens when animals humorously wear clothing as people do. The second story is about a bear who is so delighted with his birthday presents that he decides to rewrap them so he can enjoy one each day for the following months.

144. Bender, Robert (1994). *The Preposterous Rhinoceros, or Alvin's Beastly Birthday*. Illustrated by the author. New York: Holt, Rinehart, & Winston. Ages 5–7.

On his birthday, Alvin sulks in his bedroom because he thinks that no one has remembered his special day. His mother tries to cheer him up and entertains him by telling him to look outside his room to see "a rhinoceros looking quite preposterous," "a toad driving down the road," and other animals told in rhyme. Alvin isn't interested until he hears her say something about "a snake eating a cake." When Alvin takes a look and asks, "What kind of cake?" he finds that his friends are there wearing party hats and clothes decorated with animals. "A birthday cake," they all shout.

145. Bernier-Grand, Carmen T., reteller (1994). *Juan Bobo: Four Folktales from Puerto Rico*. Illustrated by Ernesto J. Ramos Nieves. New York: HarperCollins. Ages 5–8.

Here are four folktales from Puerto Rico about Juan Bobo. In each tale, he shows he is a "noodlehead:" in the first tale, Juan decides to carry water in baskets instead of buckets because baskets are lighter; in the second, he put his mother's clothes on the family pig; in the third, he follows his mother's advice when he visits a neighbor for dinner—he doesn't eat too much and ends up not having dinner at all; in the last tale, Juan is told to see his mother's sug-

arcane syrup to some widows. The widows are described as small and dressed in black dresses, carrying fans, and speaking softly. Juan mistakes flies buzzing at the window for the widows.

146. Binnamin, Vivian (1990). *The Case of the Snoring Stegosaurus*. Illustrated by Jeffrey S. Nelsen. New York: Silver Press. Ages 5–7.

Binnamin's book is an all-in-fun story useful to read before meeting the new janitor and maintenance person at school. The snoring that the students hear and their logical thinking leads the class members to the new janitor. They discover it is the new janitor who naps and snores at four o'clock every afternoon. If a librarian, teacher, or parent decides to read this story as an introduction to the children visiting the maintenance person at school, please let the janitor at the school read the story ahead of the visit.

147. Bradman, Tony (1988). *Not Like That, Like This!* Illustrated by Joanna Burroughes. New York: Oxford University Press. Ages 6–7.

Bradman offers a humorous counting book for young children. Thomas's dad gets his head stuck in the park railings and needs some help. Everyone who passes by has an idea to free him and encourages him to try to get loose with the repetitive words, *Not like that, like this*.

148. Bursik, Rose (1994). *Zoe's Sheep*. Illustrated by the author. New York: Holt, Rinehart & Winston. Ages 6–7.

In Bursik's humorous counting book story, Zoe can't get to sleep and her father suggests that she count sheep. Humor is in the details as the sheep eat the plants, toot horns, and dance, draw on the walls—all to keep Zoe wide awake. Zoe finally falls asleep only after one of the sheep dons a wolf mask and drives all the others out of her bedroom into the nearby hills. A final scene shows Zoe asleep with the sheep who saved the day and the wolf mask hanging on the bedpost.

149. Butterworth, Olive (1956). *The Enormous Egg*. Illustrated by Louis Darling. Boston: Little, Brown. Ages 8 and up.

Butterworth's humor is in the humorous situation of a hen hatching a dinosaur egg and trying to raise a dinosaur in a contemporary setting. Twelve-year-old Nathan "Nate" Twitchell takes care of the huge leathery egg and turns it every few hours. When it hatches, it is a live triceratops with warm, loose, bluish skin and a funny kind of beak like a turtle's. Nate names it Uncle Beazley because of the resemblance between the two. After a senate investigation into the question of whether raising a dinosaur is un-American, Nate leaves Uncle Beazley at the Washington Zoo with Dr. Ziemer who promises to send Nate a weekly bulletin on how Beazley is getting along. Nate promises to visit the dinosaur in his dinosaur cage in the elephant house.

150. Byars, Betsy (1994). *The Golly Sisters Ride Again*. Illustrated by Sue Truesdell. San Francisco: HarperCollins. Ages 6–8.

The Golly sisters, May-May and Rose, are a singing and dancing team in the Old West who journey in their covered wagon to entertain the people in different towns. Byars's humor is found in the situations they face as they try to get rid of a bad-luck goat in the audience, locate a magical talking rock, and hide together under their bed during a terrible thunder and lightning storm. Two other stories, *The Golly Sisters Go West* (Harper & Row, 1986) and *Hooray for the Golly Sisters* (Harper & Row, 1988) offers additional humor in different Old West situations that include trying to get their horse to start on the journey, arguing about who goes first in their song and dance show, and who should be the first singer.

151. DeFelice, Cynthia (1994). *Mule Eggs*. Illustrated by Mike Shenon. New York: Orchard. Ages 5–8.

Much of the fun by DeFelice and Shenon is in the basic expressions of the characters in the illustrations—especially the city slicker new to the country. The newcomer sees pumpkins in his neighbor's field and thinks they are apples. The neighbor-farmer convinces the newcomer that the pumpkins are mule eggs and sells him one with the advice that he would "have to sit on it, just like a mama mule." By the end of the story, the newcomer realizes that he has been fooled and after he has acquired two new mules, he names them "Tit for Tat" and "That's That."

152. De Paola, Tomie (1979). *Big Anthony and the Magic Ring*. Illustrated by the author. New York: Harcourt Brace Jovanovich. Ages 6–9.

In de Paola's story, Big Anthony, the misguided helper of *Strega Nona* (154) who fooled around with a magic pasta pot, is back in another misadventure. It is springtime and he is restless, so Strega Nona diagnoses spring fever

and recommends a little nightlife. Poor Anthony wonders who would dance with a dolt such as himself. Strega Nona assures him that Bambolona—the baker's roly poly daughter—will. Feeling a bit restless herself that night, Strega Nona uses her magic ring, sings a magic chant, and poof—transforms herself into a beautiful young lady. Big Anthony observes all this, and follows her to the village square where the young Strega Nona dances until dawn. Big Anthony waits for his chance to get the ring and when Strega Nona goes off to visit her godchildren, he finds it, puts it on his finger, and sings the magic chant. With a puff of smoke and poof—there was Big Anthony now handsome in elegant clothes. He goes to the village square where the ladies keep him dancing until he drops from exhaustion. He runs away and sings the chant to turn off the spell, but the ring is stuck fast to his finger. As Anthony runs further, the ladies chase him past the fountain, out through the gate, and into the countryside. He tries to escape up a tree but the ladies shake it until he flies off into the air and lands right at Strega Nona's feet.

153. De Paola, Tomie (1978). *Pancakes for Breakfast*. Illustrated by the author. New York: Harcourt Brace Jovanovich. Ages 5–6.

This story by de Paola has gentle humor. A persistent plump little lady wakes up to the thought of having pancakes for breakfast. To make the pancakes, she has to go to the henhouse to gather eggs, milk a cow, and then churn butter. Just when she thinks that she has all she needs to make pancakes, she discovers that she must go and buy some syrup. She returns home with a self-satisfied expression on her face only to find out an early morning crisis—her dog and cat have tipped over the milk and flour, and eaten the eggs. Just in time, the inviting smell of pancakes comes from her neighbor's house and the lady dresses in her cape and bonnet and goes to the neighbor to invite herself to a breakfast of pancakes. This is an amusing nearly-wordless book that has a recipe for pancakes at the end so that a child could try making pancakes.

154. De Paola, Tomie, reteller (1975). *Strega Nona*. Illustrated by the reteller. New York: Prentice-Hall. Ages 6–8.

The humor is in the quirkiness that de Paola creates about Strega Nona ("Grandmother

Witch") and her meddling assistant named Big Anthony who fed the goats and washed the dishes. Strega Nona, really a kindly old woman, helped cure people of their warts, headaches, lack of a husband, and warned Big Anthony *not* to touch her pasta pot. However, he heard her sing a special song, "Bubble, Bubble pasta pot," and saw her blow three kisses to the pot to make all the pasta she needed. One night when she was out of town, Big Anthony invited the town to a pasta feast. The problem was that Big Anthony did not know the secret of how to get the pot to stop. And before long, the pot had unleashed a torrent of pasta that threatened to engulf the little Italian town with its piazza, arches, and houses with tile roofs. The people barricaded the streets with mattresses and doors to try to stop the pasta. Luckily, Strega Nona returned in time to save the town and declares that Big Anthony must help clear the streets—by eating the pasta.

155. De Paola, Tomie (1982). *Strega Nona's Magic Lessons.* Illustrated by the author. New York: Harcourt Brace Jovanovich. Ages 7–8.

In this story told with hearty humor by de Paola, Big Anthony, a bumbling and sometimes greedy assistant, tries to use Strega Nona's magic. A child should enjoy this episode of Big Anthony's mistakes, his solutions, and his knack of getting himself into deeper trouble. For example, Strega Nona has to get Big Anthony to stop pretending he is a girl and poetic justice is again delivered.

156. Dinardo, Jeffrey (1989). *The Wolf Who Cried Boy.* New York: Grosset. Ages 6–8.

Much of Dinardo's humor is found in the colored ink-and-wash cartoon-style illustrations that show the wolf dressed in the "Bowery Boys" style clothing. In this version, a bored wolf plays tricks on his neighbors and pretends there is a horrible little boy after him. Yes, he does this once too often and his neighbors are angry at being fooled. They decide to trick him and it works—they are not bothered by the wolf again.

157. Fife, Dale (1979). *Follow That Ghost!* Illustrated by Joan Drescher. New York: E. P. Dutton. Ages 7 and up.

Fife's words in this narrative will remind an older child or adult of the dialogue heard in the TV show *Dragnet.* This is Chuck and Jason's first detective case and they follow people for practice until their next-door neighbor catches them following her home. Instead of being angry at the boys, Glory decides to have them find the ghost that she and her mother hear at 5 o'clock every morning. Despite their attempts to capture the ghost or to find a human reason for the ghostly sounds, the boys cannot rid the apartment of the ghost. Eventually, the ghost turns out to be a displaced woodpecker looking for a new home.

158. Foley, Louise Munro (1978). *Tackle 22.* Illustrated by John Heinly. New York: Delacorte. Ages 6–8.

Most of the humor in this story is found in lighthearted touches in Foley's text as well as in Heinly's pictures. When their quarterback comes down with the mumps, the team members of the Wildcats thought they would have to forfeit their big football game to the other team, the Spacemen. Chub's little brother, Herb, however, surprises everyone and saves the game.

159. Gackenbach, Dick (1978). *Ida Fanfanny.* Illustrated by the author. New York: Harper and Row. Ages 7–8.

Gackenbach's story humorously explores the question, "Can you imagine living where there are no seasons—in fact where there is no weather at all?" It seems that the mountains of Yurt were so high that no weather could ever pass their lofty summits—and there in the valley of Glebe lived unusual Ida Fanfanny. Ida was oblivious to the very existence of weather or seasons until she bought three magical pictures of summer, fall, and spring from Mr. Cellalotti. (Ida received winter as a bonus.) To start the magic, Ida would sing her favorite song, "She'll be coming 'round the mountain when she comes" and close her eyes. This enabled her to enter one of the pictures and try out the characteristics of each season of the year. She could experience the heavy drenching rains of spring, the pesky bugs in summer, the crispness of fall days, and the freezing cold of winter.

160. Gage, Wilson (1983). *Cully Cully and the Bear.* Illustrated by James Stevenson. New York: Greenwillow. Ages 5–6.

Silly, ridiculous situations and some irony are central to this story by Gage and Stevenson. A pioneer hunter, Cully Cully decides the ground is cold and he needs a bearskin rug to keep him warm. He finds a bear but the bear chases Cully Cully right back. Ironically, Cully

Cully finds that the bear he was chasing is now after him in a serious way. Around and around a tree they go—running so fast that sometimes the bear is ahead and sometimes Cully Cully is ahead. It is hard to know who is chasing whom. Finally, Cully Cully decides that he does not need a bearskin because the ground is softer than any rug.

161. Geringer, Laura (1985). *A Three Hat Day*. Illustrated by Arnold Lobel. New York: Harper and Row. Ages 5–8.

This is Geringer's amusing story about an eccentric character—R. R. Pottle the Third who comes from a long line of collectors in his family. His father collected canes, his mother umbrellas—but R. R. loved hats. The sadder he was, the more of them he wore—Lobel's illustrations show a different hat in each of twelve frames. On one memorable occasion, a three hat day, he met the perfect woman who wore the perfect hat in—where else?—a hat store. So they marry and R. R. the Fourth is born—a little girl who likes shoes.

162. Giff, Patricia Reilly (1981). *Have You Seen Hyacinth Macaw?* Illustrated by Anthony Kramer. New York: Delacorte. Ages 8 and up.

There are many humorous actions in Giff's story as Abby Jones tries very hard to be a detective but finds it difficult without any mysteries to solve. To keep in practice, Abby fills a memo book with her notes about anything that seems at all unusual. At the same time, Abby keeps in touch with two local police detectives who give her hints about detective work. Because of her police friends and her observations, Abby soon finds herself involved in what seems to be four or more mysteries:

- Who had moved into the apartment next door?
- What were the screams that came from there?
- What was the theft that the police were worried about?
- Who was Hyacinth Macaw and why had she disappeared?

Abby and her friend Potsie trail a suspect through the New York subway system, break into the apartment next-door, capture an unusual bird, and realize that all the mysteries are linked together. It seems that Macaw is a valuable bird stolen from Justine's Junkique shop. The daughter of Abby's landlord took the bird and put it in the empty apartment next to Abby's so that she could paint the bird's portrait. The picture was to be entered in Justine's contest. When these mysteries were all sorted out, KiKi, the bird's portrait painter, was forgiven and awarded first prize, and Abby received a reward for finding the bird.

163. Ginsburg, Mirra (1973). *The Lazies*. Illustrated by Marian Parry. New York: Macmillan. Ages 7–8.

Ginsburg's book has fifteen short humorous Russian folktales about laziness. Some are familiar, others unfamiliar to children. The stories will need some adult guidance since much of the humor is subtle—a level that could be difficult to identify even by eight-year-olds. To an interested child, perhaps initially suggest reading or listening to "Who Will Wash the Pot?" "Easy Bread," "Who Will Row Next?" or "The Princess Who Learned to Work."

164. Grossman, Bill (1991). *Donna O'Neeshuck Was Chased by Some Cows*. Illustrated by Sue Truesdell. New York: HarperCollins. Ages 5–7.

The humor is in the zaniness. Grossman's story is told in rhythmic verse that begins with "Donna O'Neeshuck was chased by some cows." It seems that in play one day, Donna patted a cow on the head. This started a ruckus and caused the animals and people to travel over field and dale and chase Donna for some unknown reason. At the end, it seems that everyone wants a pat from Donna:

"Head Pats!" they said.
"We want pats on the head.
You give such incredible head pats," they said.
They're so awfully good.
We thought that it would
Be nice if you gave us some more.

165. Hann, Jacquie (1978). *Up Day, Down Day*. Illustrated by the author. New York: Four Winds. Ages 5–8.

This is a humorous good luck-bad luck story with cartoon-style illustrations. When Jeremy and his friend go fishing, Jeremy catches three fish. His friend catches a shoe, a can, and a cold. On alternating pages, Jeremy's good luck is contrasted with his friend's bad luck. Monday when it is time to go to school, the cold has its advantages. There is a final twist as Jeremy gives his friend a fish and his friend gives Jeremy his cold.

166. Harris, Robie H. (1980). *Rosie's Double Dare*. Illustrated by Tony DeLuna. New York: Knopf. Ages 7–8.

This is a lighthearted story with lots of action. Rosie wants to play baseball with the Willard Street Gang but she cannot play well enough to play by *their* rules. She needs what her older brother calls "shrimp rules." For instance, she could not hit a pitched ball, only a grounder. In desperation to be on the team, Rosie agrees to take a dare that the gang makes up. If she actually performs the dare, the gang will let her play with them by her rules. The gang dares Rosie to sneak into cranky Mr. Quirk's apartment and borrow a set of false teeth. Rosie does but takes his wig when she cannot find any false teeth. The gang members laugh at what she did and make up another dare for Rosie—she is to untie Mrs. Samuels' dog and let it loose. When she does, Elmer the dog runs away with Rosie after him. One rainstorm later, Rosie catches him in the middle of a Red Sox game at Fenway Park. Rosie tries to catch Elmer and stops the game instead. After she is interviewed on TV, she gets a place on the Willard Street baseball team.

167. Henkes, Kevin (1986). *A Weekend with Wendell*. Illustrated by the author. New York: Greenwillow. Ages 6–8.

Most of the fun is in the humor of the characters and their relationships with one another during family visits. Henkes' story portrays what can happen when cousins get together. Sophie dreads the day that her cousin Wendell comes to visit. A visit from her overbearing cousin always makes Sophie's life miserable until she learns to assert herself.

168. Hildick, Edmund W. (1975). *The Case of the Condemned Cat*. Illustrated by Lisl Weil. New York: Macmillan. Ages 7 and up.

Ray Williams had a terrible problem when he begged the McGuirk Organization for help. His cat Whiskers had been accused of killing a neighbor's pet dove. Ray's mother decided that they couldn't risk upsetting the neighbors anymore and threatened to take Whiskers to the pound unless it could be proven that he was innocent. The organization, needing time, hid Whiskers and told Mrs. Williams that he had run away. While Whiskers was safely hidden, the group interviewed all the neighbors, surveyed the scene of the crime, and tried to decide upon the real murderer. When the remains of another bird were found while Whiskers was safely locked away, it looked as if the cat was innocent. But then McGuirk and his detectives found out that the cat had been sprung. It wasn't until they went back over all the information that had gathered that McGuirk realized who was the real culprit. The only step left was to trick old Gramp Martin, the grouch in the neighborhood, into confessing.

169. Hildick, Edmund W. (1978). *The Case of the Secret Scribbler*. Illustrated by Lisl Weil. New York: Macmillan. Ages 7 and up.

Joey's discovery in a library book of a scrap of paper with part of a letter and a strange diagram on it led the McGuirk Organization on a lively chase. Brains identified the diagram as that of a widely used security system. The part of the letter that they read told the group that there was a burglary being planned for the approaching weekend. But the youngsters knew the police would never take them seriously until they had much more evidence. By researching local alarm systems, determining who bought the unusual paper, and comparing handwriting samples, the detectives were able to convince the police of what was about to happen. In gratitude, the police loaned the organization a police monitor so that they could listen as the thieves were caught. To all but McGuirk, it seemed like the perfect way to end the case. He tried to sneak into the midst of the capture but only succeeded in getting himself in trouble.

170. Hildick, Edmund W. (1975). *Deadline for McGuirk*. Illustrated by Lisl Weil. New York: Macmillan. Ages 7 and up.

When many of the dolls in the neighborhood began disappearing, their owners went to the McGuirk Organization for help. At first, McGuirk was reluctant to take on a silly task of recovering lost dolls. But when a ransom note appeared and the organization was linked to the dolls' safety, McGuirk's reluctance vanished. The note states that if, in a written public notice, the members of the organization did not admit that they weren't good, the dolls were doomed. McGuirk's pride would never had allowed him to write such a notice. As the deadline approached, the group plotted a daring move designed to uncover the doll thief. The plan depended on Willie's supersensitive nose, a particular perfume dabbed on a stolen doll, and the curiosity of the thief. Success came only minutes before the hour of doom. Once again Sandra Ennis was the culprit.

171. Hildick, Edmund W. (1976). *The Great Rabbit Rip-off*. Illustrated by Lisl Weil. New York: Macmillan. Ages 7–8.

"Why would anyone want to put red paint on all of the clay lawn rabbits in town?" is the question that this story answers. This is the first and easier of the mysteries the McGuirk Organization had to solve. The bigger mystery was who would then steal them all and why? Almost everyone in town had purchased a rabbit to help a charity drive. Donny Towers a local social worker had thought of the idea. Donny, his fiancee, Joanne, and two reformed thieves, Sam and Ferdie, had made enough rabbits for everyone. When the rabbits disappeared, the organization began to suspect among others, Sam and Ferdie. Then when Donny replaced each one with rabbits smelling of paint remover, the group began to think Donny might have been involved. It was Wanda's sharp eyes that revealed Donny's motive. Joanne's engagement ring had been accidentally molded into one of the rabbits and Donny had retrieved the rabbits to find the ring. Knowing he couldn't return the painted rabbits, Donny had removed the red paint and told everyone he was replacing the stolen rabbits with new ones.

172. LeSieg, Theo (1974). *Wacky Wednesday*. Illustrated by George Booth. New York: Random House. Ages 6–8.

This is Le Seig's story in silly rhyme backed up by a series of picture puzzles by Booth about a day when things were out of place. When a young boy wakes up, he discovers that everywhere he turns, he finds something out of the ordinary—a shoe is on the bedroom wall that shouldn't be there, and he discovers more and more things that are wacky. Additionally, he seems to be the only one who notices the humorous mistakes. People have extra legs. Cars are driven from the back seat. Doors are placed in wrong places. Airplanes fly backwards. At the end of the day, things return to normal.

173. Lustig, Michael, and Esther Lustig (1994). *Willy Whyner, Cloud Designer*. Illustrated by Michael Lustig. New York: Four Winds. Ages 6–8.

Lustig and Lustig put sly jokes in the illustrations that accompany the text about young Willy and his invention of a cloudmaking machine. For example, the Marx Brothers are seen over Mount Rushmore, Willy's bookshelf contains copies of *The Tempest* by Shakespeare and *Clouds* by Aristophanes, and Willy's parents may remind some readers of the couple in the portrait *Americana—American Gothic* by Grant Woods. Willy experiments with his machine and makes a mammoth croissant-type cloud drift over Paris, has Moby Dick float over the pyramids, and engineers a dark rain cloud to soak the substitute teacher at school. At the end of the story, the cloudmaking fun comes to an end when Willy has to sell his invention for $14 billion and the clouds all disappear.

174. McCleery, William (1988). *Wolf Story*. Illustrated by Warren Chappell. Hamden, Conn.: Linnet/Shoe String. Ages 5–8.

Five-year-old Michael listens to his father tell a story every night—and he also dictates some of the details he wants. One night Michael interjects the character of Waldo, a wily wolf, who is determined to capture and consume Rainbow, a hen whose feathers are different colors. The hero of the story is Jimmy Tractorwheel, a farmboy (but really Michael's personality). Jimmy/Michael considers the wolf-chases-the-hen problem as only a five-year-old can do and thinks up solutions that involve such things as a baseball bat, a booby trap, and so on.

175. McKean, Thomas (1994). *Hooray for Grandma Jo!* Illustrated by Chris L. Demarest. New York: Crown. Ages 5–8.

Most of the fun is found in Demarest's exaggerated expressions and actions of the characters. In McKean's story, Grandma Jo, somewhat squinty-eyed, goes to the train station to meet her grandson. Because she cannot see without her glasses, she thinks she has her grandson but brings home a runaway *lion* instead.

176. Malkin, Michele (1988). *Blanche and Smitty's Summer Vacation*. Illustrated by the author. New York: Bantam. Ages 5–7.

Malkin's fun is packed into the absurd actions of a cat. This is the story of a mischievous cat, Smitty. His owner, Blanche, plans a vacation away from him and his antics. When she unpacks at her holiday retreat, however, she discovers Smitty there too.

177. Marshak, Samuel (1989). *The Pup Grew Up.* Illustrated by Vladimir Radunsky. Translated by Richard Pevear. New York: Holt, Rinehart and Winston. Ages 5–7.

Marshak's story shows tongue-in-cheek humor. At a train station, a woman checks her baggage—a pan, a divan, a basin, a box with three locks, a valise, and a small pekingese. At the end of the trip, the pup has turned into a Great Dane. Radunsky's comical illustrations add to the fun.

178. Mathews, Judith, and Fay Robinson (1994). *Nathaniel Willy, Scared Silly.* Illustrated by Alexi Natchev. New York: Bradbury. Ages 5–8.

In the old creaky house, Nathaniel Willy's bedroom door squeaks and it scares him silly. To comfort him, his grandmother gives him some animals for company for the night—a humorous idea by authors Mathews and Robinson. Natchev's illustrations comically convey the grandmother's actions—first she carries in the cat, dog, and pig, and, last, the cow.

179. Mayer, Mercer (1974). *Frog Goes to Dinner.* Illustrated by the author. New York: Dial. Ages 6–8.

Mayer's humor is in the slapstick situations that happen in the cartoon-type illustrations. A frog hides in a boy's pocket and, unknown to the rest of the family, goes to dinner in an expensive restaurant. Confusion and excitement result when the frog lands in the salad and knocks over the bubbly wine. The family is very embarrassed when they are evicted from the restaurant—the family is shown to the fire exit by a waiter who holds the frog by his frog legs. At home, the boy is sent to his room. The situational humor about the frog continues in the following:

- In *A Boy, a Dog, and a Frog* (Dial, 1967), the boy and the dog try to capture a frog; the frog escapes, becomes lonely, and follows the boy back home to the bathtub.
- In *Frog, Where Are You?* (Dial, 1969) the boy and his dog search for the missing frog.
- In *A Boy, a Dog, a Frog, and a Friend* (Dial, 1971), the frog's son accompanies the boy and the dog on an outing where they find a turtle. The turtle tricks them but then becomes a friend to them.

- In *One Frog Too Many* (Dial, 1975) co-authored by Marianna Mayer, the frog shows his jealousy when the boy receives a new frog for his birthday.

180. Mayer, Mercer (1987). *There's an Alligator under My Bed.* Illustrated by the author. New York: Dial. Ages 6–8.

Mayer's main character of *There's a Nightmare in my Closet* (Dial, 1969) is also in this humorous sequel. And this becomes another funny nighttime adventure in full color where the hero sits up in bed, wide awake with the bed covers pulled up, and decides to confront the intruder. Guide children to the illustration of the large alligator under the bed, his eyes and teeth gleam, his nose protrudes from the foot of the bed, and his tail sticks out beneath the head of the bed.

181. Parish, Peggy (1963). *Amelia Bedelia.* Illustrated by Fritz Siebel. New York: Harper and Row. Ages 6–8.

Parish offers a contemporary noodlehead-type story that features Amelia, the literal-minded housekeeper of the Rogers family. It focuses on the fun that happens when words have different meanings to different people and cause humorous results. Amelia, the maid, follows Mrs. Rogers's instructions to the letter—very literally. She can't understand why Mrs. Rogers wants her to "dress" the chicken or "draw" the drapes, but she goes about making clothing for the chicken so she can "dress" it and she sketches the curtains.

182. Parish, Peggy (1976). *Good Work, Amelia Bedelia.* Illustrated by Lynn Sweat. New York: Avon/Camelot. Ages 6–8.

Amelia, the maid, responds in her own upside-down manner again in this story and it is only her butterscotch cake that saves the day and the temper of Mr. and Mrs. Rogers. It seems that Mr. and Mrs. Rogers have gone out for the day and have left a list of jobs for Amelia to do. Amelia, true to her style, takes words literally:

- Bake bread (Amelia helped it rise by tying the pan with cord to an overhead light)
- Clean out the ashes in the parlor fireplace and fill the wood box (she put the ashes in the wood box)
- Make a sponge cake (she snipped a sponge into small pieces to add to the batter)

- Patch the front door screen (she stitched fabric patches on it for you "can't patch without a patch")
- Fix a chicken dinner (she served cracked corn because that's a chicken's dinner)

When Mr. and Mrs. Rogers return and discover Amelia's "work," they are angry. Amelia, however, serves them milk and cake, which leads Mrs. Rogers to remark, "we know we can't do without you." Amelia responds, "I guess I just understand your ways." For a child who is interested in more humor about the funny situations that being literal-minded brings to Amelia further, suggest one or more of the following:

- *Amelia Bedelia's Family Album* (Greenwillow, 1988) gives Amelia an opportunity to describe each member of the family from the album. Amelia has her own interpretations and tells her cousin that her relative, the boxer, packs boxes and her aunt—the bank teller—tells people where to go in a bank.
- *Amelia Bedelia Goes Camping* (Greenwillow, 1985) is the setting for Amelia as she "hits the road" in a variety of ways. She is famous for her literal interpretation of everyday expressions—"Go fly a kite;" and continues to do so in this action-filled picture book.
- *Teach Us, Amelia Bedelia (Greenwillow, 1977), Thank You, Amelia Bedelia* (Harper & Row, 1964), and *Amelia Bedelia Helps Out* (Greenwillow, 1979), are other examples of ways that words can have different meanings to different people and bring humorous results.

183. Parish, Peggy (1974). *Too Many Rabbits*. Illustrated by Leonard Kessler. New York: Macmillan. Ages 6–8.

In Parish's story, Miss Molly opens her door to find a rabbit waiting outside. The next day she finds baby rabbits, lots of them. They need care and Miss Molly keeps them all. When she tries to give them away, she finds the zoo does not need any and mothers refuse to keep them for their children. Finally a man, who owns an island, takes all the rabbits. Then a cat walks up to her and the next day, Miss Molly gets a surprise—she finds kittens—lots of kittens.

184. Ransome, Arthur (1968). *The Fool of the World and the Flying Ship*. Illustrated by Uri Shulevitz. New York: Farrar, Straus & Giroux. Ages 6–9.

In this Russian tale retold by Ransome, it is the element of superiority (i.e., the simpleton and/or helpful associates over the smug, clever people) that leads to the humor in the tale. In it, an old peasant and his wife considered their third son to be the fool of the world because he was "as simple as a child, simpler than some children" but he never did anyone any harm. The good deeds are performed by the boy and his companions can do great things—eat huge quantities, hear long distances, drink large quantities of liquids. These talents help the boy accomplish the tasks the czar has for the one who wants to win his daughter's hand. The czar has offered his daughter's hand to anyone who can build a flying ship. Being kind to an old man, the boy obtains a flying ship. With the help of his companions, the boy overcomes other obstacles that are put in his way and finally becoming important, he wins the hand of the czar's daughter. They both live happily every after.

185. Raschika, Chris (1993). *Yo? Yes?* Illustrated by the author. New York: Orchard. Ages 5–7.

Raschika's fun is shown both in the print and pictures about the start of a friendship between an African-American boy and a European-American boy when they meet on the street. They have a conversation in one- and two-word exchanges such as "What's Up?" "Not much." "Why?" "No fun." "Oh?" "No friends." They seal their friendship when they jump high in the air and yell "Yow!"

186. Raskin, Ellen (1966). *Nothing Ever Happens on My Block*. New York: Atheneum. Ages 6–8.

Sitting on a street curb, Chester Filbert, a young boy, grouses to himself that while some places are interesting, nothing ever happens on his block. In the scene to contrast with Chester's words, something exciting is going on. A house catches fire from a lightning strike and fire fighters put out the blaze. A car crashes into an armored truck and money spills out all over the street. Some children ring a doorbell and then hide when the lady answers. After two trips to answer her door, the lady pours water from her upstairs window to catch the culprits and by mistake catches the postman delivering the mail. Chester misses all of the action and still thinks nothing ever happens on his block.

187. Rosenbloom, Joseph (1985). *Deputy Dan and The Bank Robbers*. Illustrated by Tim Raglin. New York: Random House. Ages 6–8.

Rosenbloom offers a slapstick comedy set in the wild West. In the tale—historical fiction noodlehead story—Deputy Dan follows orders literally (much like Amelia in *Amelia Bedelia* does—when someone tells her to go fly a kite, she actually flies one). Dan's literal interpretation leads to silly and wacky situations shown in Raglin's illustrations—a favorite part is when Dan picks up his horse by using a crane.

188. Sachar, Louis (1994). *Marvin Redpost: Alone in the Teacher's House*. Illustrated by the author. New York: Random House. Ages 7–8.

In Sachar's story, Marvin's third grade teacher asks him to take care of Waldo, her old dog, while she is away for a few days. Marvin agrees and is proud that he has the job. He takes the job seriously and even eats a piece of dry dog food to try to tempt Waldo into eating while his mistress is gone.

189. Schubert, Ingrid, and Dieter Schubert (1994). *Wild Will*. Illustrated by the authors. New York: Carolrhoda. Ages 5–8.

Wild Will is a retired pirate, sometimes grumpy, who wants to be left alone. He is disturbed, however, by Frank, a young boy, who inadvertently has landed a kite on the roof of Will's self-made pirate house. After retrieving his kite, Frank returns daily to tell Wild Will "thanks"—words the pirate doesn't want to hear. Frank leaves homemade gifts, too, and Wild Will finally warms toward the boy, eventually enough to tell Frank some pirate adventures, which motivates the two to look for lost treasure. To search, the two build a raft and Frank learn's Will's secret—he can't swim and has a fear of the water.

190. Sharmat, Marjorie Wienman (1979). *Mr. Jameson and Mr. Phillips*. Illustrated by Bruce Degen. New York: Harper and Row. Ages 6–8.

Sharmat's story answers the question, "What might happen if you ever wanted to get away from it all?" Mr. Jameson is a writer, Mr. Phillips is an artist, and they are the best of friends. They leave the noise and traffic of the city to look for peace and quiet, and a space in which to work. They find it on a small deserted island where they each mark off a space and for many years live peacefully at their separate ends of the island, writing and painting, happy, exchanging holiday cards. One day, however, things change. A stranger arrives, stays, and invites visitors. His visitors come and they invite more people until the once-peaceful island becomes just like the city—buildings, noise, traffic. The two friends get together again and agree to leave. They pack their boat with their supplies and set sail but are unable to find a deserted island. They notice the gentle motion of the boat and realize that they have their place of solitude and peace. They each put an X to mark their space on each end of the boat, and write and paint as they wish and just send Christmas cards at holiday time.

191. Sharmat, Marjorie W. (1972). *Nate the Great*. Illustrated by Marc Simont. New York: Coward. Ages 6–8.

Sharmat's humor is in Nate's imitation of Humphrey Bogart and the way he solves a Dragnet-style mystery. Nate the Great (whose favorite food is pancakes) is hired by Annie to find the recently finished painting of her dog. It has disappeared. Nate gathers all the facts, investigates the suspects, and solves the mystery.

192. Sharmat, Marjorie W. (1974). *Nate the Great Goes Undercover*. Illustrated by Marc Simont. New York: Coward. Ages 6–8.

Nate's next-door neighbor Oliver was a pest but Nate agreed to try to solve Oliver's mystery. It seems that Oliver's garbage can was being burglarized at night and he wanted Nate to catch the snatcher of garbage. Nate makes a list of suspects and eliminates them all. He hides in the can one night and catches the thief—it is Nate's new dog.

193. Sharratt, Nick (1994). *My Mom and Dad Make Me Laugh*. Illustrated by the author. New York: Candlewick. Ages 5–7.

Young Simon, who is a conservative dresser, lives his life surrounded by dots and stripes—his mother likes dots and his father likes stripes. Their design choices make him laugh. At home, the designs—as visual jokes—are on clothing, the floors, the walls and everything in between. Away from home—even when they go on an outing to a safari theme park—Simon, who wears his conservative grey pants and shirt, notices that his mother favors the leopards and his father favors the zebras. Simon likes the elephants best of all and it is only on the last page that the child is let in on the joke and finds out why.

194. Smee, Nicola (1994). *The Tusk Fairy*. Illustrated by the author. New York: Bridgewater Books. Ages 5–6.

When Lizzie was born, Lizzie's grandmother gave her a knitted elephant, which lasted and lasted until one day, the stuffed toy was frazzled and worn, and nothing was left but some knitted fuzz and two tusks. Grandmother suggests that Lizzie put the tusks under her pillow that night and wait for the Tusk Fairy to bring a new toy elephant. Sure enough, the Tusk Fairy brings a new elephant—one with a green tip on its trunk. A child is let in on the joke when they hear the click of knitting needles in the night and infer that Grandmother ran out of grey yarn.

195. Smith, Lane (1993). *The Happy Hocky Family*. Illustrated by the author. New York: Viking. Ages 5–6.

There are both parody and jokes in Smith's illustrations with accompanying tongue-in-cheek humor in the text. The author parodies the "Dick and Jane" format of previous basal readers with eighteen short stories about the Hocky family and the family canine, Newton. For example, the family members go on a family outing to visit the zoo and visit the crocodiles in their habitat because Newton, the dog, likes them the best.

196. Whybrow, Jan (1991). *Quacky Quack-Quack*. Illustrated by Russell Ayto. New York: Four Winds. Ages 5–6.

The fun is in the rhythm and rhyme of animal noises when a toddler is given some bread to feed the ducks but decides to eat the bread himself. The ducks, of course, are irate that they aren't being feed and they quack long and loud. The quacking disturbs the geese and they start honking long and loud. The noise is louder than a nearby band whose members are tooting-tooting. Eventually, alligators, donkeys, dogs, mice, and lions are making their noises, too, and there is chaos in the countryside. In the end, the toddler's big brother restores the peace by trading the bread for an ice cream cone.

Holidays

197. Ahlberg, Allan (1985). *Funnybones*. Illustrated by Janet Ahlberg. New York: Greenwillow. Ages 7–8.

This read-aloud story by Ahlberg and Ahlberg has frolicking skeletons on the title page and a clever comic-strip format that help set the tone. Three skeletons decide to go out and scare someone. Some of the lines are great for a child to chime in on—"In the dark, dark street, there was a dark, dark house."

198. Bangs, Edward (1980). *Yankee Doodle*. Illustrated by Steven Kellogg. New York: Four Winds. Ages 4–8.

Bangs's presentation is an upbeat version of one of America's familiar patriotic songs, *Yankee Doodle*. The book is illustrated by Kellogg with humorous details that help increase the fun of the verses about the excitement, patriotism, and spirit of the day Washington took command of the American army. The well-known melody is included.

199. Brown, Marc (1983). *Arthur's April Fool*. Illustrated by the author. Boston: Atlantic/Little, Brown. Ages 7–8.

Brown's story is centered around an April fool joke and has a surprise ending. Arthur performs his best magic trick and proves to be a hero. Arthur gets back at Binky Barnes, the class bully. *Arthur's Halloween* (Little, Brown, 1983) finds fearful Arthur bravely searching for his little sister in a spooky house on Halloween night. In *Arthur's Valentine* (Little, Brown, 1980), Arthur discovers he has a secret admirer.

200. Greene, Carol (1983). *The Thirteen Days of Halloween*. Illustrated by Tom Dunnington. Chicago: Children's Press. Ages 7–8.

This is Greene's Halloween version of *The Twelve Days of Christmas* and features gifts related to the celebration given by a good friend—a vulture in a dead tree, two hissing cats, three fat toads, and so on. On the thirteenth day, the good friend is invited to lunch to receive a present in return . . . a real live creature hidden in a huge gaily wrapped present. A child will have to guess what the creature is from some pictorial clues given by Dunnington.

201. Guthrie, Donna (1985). *The Witch Who Lived Down the Hall*. Illustrated by Amy Schwartz. New York: Harcourt Brace Jovanovich. Ages 6–7.

Guthrie's tale is told with underlying humor—and had a different twist—to read aloud at Halloween. Ms. McWee, a witch, lives just down the hall from a young boy. As proof that his neighbor is indeed a witch, the boy describes her traits, one by one. He does so with the budding logic of a young lawyer and the earnest appeal of a character that might have been drawn by Judith Viorst. One, Ms. McWee, the boy says, seemed to know all about him before the two even met. She makes click-clack before the noises at night. Ms. McWee just loves Halloween. The mother refutes each bit of evidence but this does little to dispel his suspicions. His illogical reply is "I'm not so sure." The illogical logic and underlying humor of this picture story make it a compelling tale to read, and one that should please young children as they wait for the conclusion: Is Ms. McWee a witch or just a charming and captivating character?

202. Kelley, True (1981). *A Valentine for Fuzzboom*. Illustrated by the author. Boston: Houghton Mifflin. Ages 6–7.

Kelley's illustrations contribute to the humor of this comic valentine story. When Lima Bean, a young rabbit, falls madly in love with dashing Fuzzboom, she fantasizes about him and sees his image in her soup and in the clouds. Finally, she realizes that Fuzzboom is *not* dashing—he is a stuck-up cloud-brain.

203. Kimmel, Eric (1988). *The Chanukah Tree*. Illustrated by Glora Carmi. New York: Holiday House. Ages 6–9.

In this Jewish folktale retold by Kimmel, a ridiculous situation leads to the humor shown in Carmi's illustrations. The people of Chelm believe a peddler when he sells them a Christmas tree as a Chanukah tree—and says it is a special tree from America. He tells them that such trees are the latest thing so the townspeople decorate the tree with potato latkes and candles. The only star they can find for the top is on a door, so the entire door is placed on the top of the tree. When they discover that they have been deceived by the peddler, they are at first very unhappy and think that they have a ridiculous tree. The people then discover that their tree is not ridiculous, for some birds find sanctuary on the tree during a snowstorm and the latkes were food for the birds. The candles provided warmth for the feathered travelers and the door protected them from the storm.

204. Levy, Elizabeth (1982). *Something Queer at the Haunted School: A Mystery*. Illustrated by Mordecai Gerstein. New York: Dell. Ages 6–7.

In Levy's story from the popular "Something Queer" series, Gwen and Jill are trying to discover the identity of the werewolf who is haunting their school before Halloween. A child will particularly be drawn to Fletcher, the dog, who is dressed as a vampire, and the actions of the characters shown in Gerstein's illustrations in this spooky but funny mystery.

205. McDermott, Gerald, reteller (1986). *Daniel O'Rourke: An Irish Tale*. Illustrated by the reteller. New York: Viking Kestrel. Ages 6–8.

Suitable for March reading, this Irish tale retold by McDermott is bizarre, lighthearted fun as strange adventures befall Daniel O'Rourke. Daniel's troubles start when he goes to a grand party at a great mansion on the hill and on his way home, stops to rest by a stone tower that is claimed by a pooka, a mischievous spirit that can change its shape. Daniel falls asleep and his lovely summer night turns sour.

Jokes, Riddles, and Puns

206. Aber, Linda Williams (1993). *The Big Golden Book of Riddles, Jokes, Giggles, and Rhymes.* New York: Golden/Western. Ages 6–8.

This is a collection of limericks, jokes, riddles, and knock-knock jokes. There is no better book to take to read aloud on the bus while on the way to a field trip site or to leave on a display table for those odd moments of reading and browsing.

207. Adler, David A. (1988). *The Dinosaur Princess: And Other Prehistoric Riddles.* Illustrated by Loreen Leedy. New York: Holiday. Ages 6–8.

The prehistoric riddles in this collection will amuse a child with puns, plays on words, and some silliness in the familiar question-and-answer type riddles. Some of the just-for-chuckles bits are:

- *Silliness:* What does a triceratops sit on? (*His tricera-bottom.*) What would you say if you saw a three-headed dinosaur? (*Hello, hello, hello.*)
- *Pun:* How did cavemen and women make wooden tools? (*A whittle at a time.*)
- *Play on words:* How did cave men and women discover the sun? (*It just dawned on them.*)

208. Burns, L. Diane (1990). *Here's to Ewe: Riddles about Sheep.* Illustrated by Susan Slattery Burns. Minneapolis, Minn.: Lerner. Ages 7–8.

Here's to Ewe is an unusual collection since all the riddles are related to sheep and their characteristics. The questions, many with answers that are plays on words, ask, "How do sheep fall asleep?" (*By counting people.*) "What kind of trucks do sheep drive?" (*Ewe-hauls.*) "What do you say to a good-looking sheep?" (*Ewe look marvelous!*) "What do grouchy rams say at Christmas time?" (*Baaa! Humbug!*) And there are many pages of more riddles just like these.

209. Cerf, Bennett (1964). *Bennett Cerf's Book of Animal Riddles.* Illustrated by Roy McKie. New York: Random House. Ages 6–7.

Cerf's text has riddles with unexpected bursts of humor about domestic and wild animals and their characteristics. Specific animals, as well as general types, are shown in McKie's illustrations when they are mentioned in jokes about dogs, geese, fish, and others.

210. Eisenberg, Lisa, and Katy Hall (1993). *Batty Riddles.* Illustrated by Nicole Rubel. New York: Dial. Ages 6–8.

This is a collection of silly riddles that will be fun for a child to ask others and all of the questions are related to the topic of bats. One of the let's-laugh entries is:

"Why did the little bat walk around in his pajamas?"

(*He didn't have a bat-robe.*)

211. Friedman, Sharon, and Irene Shere (1988). *Make Me Laugh! Cat's Out of the Bag: Jokes about Cats.* Illustrated by Joan Hanson. Minneapolis, Minn.: Lerner. Ages 8 and up.

This is a collection of riddles related to cats and their characteristics. Madcap feline funnies include "Where did the cat get a new toaster?" (*from a cat-alog*); and "Where do cats go for fun?" (*the a-mew-sment park*).

212. Gomez, Victoria (1981). *Wags to Witches: More Jokes, Riddles, and Puns.* Illustrated by Joel Schick. New York: Lothrop, Lee & Shepard. Ages 7–8.

This is an entertaining collection of jokes, puns, and riddles that could lure a reluctant reader to read as well as challenge an independent reader. One of the grin-or-groan puns is "Why did the passenger refuse to bail out?" (*He thought they gave him a perish-chute.*)

213. Gounaud, Karen Jo (1993). *A Very Mice Joke Book.* Illustrated by Lynn Munsinger. New York: Lothrop, Lee & Shepard. Ages 7–8.

Gounaud's text is a collection of riddles that play on the word *mice.* While it might seem unfair to some children to make fun of these rodents in this way, the mouse names and related jokes are humorous to read, and Munsinger's illustrations add a great deal to the title.

214. Hall, Katy, and Lisa Eisenberg (1983). *Fishy Riddles*. Illustrated by Simms Taback. New York: Dial. Ages 7–8.

This is a collection of deep-sea snickers—there are over forty riddles related to life in the ocean. Several just-for-laughs entries are:

- "Why are fish so smart?" (*They're always in school.*)
- "How do you make a whale float?" (*Use two scoops of ice cream, some root beer, and a whale.*)
- "Why was the swordfish's nose 11 inches long?" (*If it were twelve inches, it would be a foot.*)

215. Hartman, Victoria (1993). *The Silliest Joke Book Ever*. Illustrated by R. W. Alley. New York: Lothrop, Lee & Shepard. Ages 5–8.

In this joke book, one of the joking questions is: "How did the dragon devour the computer?" (*in one byte*). And there are over eighty more jokes in a question-and-answer format like this. The book offers categories of subjects that include "food funnies," "gruesome giggles," and "techie ticklers."

216. Hoberman, Mary Ann (1978). *A House Is a House for Me*. Illustrated by Betty Fraser. New York: Viking. All ages.

Hoberman's book has upbeat rhymes about houses—some are familiar ones and others are quite unique. For instance, roses are considered houses for smell, pods are thought of as houses for peas, and pockets are seen as houses for pennies. Fraser's bright, colorful illustrations are filled with humorous details that add fun and interest.

217. Keller, Charles, compiler (1986). *Count Draculations: Monster Riddles*. Illustrated by Edward Frascino. Englewood Cliffs, N.J.: Prentice-Hall. Ages 7–8.

Outlandish puns and jokes that use the monster-and-witch theme are in this collection. The question related to the answer in the title asks, "What do you say to a new vampire?" (*Count Draculations*). Other examples: "Why do witches get A's in school?" (*They're good at spelling*); "Why did the invisible man go crazy?" (*Out of sight, out of mind*); and "Why do witches fly on broomsticks? (*It beats walking*).

218. Keller, Charles, compiler (1984). *Grime Doesn't Pay: Law and Order Jokes*. Illustrated by Jack Kent. Englewood Cliffs, N.J.: Prentice-Hall. Ages 7–8.

More outlandish puns and jokes that use the theme—Grime doesn't pay—have been collected in this book. One example: What do you call a policeman's suit? (*A lawsuit*). For those children interested further in other humorous collections by Charles Keller, guide them to *Norma Lee I Don't Knock on Doors: Knock Knock Jokes* (Prentice-Hall, 1983) or *Smokey the Shark* (Prentice-Hall, 1981). *Smokey* has pictures by Lee Lorenz and *Norma Lee* has illustrations by Paul Galdone. Both are very funny, have entertaining jokes, and will appeal to children with a zany sense of humor.

219. Lillegard, Dee (1993). *Do Not Feed the Table*. Illustrated by Keiko Hnurahashi. New York: Doubleday. Ages 5–8.

Lillegard's title is a clue to the anthropomorphism in the story and the illustrations by Hnurahashi highlight the text about a young boy, his dog, and often, his father. Both the appliances and the foods have human characteristics (hence the title) as the appliances grin and the potatoes each have two eyes and peer over the edge of a bowl, warily eyeing the potato peeler.

220. Livingston, Myra Cohn, selector (1994). *Riddle-Me Rhymes*. Illustrated by Rebecca Perry. New York: McElderry. Ages 8 and up.

Black-and-white cartoon sketches by Perry introduce each section of this riddle book compiled by Livingston. There are over eighty riddles that represent a variety of sources—Lewis Carroll, Emily Dickinson, Mother Goose, and others. The answers to the riddles appear upside down at the foot of each page.

221. Lobel, Arnold, selector (1986). *The Random House Book of Mother Goose*. Illustrated by selector. New York: Random House. Ages 7–8.

Lobel's book offers three hundred rhymes that are put together in categories. For instance, there are rhymes about clothes, food, and other topics that appear on a page spread together. Every rhyme is illustrated in a variety of comic strip shapes—panels, squares, and circles. Some of the illustrations portray some of the rhymes literally (reminding a child again of Amelia in *Amelia Bedelia*)—for Mary's garden is *really* growing pretty maids all in a row.

222. Lobel, Arnold (1985). *Whiskers and Rhymes*. Illustrated by the author. New York: Greenwillow. Ages 5–7.

This book presents thirty-five rhymes with bits of word play and sounds of language. The rhymes offer comedy and verses about selected humans (shown as cat personalities) and the incidents in their lives. There is humorous word play in such selections as "sing a song of succotash" and "George brushed his teeth with pickle paste." The cats are dressed in period costumes and are seen in full-page frame settings, vignettes, and boxed actions.

223. Maestro, Guilio (1983). *Halloween Howls*. Illustrated by the author. New York: Dutton. Ages 7–8.

The colorful, funny illustrations by Maestro are in step with the text and add to the enjoyment. Wizards, ghosts, and ghouls are featured in these riddles suitable for a "howling" good time. Perhaps some of the children will enjoy asking the questions in these riddles to friends—"How do witches stay in touch?" (*By calling poison to poison on the telebone.*)

224. Phillips, Louis (1993). *Wackysaurus: Dinosaur Jokes*. Illustrated by Ron Barrett. New York: Viking. Ages 7–8.

Phillips's book is an interesting title to share with children since there are some slapstick scenes in Barrett's illustrations that include the pie-in-the-face action. The text focuses mainly on dinosaur jokes in the question-and-answer format but there are also one-liners, two-line riddles, and word play.

225. Scheier, Michael, and Julie Frankel (1978). *The Whole Mirth Catalog*. Illustrated by the authors. New York: Franklin Watts. Ages 7–8.

This is a big book (8 1/2″ × 11″) filled with puns, jokes, and interesting things to make and do. The content has a variety of subjects ranging from parents and teachers to food and habits. Included are several humorous illustrations and some how-to sketches in red, white, and black. For a back-to-school activity, guide a child to the section about writing about "My Summer Vacation."

226. Schultz, Sam (1982). *701 Monster Jokes*. Illustrated by Joan Hanson. New York: Lerner. Ages 7–8.

One hundred riddles related to the theme of monsters are in this collection. The format is in a typical question-and-answer manner. For example, a child can look for the answers to such questions as "Do you know what to do with a green monster?" and "Do you know why vampires are like stars?"

227. Thaler, Mike (1985). *Funny Side Up!* Illustrated by the author. New York: Scholastic. Ages 7–8.

Thaler, a riddle writer, shares what he goes through to write riddles and provides some helpful tips on writing, illustrating, and publishing riddles. For a child interested further in writing original riddles or in Thaler's work, suggest *Never Tickle a Turtle!* (Franklin Watts, 1977) and *Monster Knock Knocks* (Archway/Pocket Books, 1982) by Thaler and William Cole. *Never* has puns, riddles, and jokes about such familiar creatures as the ant, the mouse, and the pig. *Monster* has simple cartoons, plays on words, and jokes in the familiar knock-knock format.

Nonsense

228. Allard, Harry (1981). *The Stupids Die*. Illustrated by James Marshall. Boston: Houghton Mifflin. Ages 7–8.

This is Allard's story of good fun about the Stupid family whose members have neat names but are indeed witless. When there is a power shortage and the lights go out, the Stupids are sure they have died. When the power returns and the lights come on again, they are convinced they are in heaven. After Grandpa tells them they still are in Cleveland, funny things happen and the characters, actions, and setting are shown in Marshall's colorful cartoons. For example, there is a picture on the wall of a dog labeled "Fish." For a child interested further in this family of zanies, suggest the following:

- *The Stupids Step Out* (Houghton Mifflin, 1978) where the weird family goes out on the town
- *The Stupids Have a Ball* (Houghton Mifflin, 1978) where the whole family decides to celebrate because the children brought home terrible report cards from school

229. Caldwell, John (1981). *Excuses, Excuses: How to Get Out of Practically Anything*. Illustrated by the author. New York: Crowell. Ages 7–8.

This is Caldwell's collection of absurd—sometimes witty—excuses and strategies that are offered for getting out of things a child does not want to do. Such things include walking the dog or doing homework. There are black-and-white sketches that highlight the absurdity of the excuses.

230. Carroll, Lewis (1977). *Jabberwocky*. Illustrated by Jane Breskin. New York: Warne. Ages 5–8.

This is Carroll's nonsense poem from *Alice in Wonderland* that is delicately illustrated in this version. A child can reflect upon his or her mental images of Carroll's "vorpal sword" and "Tumtum tree" and "Tulgey wood" and compare them to Breskin's interpretations. There appears to be a warning in some of Carroll's words—this sentence sounds serious but is really nonsense: "*Beware the Jabberwock, my son! The jaws that bite, the claws that catch! Beware the Jubjub bird, and shun the frumious Bandersnatch!*"

231. Degen, Bruce (1983). *Jamberry*. Illustrated by the author. New York: Harper and Row. Ages 5–6.

This is Degen's lilting nonsense rhyme about a boy and a bear who go on a delicious berry-picking adventure. It has lighthearted illustrations and some singsong tongue twisting lyrics about the number of berries picked—"One berry/ Two berry/ Pick me a blueberry. / Hatberry/ Shoeberry/ In my canoeberry." Words also are creatively combined and fun to roll off the tongue—"Hayberry" and "Finger and pawberry."

232. Frank, John (1993). *Odds 'n' Alvy*. Illustrated by Brian Karas. New York: Four Winds. Ages 5–8.

Frank's story is a tale about crazy fun. Alvy, a young school boy, uses all kinds of household junk to make an amazing acrobatic machine for his transportation. There is a very special reason why Alvy needs the jet-propelled machine which a child discovers, appropriately, at the ending.

233. Gwynne, Fred (1970). *The King Who Rained*. New York: Windmill Books/E. P. Dutton. Ages 7 and up.

This is Gwynne's collection of sayings that are literally interpreted in the illustrations. For example, the saying in the title is elaborated in the text to "Daddy says there was a king who rained for forty years" and the illustration shows a bearded king. He wears his gold crown and levitates in the blue sky while raindrops fall from his red robe trimmed in white fur. Additionally, oversize forks form highways and overpasses accompany "Daddy says there are forks in the road." Pigs sit around the dinner table and talk to match "Daddy says some boars are coming to dinner."

234. Hanel, Wolfram (1994). *The Extraordinary Adventures of an Ordinary Hat*. Translated from German by J. Alison James. Illustrated by Christa Unzner-Fischer. New York: North-South Books. Ages 7–8.

In Hanel's fanciful tale, a black bowler deliberately lets itself be blown away from its second owner in a search for adventure—and romance. Weeks later, the bowler sends a letter to its original owner, the owner of the hat store, and says it's happily settled in South America. The bowler is now with a new owner, Don Leonardo, and it seems that Leonardo's new bride wears a sweet straw hat that has caught the bowler's attention.

235. Joyce, William (1993). *Santa Calls*. Illustrated by the author. New York: HarperCollins. Ages 6–8.

In Joyce's humorous fantasy, Santa invites Art Atchinson Aimesworth, his little sister Esther, and his friend Spaulding, to visit him at the North Pole. On the way, they are confronted by Ali Aku, Captain of the Santarian Guard, and the Dark Elves and their evil queen in scenes reminiscent of *The Wizard of Oz*. At last, they enter Santa's toyland and have a few adventures similar to those in *The Nutcracker* until they are magically returned safely to their beds. On the final two pages, there are two letters that are attached and must be read before a child will know the reason why Art and the others were invited to the North Pole.

236. Juster, Norman (1989). *As: A Surfeit of Similes*. Illustrated by David Small. New York: Morrow. Ages 6–9.

Juster's book uses silly humor to show some of the powers of similes—as in—as exciting as a plateful of cabbage. A child learns about what something *is not* to learn about what it *is* with the various examples. For a child interested further in silly humor of this type, select Marvin Terban's books *Guppies in Tuxedos: Funny Eponyms* and *The Dove Dove: Funny Homograph Riddles* (both by Clarion, 1989).

237. Lewis, J. Patrick (1994). *The Fat-Cats at Sea*. Illustrated by Victoria Chess. New York: Knopf. Ages 6–8.

In Lewis's nonsense rhyming story, the queen of Catmandoo announces a mission for the sailing sea-cats—find some sticky-buns. The cats leave in their ship, *The Frisky Dog,* but soon run into a terrible thunderstorm that has their navigator cringing. Thus it takes a while for the cats to reach the island of Goo with its caramel waters, beaches of cinnamon, almond bushes, and doughnut-laden trees. The cats load fourteen tons of sticky-buns on board and on their return to Catmandoo are confronted by an enemy ship manned by sea-dogs—poodles wearing curls and pearls. The cats defend their cargo by firing sweet candies at the poodles who retreat "licking their wounds." Upon their successful return, the queen dubs the crew the fat-cat knights.

238. Lorenz, Lee (1983). *Hugo and the Spacedog*. Illustrated by the author. Englewood Cliffs, N.J.: Prentice-Hall. Ages 6–7.

This is Lorenz's nonsense tale about Hugo, a wandering dog, who decides to settle down as a watchdog on a farm. In his unique encounter with a space dog, he proves to be quick-witted and thinks of creative approaches to several unusual situations. Through it all, Hugo emerges as a brave and endearing hero. There are bright cartoon-style illustrations that highlight the canine's adventures.

239. Mahy, Margaret (1987). *17 Kings and 42 Elephants*. Illustrated by Patricia MacCarthy. New York: Dial. Ages 7–8.

Here are humorous illustrations by MacCarthy and enjoyable nonsense by Mahy in the rhymes and rhythmic words as kings ride on the backs of elephants who have ears like "umbrellaphants" and travel through the jungle to a rollicking beat in the text. On the royal journey, there are "tinkling tunesters" and "twangling twillicans" that flutter in the air through the great green trees and crocodiles that are as "rough as rockodiles" on the ground.

240. Most, Bernard (1978). *If the Dinosaurs Came Back*. Illustrated by the author. New York: Harcourt Brace Jovanovich. Ages 6–7.

Most's humor is in the imaginative idea that if the dinosaurs came back to modern times, they would do something unusual—scare away robbers, become playground slides for children, and give dentists plenty of teeth to work on. There are bold line illustrations with red, yellow, and purple dinosaurs to highlight the text—a dentist lies in the dinosaur's mouth to work on the giant creature's rows of teeth; kittens stuck in tall trees are rescued; and some dinosaurs help construct tall buildings in the city.

241. Most, Bernard (1979). *Whatever Happened to the Dinosaurs?* Illustrated by the author.

New York: Harcourt Brace Jovanovich. Ages 6–7.

Some unusual sights are found in Most's book. This is a humorous collection of some fanciful explanations of where the dinosaurs went. The illustrations are simple watercolor illustrations that depict the whimsical conjectures.

242. Oram, Hiawyn (1993). *A Creepy Crawly Song Book*. Illustrated by Satoshi Kitamura. New York: Farrar, Straus & Giroux. Ages 5–7.

The fun is not only in Oram's verses about bugs but also in Kitamura's humorous presentation of the rhythmic songs. For example, a page is embellished with strands of hair to draw attention to the song about lice and oversize ants. They decorate the pages for "the march of the worker ants." The titles of the songs are worth a laugh—"A Hundred Feet Ahead: The Dance of the Centipede;" "Slow, Slow Snail;" and "The Lament of the House Fly."

243. Schwartz, Alvin. *Whoppers: Tall Tales and Other Lies*. Illustrated by Glen Rounds. New York: Lippincott, 1980. All ages.

According to Schwartz in his introduction, this book is a pack of lies. This collection of humorous stories highlights the history of the frontier and the lies called the golly gloppers. The tall tales, illustrated by Rounds, are related to animals, the weather, narrow escapes, and other topics from American folklore. The tales are grouped into categories of "ordinary people," "ordinary things," "fancy clothes and narrow escapes," "animals and insects," "putrefactions and other wonders," and "the weather." Also included are notes about the tales, a list of sources, bibliography, and an index.

244. Seuss, Dr. (1937). *And to Think I Saw It on Mulberry Street*. Illustrated by the author. New York: Random House. All ages.

A small boy is warned by his father, "Stop telling such outlandish tales/ Stop turning minnows into whales." But on his way home from school, the boy sees a broken-down wagon that's drawn by a horse on Mulberry Street. He starts to embellish what he saw to tell his father when he reaches home. He wants a story that "no one can beat" and elaborates the scene into a charioteer and chariot, then into a sleigh drawn by an elephant, then into a trailer with a band pulled by two giraffes *and* the elephant. Imaginatively, the boy adds a police escort, the mayor, and other characters to the scene. Each

page shows the next addition in the boy's mind until two full-page spreads are needed to get everything in the illustration. When the boy reaches home, however, his father asks him what he saw on his way home from school that "made his heart beat." The boy's thoughts diminish suddenly under his father's cold stare, and he responds, "Nothing . . . but a plain horse and wagon on Mulberry Street."

245. Seuss, Dr. (1949). *Bartholomew and the Oobleck*. Illustrated by the author. New York: Random House. Ages 6–8.

A page boy named Bartholomew Cubbins saves the kingdom of Didd when the king gets angry with the sky. The king wishes for something to fall from the sky that no other kingdom had ever had before. His wish brings oobleck—a green menace that falls on the kingdom's inhabitants. Overwhelmed, the king asks for help and it is Bartholomew who saves the day when he suggests a remedy to the king.

246. Seuss, Dr. (1938). *The 500 Hats of Bartholomew Cubbins*. Illustrated by the author. New York: Random House. Ages 6–8.

This is a rhymed narrative filled with nonsense. Cubbins takes off his hat to the king only to find the royal coach stopping and the king sternly commanding him to take off his hat. Puzzled, Cubbins puts his hand to his head and finds another hat there. He jerks it off hastily only to find another in its place, and another, and so on. He is seized and threatened with death, but still the hats continue to arrive on his head. Finally, the king sees on Cubbins' head the most gloriously regal hat he has ever seen. In exchange for this elegant hat, he spares Cubbins's life, and Cubbins find his own head free of hats at last.

247. Seuss, Dr. (1968). *Horton Hatches the Egg*. Illustrated by the author. New York: Random House. Ages 6–8.

Horton the kindhearted elephant is faithful—one hundred percent—to his promise to hatch the egg of Mayzie—a lazy bird who wants to leave her nest and have a vacation in Florida. Horton agrees to be the egg-sitter for a while and climbs carefully up into the little tree. Mayzie enjoys Palm Beach so much she stays longer and Horton stays on the egg—through blizzard, rain, and the distractions of other peering animal observers. He asserts: "I meant what I said/And I said what I meant . . ./An elephant's faithful/ One hundred per cent!" Horton gets his reward later on when the egg hatches and it is an elephant-bird—it is about fifty percent elephant with ears, tail, and trunk just like Horton's and wings like Mayzie's. Other books with zinging verses by Dr. Seuss are Random House publications, *How the Grinch Stole Christmas* (1957) and *The Cat in the Hat* (1957).

248. Talbott, Hudson (1992). *Your Pet Dinosaur: An Owner's Manual*. Illustrated by the author. New York: Morrow. Ages 5–8.

This is Talbott's chaptered book that is a spoof on raising dinosaurs written by an unknown Dr. Rex who gives readers tips on the selection and disciplining, feeding, exercising, and training of the dinosaurs—the intellectual giants of their time. The chapter headings include such humorous topics as "the well-dressed dinosaur" and "fashion don'ts for dinos." There is even a "Dear Dr. Rex" column where the owners have sent in their letters asking questions about their dinosaur's behavior. For instance, one owner is concerned about his dino pet who keeps jumping on the mail carrier; another's concern is that his dino companion hates trombone music; and still another questions the credentials of the unknown Dr. Rex.

249. Tomkins, Jasper (1981). *The Catalog*. Illustrated by the author. San Diego: Green Tiger. Ages 5–6.

This is Tomkins's amusing story of three bare mountains who order some mountain inhabitants—twenty-seven giraffes, sixty-one turtles, and fifty-two bears from a catalog. When the animals need food, shelter, and entertainment, these are also ordered by mail from the catalog. Black-and-white drawings show the nonsense.

250. William, Jay (1980). *One Big Wish*. Illustrated by John O'Brien. New York: Macmillan. Ages 6–7.

William's humor is in the unpredictable events. This is an outlandish tale illustrated by O'Brien in cinnamon-brown and green drawings in which a kindhearted person helps to free a woman's dress from a bramble bush. In gratitude, she grants him a wish fulfillment. This results in an unexpected cause-and-effect situation and a humorous conclusion.

251. Zemach, Margot (1986). *The Three Wishes*. Illustrated by the author. New York: Farrar, Straus & Giroux. Ages 5–8.

This is a traditional English tale retold by Zemach where a woodcutter and his wife's wishes are granted by an imp whose tail was caught under a fallen tree and his rescue leads to a humorous situation. The couple free the imp and in return the imp cautions them to "wish wisely." Hungry, the woodcutter wishes for a pan of sausages for dinner. Realizing that one wish was gone, his wife becomes angry and wishes the sausages were hanging from his big nose. Now, two wishes are gone and this results in some nonsensical actions culminating in the woodcutter's dog attempting to get a taste of the string of sausages hanging from his master's nose. At the end of the tale, the satisfied couple are enjoying the sausages that they wished off the man's nose with their final wish. They agree, "We've not done too badly."

Rhymes and Verses

252. Adoff, Arnold (1985). *The Cabbages Are Chasing the Rabbits*. Illustrated by Janet Stevens. New York: Harcourt Brace Jovanovich. Ages 7–8.

Adoff offers this rhythmic accumulation of verses about what happened on a fanciful day in May when roles were reversed—the hunters became the hunted. Stevens translates the words into unusual experiences in the illustrations. For example, the garden vegetables pulled up their roots and chased the rabbits. The rabbits, cottontails of courage, chased the hunting dogs and the dogs—careful canines—chased the hunters. The hunters started chasing the trees and the trees began chasing the leaves that were blowing in the breeze. In the middle of all the chasing, the birds did not fly about to search for food but sat stubbornly on the ground and waited for breakfast to be served.

253. Belloc, Hilaire (1961). *The Bad Child's Book of Beasts, More Beasts for Worse Children,* and *A Moral Alphabet* (*In Words of From One to Seven Syllables*). Illustrated by Basil T. Blackwood. New York: Dover. All ages.

The Bad Child's Book of Beasts is how poet Belloc sees zany biology and he offers descriptions of such animals as the dromedary (*a cheerful bird*), the whale that wanders round the Pole (*is not a table fish*), and the camelopard (*who cannot stretch out straight in bed*). *More Beasts for Worse Children* offers more creature descriptions—the llama, with its indolent expression, is described as a "woolly sort of fleecy hair goat" and the microbe "is so very small, you cannot make him out at all." *A Moral Alphabet* has brief admonishments related to the late 1800s for verses from *a* to *z*. For example, a gliding waterbeetle introduces the letter *w* and "flabbergasts the human race" with its ease in the water . . . "But if he ever stopped to think,/ Of how he did it, he would sink." Belloc's moral is "Don't ask questions!"

254. Brewton, John E., and Lorraine A. Blackburn (1978). *They've Discovered a Head in the Box for the Bread*. Illustrated by Fernando Krahn. New York: Crowell. Ages 7–8.

This book is suitable for introducing limericks to a child. These limericks are humorous and some are intellectually challenging—especially those in the section, "Can You Read These? They're Especially Tricky." The vocabulary in some of the verses is sophisticated and may interest some children in searching in the dictionary. Some examples of words to investigate are *coloratura, sonorous,* and *troupial.* The last section suggests using a limerick with *no* last lines for a child who wants to explore ways of creating his or her own original lines for a limerick.

255. Brown, Beatrice Curtis (1978). *Jonathan Bing*. Illustrated by Judith Gwyn Brown. New York: Lothrop, Lee & Shepard. Ages 6–8.

In Brown's funny verse, Jonathan Bing's actions surprise a reader when he visits a royal ruler and shows his manners. He shows he can do math, read a book, and dance. The brief situation is eventually carried to a logical conclusion when he eventually moves away after he has had tea.

256. Brown, Marcia, reteller (1959). *Peter Piper's Principles of Plain and Perfect Pronunciation with Manifold Manifestations*. Illustrations by Marcia Brown, reteller. New York: Scribner's. Ages 7–8.

One of the most entertaining forms of humor to say aloud is alliterative tongue twisters and Brown has retold several in this book. The text from *a* to *z* has a bouncy nonsense rhyme with tongue-tangling lyrics. A typical piece of alliteration for the letter *B:*

Billy Button bought a buttered biscuit.
Did Billy Button buy a buttered biscuit?
If Billy Button bought a buttered biscuit,
Where's the buttered biscuit Billy Button bought?

257. Ciardi, John (1961). *I Met a Man*. Illustrated by Robert Osborn. Boston: Houghton Mifflin. Ages 5–8.

Here are Ciardi's lighthearted nonsense poems that have a controlled vocabulary of about four hundred words for the beginning reader. The poems increase from simple to complex both in words and content. For children interested further in Ciardi's original viewpoints—often short satires on children's behavior—guide them to any or all of the following:

- *Fast and Slow: Poems for Advanced Children and Beginning Parents* (Houghton Mifflin, 1975) has illustrations by Becky Gaver that emphasize the witty poems.
- *The Man who Sang the Sillies* (Lippincott, 1951) offers "summer song" where the narrator omits words and asks listeners to guess where he/she is ("By the sand between my toes,/ By the waves behind my ears,/ By the sunburn on my nose").
- *Scrappy, the Pup* (Lippincott, 1960) is a narrative in couplets. It is the story of a snoozing puppy who was supposed to be awake and on watch at the henhouse. One evening, a hungry fox gets into the henhouse, and of course, the raucous noise begins when the chickens catch sight of the unwanted intruder. The farmer hears the chicken's alarm and hurries to the rescue but through it all, Scrappy is sound asleep.
- *You Read to Me, I'll Read to You* (Lippincott, 1962) has spoofs on parent-child relations and illustrations by Edward Gorey. The poems are alternating verses where a child reads a verse and then an adult reads one. There are such unique characters as Arvin Marvin Lillisbee Fitch, Change McTang McQuarter Cat, and the narrator of the morning saga in "Mummy Slept Late and Daddy Fixed Breakfast."

258. Cole, William (1978). *Oh, Such Foolishness*. Illustrated by Tomie de Paola. New York: Lippincott. Ages 5–8.

This is Cole's collection of nonsense in verses about events and personalities such as Jimmy Jupp, Who Died of Over-Eating, The Panteater, The Hidebehind, and a Taxi Crab. Want to know what Grandpa saw when he dropped his glasses into a pot of dye? (*Purple birds were rising up/From a purple hill,/Men were grinding purple cider/At a purple mill*). Or what would happen if things grew down? (*If things grew down/Instead of up,/A dog would grow into a pup*). Or some things that have never been seen? (*I never saw a ghost on stilts/A witch wrapped up in patchwork quilts*). Cole's title poem offers original words— "Oh, such silliness!/ Silly, willy-nilliness,/ Dopey hillybilliness,/ Rolling down the hilliness!" A title and subject index are included. For readers interested in more of this type of humor, Cole has compiled:

- *Beastly Boys and Ghastly Girls* (Collins, 1964) is a volume of poems and line drawings that depict a drove of naughty yet appealing children created by John Carroll, John Ciardi, and Shel Silverstein, among others.
- The titles of *Oh, That's Ridiculous* (Viking, 1972), *Oh, How Silly* (Viking, 1970), and *Humorous Poetry for Children* (Collins, 1955) are clues to the offerings that are included. The collection of poems in these three volumes will appeal to a variety of tastes of children in the middle and upper grades—as well as to younger children as they listen to the selections read aloud.

259. Crane, Walter (1981). *An Alphabet of Old Friends and the Absurd ABC*. Illustrated by the author. New York: The Metropolitan Museum of Art and Thames and Hudson. Ages 5–8.

Exaggeration holds much of the appeal in this collection of verses and rhymes. Mother Goose characters are the focus in many of the actions—the cat that played on the fiddle when cows jumped higher than "Heigh Diddle Diddle!"; Humpty who felt "obliged to resign his seat on the wall"; and the woman (not overnice) who "made short of" the three blind mice.

260. Eichenberg, Fritz (1952). *Ape in a Cape: An Alphabet of Odd Animals*. Illustrated by the author. New York: Harcourt Brace Jovanovich. Ages 5–8.

There are rhyming words in the captions under each colored illustration that shows an animal in an odd pose or situation—an ape in a cape, a carp with a harp, a goat in a boat, and so on. Rhyming words occur in each caption— *dove* and *love, egret* and *minuet*, etc.

261. Lear, Edward (1951). *The Complete Nonsense of Edward Lear*. Collected and introduced by Holbrook Jackson. New York: Dover. Ages 7–8.

This is a collection of Lear's limericks, alphabet rhymes, nonsense botany, and narrative poems. A typical limerick from Lear: "There was an old man with a beard/ Who said, 'It is just as I feared!—/ Two owls and a hen/ Four larks and a wren,/ Have all built their nests in my beard.' " Each verse is illustrated by Lear's drawings and adds to the humor. For another example, "The Pelican Chorus" about the lovely leathery throated pelicans is accompanied by Lear's sketch of the king and queen. The nonsense words in the chorus are repeated through the verses: "Ploffskin, Pluffskin, Pelican jee!/ We think no Birds so happy as we!/ Plumpskin, Ploshkin, Pelican jill!/ We think so then, and we thought so still!"

Music for the piano is included and words to the chorus, "The Pelicans," begin with "King and Queen of the Pelicans we . . ." For readers interested in more about Lear and his humor, suggest *How Pleasant to Know Mr. Lear* (Holiday House, 1982) by Myra Cohn Livingston. In this collection, Lear's verses are arranged to highlight some of the details of his life—an unusual biographical approach.

262. Lear, Edward (1983). *An Edward Lear Alphabet*. Illustrated by Carol Newsom. New York: Lothrop, Lee & Shepard. Ages 5–8.

Newsom's illustrations and Lear's nonsense verses introduce the letters of the alphabet. The verses have families of word endings and a chubby little mouse, dressed in appropriate clothing for each scene, adds interest through humorous parallel activities as he flies on the back of a kite, plays a banjo, plays the part of a court jester. The mouse can be found in every scene from A to Z. For example for the letter *e*, the mouse dons his mask, swim fins, and swim trunks to look for the eel in the verse:

E was once a little eel,
Eely,
Weely,
Peely,
Eely,
Twirly, Tweely,
Little eel!

263. Lear, Edward (1986). *Edward Lear's ABC: Alphabet Rhymes for Children*. Illustrated by Carol Pike. Topsfield, Me.: Salem House. Ages 5–8.

These rhymes first appeared in Lear's *Nonsense Songs, Stories, Botany and Alphabets* published in 1871. The rhymes and objects from apple pie to zinc introduce the letters. There are upper- and lower-case letters in bordered inserts in full-color illustrations.

264. Lear, Edward (1967). *Lear's Nonsense Verse*. Illustrated by Tomi Ungerer. New York: Grosset and Dunlap. Ages 5–8.

Among the verses that are included in this volume are "The Table and the Chair" (they wanted to take a "little walk" and have a "little talk"), "Mr. and Mrs. Spikky Sparrow" (they flew to town and bought new clothes so they could look and feel "galloobious and genteel"), and "The Broom, the Shovel, the Poker, and the Tongs" (they all took a drive in the park; Mr. Poker sings to Mrs. Shovel and says "You have perfectly conquered my heart" and Mr. Tongs calls Mrs. Broom "the fairest of creatures").

265. Lear, Edward (1977). *The Owl and the Pussycat*. Illustrated by Gwen Fulton. New York: Atheneum. Ages 5–6.

Elegant full-page illustrations enliven this well-loved poem about the owl and the pussycat who went to sea in a beautiful pea-green boat. It continues in a melodic and chanting way and has refrains in the public domain for a child to chime in on:

They took some honey, and plenty of money,
Wrapped up in a five-pound note.
The owl looked up to the stars above,
And sang to a small guitar,
"O Lovely Pussy! O Pussy my love,
What a beautiful pussy you are,
 You are,
 You are!
What a beautiful pussy you are!

266. Lear, Edward (1968). *The Scroobious Pip*. Completed by Ogden Nash. Illustrated by Nancy Ekholm Burkett. New York: Harper and Row. Ages 7–8.

A child can speculate about the nature of Lear's strange pip in this long narrative poem as well as what attracted the different animals of the world to look at the unusual creature. When the pip goes out, it seems that all the beasts come to look but can't make out in the least if the pip is "fish or insect, bird or beast." Despite attempts to have the pip tell about itself, the creatures hear only a "whistly sound" when it says, "Wizzely wip! Wizzely wip! My only name is the Scroobious Pip!" Burkett's illustrations of the pip show a tail like a fish, wings and antennae like an insect, legs like a beast, and a beak like a bird. In the foreword, Burkett reflects that it was the idea of "harmony between ourselves and nature" which she felt was present in the rhythmic verses about the pip. This poem is accompanied by a wide variety of animal forms shown in full-color paintings and line drawings. For children interested in another creature from Lear's zany biological world, guide them to *The Pobble Who Has No Toes* (Viking, 1978) with its illustrations by Kevin W. Maddison. It is more supernonsense.

267. Lear, Edward (1970). *The Quangle Wangle's Hat*. Illustrated by Helen Oxenbury. New York: Franklin Watts. Ages 7–8.

This narrative poem, based on an uncommon experience about the comfort of the Quangle Wangle's beaver hat as a home in the top of the crumpetty tree as well as the nature of the different animals who arrived, is a favorite. The beaver hat of the Quangle Wangle attracted strange creatures who came to make their home in it since it was a hundred and two feet wide with "ribbons and bibbons on every side." Among those that arrived were the porcupine-like Attery Squash, the caterpillarlike Pobble—all green and oversize—and the Dong with the glowing luminous nose.

268. LeSeig, Theo (1970). *The Nose Book*. Illustrated by Roy McKie. New York: Random House. Ages 5–6.

Here is more nonsense than fact in the rhymes about various noses and their differences, what happens to them, and what they are used for. What would happen if we had *no* nose? The print and pictures tell the answer. A child would never smell a rose or never have a place for all eyeglasses to sit. There are bright colors in the illustrations. For a child who wants more of this kind of nonsense, suggest:

- *The Tooth Book* (Random House, 1981), with its rhymes about who has teeth and who doesn't and how to take care of them;
- *The Eye Book* (Random House, 1968). It has rhymes about eyes and what things eyes can see—down holes, up poles, bright colors, and want-to-touch animals.

269. Lobel, Arnold (1983). *The Book of Pigericks*. New York: Harper and Row. Ages 7–9.

Here are limericks about other porkers that were written by an old pig with his pen and the verses are good read-alouds. These are the results of the old pig's limerical efforts—just read the first lines of the limericks aloud to interest a reader—"There was a warm pig from Key West," "There was an old pig with a clock," and "There was a small pig who wept tears." Want, for example, to know about the slow pig from Decatur? (*Whose motto was "I'll do it later"*). Or about the sick pig with a cold? (*He sneezed into pieces/His two favorite nieces*). There are framed full-color illustrations that highlight the pigs and their behavior.

270. Merriam, Eve (1987). *Halloween ABC: Poems*. Illustrated by Lane Smith. New York: Macmillan. Ages 7–8.

Playfulness is prevalent in the twenty-six poems in this collection where each letter of the alphabet is introduced by a verse. The family pet—a companion, a pal, a friend to pat—can be the incentive to give a child the verse "pet": " . . . a pet that's not the least bit vicious/yet finds the neighbors quite nutritious." Making masks also can provide the cue to give a child a page of Merriam's "mask": "Guises/Disguises,/All kinds of surprises!" Other occasions might lead a child to try the following:

- *The Birthday Cow* (Knopf, 1978). Ages 7–8. Here are fifteen humorous poems that use nonsense sensations and sounds.
- *A Gaggle of Geese* (Knopf, 1960). Ages 7–8. This is a picture book that illustrates words that label groups of animals in the fauna kingdom.
- *There Is No Rhyme for Silver* (Atheneum, 1962). Ages 7–8. This contains bouncy verses that are nonsense.

271. Milne, Alan Alexander (1961). *When We Were Very Young*. Illustrated by Ernest H. Shepard. New York: Dutton. Ages 7–8.

Milne's humor is whimsical in these verses that will amuse many young children. For example, the words in "Market Square" are gentle ones about a child who had a bright new penny and went to the market: "I wanted a rabbit./ A little brown rabbit./ And I looked for a rabbit./ 'Most everywhere." If desired, also use the combined volume, *The World of Christopher Robin* (Dutton, 1958) or *Now We Are Six* (Dutton, 1961).

272. Morrison, Bill (1977). *Squeeze a Sneeze*. Illustrated by the author. Boston: Houghton Mifflin. Ages 6–7.

Morrison's humor is in the comical attempts of a sneezer trying to stop a sneeze. This is a lighthearted nonsensical verse that could tickle the fancies of some young children. A character, looking much like W. C. Fields, is the one trying to stop the tickling of his nose and head off the upcoming sneeze. This is zaniness in rhyme.

273. Morrison, Lillian, editor (1990). *Yours Till Niagara Falls: A Book of Autograph Verses*. Illustrated by Sylvie Wickstrom. New York: HarperCollins. Ages 8–14.

Autograph album inscriptions are as common as other end-of-the-school-year celebrations. And in this book, there are rhymes, verses, advice, and sayings for every thought—all related to subjects such as friendships, love, marriage, and success. Interested in advice? There is "Beware of boys with eyes of brown/ They kiss you once and turn you down," and "A young man's heart is like a flower/ It will wither and wilt within the hour." In friendship? "Think of a fly, think of a flea. When something tickles you, think of me." Or in success? "Don't wait for your ship to come in. Row out and meet it." Pair this as a companion to the author's *Best Wishes Amen: A Collection of Autograph Verses* (Crowell, 1974), illustrated by Loretta Lustig, or to *Remember Me When This You See* (Crowell, 1961).

274. Morrison, Lillian, editor (1955). *A Diller, A Dollar: Rhymes and Sayings for the Ten O'clock Scholar*. New York: Crowell. Ages 8 and up.

All kinds of humorous schoolroom rhymes and fun sayings are arranged by subjects that are taught in school—arithmetic, spelling, English, social studies, health, conduct, and so on. The sayings are in the familiar question-and-answer format, the couplet, and in a verse form. Examples:

Q and A

Q: How many bones in the human face?
A: Fourteen, when they're all in place.

Couplet

Two times one is two.
Just keep still 'till I get through.

Verses

Early to bed,
Early to rise,
Gives you first choice
Of your old man's ties.

An apple a day
Keeps the doctor away.
An onion a day
Keeps everyone away.

275. Oram, Hiawyn, compiler (1993). *Out of the Blue: Poems about Color*. Illustrated by David McKie. New York: Hyperion Books. Ages 5–8.

In this book, Oram has collected Mother Goose rhymes, plays on words, limericks, short couplets, and other poetic formats to celebrate colors. The verses include contributions from Shel Silverstein, Jack Prelutsky, Edward Lear, and others. In this collection, a fan of a particular poet could search for a favorite verse—a fan of Silverstein's could look for "colors," a verse told by an unknown narrator with "reddish blondish brown" hair and "greyish blueish green" eyes who says the colors held inside "have not been invented yet."

276. Orgel, Doris (1977). *Merry, Merry Fibuary*. Illustrated by Arnold Lobel. New York: Parents. Ages 7–8.

This is an unusual and zany look at the days of the month of February, humorously renamed Fibuary. For each day there is a wonderful fib told in rhyme. Each fib told by Orgel is comically shown in the accompanying drawings by Lobel. For another unusual look at things, suggest *The Good-Byes of Magnus Marmalade* (Putnam, 1966) also by Doris Orgel. Magnus says goodbye to various people including his dentist. He clearly shares his feelings about the specialist in the dental office—"It's not the drill I hate, it's you!"

277. Prelutsky, Jack (1993). *The Dragons Are Singing Tonight*. Illustrated by David Sis. New York: Greenwillow. Ages 6–8.

This collection has over fifteen poems filled with surprising and playful humor about dragons. The examples of dragons are unexpected—ancient ones, contemporary, real, and fanciful. This is a group of seventeen verses that show the author's playful imagination and has unexpected bursts of humor.

278. Prelutsky, Jack (1966). *A Gopher in the Garden and Other Animal Poems*. Illustrated by Robert Lydenfrost. New York: Macmillan. Ages 6–8.

A weasel and other animals are introduced through humorous verses. Need advice about pleasing or displeasing the weasel? (*You should never squeeze a weasel by the tail*). The humor is upbeat (*Let his tail blow in the breeze*) and unexpected (*If you pull it, he will sneeze*). For more of Prelutsky's surprising and bouncy ways of describing unusual imaginary characters, consider:

- *The Baby Uggs Are Hatching* (Greenwillow, 1982) has poetic portraits of such unusual characters as "The Sneezysnoozer," "The Dreary Dreeze," and the "Sneepies."
- *Poems of A. Nonny Mouse* (Knopf, 1989) is a collection of humorous poems written by Anon-ymous (A. Nonny Mouse) to make up the text.
- *The Queen of Eene* (Greenwillow, 1980) is an imaginative group of verses featuring unusual characters—just a few to meet are Herbert Glerbertt, Mister Gaffe, and "Pumberly Pott's Unpredictable Niece" who decided to devour her uncle's new automobile.
- *Rolling Harvey Down the Hill* (Greenwillow, 1980) is humorous verse about mischief personified as four boys become self-appointed authorities and roll the bully Harvey down the incline as their ultimate revenge. It is illustrated with black-and-white drawings.
- *The Sheriff of Rottenshot* (Greenwillow, 1982) offers humor through the characters. For instance, there are the imaginary characters found in "The Wozzit" who is hiding in the closet, in "The Grobbles" who wait to gobble someone up, and "The Lurpp Is on the Loose."

279. Prelutsky, Jack (1978). *The Mean Old Mean Hyena*. Illustrated by Arnold Lobel. New York: Greenwillow. Ages 6–8.

In this story-poem, there is no hyena meaner than the main character. This mean old mean hyena pesters all of the animals and his approach is quite different—he paints the zebra plaid, puts sneezy stuff in the elephant's trunk, ties the ostrich in a knot, and clips the lion's mane. When he is finally caught, the hyena pleads for any punishment but one—tickling.

280. Prelutsky, Jack (1986). *Ride a Purple Pelican*. Illustrated by Garth Williams. New York: Greenwillow. Ages 6–8.

These are over twenty nonsense rhymes about animals and children that roll right along on the tongue. Among others, Nennington Bunny calls for a rousing "Rumpitty Tumpitty Tumpitty Tum" before going to bed, Cincinnati Patty, a little pink pig, reveals she is from Arkansas and Grandma Bear from Delaware rocks "in a rockety rocking chair." There are full-page illustrations with eye-catching color for the poems that help make the characters and verses memorable.

281. Retan, Walter, editor (1993). *Piggies, Piggies, Piggies*. New York: Simon & Schuster. Ages 5–8.

This is a collection of more that twenty entries that celebrate pigs with stories, songs, poems, and games. For two examples, you can introduce a child to Pigling Bland in *The Tale of Pigling Bland* by Beatrix Potter and to the pig Wilbur in *Charlotte's Web* by E. B. White.

282. Rice, James (1986). *Prairie Night Before Christmas*. Illustrated by the author. Gretna, La.: Pelican. Ages 8 and up.

This is Rice's version of what happens when Santa became stranded in the southern panhandle country. With the help of two cowhands, he hitches up eight leghorn longhorn cattle and is able to finish his deliveries. Rice includes the humor of parody and flavors it with local dialect of the panhandle.

283. Rice, James (1986). *Texas Night before Christmas*. Illustrated by the author. Gretna, La.: Pelican. Ages 8 and up.

This is Rice's version of what happened one night before Christmas on the Texas prairie. Santa Claus drives scroungy longhorns (Leadfoot, Walleye, High-Hips, and such) instead of reindeer through a stormy blue Texas norther and lands them on the rooftops. As he leaves, he calls out "Y'all have a good night, y'heah?"

284. Richards, Laura (1960). *Tirra Lirra: Rhymes Old and New*. Illustrated by Marguerite Davis. New York: Little, Brown. Ages 5–8.

Humorous made-up words and nonsense verses are the favorites in this collection. There are poems that juggle creative words around—words such as ditty dotty doggumes, Orang-Outang-Tangs, and Rummy-jums. The verse "Eletelephony" is a great example of the nonsense. It considers what happened when there was an elephant who "tried to use the telephant." He got his trunk entangled in the "telehunk" and the more he tried to get it free, "the louder buzzed the telephee."

285. Robinson, Fay, editor (1993). *A Frog Inside My Hat: A First Book of Poems*. Illustrated by Cyd Moore. Portland, OR: Bridgewater Books. Ages 5–7.

Robinson has compiled over thirty light-hearted poems by well-known poets in this collection. The poems are arranged by such topics as animals, food, nonsense, seasons, and weather. The verses include contributions from Aileen Fisher, Karla Kuskin, Jack Prelutsky, and others.

286. Seuss, Dr. (1974). *Great Day for Up*. Illustrated by Quentin Blake. New York: Random House. Ages 5–6.

The different meanings of *up* are introduced humorously through a rhymed text and bright colorful illustrations. Animals and people are up to greet the day while baseballs, kites, footballs are all up in the air. Stairs, ladders, and stilts show still another definition. A final scene shows a sleeping child with the words, "Please go away. No up. I'm sleeping in today."

287. Silverstein, Shel (1974). *Where the Sidewalk Ends*. Illustrated by the author. New York: Harper and Row. All ages.

Silverstein's *Where the Sidewalk Ends* is a collection of outrageously funny verses that show where the world of Silverstein begins and about which he says, "all the magic I have known/ I've had to make myself." Among the different humorous characters that children will meet are acrobats who are admonished not to sneeze and Hungry Mungry ("who ate Boston town then drank the Mississippi River just to wash it down"). Further, children can be introduced to Silverstein's humorous view related to the holidays:

- In "The Fourth," Silverstein offers ono-matopoeia—"Oh/ CRASH!/ my/ BASH!/ it's/ BANG!/ the ZANG"—to describe the July celebration.
- In "Flag," he starts to identify Alaska and the other states that the stars represent and finally admits "there are lots of other stars/ But I forget which ones they are."
- In "Merry . . .," he says that "No one loves a Christmas tree/ On March the twenty-fifth" and

in "Santa and the Reindeer," he tells the tale of how Santa gave a gift to a reindeer on Christmas Eve.

288. Smaridge, Norah (1982). *What's on Your Plate?* Illustrated by C. Imbior Kudrna. Nashville: Abingdon. Ages 6–8.

Smaridge offers entertaining rhymes about food. Need reminders about manners? (It's *very* rude to cry, "What's *this?*"). Or about mixing a salad? (a salad *doesn't* need/ A big fat juicy caterpillar!) Or admonitions about eating unrecognized berries in the wild? (leave those berries on the bush—/ They're strictly for the birds!)

289. Smith, William Jay (1953). *Laughing Time*. Illustrated by Julia Kepes. New York: Atlantic-Little, Brown. Ages 6–8.

Limericks, rhyming ABC's, and imaginary dialogue in nonsense verse in Smith's spirited collection will entertain a child. The amusing pictures by Kepes emphasize such events as "The Land of Ho-Ho-Hum" and "The Toaster" where a dragon with "jaws flaming out" browns bread for toast. Smith's *Boy Blue's Book of Beasts* (Little, Brown, 1957) and *Mr. Smith and Other Nonsense* (Delacorte, 1968) also have good nonsense. *Boy Blue* is also illustrated by Julia Kepes with rollicking scenes of a laughing giraffe and other animals, and *Mr. Smith* is illustrated by Don Bolognese who shows a one-eyed mole, a long-haired yak, and a hopping kangaroo with boxing gloves who boxed the bad men out of town.

290. Tripp, Wallace, editor (1973). *A Great Big Ugly Man Came Up and Tied His Horse to Me. A Book of Nonsense Verse*. Illustrated by the editor. New York: Little, Brown. Ages 5–8.

There are hilarious drawings—some include puns to groan over—that accompany this selection of entertaining nonsense verses. The verse referred to in the title, author unknown, relates "As I was standing in the street,/ As quiet as could be,/ "A Great big ugly man came up/ And tied his horse to me." In the accompanying illustration, the horse appears somewhat skittish about being tied up to a badger who wears a red coat with gold buttons. The scene is carried to a finale when the horse trots away and carries the badger in a bundle under his chin. There are other animals with spirit in this collection. There is a full-page illustration where the badger proclaims "I eat my peas with honey/ I've done it all my life/ They do taste kind of funny/ But it keeps them on the knife." A bobcat in a napkin bib sits at a tree stump for a table, and looks askance at the badger while the badger gulps down sticky peas from the blade of his knife. In another example, a raccoon in a stocking cap stops a doctor in a snow-covered field and announces: "I do not love thee, Doctor Fell,/ The reason why I cannot tell,/ But this alone I know full well,/ I do not love thee, Doctor Fell."

291. Watson, Clyde (1978). *Catch Me and Kiss Me and Say It Again.* Illustrated by Wendy Watson. New York: Collins. Ages 5–7.

This is a collection of bouncy contemporary rhymes to accompany such activities as brushing your teeth or clipping your fingernails. Watson has another upbeat collection *Father Fox's Penny-Rhymes* (Crowell, 1971) with clap-along nonsense rhymes that are accompanied with watercolor and pen-and-ink illustrations that feature snatches of the conversation in cartoonlike word balloons.

292. Wescott, Nadine Bernard (1993). *Never Take a Pig to Lunch.* New York: Orchard Books. Ages 5–8.

This is a collection of bright colorful cartoons and over sixty poems by Hoberman, Prelutsky, and others, about foods that children like and dislike. For example, there is a poem about "Oodles of Noodles" that contrasts with another about eels and liver. Need advice about manners? (There are poems about table manners and eating more than you can lift.) Prelutsky is represented by "Fudge" where a father and son create a messy cooking experience, and Hoberman is represented by "School Lunch" where the school lunch-taker always wishes he/she had *bought* a school lunch but " . . . each time I buy it/ I wish I had brought it."

293. Williard, Nancy (1981). *A Visit to William Blake's Inn: Poems for Innocent and Experienced Travelers.* Illustrated by Alice and Martin Provensen. New York: Harcourt Brace Jovanovich. Ages 7–8.

Here is a collection of poems about guests — a bear, tiger, and the king of cats (who sends a postcard to his wife) — along with others who arrive at a special inn. There is a rabbit who greets guests, shows the way to the room, and makes the bed as well as two dragons who bake the bread and a man in a marmalade hat who arrives and cleans up the rooms with dusters and brooms.

Unusual Characters and Creatures

294. Agee, Jon (1988). *The Incredible Paintings of Felix Clousseau*. New York: Farrar, Straus & Giroux. Ages 6–7.

Agee's humor of surprise is shown when several paintings come to life in a Paris setting of long ago. In the chaotic uproar of a jewel heist that results, the artist, Felix Clousseau, is believed guilty and imprisoned. One of Clousseau's painted images, a dog in one of the paintings, comes to life and captures the jewel thief.

295. Ahlberg, Allan (1992). *Dinosaur Dreams*. Illustrated by Andre Amstutz. New York: Greenwillow. Ages 5–6.

Ahlberg's story captures the dreams of a night "gone right." The funnybones skeletons have dreams about the biggest skeletons of all—the dinosaur skeletons. Through the colorful illustrations and the cartoonlike humor, a child sees that the skeletons are reduced to a pile of bones—much to the dog's satisfaction.

296. Allard, Harry (1979). *Bumps In the Night*. Illustrated by James Marshall. New York: Doubleday. Ages 6–7.

Allard's story is a good read-aloud—a humorous ghost tale about Dudley, the stork. Dudley is frightened first by a bumping noise and then by something wet touching his cheek. What can Dudley do? His best friend, Trevor Hog, suggests having Madam Kreepy lead a séance during which the friends meet Donald, a ghost horse.

297. Baker, Russell (1977). *The Upside-Down Man*. Illustrated by Gaban Wilson. New York: McGraw-Hill. Ages 7–8.

Baker's story pokes fun at a mad scientist and his creations. In the kingdom of delirium, Dr. Frankenstein, and his bumbling assistant, Lazlo, attempt to create a man. The results are imaginative ones—they create an upside-down man and a girl with cow's ears.

298. Balian, Lorna (1980). *Leprechauns Never Lie*. Illustrated by Steven Kellogg. New York: Four Winds. Ages 4–8.

Balian's tale pokes fun at Ninny Nanny who is too lazy to help her Gram. Instead, she says she'll catch a leprechaun and discover his hidden gold. Gram thinks it won't work. Ninny Nanny stumbles over the wee man and catches him firmly by the seat of his britches as he wiggled and waggled and howled like a banshee. He admits to her his treasure is first under the straw pile, then under the river, and finally in the potato patch. Weary Ninny Nanny scatters the straw, bails water from the river, and digs up the plants—all but one—and fails to find the treasure. Of course, late that night, the wee man digs up his treasure from under the very last potato plant. With the refrain of "leprechauns never lie," children may join in telling this humorous story of how Lazy Ninny Nanny tries to find a captured leprechaun's gold. The text is rhythmic and catchy, and children will like finding the leprechaun highlighted in green on the pages.

299. Berenstain, Michael (1985). *The Dwarks at the Mall*. Illustrated by the author. New York: Bantam Books. Ages 8 and up.

Relying on Berenstain's drawings full of actions and fun, a child is introduced to the Dwarks—a small, furry, fun-loving family. They live in a cozy old car in a junkyard. Every night they disguise themselves as opossums and raid the houses of humans for their favorite food—garbage. One day, Mamma Dwark wants a different adventure and they visit a gigantic new mall with its attractive stores and goods with humorous results.

300. Birney, Betty G. (1994). *Tyrannosaurus Tex*. Illustrated by John O'Brien. Boston: Houghton Mifflin. Ages 5–8.

Birney's western tale is a fast-moving story about Tyrannosaurus Tex who saves the day for the Bar Double U Gang. It seems that some cattle-stealing rustlers (the lowdown kind) started a prairie fire in order to steal Double U's cattle. However, big T. Tex wipes out the varmints because the other cowhands are "too old to beat a biscuit and . . . too young to bend a bean." Tex puts out the fire with water dumped from what else—his ten thousand gallon Stetson cowboy hat. As part of the fun, O'Brien includes illustrations in earth tone watercolors that are bordered with a lariat.

301. Blackwood, Mary (1989). *Derek the Knitting Dinosaur*. Illustrated by Kerry Argent. New York: Carolrhoda. Ages 5–6.

Blackwood has a rhythmic text about Derek who lived "millions of years before man or machine/ lived Derek the dinosaur, little and green" and Argent's spotted dinosaurs stand out easily on the white backgrounds. Displayed with gentle humor in Argent's colorful illustrations, Derek knits every afternoon instead of joining his siblings who cause a great deal of uncivilized noise. He is not a rough-and-tumble dinosaur like his brothers. His best friend, a mouse, likes him just the way he is.

302. Bradman, Tony (1987). *Dilly the Dinosaur*. Illustrated by Susan Hellard. New York: Viking. Ages 6–7.

In Bradman's four easy-to-read stories that can serve as introductions to chaptered books, Dilly is a very naughty but lovable dinosaur who has an extremely tolerant and patient family. His adventures drive his family crazy but will entertain a young child. For example, in one story, Dilly's jaw is firmly set against his first trip to the dentist and he keeps his jaw shut tight, but the smart dentist changes all that and has him laughing, so Dilly gets a full examination. Other adventures of the naughty dinosaur are found in *Dilly and the Horror Movie* (Viking, 1989), *Dilly Tells the Truth* (Viking, 1988), and *Dilly Speaks Up* (Viking, 1991). In the last story, the author has Dilly win out over his bossy older sister Dorla.

303. Brennan, Patricia D. (1985). *Hitchety, Hatchety, Up I Go!* Illustrated by Richard Rayevsky. New York: Macmillan. Ages 5–8.

Brennan's story is an enjoyable read-aloud about sharing. Hitchety, Hatchety, a creature, is smaller than an elf and a sprite, and lives in a teacup house. A child can chime in and say "Hitchety, Hatchety, Up I Go! Up I Go! Up I Go!" and "Down I go, down I go, down I go," just as Hitchety does whenever he leaves and returns to his home and climbs up and down his ladders. Some suspense (and underlying humor about his attempts) builds each time he goes to get the ingredients for a pancake feast from an old woman down the lane. After successfully preparing and eating his feast, he has a craving for olives. The olives make him sick and on another trip to the old woman's house, she is waiting for him when he gets there—broom ready to sweep him away. She notices that he doesn't look well, picks him up, and gives him medicine and the two become friends.

304. Bright, Robert (1944). *Georgie*. Illustrated by the author. New York: Doubleday. Ages 5–6.

In a New England village, a friendly ghost named Georgie lived in the attic of the Whittakers' house and haunted them when he wanted to. Georgie made the loose boards creak and the parlor door squeak. The Whittakers were lucky to have Georgie as Herman the cat knew and Miss Oliver the owl knew, and it was a sad day for them when Georgie had to leave because Mr. Whittaker fixed the creaks and squeaks. Georgie tried out other places to haunt that winter—Mr. Gloams' house and an old cow barn. When the cold weather made the Whittakers' board loose again and the parlor door rusty, Georgie decided he could go home "lickety-split."

305. Bright, Robert (1975). *Georgie's Christmas Carol*. Illustrated by the author. New York: Doubleday. Ages 5–7.

Georgie, the friendly ghost, turns on the charm as he organizes an unusual Christmas surprise for two children and their uncle, gloomy Mr. Gloams. A child will chuckle at the sight of Bright's illustrations—he includes a cow with evergreen antlers pulling a sleigh and the unexpected sight of Georgie coming down the chimney. This is a good read-aloud book with gentle humor that shows a child what the spirit of giving to others accomplishes.

306. Buehler, Carolyn, and Mark Buehner (1988). *A Job for Wittilda*. New York: Oxford University Press. Ages 6–7.

The delightful illustrations show Wittilda the witch when she applies for a job at the Dingaling Pizza. She needs the job because she has forty-seven cats and wants to buy food for them. When Wittilda and the other applicants are told, "the first one back gets the job," she balances five pizza boxes with one hand as she flies over the town on her broom. Of course, she delivers the pizzas in time to be the first one back and gets the job. A final humorous scene shows Wittilda and the cats enjoying pizza together.

307. de Brunhoff, Laurent (1986). *Babar and the Ghost*. Illustrated by the author. New York: Random House. Ages 6–7.

In de Brunhoff's easy-to-read book, Babar's children encounter a friendly ghost while they are on a picnic to the black castle. Since only the children can see the nice ghost, many humorous antics occur before Babar has had enough of the tricks.

308. Cole, Joanna (1983). *Get Well, Clown Arounds!* Illustrated by Jerry Smath. New York: Parents. Ages 5–7.

In Cole's story, the humorous family of the Clown Arounds get sick. Baby Clown Arounds' capers are corrected by Grandma who prepares the cure for the family's recovery. Most of the amusement is in Smath's colorful illustrations, and the jokes and inconsistencies that are shown. For a child interested further in this funny family, guide them to Joanna Cole's *The Clown Arounds Go on Vacation* (Parents, 1984) where the Clown Arounds take a zany trip to visit Uncle Waldo's hotel.

309. de Paola, Tomie (1977). *Helga's Dowry: A Troll Love Story*. Illustrated by the author. New York: Harcourt Brace Jovanovich. Ages 8–9.

De Paola presents an entertaining humorous style both in the text and the illustrations in this tongue-in-cheek love story. Helga, attractive by any troll criteria, is an orphan with no dowry to accompany a marriage contract with the handsome troll Lars. So Helga works like a hurricane in troll land to earn a dowry of cows, gold, and land, but she soon discovers that the good-looking Lars is a gold digger—and fickle. In the end, a liberated Helga shows she has outgrown Lars and has moved on to a better life without him.

310. Delaney, M. C. (1983). *The Marigold Monster*. Illustrated by Ned Delaney. New York: Dutton. Ages 7–8.

Delaney includes plenty of jokes for a young child in this text. Any child who has told a joke will appreciate Audrey's problem—no one wants to listen to her corny jokes. When she gives up joke telling, she begins to sell marigold seeds. In this business, she meets an engaging monster and they become friends.

311. Eyles, Heather (1990). *Well I Never!* Illustrated by Tony Ross. New York: Overlook Press. Ages 5–7.

Eyles offers an imaginative getting-ready-for-school story. Polly dawdles in the morning and her mother tells her to get dressed. Mum reminds Polly where her shirt, shoes, and other items of clothing can be found, but Polly says she thinks monsters are there. Her mother goes to get the clothes herself and surprise—she finds that Polly is right—a ghost-monster is doing a dance in her shoes and a witch-monster has borrowed Polly's shirt to wear. Mom rescues Polly and after Polly dresses for school, the monsters follow her along the walk when she leaves. The humor is seen mainly in Ross' colorful illustrations of the engaging monsters.

312. Hutchins, Pat (1994). *Three-Star Billy*. Illustrated by the author. New York: Greenwillow. Ages 5–6.

Hutchins tells a going-to-school story. At first Billy, a young green monster, does *not* want to go to nursery school. Once there, however, he throws the paint, hollers instead of singing, and scares the others in the class. The teacher, however, is not upset because it seems that this is a nursery school for monsters and she gives Billy gold stars for his "monstrous" behavior. By the end of the day, Billy *loves* nursery school and does *not* want to go home.

313. Johnson, Paul Brett (1992). *The Cow Who Wouldn't Come Down*. Illustrated by the author. New York: Orchard. Ages 6–8.

Gertrude, the contented cow, doesn't know that cows don't fly and she glides over the farmland showing off her figure eights. Miss Rosemary, an elderly woman, is determined to bring Gertrude down from her flights and uses several ways to resolve her problem—but all end in near disaster. When Miss Rosemary tries a more subtle approach, it works.

314. Kennedy, William, and Brendan Kennedy (1994). *Charlie Malarkey and the Singing Moose*. Illustrated by S. D. Schindler. New York: Viking. Ages 6–8.

Barnaby is an unusual creature—a large appealing moose who sings—and his secret is discovered by Charlie and his friend, Iggy Gowalowicz, at the circus. It seems that a black necktie with white polka dots is what enables Barnaby to croon. When the two friends find the necktie on the ground, they try to return it to Barnaby, only to find that he is being held hostage by Mr. Bungaroo, Barnaby's trainer. The two boys promise to help Barnaby and get into several wacky adventures. The magical necktie plays its own special part, too, and enables other objects to sing—even a box of frozen fish and a rubber kangaroo. At the end of the story, Barnaby chooses to be an "ordinary" moose who only sings in the shower. The text includes word plays on song titles—"Mrs. Robinson" becomes "Mooses Robinson."

315. Krahn, Fernando (1977). *The Mystery of the Giant Footprints*. Illustrated by the author. New York: Dutton. Ages 6–7.

This is a wordless picture book with Krahn's visual black-and-white pencil drawings expressing wry humor. Two children run off to follow some giant footprints in the snow. Panic-stricken, their parents gather a rescue party and the villagers give chase armed with shotguns, pitchforks, and axes. After following them across a frozen lake and up the side of a mountain, the parents find their children have discovered two unusual creature friends. Fans of Krahn's sense of humor and unusual characters can also be guided to *The Family Minus* (Parents' Magazine Press, 1977) where some zaniness is found in the adventures of an unusual family. Eight long-nosed and odd-looking animal children drive to school in Mother's latest invention, a caterpillarlike car.

316. Kroll, Steven (1980). *Amanda and the Giggling Ghost*. Illustrated by Dick Gackenbach. New York: Holiday House. Ages 7–8.

In Kroll's story, Amanda's encounter with a giggling ghost leads to a chase through town as she attempts to get her possessions back. Amanda has a hard time convincing the townsfolk that it is a ghost, not she, who is responsible for all the humorous misdeeds. Kroll includes an "I told you so" ending.

317. Lobel, Arnold (1980). *The Ice-Cream Cone Coot and Other Rare Birds*. Illustrated by the author. New York: Four Winds. Ages 5–8.

Several unusual creatures are seen in Lobel's outlandish array of rare and ridiculous birds in this nonsensical book. Using objects like ice-cream cones and electric plugs, Lobel has created such unusual fowls as the Garbage Canary who lives in conditions quite unsanitary and the Key Crane who looks for doors that might need unlocking.

318. McPhail, David (1994). *Moony B. Finch, the Fastest Draw in the West*. Illustrated by the author. New York: Artists & Writers. Ages 5–7.

McPhail's humor is mainly in the fanciful actions of Moony B. Finch, a boy who draws pictures—contemporary and old-fashioned—so well that they all become animated in his real life.

Moony controls his pictures—when he wants his pictures to disappear, he erases them. One day, he draws an old-fashioned steam train and hops on it for a memorable ride. On the train, he meets an entertaining assortment of animals and a cowboy who pulls a cap pistol and demands that everyone hand over their valuable possessions. Moony decides to take care of this threat by erasing his drawing bit by bit—first, the gun, then the cowboy's hat, and finally, his pants. The embarrassed cowboy crook turns out to be modest and tries to escape from his predicament right into the arms of the conductor who captures him. Moony then draws himself right back where he belongs—at home with his parents.

319. Madsen, Ross Martin (1994). *Perrywinkle and the Book of Magic Spells*. Illustrated by Dirk Zimmer. New York: Dial. Ages 5–8.

The entertainment in Madsen's easy-to-read adventures is increased by a crow named Nevermore who is the straight-entity to Perrywinkle's funny-comic role. Perrywinkle, the son of a great wizard, suffers from "overspelling." For example, he tries the familiar rabbit trick and instead, produces a thing that eats a table. He tries to spell waterfall for his teacher and a real waterfall tumbles out of the chalkboard and threatens to flood the class.

320. Nostlinger, Christine (1977). *Konrad*. Illustrated by Carol Nicklaus. Translated by Anthea Bell. New York: Watts. Ages 8–9.

This is Nostlinger's entertaining fantasy about a robot boy. One day, Mrs. Bartolotti receives a mysterious package containing a factory-produced, seven-year-old boy. Perfect in every way, Konrad tries to adapt to living in an imperfect world. Further complications arise when the factory wants him back, and Nicklaus shows what happens in the entertaining illustrations.

321. Sadler, Marilyn (1994). *Alistair and the Alien Invasions*. Illustrated by Roger Bollen. New York: Simon & Schuster. Ages 6–8.

Bollen has cartoon-type illustrations that accompany Sadler's wacky plot about Alistair, the boy genius. Alistair blasts off in his spaceship to go in search of the most unusual plant life he can find. On the way, he notices an alien vessel that is headed toward planet Earth. He turns his ship back and is horrified to see the invaders put all the people they see into a state of suspended animation so that they, too, can collect the plant life they find. They seem to be *very* much interested in Alistair and invite themselves to his house so that they can watch him closely. In the surprise ending, readers find out why Alistair interested the invaders so much—they remove their space helmets and they all look exactly like the boy genius.

322. Seuss, Dr. (1957). *The Cat in the Hat*. New York: Random House. Ages 6–8.

The cat visits two children and a boring afternoon becomes exciting. The cat juggles objects and has two things that almost destroy the house. The cat cleans up so that mother doesn't notice. Mother asks what the children did. The children can decide what to tell her. Consider some of Dr. Seuss' other titles:

- *The Cat in the Hat Comes Back* (Random House, 1958) where the cat creates a pink mess in the house while the two children work clearing the walk of snow. Ages 6–8.
- *Hop on Pop* (Random House, 1963) where ridiculous illustrations show the silly sentence on the page. Ages 6–8.
- *One Fish, Two Fish, Red Fish, Blue Fish* (Random House, 1960) where one ordinary fish looks at the imaginative, whimsical, and silly creatures that go by and are described. Ages 6–8.

323. Shepperson, Robert (1991). *The Sandman*. Illustrated by the author. New York: Farrar, Straus & Giroux. Ages 5–7.

Shepperson's unusual character is the Sandman, dressed in denim overalls and work boots. Jay is comfortable in his bed with his comic books and a flashlight, and decides to test his parents' words that if he doesn't get to sleep right away, "The Sandman will come to sprinkle sand in your eyes." Sure enough, the Sandman arrives for his night's mission of sprinkling sand and creates chaos in Jay's bedroom. His appearance sends Jay's toys (now come-to-life) scattering when he says, "What are you doing up so late?" When Jay replies, "I'm not sleepy," the Sandman dumps his wheelbarrow and fills the bedroom with sand. Jay and the Sandman (and the mischievous toys) play in the sand that is up to their chins, eat chocolate chip cookies delivered by a phantom baker, read a book, act out a lively song, and count a stampede of sheep. When the Sandman whispers, "Someone's coming!" Jay dives under his toys and the remaining cookies to hide. Jay, of course, wakes up and discovers he has been dreaming, but notices some cookie crumbs and his toys looking very tired.

324. Small, David (1985). *Imogene's Antlers*. Illustrated by the author. New York: Crown. Ages 5–7.

Small offers a special book of silliness with the humor that is found in an absurd situation. Imogene realizes that there is nothing wrong with being different and that there may even be some advantages—when she wakes up one morning with an elaborate pair of antlers! Undaunted after surmounting the problems of dressing and getting downstairs, Imogene and the cook and the kitchen maid discover the merits of antlers as a drying rack, a bird feeder, and a candle holder. Her hefty mother, not quite so liberal, reacts to her daughter's predicament by fainting repeatedly through the story. The matter appears to resolve itself the next morning, when an antler-less Imogene appears at breakfast—she proudly shows off her new peacock tail.

325. Smith, Wendy (1986). *The Witch Baby*. Illustrated by the author. New York: Viking Kestrel. Ages 5–7.

In Smith's story, Wanda, the baby witch, has her problems. She has a broom but can't make it fly and her beginning attempt to put a spell on a wicked witch results in the wrong shape-change—Wanda wanted to turn the witch into a worm, but instead, turned her into a unicorn with spots.

326. Vesey, A. (1985). *The Princess and the Frog*. Illustrated by the author. New York: Atlantic Monthly. Ages 7–8.

Knowing the familiar fairy tale about the frog who turned into a rich and handsome prince, a silly queen is delighted when a large, ugly frog follows her daughter home to the palace one day. Nothing is too good for the frog as all hope the magical shape-changing will soon take place. He is given a beautiful bed, his own special footman to wait on him, and the most delicious foods to eat. The months pass and all begin to wonder if he will ever change into a prince. The queen remembers that her daughter must first kiss the frog to break the spell. So the princess closed her eyes and kissed the frog. When she opened her eyes she saw the same fat, bad-tempered frog who said, "I never said I was a handsome prince. I am a handsome frog. Besides which, I'm already married and have a great many little frogs."

IV

Humorous Books
for Children Ages 9–12

Animals as Humans

327. Browne, Anthony (1986). *Piggybook*. Illustrated by the author. New York: Knopf. Ages 9–12.

Browne's humor is shown mainly through this satire about Mr. Piggott who lives with Mrs. Piggott and their two sons, Simon and Patrick. The family lives in an average house with the usual possessions—a garden, a car, and a garage to house it in. But Mr. Piggott and the boys order Mom around as she prepares the meals, washes the clothes, and cleans the house before leaving for work. One day, Mrs. Piggott leaves a message informing the males that they were "pigs." After a few days without Mrs. Piggott, the boys and Mr. Piggott learn to appreciate her and she finally returns when she sees they have changed their way of thinking. Browne provides clues in the illustrations which predict the humorous transformation of the males in the Piggott family into actual pigs—images of pigs are displayed in objects such as buttons, bushes, and doorknobs.

328. Dawnay, Romayne (1994). *The Champions of Appledore*. Illustrated by the author. New York: Four Winds. Ages 9–10.

Dawnay puts slapstick humor into this fanciful story as Grunwinkle, a tired and worn-out dragon, and a Scottish mouse named Iona, help rid the town of pests. It seems that the residents of Appledore Manor are being invaded by polecats—smelly ones—and hungry wolves. The silly schemes of some of the townspeople and the lord of the manor, Sir Pomfrey de Pomme, to get rid of the pests go awry until the dragon gets involved. Sir Pomfrey, Iona, and a boy named Tom provide some needed backup against the pests.

329. Erickson, John R. (1983). *Hank the Cowdog*. Illustrated by Gerald L. Holmes. Perryton, Tex.: Maverick Books. Ages 9–10.

Hank the cowdog, head of ranch security, narrates the story of the chickenhouse murders at the ranch. Hank thinks he has a "pretty nice kind of nose that women really go for" and dreams about Beullah, the neighbor's collie, and her beautiful brown and white hair and her big eyes. He thinks about her nose that tapers down to a point and her nice ears that flap when she runs. He has to turn his thoughts away from Beullah, however, and toward solving the case. One night, he is successful and confronts the leaders of the coyotes—Rip, Scrunch, and Snort—as they head for the chickenhouse.

330. Goodall, John S. (1968). *The Adventures of Paddy Pork*. Illustrated by the author. New York: Harcourt Brace Jovanovich. Ages 9–10.

Goodall has designed this book of half-pages and full pages that show what slapstick comedy happens to a young pig after he runs away to join a traveling circus. Instead of finding the circus, he finds a friendly gentleman fox hiding behind a tree who invites Paddy home. Attacked by the fox, Paddy runs out the door and discovers the circus camped nearby. He is taken in by the bears, watches some exciting circus acts, and becomes part of one act when he is the balance on the head of the bear. In the act, he tries to juggle objects but he hits Mama bear on the nose and is sent away. A sequel is *The Ballooning Adventures of Paddy Pork* (Harcourt Brace Jovanovich, 1969).

331. Goodall, John S. (1981). *Paddy Goes Traveling*. Illustrated by the author. A McElderry Book. New York: Atheneum. Ages 9–10.

Goodall's humor is in the actions in Paddy Pork's wordless adventure as he goes on vacation. There are humorous, full-color watercolors that show Paddy traveling on a railroad and boat, and finally arriving at Monte Carlo. Later, as a result of trying to rescue a small piglet's escaping kite, Paddy finds himself zooming on a sled in the Swiss Alps and he accidentally wins a sledding contest.

332. Goodall, John (1973). *Paddy's Evening Out*. Illustrated by the author. New York: Atheneum. Ages 9–10.

Goodall's half-pages show more of Paddy's troubles at the theater. Paddy, a gentleman pig, attempts to retrieve his lady friend's fan—which she has dropped from the theater balcony. Trying to catch it, Paddy ends up on stage—to the entertainment of the audience. After he lands in the tuba in the orchestra pit, he has a series of misadventures that include hiding in a magician's box, popping up on stage with the pigeons when the lid of the box is opened, and being chased by the actors. His hiding place in a large basket of flowers is then delivered on stage where Paddy finally finds his lady friend's fan, which he hands over to her. Because of his escapades, Paddy is surrounded by news reporters and photographers.

333. Howe, Deborah, and James Howe (1979). *Bunnicula: A Rabbit Tale of Mystery*. Illustrated by Alan Daniel. New York: Atheneum. Ages 9–12.

The Howes' humor is mainly in the parody that is related to the Dracula story. In this tale, Harold, the family dog, tells the story of a bunny who was found by the Monroe family in a movie theater while watching the movie *Dracula*. Chester, the pet cat who likes to read, notices some strange nighttime behavior by the bunny and he uses two main clues—the rabbit's behavior and his long fangs—to conclude that the rabbit is really a vampire. In various ways, Chester and Harold attempt to "save" the family from the clutches of the suspected bunny vampire.

334. Howe, Deborah, and James Howe (1987). *Nighty Nightmare*. New York: Atheneum. Ages 9–12.

The Howes continue their humorous clichés from movies and their use of puns in this story of Harold and Chester, the two humorous characters introduced in *Bunnicula*. The title offers a clue to the humorous suspense that happens when the two animals decide to go on a campout with the Monroe family. They choose a site near an unusual trio. For a child interested further in humorous clichés from vampire movies, some puns, suggest the sequels, *The Celery Stalks at Midnight* (Atheneum, 1983) and *Howliday Inn* (Atheneum, 1982).

335. Landsman, Sandy (1986). *Castaways on Chimp Island*. Illustrated by the author. New York: Atheneum. Ages 9–12.

Landsman includes slapstick humor, the unexpected, and an ironic play of events to entertain a reader with this situation comedy. Danny, raised on junk food, had an easy life for a civilized chimp—and his only responsibility was to go to the language lab and learn a few new words every day. The part that Danny didn't like about his job was that he had to perform the same boring tasks over and over to prove to the researchers that he had learned his new words. When he decided that he would not learn any new words (so he would be able to get home to relax and watch TV), his idea backfires. Danny is taken to an island and left there with other primates like himself. He and the others are confronted with the challenge of figuring out how to get back to civilization.

336. Lester, Julius, reteller (1987). *The Tales of Uncle Remus: The Adventures of Brer Rabbit*. Illustrated by Jerry Pinkney and Baker. New York: Dial. Ages 9–12.

Lester's collection is a set of traditional tales from American Black traditions with over forty episodes that are accompanied by Baker's entertaining illustrations in both color and black and white. Most of the tales show different sides of Brer Rabbit's character—for example, he is a trickster in "Brer Rabbit and Brer Lion" and the trickee—the one who is tricked in "Brer Rabbit and the Tar Baby."

337. Oakley, Graham (1979). *The Church Mice at Bay*. Illustrated by the author. New York: Atheneum. Ages 9–10.

Oakley's humor is shown mainly in the hilarious battles between the mice and the government authorities. Set in the English village of Wortlethorpe, a large family of mice and their feline companion, Sampson, use the church as their home. They have an agreement with the vicar—in exchange for their services, they have a home and a weekly allowance of cheese. This all changes when the vicar's summer replacement, a man who hates mice, arrives. Humorous battles begin with Sampson helping the mice play tricks on the new vicar and the man calling the authorities to take the cat to a resettlement department. Later, the mice escape the employees of the rodent control bureau and even release Sampson from his cage. Older children interested further in the escapades of the mice can turn to the other sequels in this series entitled *The Chronicles of Wortlethorpe Church Vestry: The Church Mouse, The Church Cat Abroad, The Church Mice and the Moon, The Church Mice Spread Their Wings,* and *The Church Mice Adrift*.

338. Panek, Dennis (1978). *Catastrophe Cat.* Illustrated by the author. New York: Bradbury. Ages 9–10.

Panek's humor is in the way he develops the personality of a clever and funny feline—Catastrophe Cat. The cat is curious and mischievous which leads to several enjoyable antics during the cat's fast-moving trip around a big city.

339. Pinkwater, Daniel M. (1985). *Jolly Roger: A Dog of Hoboken.* New York: Greenwillow. Ages 9–10.

Most of Pinkwater's entertainment in this story is in the deadpan exaggerations, comic asides, and creative names. For example, a dog—thought to be part gorilla—is dubbed Brutus MacDouglas Bugleboy. In this story, Jolly Roger runs the pack called the Waterfront Dogs. He is the leader and king of the dogs and has made many friends because of his helpfulness—he teaches others how to successfully stay away from the dog catcher. Finally, old and gray around the muzzle, he retires, leaves the waterfront, and moves to Florida with his owner.

340. Smith, Jim (1977). *The Frog Band and the Onion Seller.* Illustrated by the author. Boston: Little, Brown. Ages 9–10.

Smith's wild tale is hilarious to readers who liked the "Pink Panther" movies. In a disguise reminiscent of one of Peter Sellers, Alphonse LeFlic disguises himself as an onion seller—striped shirt, beret, and tight black pants. He rides his bicycle on the top of a submarine across the English Channel into the English countryside to locate a hidden treasure. As he is pursued by a band of frogs, there are great underground scenes in a monastery and other lively illustrations filled with all sort of absurd details.

341. Yolen, Jane (1987). *Piggins.* Illustrated by Jane Dyer. New York: Harcourt Brace Jovanovich. Ages 9–10.

Yolen offers a parody that is based on a typical English mystery—diamonds are stolen when the lights go out at a dinner party. When Mr. and Mrs. Reynard invite guests to a dinner to display Mrs. Reynard's new diamond lavaliere, they explain why they must sell it. The necklace has a curse on it. When the lights go off, there is confusion, and when the lights go on the necklace is gone. All the guests are mystified, but Piggins, the butler, solves the case.

Family, School, and Community

342. Angell, Judie (1980). *Dear Lola; or How to Build Your Own Family.* New York: Bradbury. Ages 9–12.

Though Angell's story is about the sensitive topic of six orphans who want to find a place where they can be a real family, this is a surprisingly entertaining portrayal. Eighteen-year-old Arthur and thirteen-year-old James, Annie and Al-Willie (twins, age ten), and Edmund (age nine), and Ben (age five), all wanted to run away from the orphanage. One night, they escaped in a van and began living on the road until they found a house in which they thought they could live. To settle in, the children enrolled in school so they wouldn't have trouble with the local authorities and pretended to be living with their grandfather—really James. Arthur became the anonymous author of a national syndicated newspaper advice column, *Dear Lola,* and used the income to support the family. Eventually the townspeople discover no adult in charge of the household. When the court judge ruled against Arthur and said that he could not be the children's guardian, Arthur and the children raced from the courtroom and the story ends as the "family" was once more on the road and on their own.

343. Arkhurst, Joyce (1964). *The Adventures of Spider: West African Folktales.* Illustrated by Jerry Pinkney. Boston: Little, Brown. Ages 9–12.

Arkhurst's book is a collection of six humorous West African folktales about Spider and the different sides of his character—he is mischievous and clever. He loves to eat and he hates to work. Four of the short stories tell of Spider's ill-fated attempts to get food without having to work for it—"How Spider Got a Thin Waist," "How Spider Got a Bald Head," "How Spider Helped a Fisherman," and "Why Spiders Live in Dark Corners." Another tells about his greed ("How the World Got Wisdom"), and still another is complimentary ("Why Spider Lives in Ceilings").

344. Berends, Polly Berrien (1973). *The Case of the Elevator Duck.* Illustrated by James K. Washburn. New York: Random House. Ages 9–11.

Berends' humor is told in the parodied style of adult detective mysteries. Eleven-year-old Albert tells his own story beginning when he found a duck abandoned in the elevator of the apartment house where pets were strictly forbidden. He was determined to find the owner of the duck and return it. When Albert finally found the duck's owner (a young, sad child named Julio), Julio's sister forced Albert to take the duck back. Still angry at Julio's sister, Albert took the duck to the project's day-care center, where the teacher agreed to formally adopt the duck. Albert enjoyed seeing Julio's happy surprise when he arrived and found his pet.

345. Blumberg, Rhoda (1980). *The First Travel Guide to the Moon: What to Pack, How to Go, and What to See When You Get There.* Illustrated by Roy Doty. New York: Four Winds. Ages 9–12.

Much of the fun in Blumberg's guide is in Doty's cartoon-style illustrations. This is a tour of the moon in the year 2000 and the text humorously tells a reader how to take advantage of it. Blumberg gives advice on everything— from getting the most interesting seats in the space base "Windows of the World" room and what available tours to take on the moon to what equipment to take with you and what to rent when you get there.

346. Blume, Judy (1970). *Are You There, God? It's Me, Margaret.* New York: Bradbury. Ages 9–12.

Blume's story is best suited for individual reading—it is a very open and humorous treatment of the difficulties of a girl's maturation. It seemed that sixth grade was a year of "first times" for Margaret and her friends. For instance, each was kissed for the first time and they all wondered when they would start growing breasts and when they would begin menstruating. It was also a year in which Margaret tried to decide whether to be Jewish or Christian and ended up being neither. She simply remained friends with God—just as the title indicates.

347. Blume, Judy (1971). *Freckle Juice*. Illustrated by Sonia O. Lisker. New York: Four Winds. Ages 9–10.

Blume tells a very funny story that should appeal to almost everyone because it is based on the premise of a boy who *wants* freckles. Andrew wants freckles so that the dirt on his skin wouldn't show as much and he won't have to wash his face as often. As luck would have it, Sharon, a very obnoxious girl in his class, said she had a freckle juice recipe that she was willing to sell Andrew for fifty cents. Even after drinking the mixture of grape juice, vinegar, mustard, olive oil, Andrew didn't get any freckles—he got sick.

348. Blume, Judy (1972). *Otherwise Known as Sheila the Great*. New York: E. P. Dutton. Ages 9–12.

Blume's story about Sheila—Peter Thatcher's neighbor in *Tales of a Fourth Grade Nothing* (Dutton, 1972)—treats Sheila's fears realistically yet humorously. Sheila was a bundle of raw nerve endings. She had fears—among other things, she was afraid of dogs, spiders, thunderstorms, and strange noises at night. The summer that she and her family rented a house in Tarrytown, New York, she confronted each one of her fears aided by her friend, Mouse.

349. Blume, Judy (1980). *Superfudge*. New York: E. P. Dutton. Ages 9–12.

In this story, the theme of a child's life in turmoil caused by a younger sibling continues and Peter's problems with his younger brother, Fudge, go on. On Fudge's first day in kindergarten, Peter had to rescue him from the top of some storage cabinets. On another day, Fudge unexpectedly disappeared. Peter had problems with the rest of his family too. He had to cope with a baby sister, moving to Princeton, New Jersey, a new job for his mother, and his father's attempts to write a book. Although this story is a sequel to *Tales of a Fourth Grade Nothing* (Dutton, 1972), it can be read alone.

350. Blume, Judy (1972). *Tales of a Fourth Grade Nothing*. Illustrated by Roy Doty. New York: E. P. Dutton. Ages 9–12.

This is a humorous chaptered book by Blume that appeals to children, ages nine and older. The story is built around a common theme—a child whose life is in turmoil caused by a younger sibling. Peter's problems with three-year-old Fudge escalate with each chapter until the final disaster when Fudge swallows Peter's pet turtle.

351. Byars, Betsy (1981). *The Cybil War*. Illustrated by Gail Owens. New York: Viking. Ages 9–12.

Byars offers a good story with just enough humor (and romance) in it to make it appealing as a personal choice for individual reading. Simon and Tony both had a crush on Cybil, but according to Tony, Cybil liked Tony better than she liked Simon. Simon unhappily accepted Tony's word even though he knew Tony was a chronic liar. After all, Simon realized that Cybil had been the one to talk their teacher out of giving the lead in the class play about nutrition to Simon. Consequently, Simon was forced to impersonate a jar of peanut butter.

352. Byars, Betsy (1989). *Bingo Brown and the Language of Love*. New York: Viking/Kestrel. Ages 9–12.

Byars offers humorous dialogue in this sequel to *The Burning Questions of Bingo Brown* (Viking/Kestrel, 1988). Bingo, a middle school student, continues to cope with life as one of his loves (a girl in his English class) moves away and his mother becomes pregnant after twelve years with Bingo being the only child at home.

353. Byars, Betsy (1988). *The Burning Questions of Bingo Brown*. New York: Viking/Kestrel. Ages 9–13.

With humorous dialogue, Byars introduces Bingo Brown, a middle school student. As Bingo copes with what is going on in his life, he writes his questions in his journal. For instance, he questions the effect of mousse on his hair and writes about his new friends and his new loves—three girls in his English class.

354. Cleary, Beverly (1952). *Henry and Beezus*. Illustrated by Louis Darling. New York: Morrow. Ages 9–11.

Cleary introduces Henry (definitely an old-fashioned character from the 1950s) who wants to earn money to buy a bike in a very short time. He devises various moneymaking schemes—selling bubble gum; taking over a friend's paper route; and buying a used bike at the police department auction.

355. Cleary, Beverly (1953). *Otis Spofford*. Illustrated by Louis Darling. New York: Morrow. Ages 10–12.

Cleary offers six humorous episodes about Otis (another character from the 1950s who acts on every thought that comes to mind). He has a favorite activity—stirring up trouble. For example, the school fiesta turned into a disaster when Otis decided to rechoreograph the bullfight and make the bull win. His tried to liven up a reading lesson about Indians and he almost scalped a classmate. Later, everyone got a chance at the skating pond to take revenge for all the things Otis had done to them.

356. Cleary, Beverly (1982). *Ralph S. Mouse.* New York: Morrow. Ages 10–12.

Much of the amusement is in Cleary's slapstick in this fanciful story. This is a story of a fifth grader's friendship with Ralph Mouse, a dauntless talking animal. Among other antics, Ralph goes to school in the pocket of his friend, Ryan. He becomes a class project and loses his motorcycle, but gains a sports car in its place. He continues his escapades in *The Mouse and the Motorcycle* (Morrow, 1965) where he receives a small toy motorcycle, and in *Runaway Ralph* (Morrow, 1970), where he has more adventures on his motorcycle.

357. Cole, Joanna (1986). *The Magic School Bus at the Waterworks.* Illustrated by Bruce Degen. New York: Scholastic. Ages 9–10.

This is Cole and Degen's first one-of-a-kind field trip with frazzle-haired Ms. Frizzle, the magic school bus, and the students. Ms. Frizzle begins a study of the waterworks in the class and the old school bus is brought out to take the students up to the clouds to become raindrops. When the bus spins around, the students find themselves magically dressed for exploring the water cycle and a wild ride through rivers, ponds, and pipes. Wearing snorkels and scuba suits, the students follow Ms. Frizzle and go into a river, up through a sedimentation pond, down a water flow into the pipes, and then out in a burst of water when they are expelled from the water faucet at school. Through it all, Ms. Frizzle calmly explains what is going on. Degen's cartoon-style illustrations and word balloons tell part of the information and give comic asides. Other facts are represented in hand-lettered student reports, charts, and displays.

358. Cole, Joanna (1994). *The Magic School Bus in the Time of the Dinosaurs.* Illustrated by Bruce Degen. New York: Scholastic. Ages 9–10.

This is another back-in-time school trip by Cole and Degen with plenty of jokes as the magic school bus becomes a time machine that travels back in time to the Mesozoic Era. When the dial on the windshield of the bus spins around, the students find themselves suddenly dressed for exploration with hard hats and safari clothing, and are off on a wild prehistoric adventure. With her coolness and a magnifying glass, Ms. Frizzle leads the students through the lush growth to face a Tyrannosaurus Rex and other creatures. The students observe the plants and animals, photograph a videotape of the trip, and initiate the usual written reports on the topic. Through it all, Ms. Frizzle reveals current facts and statements about the reptiles. Cartoon-style illustrations and word balloons from Ms. Frizzle and the children carry part of the information about the cold-blooded and warm-blooded giants as well as humorous remarks. Other facts are given in actual-size drawings of fossil teeth, charts, and maps.

359. Cole, Joanna (1987). *The Magic School Bus: Inside the Earth.* Illustrated by Bruce Degen. New York: Scholastic. Ages 9–10.

In *Inside the Earth,* Ms. Frizzle begins a study of earth science in the class and the old school bus takes the students on a rock collecting trip. When the bus spins around, the students find themselves equipped for exploration with jumpsuits and jackhammers, and are off for a wild adventure through the earth's crust. Carrying picks and wearing hard hats, the students follow Ms. Frizzle among the stalactites and stalagmites to begin their journey. They go into the inner core where it is hot, up through a volcano, down a lava flow into the sea, and then up in a cloud of steam when the bus is expelled from the core in a volcanic eruption. The bus has a parachute and lands the class safely back in the school parking lot. Through it all, Ms. Frizzle explains vocabulary, rock formation, and the inner dynamics of the earth. A tongue-in-cheek section at the end discusses the realistic and fanciful aspects of the book. For other humorous and attractive magic school bus books, guide children to *The Magic School Bus on the Ocean Floor* (Scholastic, 1992), *The Magic School Bus Lost in the Solar System* (Scholastic, 1990), and *The Magic School Bus Inside the Human Body* (Scholastic, 1992).

360. Cone, Molly (1980). *The Amazing Memory of Harvey Bean*. Illustrated by Robert McLean. Boston: Houghton Mifflin. Ages 10–11.

In Cone's chaptered book, there is humor as well as a sensitive realism about Harvey's pain over his parents' separation, and eventually, about his redeveloping feelings of being happy again. Because Harvey thought that neither one of his parents wanted him after their separation, he told each of them that he was going to stay with the other and instead decided to spend the summer alone. Before he completely realized it, Harvey was living with a friendly couple, the frugal Mr. and Mrs. Katz. Harvey spent a happy summer eating Mrs. Katz's good cooking, and ignoring what others thought of him. When his parents finally found him, Harvey realized that they really did want him even if they were separated. He decided to live with his mother on weekdays and his father on weekends, and with the Katzs in the summers.

361. Conford, Ellen (1977). *And This Is Laura*. Boston: Little, Brown. Ages 9–12.

Conford presents a common concern—achieving—and treats it with humor and sensitivity. As a member of a family of high achievers, Laura was convinced that she was unloved and worthless because she had no talents. Then suddenly Laura discovered she had very special psychic powers—powers she began to exploit. At first it was fun to give readings after school each day. Gradually, however, as Laura foresaw her friend hurt and her brother missing, she realized that having ESP was also a frightening responsibility. Finally, her ESP became the vehicle that made it possible for Laura to tell her parents her feelings and to understand that they loved her for herself, not for her achievements.

362. Conford, Ellen (1975). *The Luck of Pokey Bloom*. Illustrated by Bernice Loewenstein. Boston: Little, Brown. Ages 9–12.

Conford offers several amusing moments in this one. A reader who likes the Judy Blume-type stories will like this one about another regular kid—Pokey Bloom. Pokey's passion was entering contests. She entered every contest she heard of and always thought she would win. Unfortunately, she never won anything. She even went so far as to practice concentrating three times each day on winning every contest she had entered because someone who had been interviewed on the radio had guaranteed

she would win that way—but she did not win. This only made more trouble for her at school and at home getting along with her older brother.

363. Conford, Ellen (1980). *The Revenge of the Incredible Dr. Rancid and His Youthful Assistant, Jeffrey*. Boston: Little, Brown. Ages 9–12.

Many readers will appreciate the common concern—bullies—that is treated here with a light touch of humor. There were two people Jeff hated and feared: Dewey Belasco, the sixth grade bully, and Lana McCabe, Dewey's female counterpart. Only in his imagination could Jeff stand up to them. In the stories Jeff wrote in a notebook, he and his friend, Dr. Rancid, were superheroes who rid the world of such scum as Lana and Dewey. In real life, Jeff ran from bullies rather than face them. Even if this meant that an eight-year-old boy and a girl Jeff's age were left to stand up to Dewey by themselves. Although the way Jeff took care of an injured child soon had most everyone thinking of Jeff as a hero, he saw that, too, as an indication of his failings at first. Finally, something inside Jeff snapped and he answered Dewey back when Dewey insulted him. Before long Jeff found himself flat on his back with a bloody nose and so many pains he could not count them. But he had finally faced Dewey and showed Dewey that he was no longer afraid. Jeff felt good.

364. Corbett, Scott (1960). *The Lemonade Trick*. Illustrated by Paul Galdone. Boston: Little, Brown. Ages 9–12.

Corbett's story is a series of humorous incidents woven together in a satisfying way. One day, Kerby was given an odd chemistry set by a strange old woman whom he helped. When he used the set to put together a brew, Kerby found himself completely under its spell. The sweet smelling liquid he had concocted forced him to be good, so good that his parents began to worry about him. Luckily, the spell wore off in a short time. But Kerby kept experimenting with the spell of being good: on his dog, on his friend, on his enemy, and finally on the entire boys' choir at church.

365. Danziger, Paula (1974). *The Cat Ate My Gymsuit*. New York: Dell/Delacorte. Ages 9–12.

Flat-chested thirteen-year-old Marcy Lewis (who hated school and hated looking like a baby blimp and dressing for physical education classes) liked Ms. Finney, her new English teacher who was willing to try anything in the classroom. For instance, she asked the class to write about what communication means to them and Marcy wrote, "Communication is NOITACINUMMOC spelled backwards." Marcy grew to like Ms. Finney and when the teacher was suspended for her controversial teaching methods, Marcy helped organize a protest, which led to a hearing and the reinstatement of the teacher. Marcy ended the year, however, by flunking gym class—she believed just getting her flat-chested body into her gymsuit was a gymnastic feat in itself.

366. Danziger, Paula (1980). *There's a Bat in Bunk Five*. New York: Delacorte. Ages 9–12.

There are more light touches in Danziger's sequel to *The Cat Ate My Gymsuit* (Dell, 1974) and it can be read alone. Marcy accepted an offer to become a junior counselor at an arts camp run by her ex-English teacher Ms. Finney and Ms. Finney's husband. After a nervous beginning, Marcy found herself enjoying the other counselors and the campers—but most of all, her first romance, Ted. Marcy's only difficulty was dealing with Ginger, a troubled ten-year-old in Marcy's cabin. Marcy couldn't seem to get through to Ginger. When Ginger ran away, Marcy was forced to consider whether she should have spent more time with the campers and not quite so much time with Ted.

366. Davidson, Carson (1978). *Fast-talking Dolphin*. Illustrated by Sylvia Stone. New York: Dodd. Ages 9–11.

This is Davidson's pleasant story that has humor, action, and originality. Eric was surprised when he found a dolphin in the ten-foot fish pond—a dolphin who spoke in poetry. He was cultured and his name was Wallingford Ullingham Lowell III. Eric kept Wallingford a secret from the others, just as Wallingford had requested. But eventually Wallingford was discovered and Eric and his brother Karl scouted the town to discover that someone, Mr. Benson, wanted to harm the dolphin. When Eric, Karl, and the local children got together to shield Wallingford from Mr. Benson, there was a struggle and Mr. Benson hit his head and rolled into the pond. With the children's help, Wallingford, Eric, and Karl were able to save Mr. Benson from drowning. Later, Wallingford was helicopter-lifted out of the pond and taken

back to his research project. The dolphin's final message was a note saying they would one day meet again.

367. Fitzgerald, Jon D. (1975). *The Great Brain Does It Again*. Illustrated by Mercer Mayer. New York: Dial. Ages 9–10.

The great brain shows an occasional bit of good will in this story, but as usual, most of his schemes are based on his interest in making money. Sometimes, the great brain shows some selfish behavior as when he hard-heartedly refuses to consider the feelings of others. Most of the time, however, the great brain is involved in the humorous incidents such as wearing a devil suit to scare a fat boy into losing weight.

369. Hurwitz, Johanna (1994). *School Spirit*. Illustrated by Karen Dugan. New York: Morrow. Ages 9–12.

Four fifth-grade friends, Julio, Cricket, Lucas, and Zoe decide to organize a save-our-school committee when they learn that the board wants to close their school. However, a bossy sixth grader takes over the committee and Julio decides to search for another worthwhile project. While looking for a new project, he sets off a fire alarm, unexpectedly frightens his grandmother, and has to come up with a birthday gift for his brother. More humorous incidents about Julio and his friends are featured in *Class Clown* and *Class President* (both Morrow, 1987 and 1990, respectively).

370. Keller, Beverly (1986). *Desdemona—Twelve Going on Desperate*. New York: Lothrop, Lee and Shepard. Ages 11–12.

Keller's story takes humor and weaves it into a sensitive home situation. Twelve-year-old Desdemona, "Des," is a honest-to-goodness person in this story and she says, "There is a reason to believe in the species if you take us one at a time." It seems that Desdemona's mother has run away to find herself and the family is about to lose its small rented house. Sherman, younger and smaller than Desdemona, wants her attention and follows her about, and Desdemona, along with all the other girls, has a crush on handsome Mike. When Desdemona and some friends earn money by preparing party food for a large group of important guests, they mix up the dog food with the truffles, which is the episode that explains the title. There are several more incidents that involve the other characters in the plot line—a hardhearted real estate agent with an interest in Desdemona's father's girlfriend, a politician, and a stray dog.

371. Kibbe, Pat (1979). *The Hocus-Pocus Dilemma*. Illustrated by Dan Jones. New York: Knopf. Ages 9–12.

Kibbe's story is really nine short episodes filled with humor. The Pinkerton family is introduced and B. J. Pinkerton tries to cultivate her newly discovered ESP talents with her family members. There are several more incidents that involve the other characters in the plot line—the dog is a target for a skunk; and the cat starts a tape recording that sounds like burglars breaking into the house.

For readers who want more about the Pinkertons, suggest *My Mother, the Mayor, Maybe* (Knopf, 1981) where B. J.'s mother wants to run for mayor. B. J. becomes the public relations coordinator and gets her mother's name in the headlines of the paper every day to create one of the most exciting elections in the town's history. She breaks into her mother's headquarters, shows her mother in a bikini photo, and illegally campaigns for her mother at the high school during the homecoming festivities. At an election rally, B. J. blows off the wig of her mother's opponent and as a reader might predict, B. J.'s mother loses the election.

372. Kline, Suzy (1986). *What's the Matter with Herbie Jones?* Illustrated by Richard Williams. New York: Putnam. Ages 9–10.

Kline's humorous realistic novel, with its short chapters and large type, begins in a school setting. Ray cannot understand why his best friend Herbie wants to spend time with Annabelle Louisa Hodgekiss, and is alarmed to discover that something is the matter with Herbie—he has the dreaded G (girl) disease. Fortunately, Herbie's infatuation with Annabelle lasts only a day and a half. The story concludes with Herbie's victory over Annabelle in a Herbie-versus-Annabelle round in the third grade spelling bee, thus ending their brief romance for good. This is a sequel to *Herbie Jones* (Putnam, 1985), an introduction to the school experiences of Herbie Jones, a third grader who is anything but a star student.

373. Lowry, Lois (1984). *Anastasia, Ask Your Analyst*. Boston: Houghton Mifflin. Ages 9–12.

This is Lowry's funny adventure that gives readers a good laugh about "touchy" situations

often felt by youngsters in their early teens. Anastasia's problems are those that most teenagers feel and Anastasia seeks psychiatric help. The book's humor will provide a good laugh over many touchy situations and their resolutions.

374. Lowry, Lois (1979). *Anastasia Krupnik*. Boston: Houghton Mifflin. Ages 9–10.

Lowry's story is told in a humorous way and focuses on growing up and adjusting to the new sibling. Ten-year-old Anastasia had a nice life until her parents tell her a baby is on the way. She was not pleased with the change. She knew that babies immediately went to a prominent place on her list of hates—a list of what she did not like. She kept lists in her notebook labeled things I love (her romance with a sixth grade boy with an Afro hair style) and things I hate (a grandmother who could never remember Anastasia's name). These helped her deal with the impending birth of a baby brother.

375. Lowry, Lois (1985). *Switcharound*. Boston: Houghton Mifflin. Ages 9–12.

Here are humorous situations, funny conversations, and text about the feuding siblings from Lowry's *One Hundredth Thing About Caroline* (Houghton Mifflin, 1983). Caroline Tate and her brother, J. P., rarely agree on anything, but when their father asks them to spend the summer in Des Moines, they suddenly agree they don't want to go. It means that they'll both have to put up with their father's three kids, Poochie and the twin baby girls. The summer starts out badly when Caroline has to take care of the messy twins, and J. P. is expected to coach Poochie's baseball team of clumsy six-year-olds, the Tater Chips. Both plan revenge, but the chance for Caroline and J. P. to use their own special talents changes the situation. Everyone gains a new perspective and all ends well.

376. Naylor, Phyllis Reynolds (1987). *Beetles, Lightly Toasted*. New York: Atheneum. Ages 9–12.

There is a subtle message from Naylor about fair play in this humorous story about research on beetles, bugs, and worms. Andy has been looking forward to the fifth grade essay contest, but he doesn't think the topic, conservation, will be a fun thing to write about. Eventually he does have some fun with his self-selected essay, "How Beetles, Bugs, and Worms Can Save

Money and the Food Supply. . . . " He does enough research to discover three topics: toasted beetles for nuts in brownies; deep-fried, breaded earthworms; and boiled mealworm larvae in egg salad. Andy himself is a picky eater so he contrives to test his products on the unsuspecting family and his classmates. Winning the contest "hoists him on his own petard," for in order to get his picture in the paper he has to be photographed eating his own meal.

377. Park, Barbara (1982). *Skinnybones*. New York: Knopf. Ages 9–12.

Two boys dislike each other and their dislike is the cause for the humor from the beginning to the end of Park's story. Alex is skinny and terrible at baseball when he is compared to T. J., a fine baseball player. These two, Alex Frankovitch and T. J. Stoner, dislike each other all through the story, and there are many humorous incidents.

378. Peck, Richard (1993). *Bel-Air Bambi and the Mall Rats*. New York: Delacorte. Ages 10–12.

This is Peck's spoof that begins when Bill Babcock, a TV producer, leaves his debts behind and takes his family back to his hometown, Hickory Fork. Once there, the family, which includes Buffie, a sixth grader, and Bambi and Brick, discover that the high school kids are "into" tearing up the local mall and use it as a meeting place. They decide to do something about the leather-wearing kids who call themselves the "Mall Rats." They all use their show business talents and do what they can to save the mall.

379. Sachar, Louis (1978). *Sideways Stories from Wayside School*. Illustrated by Dennis Hockerman. New York: Follett. Ages 9–10.

Sachar's hilarity in this chaptered book is mainly in the ridiculous situations. The architectural faux pas of constructing a thirty-story school with one classroom on each floor begins the first of the thirty chapters about Wayside School. Each of the chapters features one particular student or teacher in a humorous situation. For example, Mrs. Gorf is the teacher who changes the students into apples, and one student, John, has the ability to read only upside-down material.

380. Sharmat, Marjorie W. (1971). *Getting Something on Maggie Mamelstein*. Illustrated by Ben Shecter. New York: Harper and Row. Ages 9–11.

This is Sharmat's funny short story about Maggie who hears Thad Smith say she squeaks like a mouse and their "hate" relationship is on. To irritate her, Thad takes a role as the frog opposite Maggie who is playing the princess in a school play. Thad also finds her letter to Cary Grant—an embarrassing moment—but in return, Thad is saved from *his* embarrassing moment by Maggie's actions. For readers interested in other episodes about Maggie, suggest *Maggie Mamelstein for President* (Harper and Row, 1975). Maggie wants to help Thad Smith run for sixth grade president. When Thad refuses to let Maggie be his campaign manager, Maggie decides to run against him. Their pre-election debate turns into a shouting match and as a consequence of all the yelling, Noah, the smartest kid in the class, is elected president with a lot of write-in votes.

381. Sobol, Donald J. (1984). *Encyclopedia Brown's Book of Wacky Spies*. Illustrated by Ted Enik. New York: Morrow. Ages 9–12.

Sobol's humor is in the wacky events about these "undercover" characters. There are over one hundred anecdotes about all sorts of spies throughout history and around the world. This makes for entertaining reading that a reader can share with friends.

382. Sobol, Donald J. (1980). *Encyclopedia Brown Carries On*. Illustrated by Ib Ohlsson and Leonard Shortall. New York: Scholastic. Ages 9–12.

Set in Idaville, anywhere, U. S. A., Encyclopedia (Leroy) Brown, America's Sherlock Holmes in sneakers, and the only child of Mr. Brown, the chief of police, engages in ten mysteries filled with sleuthing fun. Leroy never forgot what he read or heard or saw, and this helped him solve the cases he faced. For example, Encyclopedia finds the key to the case of the giant mousetrap, the culprit in the case of the grape catcher, and the clue written upside-down and backward to solve the case of the upside-down witness. A final section of the book is "solutions" that explains how the ten-year-old detective solved each case. For a reader interested in matching his or her wits with Encyclopedia, additional cases are found in these books:

• *The Case of the Exploding Plumbing and Other Mysteries* (Scholastic, 1974) features a runaway elephant, worn-out sayings, a skunk-ape costume, a counterfeit bill, a silver dollar, and litterbugs.

- *Encyclopedia Brown, Boy Detective* (Thomas Nelson, 1963) features a Civil War sword, a diamond necklace, missing roller skates, and a champion egg spinner.

383. Townsend, Sue (1986). *The Adrian Mole Diaries*. New York: Grove. Ages 9–11.

Nothing goes right for Adrian and in his diary he writes about his sad state. He writes about one time when he was tempted to sniff glue while making a model airplane—and his nose stuck to the plane. Adrian's father had to take him to Casualty to have the plane removed. Adrian also was worried about turning into an intellectual and he sent poems to the BBC with lines like "Norway! Land of Difficult Spelling."

384. Yorinks, Arthur (1989). *Oh, Brother*. Illustrated by Richard Egielski. New York: Farrar, Straus, & Giroux. Ages 9–10.

In Yorinks' story, absurd situations and wry humor are found in the antics of the obnoxious twins, Milton and Morris. The twins sail from England with their parents, sneak down to the hold full of fireworks, and struggle over a skyrocket, which sets off an accident at sea. Supposedly orphaned by the accident, the boys are bumblers as they try to be pickpockets and try to learn a trade—custom tailoring. Finally invited to the court, they are recognized by their parents, the gardener and nanny.

Humorous Humans

385. Bechard, Margaret (1994). *Really No Big Deal*. New York: Scholastic. Ages 9–12.

Bechard's story offers laugh-out-loud situations about Jonah Truman, a seventh grader. It seems he thinks he has a lot of big deals to worry about and cope with—for instance, he worries that he is one of the shortest kids in his grade at school. The other big deals include figuring out how to talk to girls and earning money for the class trip at the end of the year. They also include his concern about his mother who is dating the principal of the school, Mr. Decker, and his concern about staying friends with Amy, who helps him make money by assisting at other kids' birthday parties.

386. Branscum, Robbie (1978). *Three Buckets of Daylight*. Illustrated by Allen Davis. New York: Lothrop, Lee & Shepard. Ages 9–12.

Branscum's story has humorous characters even though the setting is a sensitive one—the depression days in the Arkansas Ozarks. Jackie Lee and Jimmy Jay are close cousins. They engage in colorful dialogue (saying *smarty pants, uppity,* and *outen yer rear end*) but share everything—even the trouble that seems to be always over their heads. Jimmy is the leader—he is the one who thinks of schemes that often lead to danger. For example, when they steal apples from Ader, an old woman, she places a curse on them. In turn, the boys want to "break" the curse. To do so, they find out they have to collect some unusual things that include a bat's wings, a bobcat's tail, and a cloth that a grasshopper has spit on.

387. Brittain, Bill (1988). *The Fantastic Freshman*. New York: Harper and Row. Ages 12 and up.

In Brittain's story, Stanley Muffet has a special wish—to become a Very Important Person in school. He wants to be respected by his high school peers. Magically, he gets his wish to become a VIP in his high school. However, he finds out that this situation is not as great as he thought it would be and there are humorous consequences.

388. Burch, Robert (1980). *Ida Early Comes Over the Mountain*. New York: Avon/Camelot. Ages 11 and up.

Most of Burch's humor centers around the Mary Poppins-type character, Ida Early, who takes charge of the four motherless Sutton children. Ida is over six feet tall, wears overalls, and has unruly red hair. Though life was rough in the Blue Ridge Mountains of Georgia for the children with their mother dead and their father at work, Ida, now the housekeeper and cook, brings laughter, joking, and joy into their lives. The children are impressed by her—Ida has done many things—she tells tall tales, strikes a match on the seat of her pants, and says she tamed lions. When the summer ends and it is time to return to school, Ida agrees to accompany the twins, Dewey and Clay, on their first day of school. For more pranks, slapstick, humor, and warmth about Ida and the Suttons, select the sequel, *Christmas with Ida Early* (Avon/Camelot, 1982).

389. Byars, Betsy (1994). *The Dark Stairs: A Herculeah Jones Mystery*. New York: Viking. Ages 10–12.

Herculeah Jones likes to solve mysteries that come her way with the help of her humorous friend, Meat. Herculeah comes by this interest naturally—her mother is a private investigator and her father is a police detective. She is intrigued by a sinister-looking client of her mother's and the mystery of the long-missing owner of the Dead Oaks estate. Chapter by chapter (with titles that parody others found in mysteries), Herculeah and Meat get closer to the solution and finally solve the case, but not before exploring a dark, moldy basement, discovering a hidden staircase, and finding the owner of Dead Oaks.

390. Byars, Betsy (1993). *McMummy*. New York: Viking. Ages 9–12.

While Professor Orloff is attending a world hunger conference, Mozie has agreed to water the plants in the greenhouse and gets some assistance from Valvoline, a neighbor. Though Valvoline is mainly interested in the Miss Tri-County Pageant, she helps Mozie and the two of them hear a noise from a green bean that Mozie thinks dates back to ancient Egypt. The humor—and the mystery—continue when the familiar thunder and lightning storm in the night occurs and Valvoline and others see a large green thing (McMummy?) appear at the pageant.

391. Cleary, Beverly (1952). *Henry and Beezus.* Illustrated by Louis Darling. New York: Morrow. Ages 9–11.

In Cleary's story, Henry wants a new bicycle. At the opening of the colossal market he is delighted when he wins one of the door prizes because he thinks he will have the money for the new bike. Then he is horrified to find that it is fifty dollars worth of beauty shoppe permanent waves, facials, and false eyelashes. In the prequel, *Henry Huggins* (Morrow, 1950), Henry has several problems with a stray dog named Fibsy as he makes a compassionate effort to keep the canine around.

392. Cresswell, Helen (1978). *Absolute Zero: Being the Second Part of the Bagthorpe Saga.* New York: Macmillan. Ages 9–12.

This is Cresswell's story of how the world of advertising moves into the funny Bagthorpe family and how the Bagthorpes started competing in their efforts to win contests. It all starts when Uncle Parker wins a Caribbean cruise as a prize for a slogan-writing contest, then the rest of the family enters every contest offered. The result is chaos when the prizes start arriving.

For readers interested further in this family where disaster is the norm and nothing ever happens calmly or quietly, suggest *Bagthorpes v. the World: Being the Fourth Part of the Bagthorpe Saga* (Macmillan, 1979), the story of what happens when an overdraft bank notice sends the Bagthorpes into a chaotic survival campaign—it seems that they owe the bank billions.

393. Cresswell, Helen (1989). *Bagthorpes Liberated: Being the Seventh Part of the Bagthorpe Saga.* New York: Macmillan. Ages 10–12.

In this story, the family returns home from a holiday in Wales to find they forgot to cancel the milk and there are two hundred fifty pints in the driveway. They also forgot to lock the front door and find a tramp asleep in Jack's room. The tramp is an old man who becomes friends with Grandpa and adds to fun in the family. When the housekeeper threatens to leave, Mrs. Bagthorpe divides up the chores, an idea met with resistance by all the family—Grandma, Uncle Parker, Aunt Celia, and Daisy, four years old.

394. Cresswell, Helen (1978). *Bagthorpes Unlimited.* New York: Macmillan. Ages 9–12.

Exaggeration provides much of the humor in this story about the wacky British family first introduced in *Ordinary Jack* (Macmillan, 1977). Grandma—the undisputed and slightly unbalanced head of the clan—discovers the wacky theft of several prized but absolutely worthless family possessions. Unnerved by this catastrophe, Grandma calls for a family reunion to comfort her in her time of distress. At the reunion, the Bagthorpes share their dislike for prissy Aunt Penelope, her hen-pecked husband, and their two revolting children, and devise a series of schemes involving germs, spiders, and maggots—to drive them away.

395. Cresswell, Helen (1977). *Ordinary Jack.* New York: Macmillan. Ages 9–12.

In this story, Jack believes he has no distinguishing characteristics to compete with the talents of the others in his British family. His father is a television writer, his mother is an author of an advice column, and his siblings all pursue their favorites—sports, paintings, music, and ham radios. With the help of Uncle Parker, Jack develops the ability to prophesy and this becomes his way of being unique.

396. Denton, Judy (1987). *Angel's Mother's Wedding.* Boston: Houghton Mifflin. Ages 9–10.

Denton's humor is developed through bright characters in this story. Angel has worries through her imagination about the wedding. She thinks that her mother is not taking the upcoming wedding seriously enough. Misunderstandings occur and, of course, a series of humorous incidents. For instance, five-year-old Rudy, Angel's brother, tries to give his new father a wedding present and then tells how he believes a ring bearer should perform at the wedding.

397. Fine, Anne (1988). *Alias Madame Doubtfire.* Boston: Little, Brown. Ages 9 and up.

An unexpected situation causes the humor in Fine's story, one that many children may have seen at the movies with Robin Williams playing the role of Mrs. Doubtfire. The humor begins when an ex-husband disguises himself as a cleaning woman and babysitter in his ex-wife's house. He is the father in disguise.

398. Fleischman, Sid (1986). *The Whipping Boy*. Illustrated by Peter Sis. New York: Greenwillow. Ages 10 and up.

Some of Fleischman's humor is in the playful language of the text and the parody of the old-fashioned titles of early adventure stories. For example, Chapter 1 is entitled "In Which We Observe a Hair-raising Event" and Chapter 10 is called "In which Prince Brat Lives up to His Name." The titles parody those in *Robinson Crusoe* and the story itself is similar to *The Prince and the Pauper*. Jemmy, the orphaned son of a rat catcher, is the tough but unfortunate child who must take Prince Brat's whippings. Bored with his own pranks, the Prince decides to run away and commands Jemmy to accompany him. When the pair are kidnapped by cutthroat villains, they are briefly rescued but then lead the villains on a wild chase through the sewers that Jemmy had once used for his rat catching. The highwaymen flee the sewers when they discover the rats and stow away unknowingly on a prison ship headed for a prisoners' island.

399. Gifaldi, David (1993). *Toby Scudder, Ultimate Warrior*. New York: Clarion. Ages 10–12.

Gifaldi's story has humorous dialogue that also portrays a sensitive look at Toby, a sixth grade bully with a behavior problem. It is best suited for individual reading because of the included profanity. The story portrays Toby as a charmer in spite of his pranks, his acting out, and his fistfights. Toby has his best relationships with his pet goldfish and with Megan, his first grade partner in the school's mentoring program. At the end of the story, Toby comes to terms with his life and this includes his distracted mother, the memory of his father who deserted the family, his uncaring teenage half-brother, and his twenty-year-old sister.

400. Greene, Constance C. (1978). *I and Sproggy*. Illustrated by Emily A. McCully. New York: Viking. Ages 10–11.

Greene's story is entertaining because of its interesting characters. Ten-year-old Adam had adjusted to his parents' divorce and had even grown to like living with his mother without his dad. When his father returned from London with his new wife and stepdaughter, Sproggy, they announced that they were moving into an apartment nearby. Adam was a little worried about such closeness, but when his father asked

him to take care of Sproggy, he was furious. First of all, she did *not* need to be taken care of. She got along quite well by herself—so well that she even saved Adam from a mugger and became good friends with Adam's friends behind his back. It was only after the taller, older Sproggy proved to be vulnerable that she and Adam became friends.

401. Greene, Constance C. (1973). *Isabelle the Itch*. Illustrated by Emily A. McCully. New York: Viking. Ages 9 and up.

The amusement is mainly in the dialogue in Greene's story about Isabelle, a spunky girl in fifth grade who drove everyone around her crazy. It seems that Isabelle's fondest dream was to win the fifty-yard dash at her school's field day. Even though she took over her brother's paper route to earn money for the Addidas track shoes she needed, Isabelle still did not win the dash. However, she did make some new friends.

402. Greenwald, Sheila (1981). *Give Us a Great Big Smile, Rosy Cole*. Boston: Little, Brown. Ages 9 and up.

Greenwald's humor is mainly irony in this story about Rosy and her turn to be the subject of her uncle's book. Her uncle needed to earn money again and Rosy had just turned age ten, the age that each of her sisters had been when Uncle Ralph wrote the books *Anitra Dances* and *Pippa Prances* about them. However, Rosy could not dance like Anitra or ride horses like Pippa. Then Rosy's mother and uncle decided that Rosy could be a very little fiddler since she had been taking violin lessons—they forgot how truly untalented she was. Rosy gets an idea to stop this plan. In the park with other street musicians, she put up a sign that asked people to sign a petition if they felt she should *not* play the violin anymore. As she played her violin—badly—she drew a large crowd with her mother as one of the listeners and signers. This ended her musical career and the book, but Rosy went back to being "normal" and her uncle found another topic for his book.

403. Haas, Dorothy (1986). *The Secret Life of Dilly McBean*. New York: Bradbury. Ages 10–12.

This is Haas' just-for-fun book that is somewhere between humorous fantasy and science fiction, and it can be used as an introduction to one or the other. The entertainment is mainly in the eccentric characters (e.g., Dilly's dog is named Contrary), their actions, and some child-like humor. Orphaned Dilly has a secret legacy from his scientist father—it is the power of magnetism within his own body. It seems that anything metal flies to his fingertips if he isn't careful. Just as he is developing this "gift" with a tutor and making new friends at a new school and beginning to feel at home, Dr. Keenwit's men plot to kidnap him. Dilly is taken to Dr. Keenwit and sees the Great Harmonizer, a marvelously advanced computer that is programmed to think—for everyone! Fortunately, Dilly's new friends come to his aid and outwit the evil Keenwit.

404. Hamilton, Virginia. (1985). *The People Could Fly: American Black Folktales*. Illustrated by Leo and Diane Dillon. New York: Knopf. Ages 9–10.

The section of tall tales is filled with chuckles. "Papa John's Tall Tale," for example, recounts the time Papa John grew a turnip so large that a herd of cows could get under a turnip leaf and sleep all day. He said he had to have a pot as big and as high as a hill, and a year to get it boiled through. When young Jake asks, "How long ago was that?" Papa John says, "Been years ago." Jake replies that he sure would have liked to have tasted that turnip. Papa John says Jake had his chance. "You ate the last piece of it for your dinner, today."

405. Hildick, Edmund W. (1981). *The Case of the Bashful Bank Robber*. Illustrated by Lisl Weil. New York: Macmillan. Ages 9 and up.

Though out of print, this is one of several light, fast-moving, and humorous stories of Jack McQuirk, a shrewd leader, and his friends—Joey and Willie and Wanda and Brains—who form the McQuirk Organization. Joey is handy with words and the typewriter, and narrates each story; Willie is the one with a sensitive nose and a memory for odors; Wanda is the best tree climber and is a strong influence on the group. And Brains Bellingham is the nine-year-old scientific genius of the organization and runs the organization's crime lab. In this story, they try to protect the seven banks in town from being robbed and they patrol each bank to watch for getaway cars.

406. Hildick, Edmund W. (1981). *The Case of the Four Flying Fingers*. Illustrated by Lisl Weil. New York: Macmillan. Ages 9 and up.

In this story, McGuirk and his fellow detectives suspect that four young strangers in town are involved in break-ins and burglaries in the city and were fingering houses for someone to burglarize. The McQuirk Organization tracks down a lady suspect and her accomplice, but get caught and are taken out of town in her camper. Brains, bound and gagged, uses a flashlight and Morse code to signal help and a police car finally stops the camper for speeding. McGuirk and his friends are able to convince the police that the lady is a thief.

407. Hildick, Edmund W. (1977). *The Case of the Invisible Dog*. Illustrated by Lisl Weil. New York: Macmillan. Ages 9 and up.

This is the humorous story about the way that Brains Bellingham, the nine-year-old scientific genius, first joined the McGuirk Organization. Brains tricks the organization by making the impossible—an invisible dog—seem real. When the organization discovers the trick, it takes its revenge but McGuirk admits they all had been impressed by Brains's clever thinking. The outcome of the discussion was that Brains was invited to become a member.

408. Hildick, Edmund W. (1980). *The Case of the Snowbound Spy*. Illustrated by Lisl Weil. New York: Macmillan. Ages 9 and up.

One snowy morning McGuirk called the five members of his organization together to decipher a code. The code leads them to uncover two industrial spies who were stealing secret information about a new copying machine. For readers interested in further mysteries solved by the organization, guide them to the following:

- *The Case of the Phantom Frog* (Macmillan, 1979) where the group solves the mystery of the eerie sound of a very large frog coming from seven-year-old Bela's room. The group interviewed all the neighbors, surveyed the scene of the crime, and tried to decide upon the real murderer.

- *The Case of the Treetop Treasure* (Macmillan, 1980) where the McGuirk Organization suspected a thief was using the tree as a place to hide stolen goods and discover the culprit was the gang's long-time enemy, Sandra Ennis.

409. Horvath, Polly (1994). *The Happy Yellow Car*. New York: Farrar, Straus & Giroux. Ages 9–12.

Horvath's book introduces the humorous Grunt family and their somewhat slapstick actions that are in contrast to the story's setting in the middle of the Great Depression. Exaggerations and amusing dialogue highlight several misadventures with the family's odd relatives, as well as with family members: Ma has a secret money fund to help send Betty to college but Pa spends it for a new shiny yellow car—an act that stuns Ma and the four children; and twelve-year-old Betty Grunt has been elected Pork-Fry Queen and wants to earn money for some flowers and other things she needs.

410. Hurwitz, Johanna (1979). *Aldo Applesauce.* Illustrated by John Wallner. New York: Morrow. Ages 9 and up.

This is Hurwitz's humorous story about Aldo Sossi, a fourth grader, for whom nothing goes right. Aldo, vegetarian and new kid at school, was immediately teased and nicknamed applesauce for obvious reasons. He did not like this name or being teased. He tried to find more friends and take himself less seriously. But his attempts to make friends ended in disasters both times—at a bowling alley and at a birthday party.

411. Hurwitz, Johanna (1981). *Aldo Ice Cream.* Illustrated by John Wallner. New York: Morrow. Ages 9 and up.

Aldo got his newest nickname (Ice Cream) from his friend DeDe when she heard that Aldo not only wanted to try every flavor of ice cream at the local store but wanted to buy an ice cream freezer for his sister's birthday. The way Aldo got the money for the freezer winds itself through the story. He won a shoe store's contest by having the most worn-out pair of sneakers in town. His mother paid him the money she would have spent on a new pair of shoes for him. With this money he bought the last freezer in the store—on sale at a lower price.

412. Hurwitz, Johanna (1981). *Baseball Fever.* Illustrated by Ray Cruz. New York: Morrow. Ages 8 and up.

Ezra's father was a German-born intellectual who couldn't understand how anyone could waste so much time with baseball—watching men hit a ball with a stick. He wanted Ezra to become more interested in history and chess, but baseball was all Ezra thought about. After many humorous incidents, they finally reach a compromise where Ezra and his father learn to appreciate each other's interests.

413. Hurwitz, Johanna (1978). *The Law of Gravity.* Illustrated by Ingrid Fetz. New York: Morrow. Ages 10 and up.

Hurwitz's story has humorous treatment of a universal concern—the wish to change someone else. Eleven-year-old Margot's summer project is to get her overweight mother downstairs after nine years of staying upstairs and a determination *never* to go downstairs from their fifth-floor walk-up apartment. Though Margot is helped by her friend, twelve-year-old Bernie, none of their ideas work until Margot pretends to run away and scares her mother into going downstairs. Then Margot realizes that she loves her mother regardless of whether her mother comes out of the apartment or not, and discovers that she should not force anyone to change to suit her own ideas.

414. Kehret, Peg (1994). *The Richest Kids in Town.* New York: Cobblehill. Ages 9–10.

This is Kehret's humorous encounter with Peter Dodge III, a new kid in town, and with his new acquaintance, Wishbone Wyoming III. In the chapters, the two boys find that they have some things in common—they both want to earn money and both have the generational marker (the Third) after their names. Peter wants some money to return and visit Tommy, the best friend whom he left behind, and Wishbone wants to buy a model of a DC-3. Together, they plan several moneymaking attempts which turn into great comical romps that always leave them economically neutral—but stronger as friends. Each chapter is introduced by Peter's correspondence with Tommy and a reader sees how Peter's friendship with Wishbone grows by the way Peter signs his signature to Tommy. It changes from "Your best friend forever" in the initial chapter to "Your friend" in the final one.

415. Korman, Gordon (1992). *The Toilet Paper Tigers.* New York: Scholastic. Ages 10–12.

The contrast in the personalities of the characters provides much of the humor in Korman's story. Cory Johnson finds himself on a little league team of misfits led by Professor Pendergast, a nuclear physicist coach who is more than a little distracted all the time. The team seems destined to get clobbered in every game. However, when the professor's granddaughter Kristy (an aggressive tough-talking know-it-all from New York City), becomes the assistant coach, things change dramatically for the team members. She blackmails them with an embarrassing photograph of the players standing around in their jockstraps and thus "motivates" them into improving their performance on the field. At the end of the season, they win the big game and the little league championship.

416. Kurtzman, Harvey, and Bryon Preiss (1985). *Nuts #1*. New York: Bantam. Ages 13–14.

Kurtzman's book is ideal for satire lovers since this is a collection of parodies on teenage life that is entertainingly hilarious. The problems of teenagers and the situations in which they find themselves are illustrated in cartoon-type illustrations with the jokes sprinkled throughout. The students who like this satire also will like Kurtzman's *Nuts #2* (Bantam, 1985).

417. Law, Carol Russell (1980). *The Case of the Weird Street Firebug*. Illustrated by Bill Morrison. New York: Knopf. Ages 9–12.

This is Law's humorous story of a mystery taken on by Steffi, a girl who wants to be a detective. She attends Jeff Dangerfield's detective school. Her first lesson, trailing suspects, is a disaster, for she keeps running into a character she calls Beady Eyes. Finally, she figures out that he was the arsonist of the fire on Weir Street. Her trailing of the suspect traps her into being cornered—but she is saved in a timely fashion by the police. For her brave work, she receives a medal from the police and a partnership from Jeff Dangerfield.

418. Levy, Elizabeth (1976). *Lizzie Lies a Lot*. Illustrated by John Wallner. New York: Delacorte. Ages 9–11.

This is Levy's light touch of humor about the problem of lying a lot. There is some fun in the fact that Lizzie tells lies to get herself out of trouble or to cover up her feelings. However, when her lies cost her her only friend, Lizzie has to admit her problem to herself and to her family. They all agree to help her stop telling lies and to help her as she starts telling the truth.

419. Lowery, Lois (1981). *Anastasia Again*. Boston: Houghton Mifflin. Ages 9–12.

This is another one of Lowery's sequels about Anastasia's parents moving to the suburbs—an idea Anastasia hates. She feels better when the family moves to a house with a tower and she meets a neighborhood boy who becomes her special friend. She also involves a grouchy older neighbor with a group of lively older people at a local senior citizen center.

420. Lowery, Lois (1985). *Anastasia on Her Own*. Boston: Houghton Mifflin. Ages 9–12.

Lowery introduces a great deal of humor into this contemporary family situation—two busy professional parents try to manage a household and raise two children. Anastasia thinks that housekeeping can be easy for the family if the family can only develop and follow a household schedule. An unexpected consulting contract as a book illustrator calls her mother away from the family and this give Anastasia a chance to test her scheduling theory. She learns that it takes more than a schedule to cope with family emergencies. She finds there are unexpected interruptions to her schedule which lists the tasks for each hour from 7 in the morning to 8 in the evening. In spite of her best efforts, many things start to happen—Anastasia copes with Sam's chicken pox and an unexpected visit from her father's old girlfriend. She gets ready for her first date and prepares a romantic gourmet dinner complete with candlelight and a tablecloth that she dyed purple—along with her arms. Preparing the gourmet dinner, she is interrupted by a stranger calling to sell her dancing lessons. Anastasia also has to search for her mother's long gloves to cover the purple dye on her skin. For her first date, Anastasia had always thought of someone who looked like a handsome Laurence Olivier. When her romantic dinner guest arrives—her real-life friend, thirteen-year-old Steve Harvey—he wears a sweatshirt that reads *Psychotic State*, talks with his mouth stuffed full of peanuts, and tells her that her first try at entertaining was horrible.

Her schedule becomes increasingly simple as the story goes on and one of the last schedules for her "Housekeeping lists" . . . for hours and hours and hours. "Cry." For readers interested in further episodes in Anastasia's life, guide them to one of the following:

- *Anastasia's Chosen Career* (Houghton Mifflin, 1987), where she writes her school assignment about vocational choices. Her writing shows her humorous outlook about things.
- *Anastasia at Your Service* (Houghton Mifflin, 1982)
- *Anastasia Has the Answers* (Houghton Mifflin, 1986)

421. McCloskey, Robert (1943). *Homer Price*. Illustrated by the author. New York: Viking. Ages 9–12.

These are McCloskey's humorous tales about Homer Price, his friends, and their lives in Centerburg. In his uncle's doughnut shop, Homer helps with the new doughnut machine—but Homer can't stop it and doughnuts begin falling all over the floor and fill the shop. When they realize that the woman who helped make the batter is now missing her bracelet—the search for her jewelry shows them how to get rid of the doughnuts.

422. Merrill, Jean (1964). *The Pushcart War*. Illustrated by Dan Jones. New York: Knopf. Ages 9–10.

Merrill's story is timely today since it deals with the constant snarl of traffic and it is told with bland humor. The setting is New York City and the problem is that there are so many huge trucks that traffic on Manhattan Island is in a constant snarl. Truckers decide to eliminate other vehicles and their first plan of attack is the pushcart owners. The little army of pushcart owners, however, outwit the big business truckers.

423. Miles, Betty (1981). *The Secret Life of the Underwear Champ*. Illustrated by Dan Jones. New York: Knopf. Ages 9–10.

Miles shows a painful side to humor—teasing. One day, Dan found himself about to make a television commercial for Champ Win Knitting Mills, makers of sports clothing and underwear, because he could use the money. He did not want his school friends to see him in underwear, but to his horror, the commercial is shown the night before the first baseball game for his team. At the game, the opposing team members tease him about the commercial—so do his teammates. When he goes to bat he is mad enough to slam the ball out of the field—and he does. His winning home run earns him the name of the underwear champ.

424. Naylor, Phyllis Reynolds (1985). *The Agony of Alice*. New York: Atheneum. Ages 9–10.

Naylor's story is humorous and sensitive at the same time as motherless Alice searches for a female role model—perhaps a beautiful new teacher—to show her a roadmap on how to behave. Alice gets homely pear-shaped Mrs. Plotkins, however, who assigns a journal as a writing assignment. Alice calls her journal "The Agony of Alice" and puts in it all the embarrassing things that happen to her. Naylor has written other humorous episodes about Alice that are sure of interest to fans of Alice:

- *Alice in Rapture, Sort of* (Atheneum, 1989) is best suited for individual reading and takes place in the summer before she enters seventh grade. She discovers that love with her best boyfriend Patrick is really a mixed-up thing. Alice's friend Pamela dreams of having enough cleavage to bury a locket between her breasts, and shows Alice her new Up-Lift Spandex Ahh-Bra that "lifts, supports, and promotes cleavage." But, Alice asks, "What's cleavage?" Alice writes love letters to the departing Patrick and he makes a promise to call her on her 21st birthday to make a date for New Year's.

- *All But Alice* (Atheneum, 1992) sees Alice determined to stave off personal and social disaster by becoming part of the boring "in" crowd. She joins the all-stars fan club, the earring club, and becomes one of the "famous eight" at school. When her friends decide to take part in a talent show, Alice decides to do a magic scarf trick dressed as Wonder Woman. When she is center stage, she pulls out the scarf and a cat from the following act pounces on the end of the scarf. Alice has to walk off dragging the scarf and cat behind her to the laughter in the audience. Reflecting, she decides that there are only 272 horrible things left to happen to her in her life based on the number of horrible things that have happened already.

425. Patron, Susan (1993). *Maybe Yes, Maybe No, Maybe Maybe*. Illustrated by Dorothy Donahue. New York: Orchard. Ages 9–10.

Patron's free-floating humor is found in this story of PK's ups and downs as she sees things changing around her. She lives with her mother, who is a night waitress, and she is the middle girl between two sisters, Megan (who is gifted) and Rabbit (who is a nervous prekindergartner). PK tells stories to Rabbit each night, which, in an entertaining way, seem to come from the clothes hamper in the bathroom. When the family moves to a new apartment and a new bathroom, PK's stories come to her through a little window in her mind, and she begins to feel that she had drama in her blood (with which her mother agrees).

426. Peck, Robert Newton (1979). *Mr. Little*. Illustrated by Ben Stahl. New York: Doubleday. Ages 9–12.

In Peck's entertaining story, two boys eventually develop respect and a feeling of friendship for a new teacher. Mr. Little takes the place of Miss Kellogg as their teacher and Drag and Finley are disappointed. They decide to play tricks on the new teacher and they steal his underwear and put it on a statue in the town square. Good-natured Mr. Little, however, rescues them from this trouble.

427. Pinkwater, Daniel M. (1979). *Alan Mendelsoh, the Boy from Mars*. New York: E. P. Dutton. Ages 10–12.

This is Pinkwater's funny fast-paced story with an assortment of nutty characters. It is narrated by Leonard Neeble, a short, portly misfit who attends Bat Masterson Junior High School. Leonard's grandmother, also an entertaining character, wants to be called the Old One. Leonard's seemingly out-of-this-world friend Alan proclaims he is from Mars. The two boys get involved with another nutty character, Mr. Klugarsh, the head of Klugarsh Mind Control Associates, who sells omega meters for locating omega thought waves. The boys are intrigued by the idea that the meter plays the song "Jingle Bells" when the waves are produced.

428. Pinkwater, Daniel M. (1977). *Fat Men From Space*. New York: Dodd. Ages 9–10.

This is Pinkwater's slapstick spoof of science fiction, food fads, and junk food. It seems that William (Will) can hear the radio when the radio is off. When he wires himself to a fence, he hears space men talking. The men are on a secret mission, and they discover William and capture him. They are about to invade Earth to consume all the junk food they can find. Will is helpless to warn others until the invaders' interest is captured by a giant potato pancake floating in outer space.

429. Pinkwater, Daniel M. (1977). *The Hoboken Chicken Emergency*. New York: Prentice-Hall. Ages 9–11.

Arthur's mother gave him some money to buy a Thanksgiving turkey but it seems that the turkey reservation had been lost at the meat market and there were no other turkeys available—so Arthur returned home with a live 266-pound chicken on a leash. It seems that a strange old professor tricked him into buying the chicken. With the family's approval, Arthur renamed the friendly chicken Henrietta and kept it for a pet. When Henrietta got loose later, however, there was general hysteria in the neighborhood.

430. Quattlebaum, Mary (1994). *Jackson Jones and the Puddle of Thorns*. Illustrated by Melodye Rosales. New York: Delacorte. Ages 9–11.

There is humor in the situational tensions in Quattlebaum's story when ten-year-old Jackson Jones (who wants a basketball for his birthday) receives some birthday money to be spent on tools and seeds for his "birthday" plot of ground in the community garden. Jackson fears for his young reputation when other kids find out about the garden, but decides to plant flowers and sell them to earn the money he needs for a new basketball.

431. Robinson, Jean (1974). *The Strange But Wonderful Cosmic Awareness of Duffy Moon*. Illustrated by Lawrence DiFiori. Boston: Houghton Mifflin. Ages 9–11.

Duffy is small, loses fights, and is *not* appreciated by his uncle who was an ex-football star. So Duffy sends away for Mr. Flamel's cosmic awareness kit in hopes he can take control over the things he wants. Events finally bring Duffy and Peter to face the dreaded Boots, the leader of the Boots McAfee's gang. Things are not as bad as they seem, however, when they find out that Boots is a smart girl who, as time goes by, is more and more appreciative of Duffy's talents.

432. Robinson, Nancy K. (1980). *Wendy and the Bullies*. Illustrated by Ingrid Fetz. New York: Hastings. Ages 9–10.

This is Robinson's humorous episodic narrative about a common concern—staying away from bullies. Wendy and her friend, Karen, have a way to-and-from school so they avoid the troublesome bullies. When Karen becomes sick, however, Wendy realizes she has to face the bullies all by herself. Fearful, she hides in her basement rather than go to school. After an argument, she makes up with Karen, forms a new friendship, and gets involved in a school project—all of which helps Wendy overcome her fears.

433. Rockwell, Thomas (1973). *How To Eat Fried Worms*. Illustrated by Emily McCully. New York: Watts. Ages 9–11.

Rockwell's chaptered book has dark humor that will be gruesomely funny to some American children. At the beginning of the story, Alan bets Billy fifty dollars that Billy won't eat a worm a day for fifteen days. He takes the bet and faces his first worm (a big night crawler). He repeats the word *minibike* (an object he will buy with the money) and smothers the worm in everything in order to eat it at all. At the end of the story, Billy is hooked on worm sandwiches and has won the minibike. For children interested further in Billy's bet about worms, there is a performance version of the original story that is fun for performers and for audiences in Thomas Rockwell's *How To Eat Fried Worms and Other Plays* (Delacorte, 1980). The dialogues are easy to read and the directions are easy to follow.

434. Roos, Stephen (1990). *Twelve-Year-Old Vows Revenge! After Being Dumped by Extraterrestrial on First Date*. Illustrated by Carol Newsom. New York: Delacorte. Ages 9–12.

This is Roos's narrative war between twelve-year-olds that is told in a "read-all-about-it" format in a hilarious way. When twelve-year-old Shirley Garfield, who loves chocolate-madness cookies and reads the *National Tattletale* in history class, has a rival, Claire Von Kemp ("put a lid on it, Shirley"). Claire has lost her job at the video game arcade and Shirley takes satisfaction in the fact that *she* has a job as a summer reporter on *The Bugle,* New Eden's newspaper for kids. The two write humiliating articles about one another and end up before the town judge. The verdict is that both the girls are guilty and the judge orders them to apologize and lay off one another. They refuse and are sent to the same cell in jail until they make up—Shirley asks for a prison uniform with vertical strips since horizontal make her look fat. When the two girls finally apologize and are released, Claire says she feels they can be friends—that is, one ex-con hanging out with another.

435. Rounds, Glen (1984). *The Morning the Sun Refused to Rise: An Original Paul Bunyan Tale*. Illustrated by the author. New York: Holiday House. Ages 9–11.

When the sun doesn't rise one terrible morning, the king of Sweden contacts Paul Bunyan and asks him and Babe, the blue ox, to find the cause of the catastrophe and repair the damage. It seems that a blizzard's cold had frozen the world's axle and caused the turning earth to stop. Paul gets the world spinning again in a humorous way—with sourdough power.

436. Sciezka, Jon (1993). *Your Mother Was a Neanderthal*. Illustrated by Lane Smith. New York: Viking. Ages 9–11.

This is Sciezka's quick-paced humorous story about Joe, Sam, and Fred that begins when they find themselves in a prehistoric adventure "absolutely naked." The boys have upbeat conversations and use appropriate word play that goes along with such Stone Age icons as a saber-toothed cat, a woolly mammoth, and cave paintings.

437. Sharmat, Marjorie W. (1976). *The Lancelot Closes at Five*. Illustrated by Lisl Weil. New York: Macmillan. Ages 9–10.

Hutch, a health food fanatic, and Abby, his friend, spend the night in the Lancelot, the model home of the new housing development in which they lived. When the paper writes about the unusual vandalism at the home, several confess to spending the night there. The two friends realize that a sock with Abby's name on it was left behind and could tie Hutch and Abby to the scene of the crime at the house.

438. Singer, Isaac Bashevis (1968). *When Schlemiel Went to Warsaw & Other Stories*. Illustrated by Margot Zemach. New York: Farrar, Straus & Giroux. Ages 9–10.

In Singer's collection of folktales and original stories, there are several humorous stories. For example, there is the entertaining "Shrewd Todie & Lyzer the Miser." This is a tale that places the foolish actions of one person up against the cunning and trickery of another. With a "tit for tat" theme, the miser learns that if someone accepts nonsense when it brings a profit, someone should also accept nonsense when it brings someone a loss.

439. Sis, Peter (1993). *A Small Tall Tale from the Far Far North*. Illustrated by the author. New York: Knopf. Ages 9–11.

This is Sis's ironic story of Jan Welzl, a Czech folk hero, who journeyed to the cold Arctic regions in the late 1800s. Irony is seen not only in the Welzl's solution but also in the illustrations—there is light ridicule or light sarcasm where the intended implication is the exact *opposite* of the literal sense of the text or picture. Close to freezing to death in the harsh environment, Welzl is rescued by native people and he lives with them and develops a great deal of respect for their survival ways as they cope with the weather and icy surroundings. They learn that gold hunters are traveling into their environment. Welzl predicts that the newcomers will bring troubles along with their greed for gold, guns, and thirst for whiskey.

440. Smith, Alison (1981). *Help! There's a Cat Washing in Here!* Illustrated by Amy Rowen. New York: E. P. Dutton. Ages 9–11.

Things seem to go wrong for Henry in Smith's story. To keep Aunt Wilhemina from moving in, Henry agrees to take care of his younger brother and babysit for two weeks. His mother needs the time to prepare her art work for a portfolio to show when she interviews for jobs. Things start to go wrong in a big way—Henry burns the food, can't keep his younger sibling from misbehaving, and learns he has to make a costume for a school play. His efforts are rewarded when his mother gets a job and all ends happily.

441. Walkoff, Judie (1977). *Wally*. New York: Bradbury. Ages 9–10.

This is Walkoff's entertaining fast-moving story. For three weeks, Michael takes care of Billy's chuckwalla, Wally, and his other reptiles. Knowing his parents might not approve of his animal-care duties, Michael hides Wally in the closet and keeps Wally a secret until Wally gets out one night. Wally reappears just at the moment, of course, when Mr. and Mrs. Price are negotiating the sale of their house. He disrupts the negotiations which prevents the sale and to everyone's surprise—this makes everyone happy.

442. Wallace, Bill (1986). *Ferret in the Bedroom, Lizards in the Fridge*. New York: Holiday House. Ages 9–12.

This is Wallace's amusing situational comedy based on family relationships and their effects on life at school. Liz is a sixth grader who wants to run for class president. Jumping into school politics makes Liz realize how embarrassed she is by the many animals her father keeps for his research—this includes Fred, the ferret, and Ivan, the ibex. The two provide most of the entertainment through their antics. Liz, however, wants a home "just like the ones" her friends have.

443. Yolen, Jane (1981). *Shirlick Holmes and the Case of the Wandering Wardrobe*. Illustrated by Anthony Rao. New York: Coward. Ages 9–10.

This is Yolen's light, fast-moving mystery set in a small town. Feisty Shirlick and her friends hear that thieves have been robbing some wealthy homes of antiques. Shirlick and her friends search a burgled house for clues and stake out another house to wait for thieves. When the robbers arrive, Floria goes for help instead of hiding in the oak wardrobe with Shirlick. The wardrobe is one of the first pieces of furniture the thieves take out of the house. Shirlick can't get out when the door is wedged on the other side. Later, she finds herself in an auction and hears a familiar voice, George's father. When the wardrobe is opened, Shirlick tumbles out and the police arrest the auctioneer for selling stolen goods and give the kids the credit for solving the mystery!

444. Zemach, Margot (1977). *It Could Always Be Worse*. Illustrated by the author. New York: Farrar, Straus & Giroux. Ages 9–10.

Here is ironic humor in a Jewish folktale that tells the story of nine unhappy people who share a small one-room hut. The father asks for advice from the village rabbi and he suggests that the family bring a barnyard animal inside the hut. This continues until most of the family's livestock is inside the hut. When the rabbi suggests that the father clear the animals out, the whole family now appreciates the large and peaceful abode, for the small hut now seems larger with all the animals removed.

445. Zindel, Paul (1993). *Attack of the Killer Fishsticks*. Illustrated by Jeff Mangiat. New York: Bantam. Ages 9–11.

Zindel's story is about the peer relationships of Dave, Liz, Johnny, Jennifer and Max who call themselves the wacky facts lunch bunch. They enjoy telling one another jokes and trivia while they eat lunch. Humorous things happen after the bunch nominate Max to be the student council representative and support him as he runs against Nat, a nasty blob bully.

Holidays

446. Burch, Robert (1982). *Christmas with Ida Early*. New York: Avon/Camelot. Ages 11 and up.

With a setting in the Blue Ridge Mountains in Georgia, most of Burch's humor is in the Mary Poppins-type character, Ida. She seems as tall as a telephone pole, wears overalls, and has unruly red hair. She takes charge of the four motherless Sutton children while their father is at work, and brings laughter, joking, and joy into their lives. The children are impressed by her—Ida has done many things and she tells tall tales—but Aunt Ernestine is not impressed as Ida helps the children celebrate the holidays through the year. Aunt Ernestine makes pointed remarks and disapproves of all the fun and laughter. In spite of the pranks, slapstick, and humor, Ida finally wins the gratitude of the disapproving aunt.

447. Gondosch, Linda (1986). *The Witches of Hopper Street*. Illustrated by Helen Cogan-Cherry. New York: Lodestar/ Dutton, 1986. Ages 9–11.

Gondosch gives a funny account of what happens when three not-so-popular girls try to "pay back" their peers. When they are not invited to a Halloween party, they try to ruin the gathering through their initial attempts at "witchcraft." There is a good confrontation scene at the end.

448. Robinson, Barbara (1972). *The Best Christmas Pageant Ever*. Illustrated by Judith Gwynn Brown. New York: Harper and Row. Ages 9–11.

This is a fine read-aloud by Robinson about the meanest kids in town who take over the leads in the Christmas pageant. The six Herdman children are the terror of the school, so it is not surprising that they extend their reign of terror into Sunday school and take over the Christmas pageant. The substitute teacher cannot understand why only the Herdmans volunteer for the parts, unaware that they have threatened any children who raised their hands. Since the Herdmans have never heard of the story before, their interpretation is contemporary and humorous.

Jokes, Riddles, and Puns

449. Adler, David A. (1989). *A Teacher on Roller Skates and Other School Riddles*. Illustrated by John Wallner. New York: Holiday House. Ages 9 and up.

Adler and Wallner have packed a collection of riddles related to students and school with entertaining words. Curious about what went on when students took the bus? Read, "What happened to the children who took the school bus home?" (*They had to give it back*). Need an explanation about the use of sunglasses in the classroom? Read, "Why did the teacher wear sunglasses to class?" (*All her students were very bright*). And do you know students' attitude toward school? Read, "How do most children like school?" (*Closed*).

450. Adler, Larry (1990). *Help Wanted: Riddles about Jobs*. Illustrated by Susan Slattery Burns. Minneapolis, Minn: Lerner. Ages 9 and up.

Employment, employers, and employees are all topics in this riddle book. There are answers to such entries as "Did you hear the one about the woman who lost her job as a trapeze artist?" (*She didn't catch on*); and "Did you hear the one about the man who lost his job in the bubble gum factory?" (*He bit off more than he could chew*).

451. Agee, Jon (1993). *Flapstick: 10 Ridiculous Rhymes with Flaps*. Illustrated by the author. New York: Dutton. Ages 9 and up.

Agee's jokes are found in ten short and silly rhymes. The last line of each is not complete until a flap is lifted so a reader can see the surprising ending. The exaggerations in the illustrations add to the appeal of the book. There is more word play in Agee's *Go Hang a Salami! I'm a Lasagna Hog! And Other Palindromes* (Farrar, Straus & Giroux, 1992). In this book, the humor is in the author's imaginative use of words, the nonsense, and in the comical cartoon drawings.

452. Beisner, Monica (1983). *Monica Beisner's Book of Riddles*. Illustrated by the author. New York: Farrar, Straus & Giroux. Ages 9 and up.

Beisner encourages a reader to test his/her wit and solve the riddles, and wisely, includes a key. The key in the back of the book has the answers to such entries as "What is it? It has a mouth and does not speak/ Has a bed and does not sleep?" (*a river*) and "What always goes to bed with its shoes on?" (*a horse*).

453. Bernstein, Joanne E., and Paul Cohen (1986). *Creepy Crawly Critter Riddles*. Illustrated by Rosekrana Hoffman. Niles, Ill.: A. Whitman. Ages 9 and up.

Bernstein, Cohen, and Hoffman present a collection of riddles about ants, bees, spiders, and other creatures that crawl or slither. It includes "What do you get when you cross a bumblebee with a bell?" (*a humdinger*), "How can you tell a baby snake?" (*by its rattle*), and "Why do we forgive large snakes?" (*we let pythons be pythons*).

454. Bernstein, Joanne E., and Paul Cohen (1989). *Dizzy Doctor Riddles*. Illustrated by Carl Whiting. Niles, Ill.: A. Whitman. Ages 9 and up.

Bernstein, Cohen, and Whiting have more than one hundred riddles and jokes about medical care and diseases—both fanciful and factual. The format of the riddles includes the familiar question-and-answer kind and there are jokes in a couplet form. Examples of the couplet-as-a-joke include a doctor saying a patient's cough was sounding better (*Patient:* It should be. I practiced all night); a patient saying he thinks he is a deck of cards (*Doctor:* Sit down. I'll deal with you later); and a patient asking if the doctor will treat him (*Doctor:* No, you'll have to pay like everyone else.)

455. Bernstein, Joanne E., and Paul Cohen (1988). *Grand-slam Riddles*. Illustrated by Meyer Seltzer. Niles, Ill.: A. Whitman. Ages 9 and up.

Bernstein, Cohen, and Seltzer present an illustrated collection of jokes and riddles related to aspects of baseball, the teams and players. As examples, consider these: "Have you ever seen a house fly at the ball park?" (*No, but I've seen a home run.*) "What do you call a stadium escalator?" (*A fan belt.*) "What's the difference between an umpire and a pickpocket?" (*One watches steals, one steals watches.*)

456. Bernstein, Joanne E., and Paul Cohen (1989). *Touchdown Riddles.* Illustrated by Slug Signorini. Niles, Ill.: A. Whitman. Ages 9 and up.

The game of football, its players and rules are the focus of this illustrated riddle collection by Bernstein, Cohen, and Signorini. It includes plays on words related to contemporary situations as well as allusions to folk literature—"Which players have the worst looking hair?" (*the split ends*); "What comes after the two-minute warning?" (*a commercial*); and "Why are referees like the seven dwarfs?" (*they whistle while they work*). Signorini's black-and-white illustrations add to the appeal of the book.

457. Bernstein, Joanne E., and Paul Cohen (1990). *Why Did the Dinosaur Cross the Road?* Illustrated by Carl Whiting. Niles, Ill.: A. Whitman. Ages 9 and up.

Bernstein, Cohen, and Whiting present an illustrated collection of riddles about dinosaurs with some anachronistic additions—cave people. The riddle in the title of the book has an answer—"*There were no roads.*" Other examples are "What do you get when you cross frogs and dinosaurs?" (*leaping lizards*) and "How many books do you read to a brontosaurus?" (*Two—it's a two-story dinosaur*).

458. Bishop, Ann (1981). *Annie O'Kay's Riddle Round-up.* Illustrated by Jerry Warshaw. New York: Lodestar/Dutton. Ages 9 and up.

Bishop and Warshaw have included riddles related to a pioneer lifestyle in the West quite suitable for a student who is studying the lives of pioneers. This book has unexpected answers to riddles related to the theme: How do you mount a horse? (*Use a taxidermist.*) Name a stove used at high altitudes (*Mountain range.*) What do vultures eat for dinner? (*Leftovers.*) Interested students might make a list of words related to pioneer life (e.g., horse, mountain range, vultures) and search for riddles related to the words in the list.

Bishop has another riddle book suitable for students who are interested in humor placed in an Egyptian setting— *Cleo Catra's Riddle Book* (Lodestar/Dutton, 1981). It focuses on

cats, and flip-through "motion picture" pages are included that adds to the fun.

459. Bishop, Ann (1982). *Hello Mr. Chips!* Illustrated by Jerry Warshaw. New York: Lodestar/Dutton. Ages 9 and up.

If a student is a computer buff, invite him or her to get acquainted with Mr. Chips, the imaginary narrator in this book. Mr. Chips answers joking questions with a variety of one-liners.

460. Burns, Diane, and Andy Burns (1994). *Home on the Range: Ranch-Style Riddles.* Illustrated by Susan Slattery Burke. New York: Lerner. Ages 9–10.

This book by Burns, Burns, and Burke has surprise words and subtle humor in the answers to the riddles. Some are quite zany and all relate to a regional theme of the range and are accompanied by cartoon-type illustrations. There are more regional jokes in *Out to Dry: Riddles about Deserts* (Lerner, 1994) by June Swanson and illustrated by Susan Slattery Burke. Both are part of the series, *You Must Be Joking* (Lerner).

461. Cole, Joanna, and Stephanie Calmenson (1994). *Why Did the Chicken Cross the Road? And Other Riddles Old and New.* Illustrated by Alan Tiegreen. New York: Morrow. Ages 9–12.

After a brief introduction about the historical background of riddles, Cole, Calmenson, and Tiegreen get right into a bouncy collection of over two hundred riddles that are arranged by topics. The answers are printed upside down beneath the questions—What did one library book say to the other? (*Can I take you out?*). Tiegreen's humorous black-and-white cartoons on every page, and a subject index and bibliography of additional references for further reading, are included.

462. Emrich, Duncan, collector (1970). *The Nonsense Book of Riddles, Rhymes, Tongue Twisters, Puzzles and Jokes from American Folklore.* Illustrated by Ib Ohlsson. New York: Four Winds. All ages.

Emrich's book has five sections of humor entitled "Riddles," "Game Rhythms," "Autograph Album and Memory Book Rhymes," "Tongue Twisters," and "Nonsense and Funsense." He points out some distinctions of riddles, puzzles, and conundrums:

- A *true riddle* deals with association and comparisons where something is described in terms of another object in order to suggest something quiet different. Thus, it pretends to be one thing while it is actually something quite different—a candle, for example, is described as "little Nanny Etticoat/ in a white petticoat/ with a red nose, the longer she stands,/ the shorter she grows."

- A *puzzle* is presented clearly with all the facts and the listener figures it out—a listener is asked to guess the name of a girl in the town with "There was a girl in our town/ Silk an' satin was her gown,/ Silk an' satin, gold an' velvet,/ Guess her name, three times I've tell'd it." (*[an] Ann*).
- A *conundrum* is described as a trick question that involves a play on words—What do people call little gray cats in Tennessee? (*kittens*). The author's notes and a bibliography are included.

463. Gwynne, Fred (1980). *The Sixteen Hand Horse*. Illustrated by the author. New York: Prentice-Hall. Ages 9–12.

This is a humorously illustrated book and it portrays a young girl's mental images as her parents talk and refer to such things as bells that peel, banking a fire, and having a running nose. The jokes are in the girl's interpretations and the way they are shown in the pictures. For example, the metal cladding on a bell's side peels up like a banana peel, Dad carries a fireplace to the bank so he can bank the fire, and a small nose uses its legs and feet to run.

464. Keller, Charles, compiler (1988). *It's Raining Cats and Dogs: Cat and Dog Jokes*. Illustrated by Robert Quackenbush. New York: Pippin Press. Ages 9 and up.

Keller and Quackenbush offer an illustrated collection of riddles related to canines and felines and their characteristics. The book's title is the answer to the question "What's the worst weather for rats and mice?" "What must you know before you can teach a dog tricks?" (*More than the dog*); and "How can you tell if a cat burglar has been in your house?" (*Your cat is missing*).

465. Keller, Charles, compiler (1989). *King Henry the Ape Animal Jokes*. Illustrated by Edward Frascino. New York: Pippin Press. Ages 9 and up.

Animals and their characteristics are the featured highlight of Keller's collection of jokes that are illustrated by Frascino. The question

for the book's title which is an answer to a riddle is, "What's hairy, ruled England, and eats bananas?" Selected entries include "How do you keep a skunk from smelling?" (*Hold its nose*); "How do you talk to a giraffe?" (*Raise your voice*); and "Why does a bear sleep all winter?" (*So who's going to wake him up?*).

466. Keller, Charles, compiler (1982). *Ohm on the Range: Robot and Computer Jokes*. Illustrated by Art Cummings. Englewood Cliffs, N.J.: Prentice-Hall. Ages 9 and up.

This is a collection of riddles related to computers and robots compiled by Keller and illustrated by Cummings. It includes the question answered in the title of the book, "What's a computer electrician's favorite song?" (*Ohm on the range*); "What do you get when you cross an elephant with a computer?" (*A five-ton know-it-all*); and "What does a mechanical frog say?" (*Robot, robot*).

467. Kushner, Maureen (1987). *Funny Answers to Foolish Questions*. Illustrated by Dennis Kendrick. Toronto: Oak Tree Press. Ages 9 and up.

In this entertaining book, Kushner has packed quick, snappy answers to over eighty stupid questions and Kendrick has illustrated the pages. For instance, "Is that You?" might receive a snappy "I'm not sure, I haven't looked in the mirror lately." Other answers to chuckle over relate to questions that might be foolishly asked in the classroom: Why were you late to school? (*The car pool ran out of water*); Why are you standing on your school desk? (*I have high standards*); Where is your pencil? (*It left. It didn't want to be #2 anymore. It wanted to be #1*); Why didn't you do your homework? (*My homework was stolen and I'm waiting for the ransom note*); and Why don't you use your brain (*What? And stand out from the rest of the class?*)

The sections of riddles are entitled "Welcome Home," "Funny You Should Ask," "Keep It Clean," "Not Exactly the Teacher's Pet," "Go to Your Room," "Just Lost My Appetite," "Love That Question," "You Asked For It," and "Going Bananas." A checklist is included to help a reader find the materials he or she might be looking for in the sections.

468. Livingston, Myra Cohn, compiler (1989). *My Head Is Red and Other Riddle Rhymes*. Illustrated by Tere LoPrete. New York: Holiday House. Ages 9 and up.

Including the title riddle of "My Head Is Red," this is a collection of twenty-seven poetic descriptions that can be used as clues by the reader to determine the answers—the objects being discussed in the riddles. Each predicted answer can be cross-checked with the answer printed in capital letters that are printed upside down at the foot of the page. For instance, students can read the lines of the riddle as clues for guessing the object in the riddle. If the title riddle "My Head Is Red" is used as an example, students can read the following lines for clues: "My head is red/ My back is white/ You'll find me near the candlelight/ But once I make a shining flame/ I never ever look the same." (*A match*).

469. Maestro, Marco, and Guilio Maestro (1994). *Riddle City, USA: A Book of Geography Riddles*. Illustrated by Guilio Maestro. New York: HarperCollins. Ages 9–12.

In this book by Maestro and Maestro, there are over fifty original riddles related to geographical references and America's fifty states. Clues for the pun-based riddles are given through colorful cartoons and an accompanying map of the United States.

470. Manes, Stephen (1985). *Life Is No Fair!* Illustrated by Warren Miller. New York: Dutton. Ages 9 and up.

Manes offers a group of anecdotes about injustices in life with some satire in each one. For example, there is an anecdote about a boy's fears coming true—on a page, Bronislow Babuska's parents told him he'd never grow up big and strong. A reader turns the next page and reads, "They were half right." (Miller's illustrations show Bronislow strong enough to lift weights but still *very* short). Another anecdote is about Professor Chuzzlewit who says "There is no such thing as a flying saucer" and the next page reads, "He wasn't wrong" and the illustration shows two blue-bodied aliens with green eyes taking him away—not in a saucer but in a flying coffee cup.

471. Peterson, Scott K. (1990). *Out on a Limb: Riddles about Trees and Plants*. Illustrated by Susan Slattery Burke. Minneapolis, Minn.: Lerner. Ages 9 and up.

This is a collection of riddles about flora compiled by Peterson and illustrated by Burke. Children can identify words related to plants and trees—*pine tree, hay, vines, flowers,* and search for riddles about their suggestions or write original ones. They will find: "What do you get when you cross a barn with a pine tree?" (*a needle in a haystack*); "Why are vines so lazy?" (*all they want to do is hang around*); and "Why are flowers such good friends?" (*because they started out as buds*).

472. Phillips, Louis (1983). *How Do You Get a Horse Out of the Bathtub? Profound Answers to Preposterous Questions*. Illustrated by James Stevenson. New York: Viking. Ages 9 and up.

In this illustrated collection, the title question receives the answer, "*No problem. Just pull the plug out.*" The "profound answers" are arranged in eight categories that parody suggestions offered by newspaper advice columnists. The "advice" categories stretch from "Questions Concerning Matters Strictly Personal" to "A Little Bit of History Goes a Long Way." From "Questions" comes "I'm losing my memory—what should I do?" (*Try to forget about the problem.*) From "A Little Bit of History": "How did Alfred Nobel discover gunpowder?" (*It came to him in a flash.*); "How did he feel when he invented dynamite?" (*He got a big bang out of it.*)

473. Rosenbloom, Joseph (1985). *The Funniest Riddle Book Ever*. Illustrated by Hans Wilhelm. New York: Sterling Pub. Ages 9 and up.

This is a collection of riddles with an eclectic variety of topics. It includes "How do you talk to giants?" (*Use BIG words*); "What does a 200-pound mouse say?" (*Here, Kitty, Kitty*); and "Why is an elephant large, gray, and lumpy?" (*If it were small, white, and smooth, it would be an aspirin*).

474. Schwartz, Alvin (1973). *Tomfoolery: Trickery and Foolery with Words*. Illustrated by Glen Rounds. New York: Lippincott. Ages 9 and up.

In this illustrated collection of fooling-around-with-words are riddles, puns, and tall talk. There are examples of tangle talk—nonsense talk that involves saying the opposite of what a person means—and a phenomenon called endless tales, stories similar to "The Bear Went Over the Mountain" that have no endings. In the introduction, Schwartz points out that "No one knows who creates these tricks or just where they came from. Nor does anyone know just how old most of them are, except that some are very old." Notes, sources, and bibliography for further reading are included.

475. Schwartz, Alvin (1972). *A Twister of Twists, A Tangler of Tongues: Tongue Twisters*. Illustrated by Glen Rounds. New York: Lippincott. Ages 9 and up.

"The wild wind whipped Whit from the wharf" is just one example from this collection of one-liners, poems, stories, and alliterative twisters. The entries are arranged in sixteen sections about topics such as arithmetic, music, nature, reading, travel, and writing. Also included are the author's notes and a bibliography for further reading.

476. Schwartz, Alvin (1983). *Unriddling: All Sorts of Riddles to Puzzle Your Guessery*. Illustrated by Sue Truesdell. New York: Lippincott. Ages 9 and up.

In this illustrated collection, Schwartz has included eighteen different kinds of traditional riddles. He gives examples of riddles with queer words, hidden answers, pictures that show something from an unusual angle (droodles) and tricky questions.

477. Schwartz, Alvin (1973). *Witcracks: Jokes and Jests from American Folklore*. Illustrated by Glen Rounds. New York: Lippincott. Ages 9 and up.

In this illustrated collection, Schwartz has gathered many types of jokes—conundrums that are answered by a pun or play on words, the elephant jokes, knock-knock jokes, moron jokes, shaggy dog tales, and tall tale (exaggerated lies) jokes. The author's notes, sources, and bibliography are also included.

Nonsense

478. Keller, Charles, compiler (1979). *The Best of Rube Goldberg*. Illustrated by Rube Goldberg. Englewood Cliffs, N.J.: Prentice-Hall. Ages 9–11.

Keller has compiled a book of Goldberg's cartoons that show his tongue-in-cheek humor and the wonderfully complicated mechanical solutions Goldberg developed for everyday problems. There are over ninety inventions inserted, which appeared in his cartoons over his career from 1914 to 1944. Some of the mechanical inventions in this collection include a solution for closing a window, swatting a fly, and making a simple alarm clock.

479. Mahy, Margaret (1989). *Nonstop Nonsense*. Illustrated by Quentin Blake. New York: Macmillan. Ages 9–11.

Mahy and Blake offer a collection of short stories and poems that support the theme that poetry can be "very tricky stuff." For example, in the story entitled "The Cat Who Became a Poet," Mahy lets the cat speak in poetic words—"Perhaps all this poetry stuff is just the world's way of talking about itself." When the cat recites words about catching a mouse and tricking the dog, the feline says that "poetry is very tricky stuff and can be taken two ways."

480. Meggendorfer, Lothar (1985). *The Genius of Lothar Meggendorfer*. Foreword by Maurice Sendak. Introduction by Waldo H. Hunt. New York: Random House. Ages 9–11.

In this book, it is the ingenuity of Meggendorfer's illustrations that surprises the reader. There are illustrations of movable paper parts to accompany the verses. For instance, a silly fellow likes to play his musical horn all through the night and sets his music on a stand and plays by moonlight and candlelight. A pull-tab activates a cat sitting on the rooftop and moves the man's body as he takes a breath to blow his horn. In another illustration, a helpful maid cleans a mirror and thinks that her mistress's face will "likely break it." A pull-tab activates the maid's arm and she wipes the mirror's sur-

face. A final page shows how Meggendorfer devised the paper levers and tiny metal rivets to make his characters move.

481. Peet, Bill (1983). *No Such Things*. Boston: Houghton Mifflin. Ages 9–11.

Peet offers humorous reading through nonsense rhymes and nonsensical illustrations of nonsensical imagined things such as the "blue-snouted twumps." It seems that when the twumps are engaged in weeding and seeding, the seeds sprout into weeds on the twumps' backs. This makes the twumps look like walking "haystacks."

482. Seuss, Dr. (1984). *The Butter Battle Book*. Illustrated by the author. New York: Random House. All ages.

Dr. Seuss's story considers the nonsense of war. Although he is writing about people called Zooks and their enemies the Yooks, and the issue that divided them—whether bread should be eaten butter-side up or butter-side down, Dr. Seuss is actually commenting on the absurdity of war. A boundary called the wall separates the Zooks and Yooks and their weapons escalate from a snick-berry switch and triple-sling jigger to a jigger-rock snatchem and the eight-nozzled, elephant-toed boom-blitz. The final weapon is the big-boy boomeraoo—seemingly a deterrent to further escalation.

483. Seuss, Dr. (1950). *If I Ran the Zoo*. Illustrated by the author. New York: Random House. Ages 9–11.

In this story, there are new words and names to describe the animals in the nonsensical rhyming text. Gerald McGrew imagines a fanciful zoological habitat that has an elephant-cat, a bird called a bustard, a beast called flustard, and bugs with names of thwerils and chugs. The boy searches for the imaginary animals in their imaginary habitats—the wilds of Nantasket, the desert of Zind, and region of motta-fa-potta-pa-pell.

484. Seuss, Dr. (1984). *The Lorax*. Illustrated by the author. New York: Random House. All ages.

This story considers the nonsense of destroying trees. Although he is writing about people called the Once-ler family and the brown Bar-ba-loots, and whether trees should be cut or kept, Dr. Seuss is actually commenting on the absurdity of destroying nature.

485. Seuss, Dr. (1990). *Oh, The Places You'll Go!* Illustrated by the author. New York: Random House. All ages.

The text gives humorous advice in rhyme about going forward in life and confronting fear, loneliness, and being in charge of one's actions. Although Seuss is writing about imaginative places called the Lurch, the Slump, the Waiting Place, and the Hakken-Kraks Howl, he is actually giving advice about coping in unusual situations—"unslumping yourself is not easily done" and "simple it's not, I'm afraid you will find, for a mind-maker-upper to make up his mind."

486. Wrede, Patricia (1992). *Dealing with Dragons*. New York: Scholastic. Ages 9–12.

Wrede's story has a wry sense of humor that pokes fun at fairy tales. Princess Cimerone is not a proper princess but a marvelous plucky heroine who knows her mind and sets out to get what she wants. She's had the proper training for a princess, of course—how to dance, classes on how to curtsy to a prince, and practice in screaming loudly when something or someone carries her off. She finds this boring and prefers to learn fencing and magic and Latin, economics, and philosophy. Her parents object to her preferences and Cimerone accepts the help of an enchanted frog to escape—and become a dragon's princess with the desire *not* to be rescued.

487. Wrede, Patricia (1992). *Searching for Dragons*. New York: Scholastic. Ages 9–12.

Wrede offers more fun and humor in this mystery and adventure about Princess Cimerone. Cimerone discovers that Kazul, the dragon, is missing and believes he has been captured by the wicked wizards. She meets Mendanbar, king of the enchanted forest, who refuses to be kingly. Mendanbar objects to the procedures of the court—especially the dictate that he must marry a princess (for the king thinks that they are all silly, stupid, and rather useless). Mendanbar knows that unusual things are happening in the forest and he thinks the wicked wizards are responsible. The king and princess meet when they each try to solve the mystery facing them. During their adventures, Mendanbar discovers that Cimerone is not silly, stupid, or useless, and Cimerone finds out that Mendanbar is not the usual prince.

Rhymes and Verses

488. Bodecker, Neils Mogens (1978). *Hurry, Hurry, Mary Dear! and Other Nonsense Poems*. Illustrated by the author. New York: Atheneum. Ages 9–11.

Bodecker presents rhythm and humor of poetry together with line drawings and makes his collection very appealing to readers. There are a variety of moods—joyful, protesting, sobering. As an example of quiet protest, the title poem portrays Mary who is given orders to do this and that by a man who sits in his rocking chair the entire time. He wants her to do the chores—pick apples, chop trees, churn butter, brew tea, and so on. She finally makes her unspoken protest by putting the teapot on the man's head. For readers interested further in some of Bodecker's limericks and satire, there is *A Person from Britain and other Limericks* (Atheneum, 1980) and *Pigeon Cubes and Other Verse* (Atheneum, 1982).

489. Bodecker, Neils Mogens (1974). *Let's Marry Said the Cherry and Other Nonsense Poems*. Illustrated by the author. New York: Atheneum. Ages 9–12.

Bodecker's book is just the one for serendipitous finds. There are words of happy nonsense, tongue twisting word play, some irony, and nonsensical rhymes. The more-than-forty verses are entertainingly illustrated with sketches.

490. Booth, David (1993). *Dr. Knickerbocker and Other Rhymes*. New York: Ticknor & Fields. Ages 9–12.

Booth presents parodies of traditional rhymes and some nonsense along with jump rope rhymes. The playground rhymes were collected from school yards and written sources and printed on the pages in unusual ways—on banners, on the bases of statues, on postcards, on signs, and on word bubbles.

491. Brewton, Sara, and John E. Brewton, editors (1975). *Laughable Limericks*. Illustrated by Ingrid Fetz. New York: Crowell. Ages 9–12.

With an opening acknowledgment to Edward Lear, Brewton and Brewton present a collection of limericks in groups that include "Bugs, Bees, and Birds" and "Try Singing These." Wisely included are the final two sections about how to write your own limericks and how to set limericks to music.

492. Carroll, Lewis (1970). *The Hunting of the Snark*. Illustrated by Helen Oxenbury. New York: Merrimack. Ages 9–12.

This is Carroll's nonsense poem about the Snark that has "those frumious jaws" that is imaginatively illustrated by Oxenbury in this oversize book. Carroll himself said that the scene of the *Snark* poem was an island frequented by the Jubjub bird and the "fruminious" Bandersnatch—no doubt the very island where the whiffling, burbling Jabberwock was slain (see *The Annotated Alice: Alice's Adventures in Wonderland* and *Through the Looking Glass* [Bramhall House/Clarkson N. Potter, 1940]). For readers who are intrigued and want more of Carroll's words, suggest *Poems of Lewis Carroll* (Crowell, 1973) compiled by Myra Cohn Livingston, a fine collection illustrated with original illustrations that includes explanatory notes for each poem and a biographical sketch of the author.

493. Carroll, Lewis (1977). *Jabberwocky*. Illustrated by Jane Breskin Zalben. New York: Warne. Ages 9–12.

Much of Carroll's humor is in the nonsense words of this poem that first appeared in reversed form —a looking-glass book—to Alice and when she held it up to a glass, she saw the words in the right way. It describes a battle between a conqueror with his "vorpal" sword in hand and his foe—the Jabberwock with the "jaws that bite, the claws that catch" and the "eyes of flame." Alice mentioned the effect of the poem on her and said it seemed to "fill my head with ideas—only I don't know exactly what they are." In *The Annotated Alice: Alice's Adventures in Wonderland and Through the Looking Glass* (Bramhall House/Clarkson N. Potter, 1940), Carroll himself defined some of the words he used in *Jabberwocky*—*brillig* meant the time of broiling dinner, *slithy* was a combination of slimy and lithe, which meant smooth and active, and *borogoves* was an extinct kind of parrot.

494. Cassedy, Sylvia (1987). *Roomrimes*. Illustrated by Michele Chessare. New York: Crowell. Ages 9–12.

In Cassedy's collection, there are twenty-six verses about rooms and places arranged in alphabetical order from attic to zoo. Some unusual choices are *haunted room* (who?), *shell* (a parlor to the clam), and *upstairs* (. . . where the doorbell rings).

495. Cassedy, Sylvia (1993). *Zoomrimes: Poems about Things that Go*. New York: HarperCollins. Ages 9–12.

This is Cassedy's alphabetical collection of twenty-six poems about things that go from an ark to a zeppelin. The poems—some metered rhymes and others free verse—are fun to read aloud. They introduce students to ways to see ordinary objects and subjects in an extraordinary way, since creative word play and humorous twists are found in the verses.

496. Ciardi, John (1985). *Doodle Soup*. Illustrated by Merle Nacht. Boston: Houghton Mifflin. Ages 9–12.

Here are Ciardi's light poems that are witty (and sometimes caustic) and they are good read-alouds. Need, for example, to know why pigs don't write poems? (nothing rhymes with *oink*). Or what happened when the ice-cream truck got stuck? (. . . *first, we had to lighten the load/ When we had helped a gallon apiece/ The driver phoned the Chief of Police/*). Or what happened when I asked my sister the question, Why is water wet? (*How could you drink it if it were dry?/It would sting like sand and make you cry/*). A reader will appreciate the mischief in the poetic anecdotes and the surprises—just read the titles aloud to generate interest—"The Best Part of Going Away is Going Away from You," and "I Picked a Dream Out of My Head." There are pen-and-ink drawings, some with washes in shades of gray, that show the zany characters and actions.

497. Kennedy, X. J. (1985). *The Forgetful Wishing Well: Poems for Young People*. New York: Atheneum. Ages 9 and up.

Kennedy's verses focus on children's relationships as they grow up, but also introduce some poetic snapshots of such humorous personalities as "Agnes Snaggletooth" and "Wilberforce Fong." For readers who like Kennedy's weird sense of humor in his other poetic descriptions, guide them to any or all of the following:

- *One Winter Night in August and Other Nonsense Jingles* (Atheneum, 1975) has nonsense jingles with titles related to characters and objects. Humorous verbal portraits are found in such verses as "The Up-to-Date Giant" and "The Muddleheaded Messer," the bird that lives in dresser drawers and delights in messing them up. Entertaining descriptions of places are in "Terrible Troll's Tollbridge" and others.
- *The Phantom Ice Cream Man: More Nonsense Verse* (Atheneum, 1979) is a collection of verses—some with dark humor—with titles such as "Mother's Nerves," "Father and Mother," and "A Social Mixer."

498. Lear, Edward (1965). *Lear Alphabet Penned and Illustrated by Edward Lear Himself*. Illustrated by the author. New York: McGraw-Hill. All ages.

In this edition, Lear's original verses from 1871 are bordered in red and blue beginning with *A* for busy ants trying to build a hillside home. Lear's zany animals continue to be busy through the verses—a cat chases a rat, a rabbit eats flowers in the bowers, and a whale swims the Pacific. Several other versions of Lear's verses are suitable book companions for this one and can be found in *Edward Lear: A Nonsense Alphabet* (Doubleday, 1961) illustrated by Richard Scarry, in *The Nonsense Alphabet* (Grosset & Dunlap, 1961) illustrated by Art Seiden, and in *The First ABC* (Watts, 1971) edited by Frank Waters and illustrated by Charles Mozley.

499. Lear, Edward (1988). *Edward Lear: A New Nonsense Alphabet*. Edited by Susan Hyman. London: Bloomsbury. All ages.

In 1862 Lear promised an alphabet to a new baby, the granddaughter of friends. The alphabet gift was drawn in deep blue ink on pale blue linen. It is reproduced in the book along with its accompanying letter to the child, Lear's original sketches, Lear's photograph, and an addendum of his humorous discoveries. Lear describes one of his discoveries (which looks like a coat and hat stand) as an object of antiquarian interest and his words are in the public domain: " . . . there are others who contend that the singular object in question is the Gigantic & Fossil remnant of an extinct brute partaking of the nature of an ostrich & the domestic caterpillar habitually walking on 3 feet, its neck, head, and expansive antennae fixed on the summit of its elongated body & its general appearance at once surprising & objectionable."

500. Lear, Edward (1994). *There Was an Old Man . . . A Gallery of Nonsense Rhymes*. Illustrated by Michele Lemieux. New York: Morrow. Ages 9–12.

Lear's nonsense verses, now in the public domain, engage children in meeting Lear's silly limerical personalities and their peculiar habits—"There was an old person of Bromley/ Whose ways were NOT (*sic*) cheerfully or comely/ He sate (*sic*) in the dust, eating spiders and crust/ That unpleasing old person of Bromley./" There is also amusement in seeing the nose ring worn by the moon-gazing "Old Person of Tring/ Who embellished his nose/" and in the highlighted humor of various personages from other places who have interesting attributes. Each limerick is accompanied with a full-color illustration.

501. Lee, Dennis (1978). *Garbage Delight*. Boston: Houghton Mifflin. Ages 9–12.

Lee offers a collection of poems—some with dark humor—that children like because the book is great fun. Children meet such characters as the narrator in "I Eat Kids Yum Yum!," Inspector Dogbone in "Inspector Dogbone Gets His Man" and the winged insect in "The Last Cry of the Damp Fly." There is nonsense with a lot of exaggerations in the strong rhythmic verses. For readers who like these rollicking verses, suggest either of the following:

- *Jelly Belly* (Macmillan, 1983) includes its collection of counting-out rhymes, finger plays, and nursery rhymes;
- *Alligator Pie* (Macmillan, 1974). One of the favorite poems and best known is "Alligator Pie."

502. Livingston, Myra Cohn (1985). *A Learical Lexicon*. Illustrated by Joseph Low. New York: Atheneum. Ages 9 and up.

Livingston selects some of Lear's outlandish words and introduces them in alphabetical order. A reader finds words with unusual spellings (*carrotable*), hidden meanings (*ted bime* for *bed time*), transposed letters (*Ossifers*), and onomatopoetic sounds.

503. Livingston, Myra Cohn, editor (1971). *Speak Roughly to Your Little Boy: A Collection of Parodies and Burlesques, Together with the Original Poems, Chosen and Annotated for Young People*. Illustrated by Joseph Low. New York: Harcourt. Ages 11 and up.

Livingston has put together a collection of original verses and their parodies. This unique approach offers an entertaining diversion for readers. For example, A. A. Milne's verse "Now We Are Six" can be paired with its parody—J. B. Morton's "Now We Are Sick." Longfellow's Song of Hiawatha ("By the shores of Gitchee-Goomie") can be paired with Carroll's burlesque of the verse.

- A *Lollygag of Limericks* (Atheneum, 1978) is a collection of these special types of 5-line rhymes that is humorously illustrated by Joseph Low.
- *What a Wonderful Bird the Frog Are: An Assortment of Humorous Poetry* (Harcourt Brace, 1973) is an entertaining anthology on a variety of subjects and offers a range of poetry models from Haiku to nonsense jingles.

504. McCord, David (1980). *One at a Time*. Illustrated by Henry B. Kane. Boston: Little, Brown. Ages 9 and up.

This is an upbeat collection of McCord's poems that has a full subject index and an index of first lines. It includes a reprint of his verses from *Far and Few, Take Sky, All Day Long,* and others. Many selections are playful. Want to learn how to write poetry? In a final section, Professor Brown explains how to write a couplet, quatrain, the triolet, and the limerick in words that are written *in the form of the poems themselves.*

505. Nash, Ogden, compiler (1980). *Custard & Company*. Illustrated by Quentin Blake. Boston: Little, Brown. Ages 9–11.

In this collection of over eighty poems, readers will meet many humorous characters. There is the cowardly dragon, "Custard," Isabel who eats a bear in "The Adventures of Isabel," and an unfeeling child in "The Boy Who Laughed at Santa Claus." "The Panther" and "The Centipede" and "The Eel" also will have special appeal.

506. Prelutsky, Jack (1990). *Something Big Has Been Here*. New York: Greenwillow. Ages 9–11.

In this collection, readers meet such unusual characters as "Super Samson Simpson" who is "superlatively strong" and can carry elephants, a meat loaf that defies a hammer, brick, and drill in "My Mother Made a Meat Loaf," and five flying hotdogs who call themselves the "Unflappable Five" in "We're Fearless Flying Hotdogs." Several characteristics are discussed in humorous ways—in "The Turkey Shot Out of the Oven," the unknown narrator promises to plan ahead the next time he or she stuffs a turkey and promises "never again to stuff a turkey with popcorn that hadn't been popped." For older readers who enjoy Prelutsky's comical words, suggest additional collections:

- *The New Kid on the Block* (Greenwillow, 1984). Illustrated by James Stevenson. Nonsense verse is taken from everyday situations and sibling relationships—"I'm Disgusted with My Brother" and "My Sister Is a Sissy."
- *The Snoop on the Sidewalk* (Greenwillow, 1977). This collection introduces some darkly humorous creatures through the Lurpp in "The Lurpp Is on the Loose" and the human-gobbling Grobbles in "The Grobbles."

507. Rosen, Michael (1983). *You Can't Catch Me*. Illustrated by Quentin Blake. New York: Dutton. Ages 9–11.

Rosen, a British humorist, shares his wit about family relationships and the humor that can result. For example, two siblings race to see which one is going to be "last" to get undressed and be the one to have to turn out the light, and two others argue about who is going to clean the "fluff" out from under the bed. For readers interested further in Rosen's humor, suggest Rosen's other poems found in *Mind Your Own Business* (S. G. Phillips, 1974), *Wouldn't You Like to Know* (Dutton, 1980), and *Quick, Let's Get Out of Here* (Dutton, 1984).

508. Silverstein, Shel (1981). *A Light in the Attic*. Illustrated by the author. New York: Harper and Row. Ages 9–11.

Much of the humor in Silverstein's upbeat verses is based on the sounds children hear in the words, the unusual characters, and the entertaining situations—many are slapstick. For example, children consider a bear of the Arctic in a refrigerator and a character who digests what he eats quickly and becomes known as the "Quick-Digesting Gink." A companion volume of rollicking verses and slapstick humor is *Where the Sidewalk Ends* (Harper & Row, 1981) with the title poem about "Where the Sidewalk Ends," as well as "The Invitation" and "Listen to the Mustn'ts."

509. Thayer, Ernest Lawrence (1988). *Casey at the Bat: A Centennial Edition*. Illustrated by Barry Moser. Boston: David R. Godine. All ages.

In Thayer's poetic narrative, things are not looking promising for the team—the Mudville Nine. It is the bottom of the ninth inning with two outs and they are behind, 4–2. Flynn hits a single and Blake hits the ball so hard he takes the cover off the ball. When the uproar settles, the runners are on second and third and Mighty Casey steps into the batter's box with defiance in his eyes and a sneer on his lips. A speeding ball results in "strike one" and a flying spheroid results in "strike two." On the next pitch, "the air is shattered by the force of Casey's blow" but there was no joy in Mudville that day—mighty Casey had struck out.

Unusual Characters and Creatures

510. Babbit, Natalie (1987). *The Devil's Other Storybook*. Illustrated by the author. New York: Farrar, Straus & Giroux. Ages 9–12

Black-and-white drawings show a slightly paunchy devil with a very long pointed tail, first seen in *The Devil's Storybook* (Farrar, 1974). In these ten read-aloud stories he shows himself in his familiar form—and creates trouble and misfortune for the world's inhabitants. Sometimes the tables are turned, however, and the devil gets a surprise. These surprises make the stories humorous, but some have a beyond-the-lines sensitivity and sadness. Interested readers will meet such characters as an opera singer named Doremi Faso and a talented parrot who poses as a bumbling fortuneteller.

511. Carey, Valerie Scho (1987). *The Devil and Mother Crump*. Illustrated by Arnold Lobel. Harper and Row. Ages 9–12.

"Once there was a baker woman by the name of Mother Crump." So begins the colloquial dialogue in this lively and original tale that goes on to say that stingy, mean Mother Crump got three wishes from the devil but used them to trick herself out of his clutches. When she died she tricked her way into heaven and built a bake oven among the clouds, which still glows in the form of heat lightning on warm summer nights.

512. Ericksen, Clarie (1988). *A Monster is Bigger Than 9*. Illustrated by Mary Ericksen. San Diego: Green Tiger Press. Ages 9–12.

Humorous to older students and adults, this book is a collection of the sayings of preschoolers as recorded by their teachers. Several relate to unusual creatures and characters: Want to know if a skeleton has bones? (*Skeletons don't have bones . . . only Indians do. They have bone-arrows.*) Or how dinosaurs cook people? (*They roast them over volcanoes.*) Or about heroes? (*Worms are never heroes. Worms are always losers.*)

513. Jones, Diana Wynne (1989). *Howl's Moving Castle*. New York: Greenwillow. Ages 9–12.

Unusual characters—Wizard Howl and bossy Sophie who both want their own way—and their interactions provide the humor in this one. Sophie, cranky creature, has her hair dyed by Wizard Howl and it turns an ugly color which makes her miserable. Sulking, Wizard Howl does his green slime trick and creates mountains of it. Additionally, changes in historical time periods, a magic suit, and seven-league boots are all part of the entertainment in this story.

514. Kraus, Roberts (1988). *Mummy Knows Best: A Mummy Dearest Creepy Hollow Whoooooooo Dunnnit?* Illustrated by the author. New York: Warner. Ages 9–10.

In a slapstick mystery, Detective Mummy investigates the disappearance of Mr. Milkghost's sheets. There are plays on words and visual jokes in the cartoon-style illustrations and the cartoons can help a reader solve the mystery right along with Mummy. Other sleuthing antics in this series include:

- *Mummy Vanishes: A Mummy Dearest Creepy Hollow Whoooooooo Dunnnit?* Illustrated by the author. Warner, 1988. Noah, the vampire detective, rescues Mummy Dearest and her big ape, and returns them to the Bronx.

- *The Phantom of Creepy Hollow: A Mummy Dearest Creepy Hollow Whoooooooo Dunnnit?* Illustrated by the author. Warner, 1988. The question basic to this mystery is, "Who put the bubble bath in the brass section at the opry?" Detective Mummy finds out, of course. The illustrations and allusions to literature can help a reader figure out the mystery right along with Mummy.

- *Private Eyes Don't Blink: A Mummy Dearest Creepy Hollow Whoooooooo Dunnnit?* Illustrated by the author. Warner, 1988. This is a slapstick mystery with Detective Mummy Dearest, Mister, the monster, Ol' Professor, Lois Lips, and Private Eye. The humor in the cartoon-type illustrations add to the story's appeal.

515. Lindgren, Astrid (1950). *Pippi Longstocking*. Illustrated by Louis S. Glanzman. New York: Viking. Ages 9–10.

Pigtailed Pippi, a nine-year-old orphan of "supergirl" fame, is the strongest girl in the world. Her full name is a mile long—Pippillotta Delicatessa Windowshade Mackrelmint Afraim's Daughter Longstocking. In this story full of humorous exaggerations and lively misbehavior, Pippi can lift her horse up onto the porch of her house—Villa Villekulla—or throw a man into the air. Without hurting herself, she can dive from the villa's roof into a tree. She never lets anyone else get the better of her, says what she thinks, and lives all by herself with a monkey (called Mr. Nilsson) and a horse. She scrubs the floor with brushes tied on her feet and wears stockings of different colors. Pippi also sleeps on a bed with her feet where her head should be and decides to go to school so she won't "miss" having a Christmas and Easter vacation when school is "out." The exaggerations continue in *Pippi Goes on Board* (Viking, 1957), *Pippi in the South Seas* (Viking, 1959), and *Pippi on the Run* (Viking, 1976).

516. Mitchell, Adrian, reteller (1986). *The Baron on the Island of Cheese*. Illustrated by Patrick Benson. New York: Philomel. Ages 9–12.

Mitchell presents a group of tall tales that sequence one another in the book. For example, there is the adventure of the baron who shoots the stag without a bullet in his gun. The baron, without ammunition, shoots the stag with a cherry pit. The stag sprouts a cherry tree ten-feet-tall after the shooting.

517. Pene du Bois, William (1966). *Lazy Tommy Pumpkinhead*. New York: Harper and Row. Ages 9–12.

This story is a humorous warning against dependence on electrical gadgets. Tommy lives in an all-electric house. In a Rube Goldberg arrangement, an electric bed wakes him up and slides him out of his night clothes and into a tub of warm water. The tub splashes him and tips him out and into a drying room—a harness holds him up while other machines dry him. Still others comb his hair, brush his teeth, dress him, and feed him. One day, his life changes. Rain and wind put an end to the electric gadgets and all goes wrong. His feet are cleaned and combed, and his clothes are put on upside down. The feeding machine wipes his feet and the tooth machine brushes his toes and he asks, "How did I get myself in this mess?"

518. Sandburg, Carl (1988). *Rootabaga Stories*. Illustrated by Maud and Miska Petersham. New York: Harcourt Brace Jovanovich. Ages 9–12.

Sandburg's collection consists of brief stories in a setting called Rootabaga Country where the train tracks zig and zag. The largest village is called Liver and Onions. The countryside is called Over and Under, and some animals wear clothing. The residents have names that are tongue twisters such as Ax Me No Questions, Henry Hagglyhoagly, and Miney Mo; and they all talk in alliterative words.

519. Schwartz, Alvin, compiler (1976). *Kickle Snifters and Other Fearsome Critters Collected from American Folklore*. Illustrated by Glen Rounds. New York: Lippincott. Ages 9–12.

All of the fearsome critters in this book are imaginary beasts of the tall tale variety. A collection of riddles accompanies creatures, and there is a list of illustrated definitions with notes on sources included at the back of the book.

520. Thomas, Kathleen (1981). *Out of the Bug Jar*. Illustrated by Tom O'Sullivan. New York: Dodd. Ages 9–10.

Awakened in the night by an unusual creature grumbling and crawling under his pillow, Tom Jenkins meets Marvin, the tooth fairy. Tom scoops him into a bug jar but Marvin begins to run Tom's life. Marvin makes life difficult for Tom—he badgers Tom about brushing his teeth, doing his homework, and telling the truth. He tells Tom he can take care of Tom's teeth in retaliation for being held prisoner in the jar. When Marvin finally gets loose, Tom is afraid of losing his teeth and sleeps with tape over his mouth. When Marvin is found, he admits he likes his new lifestyle and wants to stay with Tom.

521. Yorinks, Arthur (1983). *It Happened in Pinsk*. Illustrated by Egielski. New York: Farrar, Straus & Giroux. Ages 9 and up.

Yorinks introduces readers to Irv, a man who feels he is not as important as everyone else. One morning, he realizes that his head is missing. His wife makes him a head of a pillowcase made with socks and sends him off to work. Poor Irv is desperate about what is going on until he sees his head being used as a dummy's head in a hat shop. He runs in and grabs it and is delighted that at last he has "found himself." The main comic aside of the story is that the head is a representation of Maurice Sendak, a friend of the author's.

Glossary

Absurdity The idea of being foolish or unwise, silly and lacking in good sense, and preposterous or irrational.

Animal traits The humorous idea of exaggerating a trait or characteristic of an animal to make a story or joke fun.

Antics and pranks Jokes and tricks—humorous acts.

Being in on the joke This is the act of knowing what might happen that could be funny.

Cartoonlike illustrations Pictures often filled with hyperbole and exaggerations that are used by artists to show something to cause laughs.

Conundrum A trick question that involves a play on words.

Exaggeration The idea of making something seem more than it really is that is often used to create certain effects of humor.

Misadventures "Bad" adventures or adventures that go humorously wrong and askew.

Nonsense Words, language, or actions that have no sensible meaning.

One-liners Witty replies.

Parody Writing in which the language and style of an author is imitated especially for comic effect or for ridicule.

Personification Giving an inanimate object some human attributes for a comic effect.

Pun Joking way of saying something by using a word (or a saying) that has two different meanings.

Puzzle A presentation of facts that have to be "figured out."

Quirkiness A sudden humorous turn or twist in language or behavior.

Ridiculousness Situations that are shown through characters, objects, and actions that are *not* worthy of serious consideration.

Satire A way to ridicule or scorn or expose or discredit a human vice or folly. Wit, irony, and sarcasm are often used.

Silliness A lack of sense as we know it.

Slapstick Rapid, physical activity for comic effect; includes rough-and-tumble actions, and sometimes cause-and-effect situations.

Spoof A take off on a subject.

Straight person/funny person A contrast in two characters that builds the humor by provoking laughter and mirth.

Surprise endings Something unexpected; a finale without warning.

Tongue-in-cheek Saying something humorous or portraying something funny in a serious manner knowing full well it really didn't happen or couldn't happen. Also known as "kidding around."

Tongue twisters Alliterative words strung along in a sentence or verse format.

Tricks Humorous acts that involve cleverness and skill, and can be intended to fool someone (or even to cheat a deserving villain).

True riddle The words pretend to describe one thing while actually describing something quite different—something is described in terms of another object in order to suggest something else; deals with association and comparisons.

Verbal and visual jokes Something said or done or shown to get a laugh—to excite mirth.

Weird and wacky Unusual, sometimes crazy and definitely mixed-up actions.

Wittiness Saying amusing congruities (harmonious things, things in agreement) and incongruities about people, places, and things.

Word play To amuse or divert oneself with words and their meanings, sounds, and spellings.

Zaniness Behavior that reflects some buffoonery, irrational words, and ludicrous behavior and antics intended to amuse readers.

Index

References are to entry numbers, not pages.

About the Author

After receiving her Ed. D. at the University of the Pacific, Patricia L. Roberts received the Distinguished Alumnus of the Year award and joined the faculty in the School of Education at California State University, Sacramento, where she received the California State University's Award of Merit for Teaching. The Award of Merit is given for a superior teaching record and outstanding service to the institution and to the community. She has taught graduate courses in children's literature, language arts, and reading and served as coordinator of an elementary Teacher Education Center. She also has served as the Chair and Associate Chair of the Department of Teacher Education at California State University, Sacramento.

Dr. Roberts is the author of *Alphabet: A Handbook of ABC Books and Book Extensions for the Elementary Classroom, Second Edition* (Scarecrow Press, 1994) and numerous other textbooks and resources for librarians, teachers, and parents. She currently serves as a national reviewer of adolescent literature for SIGNAL (International Reading Association Special Interest Group) and an educational consultant, writes for professional journals, and is a member of the International Reading Association, National Council of Research on the Teaching of English and other professional groups. Her current research has centered on multicultural children's literature and literature-based instruction, and this research is reflected in her book *Multicultural Friendship Stories and Activities for Children Ages 5–14* (Scarecrow Press).